Issues in Historiography
General editor
R. C. RICHARDSON
University of Winchester

Debates on Stalinism

Manchester University Press

Issues in Historiography

Already published

The Debate on the Norman Conquest
Marjorie Chibnall

The Debate on the French Revolution
Peter Davies

Debates on the Holocaust
Tom Lawson

The Debate on the English Reformation: new edition
Rosemary O'Day

The Debate on the Decline of Spain
Helen Rawlings

The Debate on the English Revolution: third edition
R. C. Richardson

The Debate on the American Civil War Era
H. A. Tulloch

The Debate on the Crusades
Christopher Tyerman

The Debate on Black Civil Rights in America
Kevern Verney

The Debate on the Rise of the British Empire
Anthony Webster

Issues in Historiography

Debates on Stalinism

MARK EDELE

MANCHESTER
UNIVERSITY PRESS

Copyright © Mark Edele 2020

The right of Mark Edele to be identified as the author of this work has been asserted by him in accordance with the Copyright, Designs and Patents Act 1988.

Published by Manchester University Press
Altrincham Street, Manchester M1 7JA
www.manchesteruniversitypress.co.uk

British Library Cataloguing-in-Publication Data
A catalogue record for this book is available from the British Library

ISBN 978 1 7849 9430 3 hardback

ISBN 978 1 7849 9431 0 paperback

First published 2020

The publisher has no responsibility for the persistence or accuracy of URLs for any external or third-party internet websites referred to in this book, and does not guarantee that any content on such websites is, or will remain, accurate or appropriate.

Typeset
by New Best-set Typesetters Ltd

CONTENTS

List of figures	*page* vi
General editor's foreword	vii
Acknowledgements	ix
Debates on Stalinism: an introduction	1
Part I: Biography and historiography	**11**
1 A 'withering crossfire': debating Stalinism in the Cold War	13
2 Marxism–Lewinism and the origins of Stalinism	34
3 The Russian origins of totalitarianism: empire and nation	62
4 Unrevisionist revisionism	89
Part II: Cold War debates	**119**
5 Stalinism with Stalin left in	121
6 Totalitarianism and revisionism	150
7 After revisionism	176
Part III: Contemporary debates	**205**
8 Fighting Russia's history wars	207
9 Holodomor: a transnational history	235
New perspectives on Stalinism? A conclusion	270
Further reading	282
Index	291

LIST OF FIGURES

4.1	Google Ngram for 'Sheila Fitzpatrick' and 'Moshe Lewin'	*page* 104
4.2	Google Ngram for 'Sheila Fitzpatrick' and 'Richard Pipes'	105
9.1	Google Ngram for 'Ukrainian famine'	247
9.2	Google Ngram for 'Holocaust' shows the rise and rise of the concept	248
9.3	Google Ngram for 'Ukrainian famine' and 'Soviet genocide'	249

GENERAL EDITOR'S FOREWORD

History without historiography is not only oversimplified and impoverished but a contradiction in terms. The study of the past cannot be divorced from a linked investigation of its practitioners and intermediaries. No historian writes in isolation from the work of his or her predecessors, nor can the commentator – however clinically objective or professional – stand aloof from the insistent pressures, priorities and demands of the ever-changing present, and sometimes is deliberately prevented from doing so. In truth, there are no self-contained, impregnable, 'academic towers'. Historians are porous beings. Their writings are an extension of who they are, where they are placed, and who they speak for. Though historians address the past as their subject they always do so in ways that are shaped – consciously or unconsciously as the case may be – by the society, politics and systems, cultural ethos and pressing needs of their own day, and they communicate their findings in ways which are specifically intelligible and relevant to a present-minded reading public consisting initially of their own contemporaries. For these reasons the study of history is concerned most fundamentally not with dead facts and sterile, permanent verdicts, but with highly charged dialogues, disagreements, controversies and shifting centres of interest among its presenters, with the changing methodologies and discourse of the subject over time, and with audience reception. *Issues in Historiography* is a well-established, well-stocked series designed to explore such subject matter by means of case studies of key moments in world history and the interpretations, reinterpretations, challenges, debates and contests they have engendered.

Written by a key player in the field, Mark Edele's book takes the series into new geographical territory, as well as into what by any standards has been a historiographical battlefield. Edele bravely takes on the incredibly complex and disturbing multilayered subject of Stalin and Stalinism and locates it securely in its volatile, sometimes dangerous, political setting. Chiefly concerned with the three decades of historiography after 1980 – though with many backward glances – the author takes stock of historical writing produced within and outside the Soviet Union and its successor

GENERAL EDITOR'S FOREWORD

states. His subject is one that is emphatically plural in its many-sided relations with multiple national, political, ideological and temporal contexts. Changing access to sources, changing paradigms, changing fashions come under discussion, as does the adequacy of classifying historians as totalitarians, revisionists or post-revisionists. The Cold War and *glasnost* necessarily figure prominently in these pages. So do the many implications of the postcolonial splintering, re-formations and renationalization of component parts of the former Soviet Union. The particularly important role played in these debates by historians – sometimes transplanted – in America and Australia, is carefully examined. Leading contributors like Moshe Lewin (1921–2010) and Richard Pipes (1923–2018) – politically contrasting Polish Jews who both escaped to the United States – and Australian-born Sheila Fitzpatrick (i.e. 1941–), and the heated debates in which they engaged come under extended scrutiny. Transnationalism in a number of ways – both as subject matter and in terms of the background and baggage of historians themselves – is a conspicuous component of Edele's analysis.

That the historiography of this field has been marked by such bitter disagreements and intense hostilities is unsurprising given the brutal, looming presence of Stalin himself and his dictatorship, his ruthlessness in disposing of individual political opponents like Trotsky, of awkward, unwanted *cadres*, or indeed of whole populations. Historians' treatments of the Great Famine of 1932–33, the Great Terror of 1937–38, the impact of the Stalinist regime in Poland and Ukraine, are all carefully explored. So, too, is the Great Patriotic War and its historiographical legacy. More than a codicil to the Stalin story the later implementation of Putin's Memory Law makes for chilling reading.

Edele's treatment of his subject works well at both the micro and macro levels, and he succeeds admirably in placing Stalin and Stalinism in the broad sweep of Tsarist and post-1917 Revolution Russian history. Readers will find this text an incredibly helpful, well-structured, well-signposted guide, one that in its conclusion signals what might be expected to be some of the key future directions of research and writing in this teeming, controversial, and pressingly relevant field.

R. C. Richardson
July 2019

ACKNOWLEDGEMENTS

The account that follows builds on earlier work. Important English-language contributions include a seminal study of the history of totalitarianism,[1] an important book on America's Soviet experts,[2] and an essay about the founding fathers of the field.[3] Several authors have explored the historiography on Stalinism in the Soviet Union[4] and post-Soviet Russia.[5] Two now dated books give good introductions to debates,[6] while a series of essays inform a Russian-reading audience of the oddities of Americans writing about Soviet history.[7] The pages of the journal *Kritika* have lifted discourse on historiography to new qualitative levels.[8]

I began writing this book during my final half year at the University of Western Australia. An Australian Research Council Future Fellowship allowed me to ignore much of the turmoil which consumed the waking hours of most of my colleagues, and I taught a wonderful honours course on the topic of this book in 2017. UWA had been good to me for much of the thirteen years it employed me, but I was relieved to move on when I did. It was painful to leave behind good friends and wonderful colleagues, first among them Andrea Gaynor, Tijana Vujosevic, and the now blissfully retired Robert Stuart.

The manuscript was finished during the first year and a half of my tenure as the inaugural Hansen Professor at the University of Melbourne in 2017–18. My colleagues, in what continues to be the best history department in Australia, have been a source of inspiration. In particular, David Goodman, Kate McGregor and Julie Fedor have taught me new ways to think about teaching and writing history. Trevor Burnard was an incredibly supportive 'boss', always concerned that all went well with the multiple tasks he had entrusted to me.

George Liber, Julie Hessler, Sheila Fitzpatrick, Julie Fedor, Paula Michaels, David Brandenberger, Jonathan Daly and James Heinzen have taken on the thankless task of commenting on draft chapters. They will not find all their comments reflected in the final version, but they have saved me from some blunders. I am extremely thankful for their help. Series editor Roger Richardson, a quick reader, reliable correspondent, and gentle critic, followed the gestation of this book from the outset.

Research was assisted by Oleg Beyda and Rustam Alexander. Scholars of the Soviet Union in their own right, they have made my life as a writer much easier, while Nathan Gardner and Fallon Mody have helped in keeping the workload of the Hansen Professor in more or less sane boundaries. Tim Horning accommodated me at short notice in the UPenn archives, and gave permission to quote from the Lewin papers. The staff of the Harvard Archives and the University of Chicago's Special Collections deserve praise for their professional help. Daniel Pipes gave permission to work with his father's papers. Jonathan Daly shared proofs of his book on the Pipes–Raeff correspondence and made himself available for an interesting discussion of our work over breakfast on a rainy Chicago morning. Simone Bellezza and Marta Havryshko advised on debates surrounding the Holodomor, and Terry Martin might not know that, over a pint outside Harvard Yard, he pointed me towards an important source. Ara Keys bequeathed me her copy of Ulam's *Stalin*, 'to make space on the bookshelf'. It took up valuable real estate on mine, but was well worth the investment.

Chapter 2 was presented in an earlier and shortened form throughout 2018 at history seminars at the University of Melbourne, UNSW Sydney and Monash University. I thank all participants for their comments, and especially Stephen Wheatcroft, who took the time to give me a long and detailed explanation of his take on this chapter and on the history of the R. W. Davies group. Sheila Fitzpatrick answered queries and bravely read chapters about herself. Caroline Maxwell created the index with her usual precision and speed.

Earlier versions of several sections in chapters 4, 6 and 7 have been published before as 'What is a School? Is There a Fitzpatrick School of Soviet History?', *Acta Slavica Iaponica* 24 (2007): 234–37; 'Soviet Society, Social Structure, and Everyday Life. Major Frameworks Reconsidered', *Kritika: Explorations in Russian and Eurasian History* 8, no. 2 (2007): 349–73; 'Stalinism as a Totalitarian Society. Geoffrey Hosking's Socio-Cultural History', *Kritika: Explorations in Russian and Eurasian History* 13, no. 2 (2012): 441–52. Book reviews published in *Slavonic and East European Review* 92, no. 1 (2014): 65–67, and in *Jahrbücher für Geschichte Osteuropas* 58, no. 2 (2010): 302–03 formed the first draft of two other sections.

ACKNOWLEDGEMENTS

Chapter 8 is a substantially revised version of 'Fighting Russia's History Wars: Vladimir Putin and the Codification of World War II', *History and Memory* 29, no. 2 (2017): 90–124.

Notes

1. Abbott Gleason, *Totalitarianism: The Inner History of the Cold War* (Oxford, 1995).
2. David C. Engerman, *Know Your Enemy: The Rise and Fall of America's Soviet Experts* (Oxford, 2009).
3. Jonathan Daly, 'The Pleiade: Five Scholars Who Founded Russian Historical Studies in the United States', *Kritika: Explorations in Russian and Eurasian History* 18, no. 4 (2017): 785–826.
4. R. W. Davies, *Soviet History in the Gorbachev Revolution* (Basingstoke, 1989); Roger Markwick, *Rewriting History in Soviet Russia: The Politics of Revisionist Historiography, 1956–1974* (Basingstoke, 2000); Polly Jones, *Myth, Memory, Trauma: Rethinking the Stalinist Past in the Soviet Union, 1953–70* (New Haven, 2013).
5. R. W. Davies, *Soviet History in the Yeltsin Era* (Basingstoke, 1997); Thomas Sherlock, *Historical Narratives in the Soviet Union and Post-Soviet Russia: Destroying the Settled Past, Creating an Uncertain Future* (New York, 2007); Nikolai Koposov, *Pamiat' strogogo rezhima: Istoriia i politika Rossii* (Moscow, 2011); and David Satter, *It was a Long Time Ago and it Never Happened Anyway: Russia and the Communist Past* (New Haven, 2012).
6. Giuseppe Boffa, *The Stalin Phenomenon* (Ithaca, 1992); Chris Ward, *Stalin's Russia*. 2nd ed. (London, 1999).
7. Alfred J. Rieber, 'Izuchenie istorii Rossii v SShA', *Istoricheskie zapiski* 3, no. 121 (2000): 65–105; Michael David-Fox (ed.), *Amerikanskaia rusistika: vekhi istoriografii poslednikh let, sovetskii period: antologiia* (Samara, 2001).
8. An important editorial which anticipated some of my arguments about continuity in the field is 'From the Editors: Really-Existing Revisionism?', *Kritika: Explorations in Russian and Eurasian History* 2, no. 4 (2001): 707–11.

DEBATES ON STALINISM: AN INTRODUCTION

Stalinism

The historiography of the Soviet Union contains three major fields of contention. The first is the Revolution of 1917, a debate about origins and legitimacy. Why did the Revolution happen? Who supported it? Could it have been avoided? Was it a legitimate revolution or an illegitimate coup?[1] The Soviet Union's end is also controversial, a debate about the future of socialism as much as its history. Was the Soviet Union reformable? Could 1991 have been avoided? Was it doomed from the start, or could it have developed into a more humane version of socialism?[2] The third debate focuses on the years of Stalin's brutal reign, from the end of the 1920s to the dictator's death in 1953: the years of Stalinism. This debate is about the destination of the Soviet project and its essence. It is the topic of this book.

Beginning in 1928, Stalin and his leadership team launched a major revolutionary assault on the society they ruled. This revolution from above had three prongs: quick industrialization of the urban economy, forced collectivization of the peasantry, and the replacement of elites of pre-revolutionary vintage with new Red cadres. The goal was to build a socialist industrial state which could withstand modern war. The immediate results were plummeting living standards, famine, a growing police state, increasing levels of coercion, and a sprawling concentration camp empire. Not content with his first revolution from above, Stalin soon launched a second assault, a peak of state violence known as the Great Terror of 1937–38, when millions were arrested and sent to concentration camps. Some 700,000 were shot.[3]

If calamity and horror were the immediate results of Stalin's policies, in the medium term they allowed the mobilization of the resources of an industrializing agrarian country for modern war. The system focused on heavy industry and armaments, ignoring the needs of the population. It was based on suffering and exploitation and created enormous waste. Shortages and inefficiencies were built into the command economy. But it did get the job done, as became obvious between 1941 and 1945, when the Soviets won the war against Nazi Germany. In the long-term, however, the Stalin revolution created an economy of scarcity and a dictatorial system of government which proved impossible to transform into a socialism with a more human face.[4]

This history of the Soviet Union under Stalin has produced enormous debate. Did 'Stalinism' form a system in its own right or was it a mere stage in the overall development of Soviet society? Was it an aberration from Leninism or the logical conclusion of Marxism? Was its violence the revenge of the Russian past or the result of a revolutionary mindset? Was Stalinism the work of a madman or the product of social forces beyond his control? Could it have been avoided? Could the war have been won without it? What was it like to live within it? The answers to such questions form the historiography of Stalinism.

Definitions

But what does 'Stalinism' mean? For twentieth-century intellectuals on the political Left, the concept was attractive because it allowed them to isolate (good) Marxism from its totalitarian instantiation. That Stalinism was 'bad' was the only judgement everybody using the word seemed to agree on.[5] It was 'the mongrel offspring of Marxism and primitive magic', wrote one prominent writer. Displaying his European prejudices, he added that it was produced 'by the impact of a Marxist revolution upon a semi-Asiatic society'.[6] It was divided from Leninism by 'a whole river of blood', wrote another of Stalin's victims.[7]

Beyond such demarcations, critics differed in what they saw as the actual content of Stalinism. Was it the class rule of the bureaucracy,[8] or the personal despotism of one man?[9] Was it a political system, exemplified not only by the Soviet Union under Stalin but also by 'Eastern Europe, China and Indo-China', the 'internal mode of functioning of many Communist Parties as well as various political sects of the far Left'?[10] Could Stalinism exist without Stalin? Or was that a contradiction in terms and the term denoted 'a special political formation' in which 'the psychopathological personality of Stalin was a powerful driving force'?[11]

Whatever it was, it was a system of rule characterized by 'excess' and 'extraordinary extremism'. Stalinism, to such critics, was 'not merely coercive peasant policies, but a virtual civil war against the peasantry; not merely police repression, or even civil war-style terror, but a holocaust by terror that victimized tens of millions of people for twenty-five years; not merely a ... revival of nationalist tradition, but an almost fascist-like chauvinism; not merely a leader cult, but deification of a despot'.[12] This peculiar combination did not exist before Stalin built his personal power between 1928 and 1938. And, at least in the Soviet Union, it disappeared with his death in 1953. 'Stalinism', then, was the totalitarian phase of Soviet socialism, 'a form of personalized, terroristic rule with totalitarian aspirations, which emerged under conditions of socio-economic change, ethnic-cultural conflicts, institutional underdevelopment and societal mobilization'.[13]

Such definitions seek to grasp the essence of a phenomenon in motion. Neither Stalin's own position,[14] nor the situation of his closest entourage, remained fixed between 1928 and 1953.[15] The society they ruled transformed dramatically under the impact of two revolutions from above (1928–32 and 1937–38), famines (1932–33 and 1946–47), and war (1938–49). People and peoples were moved around, social structures dissolved and reformed, humans were killed, personalities 'reforged'. Terror came in waves, with periods of relative calm in between, and the police forces underwent remarkable evolution, both institutionally and in terms of their repressive practice.[16] Even the physical borders of Stalin's realm changed repeatedly between 1939 and 1951.

Thus, historians view Stalinism simply 'as that which happened during Stalin's tenure as General Secretary'.[17] More precisely, most begin Stalinism in 1928 – that is, with the moment Stalin and his team won the factional fights after Lenin's death. Such a definition, of course, just describes the boundaries of the phenomenon under review, not its content. Therefore, this book does not include a discussion of the 'export of Stalinism' to other places or times. It is a book not about a political model or an ideological construct, but about attempts to understand a concrete society in a concrete space and a concrete time: the historiography of the Soviet Union under Stalin.

Historiography

'Historiography' has at least three meanings. The term can denote an honest account of the state of a field of historical research, of the findings of fact and the changing approaches of those who came before: the kind of review essay one finds at the beginning of good doctoral dissertations. It maps the current state of knowledge for a particular topic in order to define an agenda: What is there still to be known? What contribution will this particular piece of history-writing make? Historiography can also be a narrative of a field of historical study – a history of history. Such accounts sometimes lapse into myth: historians tend to tell a particular story which places their own work at the apex of a historical development. The writer's own approach, it usually turns out, is the latest paradigm all other scholars are to follow. A third approach to historiography sees it as debate: between scholars and between the present and the past. This approach focuses on disagreements and their underlying logic. It does not assume that the truest account of the past wins: history is political.[18]

This book owes something to each of these approaches. It tries to provide a sketch of the history of my field which is based on evidence, on sources, and on plausible interpretation. *Debates on Stalinism* also gives readers a general orientation of where the study of Stalinism is, what we know, and what we have learned collectively. It tries to dispel myths about the field's own past, not promote one version of it. It does not tell a story from darkness to light, but shows the complexities in the development of the field. At times, *Debates on Stalinism* comments on what I see as the current consensus on a matter, and in the conclusion I offer my own view of what are the most promising avenues of further research. But Stalinism is such a wide field of research that giving a full account would be impossible in a book of this length. It would also be tedious. Hence, the focus is on particular debates and their implications. Other historians would have written different chapters. They should do so.

Overview and arguments

The book begins with a debate among anglophone scholars in the mid-1980s, which marked the point when historians had left enough of a mark on Stalinism that they could claim this field of study as rightfully theirs. The 'revisionism debate' erupted just when the Soviet Union began to embark on its most determined attempt

DEBATES ON STALINISM: AN INTRODUCTION

yet to get rid of the legacy of Stalinism: General Secretary Mikhail Gorbachev's reforms, known as '*glasnost*' (openness) and '*perestroika*' (reconstruction). They would lead to the breakdown of the Soviet empire, an event with far-reaching consequences for the study of Stalinism. But in 1986 none of this was clear, and the debate reflected all the bitterness of the Cold War. The chapter also introduces a major myth about the history of this field: a narrative about a succession of generations – totalitarians, revisionists, post-revisionists.

Next come three biographical studies. Chapter 2 recounts the life and work of Moshe Lewin, a scholar who marked the extreme Left of polite academic discourse about Stalinism in the United States. His equivalent on the Right was Richard Pipes (Chapter 3), a scholar of Russian history and the Russian Empire whose work also had enormous influence on how the wider public understood both Stalinism and the work of the so-called 'revisionists'. Chapter 4 moves on to the most iconic of them – Sheila Fitzpatrick.

Together, these three chapters make several points. One is that the generational narrative of totalitarianism-revisionism-post-revisionism is inadequate to describe the history of this field; another, that this historiography is transnational in more than one respect. Not only do scholars in different countries read each other's works. The scholars themselves are products of international lives: all three of the major American historians of Stalinism these chapters explore were recent immigrants who brought sensibilities from other contexts with them.

This transnational nature of much of the debate is a main theme of this book. Displaced scholars, circulating ideas, and a multiplicity of national, political, ideological and temporal contexts explain the particular richness of this historiography, but also the often acrimonious debate, fuelled by ideological and political confrontations, but also by mutual misunderstandings.[19] Given that this book is written for an anglophone audience, a bias towards English-language historiography remains: a German, French, Russian or Ukrainian history of the field of Stalinism studies would look different. Nevertheless, the deeper I got into writing the book, the more did the theme of transnationalism assert itself – not so much by design or by dictates of fashion, but because it was such a defining aspect of the historiography.[20]

5

Third, the biographical studies complicate the phrase 'history is political' – an assumption of the series *Issues in Historiography*. In the writing of history politics is personal and hence often idiosyncratic. Political positions are entangled with personality, biography, and the environment historians move in. Personal experiences, individual resentments, fears and hopes all shape a historian's outlook on life, the world and the past. Changing fashions and changing source bases, too, have their impact. Academic politics – the struggle for recognition, for positions, for book contracts, for good reviews, for readers, for influence – is as significant as ideological commitments, sometimes more so. Thus, we need to know something about the historians involved, about their life paths, personalities and careers, not just their politics, presumed or real.[21]

The rest of the book shifts from studying individuals and their work to debates and literatures. The first is about Stalin, the centre of Stalinism (Chapter 5). Biographies of the dictator often serve as ways into the history of this society more broadly. We observe not only how topics of 'totalitarians', 'revisionists', or 'post-revisionists' appear at inopportune moments in this literature, but also how historians learn from each other despite polemical oppositions. This process of learning and forgetting is another theme the book explores throughout.

Chapters 6 and 7 investigate in a more systematic fashion the debate about totalitarianism, revisionism, and what came after. The themes of learning and forgetting and of personal idiosyncrasies reappear, but the inadequacy of the established narrative about the development of the field is at the centre of attention. Rather than totalitarians being replaced by revisionists only to be overcome by post-revisionists, the two chapters demonstrate that neither revisionism nor post-revisionism really broke free from the framework drawn up by earlier scholarship. Far from being overcome, the concept of totalitarianism in its empirical application captured something essential about Stalinism. Rather than a series of ruptures, then, the two chapters of Part III narrate the unfolding of one larger paradigm. This way of telling the story explains why explicitly totalitarian approaches could so easily be reappropriated by scholars in the 1990s. The concept continues to serve political purposes in a world where open societies are again under attack by their enemies.

DEBATES ON STALINISM: AN INTRODUCTION

The final two chapters are devoted to highly charged contemporary debates. Chapter 8 explores how the history of Stalin's Second World Wars have become a battleground for identity politics in today's Russia. Chapter 9 focuses on similar processes in Ukraine, where the Great Famine, known now as Holodomor, has taken the status of a central national myth. In both chapters we see that the end of the Cold War has not depoliticized the debates about the Stalinist past. It merely recast their politics.

That these debates are highly transnational makes them, if anything, fiercer. Passions flare in Twitter storms. Russian, Ukrainian, Polish, and Baltic nationalisms are ever-present. Outside the successor states, other identities muddle the picture. Many of the intellectuals involved are cosmopolitans with more than one loyalty. Few have easily identifiable identities; most have complex careers; and all are – to one extent or another – products of transnational debates, and often transnational lives. Transnationalism and the increasing cosmopolitanism of historical debate, while exciting to intellectuals, also heighten the risk of saying something that someone, somewhere, will find offensive. In many ways, historians today face the often complex choice of whom, not whether, to offend.

Overall, this book combines a thematic with a chronological approach. Each chapter tells the story of the life of one person or the changes over time to one particular topic. The book, overall, begins in the 1980s and ends in the 2010s, with various flashbacks as far back as the 1930s along the way. Taken together, the chapters narrate the increasing internationalization and professionalization of the field, but also stress countervailing forces of renationalization and repoliticization. Hence, no upward movement towards greater enlightenment, no clear shift between paradigms, but also no story of rise and fall structures this book. Instead, the reader will follow this history in all its complexity.

The final verdict is decidedly mixed: while historians today have a much larger source base and a much better secondary literature about Stalinism at their disposal than ever before, many chose to forget about the work of their predecessors. Moreover, while a large part of the field has become professionalized, Stalinism remains full of political touchstones, both within the region of the former Soviet Union and without. While these help to engender debates and keep this history relevant, they also often create roadblocks to understanding.

DEBATES ON STALINISM: AN INTRODUCTION

Notes

1. See Ronald G. Suny, *Red Flag Unfurled: History, Historians, and the Russian Revolution* (London, 2017).
2. For introductions, see David Rowley, 'Interpretations of the End of the Soviet Union: Three Paradigms', *Kritika: Explorations in Russian and Eurasian History* 2, no. 2 (2001): 395–426; and David R. Marples, 'Revisiting the Collapse of the USSR', *Canadian Slavonic Papers* 53, no. 2/4 (2011): 461–73.
3. For my own summary see Mark Edele, *Stalinist Society 1928–1953* (Oxford, 2011).
4. I tell this overall story in Mark Edele, *The Soviet Union: A Short History* (Oxford, 2019).
5. Cf. Giuseppe Boffa, 'The Problem of Stalinism', *The Stalin Phenomenon* (Ithaca, 1992), 1–13.
6. Isaac Deutscher, *Russia After Stalin: With a Postscript on the Beria Affair* (London, 1953), 52.
7. Leon Trotsky, 'Stalinism and Bolshevism', (August 1937), https://www.marxists.org/archive/trotsky/1937/08/stalinism.htm (accessed 6 June 2019).
8. Leon Trotsky, *The Revolution Betrayed: What Is the Soviet Union and Where Is It Going?* (New York, 1972); Milovan Djilas, *The New Class: An Analysis of the Communist System* (New York, 1957). The rule of the bureaucracy, of course, continued after Stalin's death: M. S. Voslenskii, *Nomenklatura: Anatomy of the Soviet Ruling Class* (London, 1984).
9. N. S. Khrushchev, 'On the Cult of Personality and Its Consequences', in: *The Stalin Dictatorship: Khrushchev's 'Secret Speech' and Other Documents*, ed. T. H. Rigby (Sydney, 1968), 23–89.
10. Tariq Ali, 'Preface', in: *The Stalinist Legacy: Its Impact on Twentieth-Century World Politics*, ed. Tariq Ali. 2nd ed. (Chicago, 2013),7–8, here: 7.
11. Robert C. Tucker, *The Soviet Political Mind: Stalinism and Post-Stalin Change.* Rev. ed. (New York, 1971), xi.
12. Stephen F. Cohen, 'Bolshevism and Stalinism', in: *Stalinism: Essays in Historical Interpretation*, ed. Robert C. Tucker (New York, 1977), 3–29, here: 12.
13. Jörg Baberowski, Wandel und Terror: Die Sowjetunion unter Stalin 1928–1941. Ein Literaturbericht', *Jahrbücher für Geschichte Osteuropas* 43, no. 1 (1995): 97–129, here: 129.
14. S. G. Wheatcroft, 'From Team-Stalin to Degenerate Tyranny', in: *The Nature of Stalin's Dictatorship: The Politburo, 1924–1953*, ed. E. A. Rees (Basingstoke, 2003), 79–107.
15. Sheila Fitzpatrick, *On Stalin's Team: The Years of Living Dangerously in Soviet Politics* (Melbourne, 2015).
16. Paul Hagenloh, *Stalin's Police: Public Order and Mass Repression in the USSR, 1926–1941* (Baltimore, 2009); David R. Shearer, *Policing Stalin's Socialism: Repression and Social Order in the Soviet Union, 1924–1953* (New Haven, 2009).
17. Chris Ward, 'Introduction', in: *The Stalinist Dictatorship*, ed. Chris Ward (London, 1998), 1–3, here: 2.

18 A famous exponent of this view was also a historian of the Soviet Union. E. H. Carr, *What Is History? The George Macaulay Trevelyan Lectures Delivered at the University of Cambridge January–March 1961* (New York, 1961).
19 The issue of the international nature of the field has been raised by Michael Confino, 'The New Russian Historiography and the Old – Some Considerations', *History and Memory* 21, no. 2 (2009): 8–33, here: 21–26.
20 Akira Iriye, *Global and Transnational History: The Past, Present, and Future* (Basingstoke, 2013).
21 For this approach to historiography, see also R. J. B. Bosworth, *Explaining Auschwitz and Hiroshima: History Writing and the Second World War 1945–1990* (London, 1993).

Part I

Biography and historiography

1
A 'withering crossfire': debating Stalinism in the Cold War

A modest proposal

In 1986, a 45-year-old scholar, a professor at the University of Texas in Austin with three major books and an important edited collection under her belt, published a survey of emerging social history scholarship on Stalinism. This article, she pleaded, 'should not be read as a New Cohort manifesto'. Rather, it was an investigation of 'the likely impact of historians, particularly social historians, on the study of the Stalin period'. Her claims were modest: 'What has emerged from the recent scholarship', she wrote, 'is an appreciation that no political regime, including Stalin's, functions in a social vacuum.' At the end of the essay she made a proposal for a methodological innovation, which, from our vantage point in the early twenty-first century, seems as unadventurous as her treatment of the historiography. Instead of exclusively focusing on state–society relations, social historians should look at social relations relatively independent of the state. Removing the state 'from centre stage' would allow scholars 'to formulate new questions and develop a real social-history perspective on the Stalin period'.[1]

What happened next is hard to understand for those who have grown up after the Soviet Union ended. In the words of the then editor of the scholarly journal in which Sheila Fitzpatrick's 'New Perspectives on Stalinism' was published, she had been 'lured … into a withering crossfire'.[2] This chapter reviews this fight, which played out in the pages of *The Russian Review* in 1986 and 1987. It introduces many influential players in anglophone Stalinism studies and gives readers a first glimpse of the fierceness of the Cold War debate which is often referred to – misleadingly as we shall see – as a debate between 'revisionists' and 'totalitarians'.

We can learn several basic lessons from the spectacle of the 1986–87 brawl: first, that history can be deeply political – for better or for worse; second, that once academia becomes politicized to the extent it was in the 1980s, things can turn very nasty. In academic debates, as we will see again and again in this book, personality, politics and disciplinary identity are entangled so strongly with each other and with feelings of loyalty and betrayal, vanity and resentment, that reducing an exchange to one of these dimensions makes little analytical sense. Historians are human beings. This simple fact means that we can try to understand their behaviour and their writing – the task of this book.

'Deeply troubled'

The attacks on Fitzpatrick's article were kicked off by Stephen Cohen, a political scientist teaching at Princeton. Cohen had the distinction of having invented the 'Bukharin alternative' – the thesis that Stalin was not really necessary. Had only his more learned colleague in the Politburo, Nikolai Bukharin, won the factional fights of the 1920s, Bolshevism would have had a much more human face.[3] Cohen, then, was a man of the Left. His defence of Leninism against the charge of guilt by association with Stalinism remains the most eloquent exposé of the differences between the two regimes ever since Leon Trotsky had separated them by 'a river of blood'.[4]

Cohen was 'deeply troubled', he charged, 'by two important omissions in Fitzpatrick's article', which despite her disclaimer he declared a 'New Cohort manifesto'. Fitzpatrick's first fault was that she had not quoted Cohen enough. Part of her target had been the 'totalitarian model', a social science approach to Stalinism which had helped frame much of the earlier research. There were, however, some political scientists working on the Soviet Union, Cohen among them, who had 'rejected the totalitarian model's blinkered obsession with "the Kremlin"'. It did not matter that these scholars had not written about Stalinism or that they had 'not actually investigated Soviet society itself', as Cohen admitted. They should have been quoted anyway. Fitzpatrick's craft consciousness as a historian – the essay had asked what would change with historians taking over the interpretation of Stalinism – clearly irritated the political scientist.

Secondly, Fitzpatrick had not paid tribute to the establishment. Moshe Lewin, 'the *doyen* of social history in Soviet studies', had not received the respect he deserved. This criticism was somewhat odd. After all, Fitzpatrick was writing not about old men but about a new cohort, to whom Lewin, born in 1921, patently did not belong. Moreover, his work had not been ignored. Instead, she had gently criticized Lewin as a follower of Trotsky, a classification which Cohen dismissed. This denial of Lewin's Trotskyite tendencies was even odder, as the founder of the Red Army was one of Lewin's 'admired predecessors', as one of 'Misha's' friends would write later.[5]

Fitzpatrick's article had created, Cohen continued, 'the impression that the new social historians have no scholarly predecessor or intellectual debts'. 'The golden rule of revisionist scholars must be', he mansplained, 'credit others as you would have others credit you.' Somewhat contradictorily, however, he also repeated what Fitzpatrick had stated in her own essay: social history research was only beginning. It would require 'dozens of scholars, many diverse monographs, and years of work'. Fitzpatrick should publish less, he implied, and not formulate hypotheses: 'ample data should precede large generalizations'.[6]

Cohen then hit her with the greatest stick in the arsenal of polemics on the Soviet Union: the Terror. In all revisionist writing, he claimed, 'the terror is ignored, obscured, or minimized in one way or another'. In *The Russian Revolution* (1982), Fitzpatrick had indeed expressed scepticism about estimates of millions of repression deaths (executions plus deaths in custody) during the Great Terror of 1937–38. Following calculations made by her former husband, the political scientist Jerry Hough, who had used available census data, she wrote that 'a figure in the low hundreds of thousands seems more plausible'. We now know that this number was way off the mark – as were the estimates in the millions. The NKVD (People's Commissariat for Internal Affairs) registered 681,692 executions in 1937–38. Adding liquidations of non-political prisoners and mortality in detention leads to an overall number of repression deaths during these two lethal years of between 950,000 and 1.2 million.[7]

The Great Terror played a major role in the argument of *Education and Social Mobility* (1979), however, which showed that the Stalinist 1930s were a period of immense social mobility. The Terror, in Fitzpatrick's narrative, was the moment when cadres of working-class origins, who had been trained in the late 1920s and early 1930s, got the good jobs because their elders had been shot. In *The Russian Revolution* too, the supposed whitewasher of Stalin had called the Great Purge of 1937–38 a 'monstrous postscript' to the Revolution with a 'casualty rate ... as high as 70 per cent' among top administrators.[8]

Cohen did not seem to remember such statements. Fitzpatrick and 'her cohort' were guilty of minimizing the Terror, were using the wrong words, and did not follow in every word previous critiques by Cohen, who, 'unable to rephrase the point better' again resorted 'to quoting myself'. On and on it went: Why did social historians not focus on what was already well known – that Stalin's was a regime of terror producing large number of victims? Why did they not write with moral disgust about this system? Why did they focus on social processes rather than fear? He ended dogmatically: 'The terror must be a central feature of the social history of Stalinism not because it was more important than anything else, but because it was an essential part of almost everything else.' Before social history had actually been done – as he had pointed out only pages before – Cohen already knew the answer.[9]

'Rather shocking'

If the first attack on Fitzpatrick's proposal for a social history of Stalinism came from a non-historian, the next charge came from a scholar with no expertise in the Soviet Union: Geoff Eley, a historian of Germany. He compared the development of social history in his own field with what seemed to be taking place in the history of Stalinism. Assuming a universal history of method and approach, he painted Soviet history as backward, which came with the distinct advantage that 'key methodological and conceptual debates have already taken place among British, French, and American historians'. In particular, Fitzpatrick should read more German history, where similar debates had already taken place. Having thus defined Fitzpatrick's task in his own terms, he asked:

'How successfully does Sheila Fitzpatrick meet this challenge?' Not very well, was his unsurprising conclusion.[10]

Like Cohen, Eley chided Fitzpatrick for not honouring her elders and dismissing the totalitarianism literature too quickly. He listed other scholars who should have been cited, including the history-writing economists Alec Nove and R. W. Davies, and, again, Lewin. Unaware that what Lewin had written was largely political rather than social history, he exclaimed: 'To go through an entire survey of the prospects for a social history of Stalinism without once mentioning the work of Lewin, except to lump it misleadingly with Trotskyist discussions of bureaucracy, is rather shocking.' He even made Fitzpatrick responsible for Cohen's 'outrageous dismissal' of a scholar she had neither mentioned nor attacked: E. H. Carr.[11]

Eley ignored, like Cohen before him, Fitzpatrick's disclaimer that she was not writing a manifesto for the new cohort. Reading her mind rather than her essay, he declared that the latter was 'clearly intended as a manifesto of social history'. As such, it was wanting: not theoretical enough, and too interested in the history from below. The state must not be removed from the centre of analysis, because in Stalinism it was central. 'The state', he lectured, 'is not something that can be removed or restored by historians at will.' Mistaking Fitzpatrick's methodological tactic for an overall theory of society, he criticized her for lacking a 'totalizing social-history perspective'. Her essay displayed a 'deficit of theory'. She should read Lewin, who had already given all the answers 'with a singular intelligence'. Fitzpatrick's ideas, by contrast, were 'banal'.[12]

'Outlandish'

Next in line was finally a historian of Russia, although not of the Stalin years: Peter Kenez (born 1937), an immigrant of middle-class Jewish-Hungarian extraction. The Nazis had murdered his father at Auschwitz. He had survived the Second World War, and for a while indulged in his social resentments as a young communist after the war before becoming disillusioned with this bleak utopianism. Eventually he emigrated to the United States, ideally suited to embrace the notion of totalitarianism. Fittingly, Kenez became a student of the Harvard professor Richard Pipes, a major exponent of this approach (and later an adviser to Ronald Reagan). By the time he joined *The Russian Review* debate, Kenez was an accomplished scholar. He had written two important books on the Whites in the Civil War, and one on *The Birth of the Propaganda State* (which ended in 1929 but called Stalinism 'totalitarian'). He had not published research on Stalin's years in power, however.[13]

Kenez was nearly kind. He acknowledged that Fitzpatrick was 'correct in identifying a new and self-consciously revisionist group of historians of the era of Stalin', which included J. Arch Getty, Roberta Manning, Gabor Rittersporn, Lynne Viola and William Chase. 'Clearly, something noteworthy is happening in rewriting the history of Stalinism.' A careful reader, Kenez picked up the extent to which Fitzpatrick was positioning herself outside the group she was describing. 'If the revisionists were as reasonable as she, I would have fewer disagreements with them', he concluded. He pointed out that Fitzpatrick's own preoccupation with 'an analysis of social relations and social mobility' was singular among the revisionists: 'It is she alone ... who has made a lasting contribution' to this field of study. Meanwhile, if social history was 'an examination of how simple people actually lived, then the best book on that topic still is the old classic of Merle Fainsod, *Smolensk under Soviet Rule*'. The revisionists – with the exception of Fitzpatrick – were 'just as interested in the question of power, hence, politics, as those whose works they choose to attack'. Their views, however, were 'so outlandish that I wonder what makes them see the past the way they do'.[14]

The first round of the debate came to an end with the intervention of Alfred G. Meyer, a political scientist who had written extensively on the Soviet political system as well as Marxism, socialism and feminism. His role had presumably been to represent, like Kenez, the position of the 'totalitarians'. He was indeed a representative of the generation of Sovietologists, who largely worked within this framework. He knew Fitzpatrick personally, and turned out to be tolerant. He began with the assertion that there was no unpolitical history-writing: 'all history-writing is a projection of present-day politics into the past'. What followed was a thoughtful discussion of the extent to which the totalitarian model reflected historical reality while at the same time 'celebrating Americanism ... and succumbing to cold-war hysteria'. He gently reminded 'scholars of Fitzpatrick's generation' of 'the profound effect that the cold-war hysteria of the 1940s and 1950s had had on scholarship', illustrating his point with memorable anecdotes. He saw the new social history as an 'attempt to exorcise McCarthyism and knee-jerk anticommunisn. As such, it should be hailed as a healthy and long-overdue reaction.' Meyer presented a sympathetic reading of revisionists like Getty and Rittersporn, pointing out that 'neither the older cohort of the totalitarian school nor the present-day revisionists deny that some dreadful things happened during the reign of Stalin. Their argument is only over who is to be blamed for them.' His only criticism was Fitzpatrick's somewhat caricatured view of the totalitarian model, which he corrected in a tour de force through the intellectual history of confronting the Soviet past.[15]

'Not much use'

Fitzpatrick must have been furious after reading these criticisms which, as she remembered two decades later, 'assailed me ... from every possible direction'.[16] Nevertheless, when given the chance to reply she remained remarkably calm, assuming an air of aloofness. Her response showed, in the words of the journal's editor, that 'her own weapons are still in good order'.[17]

Her critics 'were obviously confused about the point of my article', she began. She was not a 'young revisionist' any more. Like Cohen, she belonged 'to the middle-aged cohort'. And she did not write a manifesto for the new scholarship. 'The new cohort is quite capable of writing its own manifestos. I was giving a friendly account of its members' work, as Kenez notes. But I was also giving a friendly account of my disagreements with them on a number of points I consider important.' And yes, she had not discussed 'Carr or Lewin or Fainsod', but then their work was 'surely familiar to everybody with an interest in the field, and my article was about new perspectives on the social history of the Stalin period'. She also added a footnote on two other important 'young revisionists' – Lewis Siegelbaum and John Barber – who she did not mention 'in the final version of the article', because she had no disagreements with their work.[18]

The totalitarian model did explain certain things quite well, she noted: yes, terror was 'a pervasive presence affecting all the other parts' and social historians should work on it. 'That is why I organized a workshop of social historians on the subject in Austin last spring.' In order to lessen her critics' confusion she made explicit her anti-Marxism, calmly reasserted her classification of Lewin as a Trotskyite – which had so agitated Eley and Cohen – and waved away the 'ponderous scholasticism', 'semantic orthodoxy' and 'intellectual jargon' often associated with the neo-Marxist 'general theory' advocated by Eley. His universal view of historiographical progress was ridiculous: 'He evidently thinks in terms of upward progress through stages of increasing enlightenment and offers Soviet historians a preview of the Western (higher) stage.' Her own concerns were much more modest: she had made a point about 'short-term scholarly research tactics'.

As far as Cohen was concerned, his method of repeating 'familiar data (and pseudo-data) ... framed by restatement of familiar moral judgments' was more 'appropriate for polemics and advocacy journalism'. It was 'not much use to scholarship, whose purpose', she lectured, 'should be the advancement of knowledge'. This endeavour required critical examination of data and thorough source critique, 'otherwise there is no point in doing research in this area'. Did Cohen really mean, she asked rhetorically, 'that hypotheses should never be put forward or tested? That historians should start with a priori conclusions about everything and spend their time confirming them?'

She did not leave these questions in the realm of the rhetorical: 'I suspect that, up to a point, this is indeed what he means.' That was fine, she added tolerantly. Scholars often had ideological commitments and then went on to find the evidence to support their preconceptions. But there was 'no requirement' to follow this method. She herself was a '"so-called objective" type' who did not have 'a political or ideological position that I value equally or more' than the 'illusion of objectivity'. There were, she added, 'ideological revisionists' (like Cohen) and 'iconoclastic revisionists' (like herself).[19]

Betrayal

If Fitzpatrick thought her counter-attack had ended the matter she was mistaken. Indeed, in the introduction to the issue of *The Russian Review* in which the initial brawl took place, the editor had already noted that 'passions are boiling in other breasts. I write some ten weeks before this issue will be published; four colleagues have already written to request space to comment on the exchange.' A year later, Daniel Field began to become mildly disgusted with the debate he had started. 'Almost all the contenders seek to advance the debate', he wrote in the editorial which introduced round two of the fight, 'but also to defend and vindicate their own writings. The proportion of footnotes in which the author cites his or her own work seems high.' There was 'a tincture of vanity' in these responses which became 'conspicuous' when reading them all together.[20]

Part of the second round was a replay of the first. Again, Fitzpatrick was scolded for not quoting this or that scholar, sometimes by the historian in question. Again, the revisionists were accused of downplaying the Terror. Again, they were charged with making straw men out of the older literature on totalitarianism. Dismissive attacks on the character of the historians in question were also nearly standard: revisionists were displaying 'parochialism, limited vision, and ignorance of the nature of historical (or other) evidence', wrote the always reliable totalitarianism scholar, Robert Conquest.[21]

However, there was also a new element to the debate: a visceral reaction by 'young revisionists' themselves. Most of them seemed annoyed to be added to that group. 'I read with great interest the … discussion … about a new school of young revisionists emerging in the field of Sovietology', quipped the 32-year-old Lynne Viola, in a contribution Field found 'defensive'. There was 'no clearly identifiable cohort', Viola declared, and she certainly was not 'young'. At the time, Viola was an untenured assistant professor at the State University of New York, whose dissertation on collectivizers had just been published as a book. Fitzpatrick had been a long-term supporter of her work and had smoothed her way in the archives.[22]

Others protested too: 'For everyone's sake', wrote an exasperated William Chase (whose dissertation book on the Moscow working class between revolution and Stalinism had just left the printing press) 'can we all agree to drop the appellation "Fitzpatrick's cohort".' Yes, her work was important, but no, she was 'not the founder of any school or cohort'. Hiroaki Kuromiya, a 1985 Princeton PhD, at the time a fellow of King's College, Cambridge, whose doctoral thesis was about to hit the bookshelves as a major monograph on Stalin's industrialization, also complained that his cohort was 'not a cabal of Fitzpatrickists'.[23]

Had she betrayed the cause? It seemed so to Rittersporn, a researcher based in France: 'Brandishing so many olive branches in so many directions that she is about to metamorphose into a dreadful Shiva', he wrote, 'Fitzpatrick risks destroying promising paradigms she helped to construct.'[24]

There was universal condemnation of Fitzpatrick's proposed research tactic among those she tried to influence: 'I have trouble supporting Fitzpatrick's desire to see scholars write social history devoid of politics', wrote Chase. 'To suppose that we can study society without addressing politics is quixotic.' Getty, too, labelled moving the state away from the centre of analysis 'unworkable', agreeing 'completely with Eley on this point'. 'We are not likely to abandon the study of politics as a matter of little concern to social historians', added Roberta Manning, while Viola labelled 'leaving politics out of history' a 'most objectionable practice'. Fitzpatrick was 'the only person' proposing any such thing.[25]

Both Fitzpatrick and Field were taken aback by the responses. 'I have had many compliments for sponsoring the first exchange', wrote Field in October 1987, 'but vanity and pettiness seem to permeate this round.' Conquest's first response Field sent back: 'I wrote to Conquest saying, somewhat more politely, that his contribution was asinine and he would do well to withdraw it, [and] he responded with a new version.' The contribution by another scholar on the Right he rejected out of hand as 'a thinly disguised review-essay on Lynne Viola's new book' which he could not have reviewed because his professional links to her were too close. 'His theme is that you are a demon, Arch [Getty] is Mephistopheles, and Lynne Viola is the devil herself.'[26] Fitzpatrick wrote back: 'I hope you will include Conquest's piece, even if he does not add footnotes. It adds a missing dimension to the discussion.'[27] This apparently generous response hid more negative psychological reactions, as we shall see in Chapter 4.

The context

The 1986–87 exchange (if that is the right word) was extraordinary in its fierceness, the lack of restraint of the tussling parties, and the anger which drove much of the debate. Many participants quite clearly forgot their manners and lashed out in ways not usually seen in academic debate. Why did Fitzpatrick's relatively modest proposal for a change of research tactics provoke such fury?

The explanation lies in the context of the debate rather than its substance. For most of the participants, what was at stake was not a methodological tactic for scholarly research. What was at issue was socialism, as the journal's editor pointed out:

> For some, it is a matter of moral urgency to link the victims of Stalinist terror to socialism; for others, it is no less urgent to detach the terror from the socialist cause and show it to be an aberration. And because our colleagues in the USSR generally seek to uphold the honor of Soviet socialism by ignoring the terror, it seems all the more important to scholars in the West to keep it in the foreground of any discussion of the Stalin era.[28]

Chase was more precise: what was at stake was Stalinism. Critics of revisionism used 'their commentaries to reaffirm their hatred of Stalinism and sublimating their moral indignation with that system into an unjust condemnation of those who seek to clarify our understanding of it'.[29]

Understanding this debate, then, presupposed knowledge of the history of socialism, its detractors, supporters and fellow-travellers, as well as the role Stalinism played in this ongoing debate. What we need to get a handle on, in other words, is nothing less than 'the inner history of the Cold War' – a topic we return to again and again in this book.[30]

The debate was political in another sense, an aspect which is often overlooked: Fitzpatrick was a woman; the vast majority of her critics were men. For scholars trained in detecting gendered forms of discourse in academic encounters, it is hard not to suspect barely concealed male panic in some of the responses.[31] Cohen, for one, was only a few years Fitzpatrick's senior (he was born in 1938, she in 1941); they had published a similar number of books; and yet he felt he could tell her that it was 'too early' to claim to have 'revised scholarly thinking about Stalinism in an original or substantial way'.[32] Lewin, the man, had published one substantial monograph on the decision to collectivize[33] and a collection of essays also focusing on the making of Stalinism (his third book was concerned with post-Stalinist affairs).[34] He was the 'doyen' of the history of Stalinism. Fitzpatrick, the woman, had also written one substantial monograph on Stalinism (and one on the Civil War), a best-selling textbook locating the 1930s in the large sweep of the Russian Revolution, had edited a collection of essays on the Stalin revolution, and was working on a second book on Stalinism. She had no right yet to speak, let alone would be called a *doyenne* any time soon.[35] Indeed, her critics constantly acted as if she was a 'young revisionist', rather than an established scholar.

Nor did it help that Fitzpatrick's demeanour was likely to alienate others. As she wrote decades later:

> I have often denied being an ideologist or crusader for a cause, but in fact in the 1970s I was a one-woman crusade to establish the discipline of history in the study of the Soviet past. The word 'discipline' should here be taken in its broad as well as narrow meaning; I thought American Sovietologists needed the discipline (even the punishment?) of data and primary sources to make honest scholars out of them. (It seems unsurprising, looking back, that this amazing arrogance often annoyed people.)[36]

Fitzpatrick's footnotes were lean and, as we shall see in Chapter 6, the image of the totalitarianism literature she painted was caricatured. Effectively, she was discarding, in the words of Eley, 'the baby of analysis with the bathwater of the model'.[37] Several scholars – Cohen, Eley, Nove – were annoyed that their work had not been cited, a common complaint among scholars, and one which Fitzpatrick made no attempt to pre-empt by fattening up her footnotes.

Finally, Fitzpatrick did not simply take sides with the revisionists, who did have what Eley called a 'totalizing social-history perspective'. In their view, the state was a fundamental part of the overall structure of social relations ('society'), not something opposed to it. To them the government, its institutions, and means of coercion were part and parcel of the overall social formation. Everything was linked to everything else, and the borders between the state and 'the rest of society' were complex, fuzzy and shifting. The new cohort embraced a theory of power reminiscent of what would later be popularized by English translations of the work of French philosopher Michel Foucault: it moved, wrote Getty, 'from the top down, from the bottom up, and in a variety of lateral directions'. Politics was 'practiced everywhere and at all levels of Soviet society in the Stalin period'.[38]

Given such a vision of the Soviet polity it made no sense to hypothesize, like Fitzpatrick, that there could be political processes which followed their own logic and social processes which might be driven internally. 'It is disappointing', wrote Getty, that Fitzpatrick 'resurrects the old bipolar state–society model in the form of Revolution from Above or Below.' He labelled this scheme 'retrogressive'. Viola used the term 'trite'.[39]

The more emotional reactions, however, were prompted by something other than theoretical disagreements. They were also not triggered by the original essay but by an aside in her response to the critics: what Fitzpatrick described later as her 'gratuitous slaps at fellow revisionists', which she had made in the heat of debate. In her riposte, the criticism of the young cohort had become much sharper than in the initial essay, accusing them of 'counter moralizing' and of diverting 'blame for terror from the regime'. 'Not surprisingly', she later conceded, the admonition of alleged political bias

> produced angry responses from … 'new cohort' members asserting that, if they belonged to any school, it certainly was not mine. A sense of betrayal came through clearly in this exchange, prompting Stephen Kotkin to remark unkindly a decade later that I had led the revisionists into the wilderness and abandoned them there. Of course, I felt somewhat abandoned myself, with the young revisionists joining everyone else in beating up on me; for some reason I did not see how hefty a provocation I had offered in my 'Afterword'.[40]

While some revisionists felt betrayed, nothing less than subjection to the authority of the elders would do for some of the totalitarianism scholars. In the polarized atmosphere of the Cold War, Fitzpatrick's independence incensed all sides. Her unwillingness to join a faction had a longer history, as we shall see in Chapter 4: she was an anti-Marxist revisionist, while many of the other revisionists were Marxists of some shape or other. As a result, she effectively fought a two-front scholarly campaign: against Marxists on the Left, and the totalitarian model on the Right.

Results

Eventually, the debate died down. What could be said had been said. Indeed, often more had been said than should have in public. Certain aspects would linger, such as the nearly ritual incantation that one must not 'leave the state out' of analyses of Stalinism, a refrain for a long time to come. The notion that totalitarianism was useless and dead, a central assumption of the revisionists, would be disproved by some of their students who would reinvent the concept for their own ends, as we shall see in Chapter 7.

After the opening of the archives, the questions about the number of victims and the extent of the Terror – so central to the debate – could finally be investigated empirically. These studies proved the totalitarians and the left-wing revisionists like Cohen correct, both in their view of the Terror as driven from above, and as broadly victimizing ordinary Soviet citizens well beyond the elite. At the same time they were patently wrong in the enormous numbers they had cited without much evidence.[41]

What remained was the thesis that there were 'cohorts' in the writing of Soviet history, and that these generations were separated by methodological approaches: totalitarians were followed by revisionists. This scheme was, at best, a simplification of the real intellectual history of the field, as many in the debate had pointed out; at worst, it was a misleading myth which served only to diminish the incentives to read the rich literature of the 1950s and 1960s. This myth was so deeply engrained in anglophone historiography, that when a new cohort of scholars made their debut in US academia in the 1990s, some of them felt compelled to write themselves into the historical narrative as the next step of historiographical progress: 'post-revisionism'. We shall return to this phenomenon in Chapter 7.

In the long-term, the scuffle in *The Russian Review* helped confirm Fitzpatrick as one of the leaders in the anglophone social history of Stalinism. If a little methodological essay leads to fierce reactions by nearly everybody with a name in the profession, then the author must clearly have something to say. This reputation attracted research students, who would flock to Fitzpatrick, particularly after she took up a position at the University of Chicago in 1990. Twelve years later her work would be honoured with a Mellon Foundation Distinguished Achievement Award, a rare distinction for a historian of Russia. By then, there could be no confusion: the former revisionist had joined the establishment. But these eventual victories came at a price, as we shall see in Chapter 4.

Her chief opponent, Cohen, would continue to treat Stalinism as something of a dreadful black box into which Soviet history had descended, despite the availability of the gentler Bukharin alternative. He would never do research on Stalin's years, but instead jumped straight to the post-Stalin period and the return of the surviving victims. Soon, he shifted to contemporary politics, leaving history to the historians. Excited by the newfound dynamism of the Soviet Union under Mikhail Gorbachev (reforms initiated in the year *The Russian Review* debate began) he interviewed, together with his wife, *The Nation* editor Katrina vanden Heuvel, Soviet leaders about their political struggles. Soon after the book was published, the Soviet Union broke apart. Cohen became a major critic of what followed. In a 2000 book, a withering indictment of the Yeltsin government, the Russia policies of the Clinton administration, and political science ('transitology'), he accused fellow Russianists of 'Orwellian' doublespeak and professional 'malpractice'. American triumphalism and maltreatment of Russia was the reason for the new cold war, which needed to be stopped urgently. Against the destructiveness of the post-Soviet 'shock-therapy' capitalism on the one hand, and Stalin-inspired neo-authoritarianism on the other, he again hoped a 'Bukharinist alternative' might gain traction – New Economic Policy (NEP)-style socialism, which he had long seen as a viable option. President Vladimir Putin's reassertion of control over the economy could 'plausibly' be represented as 'a neo-NEP' – an incredibly hopeful reading.[42]

Cohen transferred what he used to call 'an intellectual passion for Russian-Soviet civilization' to the largest of the fifteen successor states: the Russian Federation. He began to appear regularly on the Russian foreign propaganda station *RT* (formerly *Russia Today*), which critics chalked up as pro-Putin behaviour. His insistence that Russia's militant Ukraine policies (including the annexation of Crimea and the support of separatists in the east) might be an understandable reaction to NATO and EU 'velvet aggression', that

Kyiv's Euromaidan was 'a coup', and that 'Putin's actions have been mostly reactive', rankled critics who saw Russia, not Ukraine or the West, as the culprit. Thus, the man who had accused revisionist historians of apologetics for Stalin was now denounced as one of the 'pathetic lot' of 'Putin's American dupes': one of 'Putin's useful idiots'.[43]

Such escalating name-calling soon also reached the academy. When Cohen and vanden Heuvel tried to endow a PhD scholarship, the peak body of post-Soviet scholars refused to take the money as long as it had Cohen's name on it. An outcry by a large section of its membership followed. Well over one hundred scholars, including myself, signed an open letter which eventually was successful: the gift was accepted. It is named the Cohen–Tucker Dissertation Research Fellowship. This solidarity should not be seen as support for his positions, though, which many find deeply problematic. That so many chose to stand up for a colleague they disagreed with politically and intellectually shows how far at least part of the field had travelled since 1986: today, scholars who are attacked because of their presumed politics are protected by their colleagues, not savaged – maybe a lesson learned from the fallout of the 1980s.[44]

The group under attack in the 1986–87 brawl had the last laugh. Their careful empirical work made them into leaders in their field. Chase continued his career at the University of Pittsburgh, where he became a full professor in 2000. His research moved into the 1930s and began to focus on repression, a topic 'the revisionists' had been accused of ignoring.[45] Viola went on to a chair at the University of Toronto, where she trained a large crop of historians of the Soviet experience. Her work continued to focus on collectivization, but – maybe to avoid further pummelling by the academic Right – shifted to studying the victims of the policy rather than its perpetrators. When, in the 2000s, she returned to the study of perpetrators, she was remarkably defensive about this choice at a time when nobody batted an eyelid about books on perpetrators in the Holocaust. Clearly, the wounds of the 1980s were still only scabbed.[46]

Getty eventually moved from Riverside to UCLA, where he, too, became a full professor. Like Fitzpatrick, he had a period of low productivity in the 1980s, but recovered once the central archives of the Soviet Union were flung wide open after 1991. Together with Rittersporn and a Russian colleague, V. N. Zemskov, he published the first in-depth study of the most contentious issue of the revisionism debate: the numbers of victims of the Terror, which were lower than sometimes estimated by totalitarianism scholars. Elsewhere, however, the new evidence forced Getty to revise his views, which he did in a major annotation of archival evidence on the road to terror (1999). Two further explorations of the 1930s followed, one focusing on Stalin's executioner, N. I. Yezhov, the other exploring informal practices as central aspects of the Stalinist political system (and Russian political culture more generally).[47]

The influence of the revisionists on the profession was salutary in many ways. Having felt the stick themselves, they worked hard to limit nastiness in the field.[48] Even when provoked by younger scholars keen to make a mark, the revisionist establishment would reply with polite interest and, at worst, mild rebuke. By the time I entered graduate school in the US in the late 1990s there were widely accepted rules of behaviour, intended to limit harm. They included, for example, to quote doctoral dissertations only favourably, or not quote them at all. Only once a thesis was published as a book was it legitimate to go after it in print. The next generation of scholars, trained overwhelmingly by the former revisionists, would have the good fortune to grow into a much more mature and much more professional field than it had been in the 1980s.

Notes

1 Sheila Fitzpatrick, 'New Perspectives on Stalinism', *The Russian Review* 45, no. 4 (1986): 357–73, here: 358, 372, 373. Spelling adjusted.
2 Daniel Field, 'From the Editor: Controversy', *The Russian Review* 45, no. 4 (1986): V–VI.
3 Stephen Cohen, *Bukharin and the Bolshevik Revolution: A Political Biography, 1888–1938* (New York, 1973).
4 Stephen F. Cohen, 'Bolshevism and Stalinism', in: *Stalinism: Essays in Historical Interpretation*, ed. Robert C. Tucker (New York, 1977), 3–29.
5 Stephen F. Cohen, 'Stalin's Terror as Social History', *The Russian Review* 45, no. 4 (1986): 375–84, here: 376, 377; Fitzpatrick, 'New Perspectives', 361 n. 8, 361–62; Ronald Grigor Suny, 'Living in the Soviet Century: Moshe Lewin, 1921–2010', *History Workshop Journal* 74, no. 1 (2012): 192–209, here: 193.
6 Cohen, 'Stalin's Terror', 377.
7 Cohen, 'Stalin's Terror', 378; Sheila Fitzpatrick, *The Russian Revolution* (Oxford, 1982), 157; Michael Ellman, 'Soviet Repression Statistics: Some

Comments', *Europe–Asia Studies* 54, no. 7 (2002): 1151–72. See also the substantially rewritten section on the Terror in the second edition, after the archival data had become available: Sheila Fitzpatrick, *The Russian Revolution*. 2nd ed. (Oxford, 1994), 166.
8 Sheila Fitzpatrick, *Education and Social Mobility in the Soviet Union 1921–1934* (Cambridge, 1979), 242; Sheila Fitzpatrick, 'Stalin and the Making of a New Elite, 1928–1939', *Slavic Review* 38, no. 3 (1979): 377–402; Sheila Fitzpatrick, *The Russian Revolution* (1982), 3, 157, also: 153.
9 Cohen, 'Stalin's Terror', 379, 383–84.
10 Geoff Eley, 'History with the Politics Left Out – Again?', *The Russian Review* 45, no. 4 (1986): 385–94, here: 387.
11 Eley, 'History with the Politics Left Out', 391; Cohen had indeed dismissed Carr as a 'flawed' precursor of the equally flawed Fitzpatrick: Stephen F. Cohen, *Rethinking the Soviet Experience: Politics and History Since 1917* (New York, 1985), 34, 171 n. 107.
12 Eley, 'History with the Politics Left Out', 391, 392, 393, 394.
13 Peter Kenez, *Varieties of Fear: Growing up Jewish under Nazism and Communism* (Washington, 1995); id., *Civil War in South Russia, 1918: The First Year of the Volunteer Army* (Berkeley, 1971); Peter Kenez, *Civil War in South Russia, 1919–1920: The Defeat of the Whites* (Berkeley, 1977); Peter Kenez, *The Birth of the Propaganda State: Soviet Methods of Mass Mobilization, 1917–1929* (Cambridge, 1985), for Stalinism as totalitarian: 12.
14 Peter Kenez, 'Stalinism as Humdrum Politics', *The Russian Review* 45, no. 4 (1986): 395–400, here: 395–96, 400. Merle Fainsod's classic *Smolensk under Soviet Rule* (New York, 1958) is discussed in Chapter 6.
15 Alfred G. Meyer and Gustav Hilger, *The Incompatible Allies: A Memoir-History of German–Soviet Relations* (New York, 1971); Alfred G. Meyer, *Marxism: The Unity of Theory and Practice* (Cambridge, Mass., 1954, 1970), *Leninism* (Cambridge, Mass., 1957; New York, 1962; Boulder, 1986), *Communism* (New York, 1960, 1963, 1985), *The Soviet Political System: An Interpretation* (New York, 1965), and *The Feminism and Socialism of Lily Braun* (Bloomington, 1986); Meyer to Fitzpatrick, 17 August 1981, Sheila Fitzpatrick Papers (SFP), The University of Chicago Special Collections, box 26; Alfred G. Meyer, 'Coming to Terms with the Past… and with One's Older Colleagues', *The Russian Review* 45, no. 4 (1986): 401–08.
16 Sheila Fitzpatrick, 'Revisionism in Retrospect: A Personal View', *Slavic Review* 67, no. 3 (2008): 682–704, here 690.
17 Sheila Fitzpatrick, 'Afterword: Revisionism Revisited', *The Russian Review* 45, no. 4 (1986): 409–13; Field, 'From the Editor: Controversy', V.
18 Lewis Siegelbaum's two major contributions to the study of Stalinism are *Stakhanovism and the Politics of Productivity in the USSR, 1935–1941* (Cambridge, 1988) and, with Andrei Sokolov (eds), *Stalinism as a Way of Life: A Narrative in Documents* (New Haven, 2004). Students and teachers also appreciate the incredible resource he helped put together: *17 Moments in Soviet History. An on-line Archive of Primary Sources,* http://soviethistory.msu.edu. John Barber contributed *Soviet Historians in Crisis, 1928–1932* (Basingstoke, 1981); with Mark Harrison, *The Soviet Home Front, 1941–1945: A Social and Economic History of the USSR in World War II* (London, 1991); and, with

Andrei Dzeniskevich (eds), *Life and Death in besieged Leningrad, 1941–44* (Basingstoke, 2005).
19 Fitzpatrick, 'Afterword: Revisionism Revisited'.
20 Field, 'From the Editor: Controversy'; Daniel Field, 'From the Editor: More Controversy', *The Russian Review* 46, no. 4 (1987): 375–78, here: 376.
21 Alec Nove, 'Stalinism: Revisionism Reconsidered', *The Russian Review* 46, no. 4 (1987): 412–17, here: 12–13; Robert Conquest, 'Revisionizing Stalin's Russia', *The Russian Review* 46, no. 4 (1987): 386–90.
22 Field to Fitzpatrick, 15 July 1987, SFP, box 30; letters from Viola to Fitzpatrick, 1981–1984, SFP, box 9, box 26. Fitzpatrick to Selivanova regarding Viola's archival access, 23 November 1981, SFP, box 26; Lynne Viola, 'In Search of Young Revisionists', *The Russian Review* 46, no. 4 (1987): 428–31, here: 428. Lynne Viola, *The Best Sons of the Fatherland: Workers in the Vanguard of Soviet Collectivization* (Oxford, 1987).
23 William Chase, 'Social History and Revisionism of the Stalinist Era', *The Russian Review* 46, no. 4 (1987): 382–85, here: 385. William Chase, *Workers, Society and the Soviet State: Labor and Life in Moscow, 1918–1929* (Urbana, 1987); Hiroaki Kuromiya, 'Stalinism and Historical Research', *The Russian Review* 46, no. 4 (1987): 404–06, here: 404. Hiroaki Kuromiya, *Stalin's Industrial Revolution: Politics and Workers, 1928–1932* (Cambridge, 1988).
24 Gabor Tamas Rittersporn, 'History, Commemoration and Hectoring Rhetoric', *The Russian Review* 46, no. 4 (1987): 418–23, here: 420–21.
25 Chase, 'Social History and Revisionism of the Stalinist Era', 384; J. Arch Getty, 'State, Society, and Superstition', *The Russian Review* 46, no. 4 (1987): 391–96, here: 395; Roberta T. Manning, 'State and Society in Stalinist Russia', *The Russian Review* 46, no. 4 (1987): 407–11, here: 408; Viola, 'In Search of Young Revisionists', 428.
26 Field to Fitzpatrick, 14 October 1987, 4 October 1987, 15 July 1987, SFP, boxes 6 and 30.
27 Fitzpatrick to Field, 8 October 1987, SFP, box 30.
28 Daniel Field, 'From the Editor: Controversy', V.
29 Chase, 'Social History and Revisionism of the Stalinist Era', 385.
30 Abbott Gleason, *Totalitarianism: The Inner History of the Cold War* (Oxford, 1995).
31 On the gendered dimension of the power struggle in the field Fitzpatrick faced, see the reminiscences by Barbara Gillam and Katerina Clark in *Writing the Stalin Era: Sheila Fitzpatrick and Soviet Historiography*, ed. Golfo Alexopoulos, Julie Hessler and Kiril Tomoff (Basingstoke, 2011), 211, 232.
32 Cohen, 'Stalin's Terror as Social History', 377. Cohen had published *Bukharin and the Bolshevik Revolution* (1973); *Sovieticus: American Perceptions and Soviet Realities* (1985); and *Rethinking the Soviet Experience* (1985). Fitzpatrick had published *The Commissariat of Enlightenment* (1970); *Education and Social Mobility* (1979); and *The Russian Revolution* (1982). She had also edited *Cultural Revolution in Russia* (1978).
33 Moshe Lewin, *La paysannerie et le pouvoir sovietique* (Paris, 1966), translated as *Russian Peasants and Soviet Power: A Study of Collectivization* (London, 1968), was an overwhelmingly political history of the decision to collectivize. Insofar as it was social history, it was concerned with the pre-Stalin Soviet

Union. Lewin's second book, *Political Undercurrents in Soviet Economic Debates From Bukharin to the Modern Reformers* (Princeton, 1974), had one chapter (97–124) sketching the Stalinist economic model. Otherwise it was devoted to post-Stalinist debates and their political implications.
34 Moshe Lewin, *The Making of the Soviet System: Essays in the Social History of Interwar Russia* (New York, 1985).
35 She would, eventually, be called exactly that. See, for example, Orlando Figes, 'Stalin's Oblomovs', *The Times Literary Supplement* (13 January 1995), http://www.the-tls.co.uk/articles/private/stalins-oblomovs/ (accessed 5 April 2017); and Martin Malia, 'The Archives of Evil. Soviet Studies after the Soviet Union', *The New Republic* 291, no. 22–23 (2004): 34–41, here: 36.
36 Sheila Fitzpatrick, 'Cultural Revolution Revisited', *The Russian Review* 58, no. 2 (1999): 202–09, here: 205.
37 Eley, 'History with the Politics Left Out – Again?', 390.
38 Getty, 'State, Society, and Superstition', 393. For the juxtaposition of the state apparatus and 'the rest of society', see Gabor T. Rittersporn, *Stalinist Simplifications and Soviet Complications: Social Tensions and Political Conflicts in the USSR 1933–1953* (Chur, 1991), 321, 322.
39 Getty, 'State, Society, and Superstition', 391, 393. Similarly: Manning, 'State and Society in Stalinist Russia', 408–10; and Viola, 'In Search of Young Revisionists', 429, 430.
40 Fitzpatrick, 'Revisionism in Retrospect', 691; Fitzpatrick, 'Afterword: Revisionism Revisited', 411.
41 For a summary see Edele, *Stalinist Society*, chapter 2.
42 Stephen F. Cohen and Katrina vanden Heuvel, *The Voices of Glasnost* (London, 1990); Stephen F. Katrina, *Soviet Fates and Lost Alternatives: From Stalinism to the New Cold War* (New York, 2009), 28; Stephen F. Cohen, *Failed Crusade: America and the Tragedy of Post-Communist Russia* (New York, 2000), 5, 33; Stephen F. Cohen, *The Victims Return: Survivors of the Gulag after Stalin* (London and New York, 2010).
43 Cohen, *Rethinking the Soviet Experience*, 10; Stephen F. Cohen, 'The New Cold War and the Necessity of Patriotic Heresy', *The Nation* (12 August 2014), https://www.thenation.com/article/new-cold-war-and-necessity-patriotic-heresy/ (accessed 5 April 2017). For more, see: https://www.thenation.com/authors/stephen-f-cohen/ (accessed 3 November 2019); Jesse Zwick, 'Pravda Lite', *New Republic* (14 March 2012), https://newrepublic.com/article/101703/russia-tv-rtv-cohen-alyona (accessed 31 March 2017); Slawomir Sierakowski, 'Putin's Useful Idiots', *New York Times* (28 April 2014), https://www.nytimes.com/2014/04/29/opinion/sierakowski-putins-useful-idiots.html?_r=0 (accessed 5 April 2017).
44 The letter can be accessed here: http://academeblog.org/2015/02/09/russia-scholars-reply-to-aseees-detailed-clarification-regarding-cohen-tucker-fellowship-controversy/ (accessed 31 March 2017); Joshua Sanborn, 'Dear Stephen Cohen: I Love You; I'm Sorry; You're Wrong', *Russian History Blog* (5 February 2015), http://russianhistoryblog.org/2015/02/dear-stephen-cohen-i-love-you-im-sorry-youre-wrong/ (accessed 31 March 2017).
45 William Chase, *Enemies within the Gates?: The Comintern and the Stalinist Repression, 1934–39* (Yale, 2001).

46 Lynne Viola, *Peasant Rebels under Stalin: Collectivization and the Culture of Peasant Resistance* (Oxford, 1999); Lynne Viola, *Contending with Stalinism: Soviet Power and Popular Resistance in the 1930s* (Ithaca, 2002); Lynne Viola, *The War against the Peasantry, 1927–1930: The Tragedy of the Soviet Countryside* (New Haven, 2005); Lynne Viola, *The Unknown Gulag: The Lost World of Stalin's Special Settlements* (Oxford, 2007); Lynne Viola, 'The Question of the Perpetrator in Soviet History', *Slavic Review* 72, no. 1 (2013): 1–23; Lynne Viola, *Stalinist Perpetrators on Trial: Scenes from the Great Terror in Soviet Ukraine* (Oxford, 2017).

47 J. Arch Getty, Gabor T. Rittersporn and V. N. Zemskov, 'Victims of the Soviet Penal System in the Prewar Years: A First Approach on the Basis of Archival Evidence', *American Historical Review* 98, no. 4 (1993): 1017–49; J. Arch Getty and Oleg V. Naumov, *The Road to Terror: Stalin and the Self-Destruction of the Bolsheviks, 1932–1939* (New Haven, 1999); J. Arch Getty and Oleg V. Naumov, *Yezhov: The Rise of Stalin's 'Iron Fist'* (New Haven, 2008); J. Arch Getty, *Practicing Stalinism: Bolsheviks, Boyars, and the Persistence of Tradition* (New Haven, 2013).

48 Kiril Tomoff, 'Reminiscences', in: *Writing the Stalin Era*, 234.

2
Marxism–Lewinism and the origins of Stalinism

A loud silence

One voice was conspicuously absent from the 1986–87 debate on Stalinism: Moshe Lewin, then at the University of Pennsylvania. An unorthodox Marxist scholar of the Soviet experience, a social historian well before 'revisionism' emerged, Lewin had become a mentor to many who thought of themselves as 'socialist historians', and 'Marxist–Lewinists'.[1] Sheila Fitzpatrick was neither, and Lewin had never been very impressed by the Australian. In 1979, after he had read her nearly decade-old volume, *The Commissariat of Enlightenment* (1970), he described her as 'a competent professional and a diligent researcher' who had a knack for digging up new sources. She had even been to the Soviet archives, which 'other people found impenetrable'. Her interpretations, however, were characterized by 'conceptual fuzziness', and he was 'not yet sure how bright she is'.[2]

As time went on, he made up his mind. Fitzpatrick was, he wrote in a 1986 letter about *The Russian Review* exchange, 'an obsessed but unintelligent *khalturshchitsa*' – a hack.[3] She was part of a group of amateurs, who undeservedly got the limelight, while his own contributions to the study of Stalinism were ignored:

> I wrote four interpretative essays on Stalinism and they are all gathered, with others, in my book of essays called *The Making of the Soviet System* (N.Y, 1985) and the fact that they do not draw attention as a contribution to the understanding of the phenomenon in question certainly points to some kind of failure on my part. The attention is rather drawn to some 'revisionist' with whom I did not polemicise

... and I didn't so far because these authors are not worth it yet. They are novices who should first learn a little bit more. I thought that making a fuss about them is actually building them up before they merit it.[4]

In public, Lewin chose the path of maximum insult: of criticizing a colleague without citing her. That way, everybody in the know understands who is being dismissed, but non-initiates (and undergraduate students) are not tempted to read the work in question.[5] Such advanced citation tactics are likely to lead to retaliation. By studiously ignoring his work, Fitzpatrick gave Lewin a taste of his own medicine – to the annoyance of his supporters.[6]

Lewin's silence was an active choice. Daniel Field, the journal's editor, had sent him the first round of the exchange with a note asking for a contribution.[7] Lewin declined. As he wrote in his response, he was done with 'Stalinism' and 'ready to move on to other business'.[8] He also saw Fitzpatrick's work as 'maneuvering to dis-stalinize (sic) Stalin and Stalinism'. It needed to be opposed on political grounds because it was

> actually a pretty stupid device. It is not good for Russia, not good for the profession, not good at all for the Left – if these bizarre operators think they are some kind of 'a left'. And it makes the life of hawks much easier, making all of us look like some amateur-fellow-travelers, and utterly unprofessional at that.[9]

Polish heritage

Lewin, then, was a highly political man who marked the left edge of polite discourse about the Soviet past and its present in Cold War America. He had been born on 7 November 1921, on the fourth anniversary of the Bolshevik revolution, as he liked to point out. He hailed from Wilno (now Vilnius in Lithuania), a city which once had been part of the Russian Empire, but had fallen to the new Polish state as a result of war, revolution and imperial breakdown.

Vil'na, as it was spelled in Russian, the 'Jerusalem of Lithuania', had been a major centre of Jewish culture, religion and learning in the Russian Empire. By the late nineteenth century, Jews constituted approximately 40 per cent of the population, Poles 31 per cent and Russians 20 per cent.[10] Occupied by German troops in the First World War, Vilno changed hands and names several times in the confusing years to follow. Lithuanian, Polish and Bolshevik Russian forces all, at one time or another, took charge. By the middle of 1920, it was part of Lithuania, only to be conquered by Polish troops later that year and annexed to the Polish state in 1922.[11] It would remain Polish until the Second World War, but continued to be a multiethnic city. By 1939, about 45 per cent of the population were Polish, 37 per cent Jewish, and 10 per cent Lithuanian.[12]

An embodiment of the multiculturalism of his home city, Lewin was the son of a Jewish father involved either with the Jewish underworld or with acrobatics and the circus, or both – depending on which source we like to believe. His Russian-speaking Ukrainian mother kept a kosher household and brought the boy up in the Jewish religious tradition (although she did not convert herself). Lewin did not write memoirs, and what little we know about his background comes from what he told people close to him as well as from a formal interview conducted in 1982. What is clear is that of the basic political choices Jews could make in interwar Poland – to assimilate into Polish culture or to assert Jewish identity – he chose the latter. [13]

Polish anti-Semitism was tough, remembered Lewin – 'zoological': it involved 'the frequent applications of physical violence against Jews, not only fists but also knives and stones'. Given this context, Zionism came 'quite naturally' to Lewin, 'almost in my childhood'. Lewin gravitated towards the Left, joining *Hashomer Hatsair*, or the *Young Guard*, a movement which combined Zionism with socialism and hoped to build a binational state for Arabs and Jews in Palestine. Lewin described this group as 'pretty eclectic: 'left-wing Zionist, ... Marxist, Socialist, quite pro-Soviet..., Freudian'.[14] He would remain an admirer of Lenin to the very end of his life. Thus he acquired the theoretical and political framework he would put to use, eventually, in his chosen academic field. But first, he had to survive the war.

In Stalin's Soviet Union

After the German attack on Poland on 1 September 1939, and the Soviet Union's incursion from the east from 17 September, Wilno was occupied by Soviet troops on 19 September. By 30 October, however, the city was handed over to still independent Lithuania as part of a deal to allow Soviet troops into the country. Nine months later, the Soviets were back. The treaty had just been the first step towards outright annexation of Lithuania on 3 August 1940. Vilnius became the capital of the Lithuanian SSR, one of the new republics in the west of the enlarged USSR.[15]

It is unclear what Lewin's encounters with the occupying Soviet forces were in 1939–41. The standard accounts of his life omit the Soviet occupation and the 1982 interview is vague on the issue. His unpublished papers in the University of Pennsylvania's archives offer no clues. Was he among those who cheered Soviet troops as the lesser of the two evils? Was he among the enthusiasts from the Left who imagined the Soviet Union as a socialist paradise? It appears so. The Red Army, Lewin noted, 'was giving us a sanctuary from war'.[16] Lewin did not further dwell on the short first Soviet occupation, and the interviewer did not press him on the issue. Instead, the conversation moved on swiftly to the handover of Vilnius to Lithuania before omitting the second Soviet occupation entirely, jumping straight to the German attack in the summer of 1941.[17]

As a Zionist in Soviet Vilno, however, Lewin was at best in an ambiguous position, notwithstanding his admiration for Lenin. Zionism, even in a socialist variant, was construed as 'bourgeois nationalism', and activists of political organizations other than the Communist Party were arrested or deported. Already, in September and October 1939, mass arrests ripped through the Jewish population, targeting community leaders, entrepreneurs and political activists. The Jewish Bund, a major competitor to Bolshevism on the Left, was a particular target of this first wave, but by no means the only one.[18] Once the Soviets returned, the arrests gained in systematicity. In May 1941, the Soviet government empowered the security services of Latvia, Lithuania and Estonia to arrest, besides the 'criminal element', all kinds of 'socially dangerous' people: 'active members of counterrevolutionary parties and participants in anti-Soviet, nationalist, white-guardist organizations', former policemen and prison guards, factory owners, large-scale land owners, high-level state functionaries of the old regime, and officers of the old army. These supposed enemies of the Soviet regime had their property confiscated and received five- to eight-year labour camp sentences followed by twenty years of exile 'in remote regions of the Soviet Union'. Their families were deported straight away, as were family members of 'counterrevolutionaries' in hiding, or those who had been sentenced to death, had repatriated from Germany, or registered to emigrate.[19]

By the end of the operation, in June 1941, the security services had arrested 14,467 and deported another 25,711 people in all three Baltic republics. Lithuania saw 5,664 arrests and 10,187 deportations. In addition to the groups listed in the initial resolution, the victims included refugees (overwhelmingly Jewish) from Poland, who had refused to accept Soviet citizenship.[20] Jews were also arrested as class enemies (capitalists, factory owners, etc.) or political activists of 'anti-Soviet' parties, including Zionists like Lewin.[21] One of his uncles became a victim of the deportations,[22] but Lewin did not. He avoided arrest, survived the entry of Lithuania's army on 28 October 1941, and was still in Vilnius when the Germans broke their non-aggression treaty with Stalin and marched into the Soviet Union on 22 June 1941.

When Hitler's troops approached Vilna, Lewin fled.

> My city was conquered by the Germans coming from East Prussia only a few days after the beginning of the German attack. I, along with three friends, managed to get far away, unlike many others who were caught by German troops, especially by their motorcyclists. Those who were not shot on the spot were returned to their homes; Jews to ghettos. My success and that of my friends was due to retreating Russian soldiers who allowed us to climb onto their trucks. I remember this scene vividly, it was a crucial moment in my life. I was about twenty at the time. The officer forbade the soldiers to take civilians on the trucks, but the peasant-soldiers, sitting there, terribly tired, waited till the officer went back to the driver's cabin, winked to us, and called us in: 'The young guys don't understand much of life.' (They meant the officers.) 'Tomorrow you will be our soldiers too.' And so, thanks to their disobedience, we were taken into pre-1939 Russia.[23]

His escape left Lewin with a complex mixture of gratitude and survivor's guilt, as one of his friends pointed out after his death. 'Clearly to his last day he remained grateful to those soldiers who enabled him to escape the Nazis by the skin of his teeth', wrote Omer Bartov in a moving obituary. 'But I believe that he was also left with an intense sense of guilt for having abandoned his parents.'[24]

Initially a refugee fleeing on his own initiative, Lewin was soon swept up in the Soviet effort to save men of military age. He observed life and work on collective farms, both successful ones and those which were 'real wrecks'. As the Germans approached again, he was evacuated, on foot, together with the youth of his farm. 'We marched a whole month from Tambov to Penza where a train was waiting to take us to an induction center in the Urals.' Because the authorities distrusted people from the newly acquired western territories, Lewin was not drafted into the army but sent to work: first as 'an iron ore miner', then 'as a blast furnace operator, doing pig iron in a metallurgy plant'. He worked in the hot shop under horrible conditions for two long years, nearly dying of starvation, regularly fainting from the heat and the hard work, having his eyebrows permanently burned off. Unlike many others, however, who died in accidents or of pneumonia, he survived. In the summer of 1943, he was sent a thousand kilometres from his plant to help with the harvest. He took the opportunity to desert from the labour front, found a friend near Perm, and volunteered for the army. This time he was accepted and trained as an officer. He returned to Vilnius at war's end, and left for Poland as part of the post-war repatriation of Polish citizens.[25]

Saving Lenin from Stalin

Lewin did not stay in Poland long. Like many of his peers he soon left a country which had erupted into pogroms once it became clear that the Final Solution had not killed every Polish Jew, as the Germans had promised.[26] Lewin went to France, working odd jobs, and from there to Israel, where he arrived in 1951, 'pursuing my ideological commitments'. After working on a kibbutz – 'driving a tractor with a rifle slung over his shoulder' – and as a journalist he completed a BA at Tel Aviv University in 1961. Disillusioned with Zionism he moved back to Paris, where he studied for his doctorate at the Sorbonne. He gained his degree in 1964. Turned into a book, *Russian Peasants and Soviet Power* was published in French in 1966, then in an English translation in 1968.[27]

The book was the start of a lifelong quest to reconcile the Leninism of his youth with the terrible things he had experienced in the Soviet Union. How could this Stalinism – which deported his uncle and arrested his friends, which exploited the working class mercilessly and fed engineers and managers in separate canteens – be brought into harmony with the inspiring ideals of the Revolution?

Russian Peasants and Soviet Power was among the best pieces of history Lewin would ever write: an in-depth study of Bolshevik debates about, and policies towards, the peasantry in the 1920s. It began with a sociological sketch of the world of the 'Russian' peasant (who turned out to be at times Central Asian or Ukrainian as well) in the 1920s. After this social history background, Lewin devoted the bulk of the book to the history of politics and ideology. Chapter 6, on what Bolsheviks called the 'accursed question' of how to deal with the peasantry, remains one of the most detailed explorations of the policy debates within the ruling circle.

Lewin demonstrated that nobody had ever contemplated forced collectivization as it eventually emerged.[28] All participants agreed that there would be an evolutionary change towards a more and more industrialized country. The disagreement was over the extent to which state-run industry should accommodate itself to the needs of the peasants, or if the agriculturalists instead should be squeezed by fiscal and economic policy, to pay for investment in industry. Stalin, to Lewin, took positions that were most expedient for his 'main objective', which was 'victory over possible rivals'.[29]

Stalin won in the power struggle after Lenin's death, asserted Lewin, because he was 'primarily a tactician', a 'past master' in the art of internal party struggle. The losers on the 'left' and on the 'right' meanwhile, were exhausting themselves with strategic thought, which, while possibly sound, was never tested in practice. Had they been given a chance, 'the history of their country would have, or might well have, taken a different turn'.[30]

The question of alternatives to Stalinism was also at the centre of Lewin's second book, *Lenin's Last Struggle*, also written during his Paris phase.[31] Based substantially on Richard Pipes's first book and on the then newly published 1922 writings of Lenin, it developed what we might call the 'Lenin–Trotsky alternative' to Stalin:[32] Had Lenin not died in 1924, Lewin claimed, he would have teamed up with Trotsky and removed Stalin. History would have taken a different turn.³³ The ideals of Lewin's youth were thus saved from his wartime experience.

Supporting dictatorship

While Lewin tried to save Lenin from Stalin, he did not attempt to make Lenin into a democratic socialist. At stake was not democracy but how best to 'develop a backward country'.³⁴ In *Russian Peasants*, Lewin had observed that Bolshevik leaders had the tendency to participate 'in anti-democratic and even totalitarian practices' while in control of affairs, only to become inner-party democrats once they had lost power.³⁵ This insight also applied to Lenin during the phase of his 'final struggle' in 1922 when, due to his quickly deteriorating health, his participation in events 'was very limited'.³⁶ As far as the peasantry was concerned, Lenin was unapologetic: 'we promise neither freedom nor democracy'.³⁷ Lenin also continued to promote the possible use of terror.³⁸

Lewin put this authoritarianism in a dual perspective. For one, he claimed that 'this denial is clearly intended as provisional, applicable only so long as the threat of war persists and the regime is not entirely secure from attack'.³⁹ To Marxist–Leninists, of course, everything in the present was temporary. Only after the final struggle and the victory of world revolution would things settle into permanency: communism would break out, money, the state, religion and housework would disappear, and each would work according to ability and receive according to need. In practice, however, this position meant postponing democracy forever. But Lewin went further, praising Lenin for his explicit opposition to democratization. The leader, he wrote, 'was very far from being a weak liberal, incapable of taking resolute action when necessary'.⁴⁰

At the heart of Lewin's politics in *Lenin's Last Struggle*, then, was open support for dictatorship, as long as it was developmental and politically on the Left. After 'fifty years of socialist experience', he wrote, 'the first proletarian dictatorship' should be a lesson to new 'left-wing dictatorships'.⁴¹ These proliferated at the time. After communist regimes were established in Eastern Europe and North Korea after the Soviet victory in the Second World War, the communists had won the civil war in China by 1949. Cuba had led the next wave of communist victories in 1959. In Vietnam and

Laos, the struggle was ongoing in a brutal civil war involving the United States.

Lewin supported this anti-democratic tide: 'Left-wing dictatorship is one of the most significant political phenomena of our time', he wrote in *Lenin's Last Struggle*. 'There was nothing essentially utopian about Lenin's aim of achieving a rational dictatorial regime, with men of integrity at its head and efficient institutions working consciously to go beyond both underdevelopment and dictatorship.'[42] The dreams of his youth were still dreamable, Stalin or no Stalin.

Remarkably, Lewin did not retract such statements when his book was reissued five years before his death, in a world where the Soviet Union had ceased to exist, China, Laos and Vietnam had turned capitalist (but not democratic), and the remaining left-wing dictatorships were a grim totalitarianism in North Korea and a struggling socialism in Cuba. In the introduction to the 2005 edition of the book, he again wrote that Lenin's 1922 programme 'could still be of value in a world where backward, still-rural countries are living in misery and are commanded by inept, oppressive regimes'.[43]

Lewin would never drop his support for dictatorship as one of the possible, and at times necessary, developmental options. It was too deeply engrained in his original politics, which had led him from Poland to Russia and beyond. Essential to this support for Leninist dictatorship, however, was the assumption that Stalinism was not its logical outcome. The world he had experienced during his Second World War was too brutal and too depressing to be embraced as a positive model. Hence the recurrent assertion that 'dictatorial regimes come in different shapes and colours, just like other political regimes'. Stalinism was an outlier.[44]

Success and failure

Lewin's first two books, and in particular the brilliant dissertation, made his name and allowed him to start an academic career in his mid-40s. Eventually, it would bring him to the United States, where he became the most prominent opponent of Pipes and other 'totalitarians'. But first, further detours followed. After a one-year stint as director of study at the Paris *École pratique des haute études* (1965–66) and a fellowship at Columbia University (1967–68) he secured a position, which eventually became a chair, at Birmingham University (UK) in 1968, where he joined the team around the former communist R. W. Davies. After ten years at Birmingham's Centre for Russian and East European Studies, then the premier research institution on the Soviet Union in the English-speaking word, he was appointed to a chair at the University of Pennsylvania in 1978. He retired in 1995.[45]

His years in Birmingham did not yield another book on Stalinism. Nor was one forthcoming in Philadelphia. Not that he lacked the ambition to write. He had planned a follow-up study to *Russian Peasants*, which would tell the story of collectivization and its effects – a second volume bringing the story to 1934.[46] He never completed it. Instead, he fell into a pattern that would define most of his scholarly life: rethinking an ongoing project before it was finished, moving on to the rethought version, only to rethink it again.

What started as a second volume of *Russian Peasants* thus soon became a much more ambitious project: a social history of the 1930s more generally. As he described the project in 1975, it was to be 'a very detailed history of Soviet society from about 1928 till the war'.[47] This expansion of the original ambition soon merged into a study of the entire Soviet experience. By 1983 he no longer mentioned the Stalinism book but 'a large scale research program in the history of Russian society in the 20th century'. It would demand 'many years for collecting materials and more years for coming up with something reasonably good in print'.[48] This project yielded several preliminary essays and book-length ruminations, just as he began to move on to embedding the Soviet experience in a longitudinal study of Germany and Russia from the nineteenth century to the present.[49]

The enduring result of these efforts was a book-length essay, written in a mad rush in six weeks in early 1987, despite Lewin losing two chapters in the bowels of his new computer, which had replaced the typewriter as his writing tool.[50] After rewriting them, *The Gorbachev Phenomenon* (1988) became his most resounding commercial success, translated into several languages and reissued in a revised edition just before the fall of the Soviet Union.[51] One of his two best books, it remains a major contribution to our understanding the social and historical context which shaped the final decade of the Soviet Union.

The book project on Stalinism, meanwhile, dropped off the agenda. One reason was his unsteady life. Paris continued to be Lewin's favourite city, where he spent several months every year. In a time before emails and computers this transatlantic life caused severe problems of logistics, as notes and copies needed to be lugged around, his mail forwarded or held, and time spent on organizing housing and travel. Book writing requires a sustained effort, organized notes, a stable work environment. Lewin never allowed himself this space, but travelled back and forth between Paris, the UK, Italy and Philadelphia, eventually adding Moscow to his itinerary. He could squeeze out essays that way, even book-length ones, but a scholarly monograph based on primary sources was another matter.

Lewin also did not like the kind of research necessary to write a social history of Stalinism. With at best restrictive access to archives on the 1930s, historians had to work from published sources. Their quality declined massively as the political system became more secretive under Stalin. In the 1920s, scholars could still draw on fairly thick sociological studies and public debate of policy options – sources which had formed the empirical bedrock of *Russian Peasants*. Lewin enjoyed reading policy debates and economic and sociological works of Soviet scholars, which he would again mine for alternatives to Soviet reality for the 1960s and 1970s, but such sources were absent for the 1930s.[52]

For the pre-war Stalin years, information on social structure and social dynamics had to be cobbled together from multiple, often contradictory, and always incomplete sources, a labor-intensive quest executed successfully by Fitzpatrick in *Education and Social Mobility* (1979), or by Lynne Viola in her study of the collectivizers (1989).[53] Lewin had no patience for such research; it made 'the brain decompose', as he complained in late 1975.[54] Early the next year, he expanded on this theme, displaying doubts about the feasibility of the project:

> I am drowning in a lot of microfilms and xeroxes, and actually have a bad time with all this. I decided to break the back of it – i.e. of the drudgery side of my project, to get over with the bulky sources, during the current year. As these sources yield a mass of disconnected bits of information, it is all a pure filtering job, no intellectual effort involved, the brain is asleep, just drudgery. If it lasts too long – and it does – there could be a permanent brain damage – loss of capacity

to think. I hope to see the end of this, and then begin to assimilate the stuff, which is exacting but more rewarding. One point is nagging me – whether a history of this society, without a mass of predecessors, monographs etc. is at all feasible, whether I don't overshoot. No way of knowing other than either by dropping it – or just continuing.[55]

Eventually, he would drop it – but only to pick up an even broader and – given the state of the historiography at the time – even less doable topic.

Most of his research was done in Paris, where he returned each summer. The libraries there were better than what he had in Philadelphia, but his routine also precluded the use of other available sources. Interviews with former Soviet citizens had been conducted after the war, and their transcripts continue to provide a rich source for all kinds of everyday life issues.[56] But they were held in a library at Harvard – the institutional home of the conservative Pipes.[57] Others used the archives of the Party organization of Smolensk, which had found its way west during the Second World War.[58] They were available in the US National Archives.[59] To use these sources would have required Lewin to give up his summers in Paris and spend them in Cambridge, Mass., or College Park, VA. As for gaining access to Soviet archives, Lewin did not even try until the late 1980s.[60]

Then there was politics. What could one really learn from a detailed study of Stalinism? That things had been terrible? That would just play into the hands of the 'hawks'. When a younger scholar wrote to him with considerable excitement about new sources on the 1932–33 famine, Lewin dampened his enthusiasm.[61] Such 'horror stories', he wrote

> are easily misused. ... The incredible misuse to which right-wing Ukrainians in the US and Canada tried to put 'the Ukrainian holocaust', with an obvious aim of poisoning the atmosphere against signing disarmament treaties, as well as stealing a thunder from the Jews (who had good reasons to accuse the same Ukrainians of mass-slaughtering Jews at different times) – is just an example of irresponsible treatment without any contribution to scholarship – including understanding Stalinism. So I would propose being careful with publication.[62]

Writing about the 1930s would have put Lewin in an impossible position: as an anti-Stalinist he was devoted to showing the brutality of the regime, but as a socialist he did not want to play into the hands of the conservatives, who loved to write about Stalinism because it implied that socialism was 'totalitarian'.

Stalinism in historical perspective

Occasionally, Lewin continued to write on Stalinism, but he switched to what would become his favourite literary form: the essay. Some of the many think-pieces he wrote stood the test of time, including a summary of the political economy of Stalinism, which drew substantially on the work of old 'totalitarian' scholars of the Harvard Interview Project;[63] an overview of grain-taking policies in the 1930s, which could well have become part of either of the never-written books;[64] an exploration of the politics of labelling during dekulakization, which drew together material and analyses from *Russian Peasants*;[65] and a lucid explication of how, in the Stalinist context, planning 'disappeared in the plan'.[66] Others were restatements of what he had already said, and some are best characterized as political pamphleteering.[67] Many of them were republished in collections, sometimes several times, making his output look more impressive than it actually was.[68] The majority of these essays drew on the same source base as his first two books and circled around the same questions he had raised in them: the origins of Stalinism and its alternatives and the difference between Leninism and Stalinism.

Two new problematics interested Lewin after he left Paris: the position of the Stalinist years in the longer sweep of Soviet history, and the nature of Stalinism. These would become central concerns in his final two books, *The Gorbachev Phenomenon* (1988) and *The Soviet Century* (2005), a book which drew on newly available archival documents he had gathered during research trips to what turned out to be a quickly dying Soviet Union.

The first problematic was connected to what his friend, Ron Suny, described as a quest 'to save the Soviet Union, which was the country that had saved him'.[69] As terrible as Stalinism was, it was only one stage – and an avoidable stage at that – of the transformation of 'Russian' society in the twentieth century.[70]

Thus, there was always hope. A better, more humane socialism was always just around the corner. Bukharinism was alive and well behind the scenes, as he showed in *Political Undercurrents to*

Soviet Economic Debate (1974). Maybe a new NEP was possible? Such hopes grew with Gorbachev's rise to power, and two research trips to the Soviet Union in 1987 and 1989.[71] By 1988, it seemed to Lewin that the preconditions to building NEP-style socialism had finally been attained. Maybe finally the system could 'reclaim some of the hopes of its idealistic revolutions'?[72] Even the evident failure of Gorbachev did not dampen his optimism. In 1991, with the Soviet Union edging closer and closer to implosion, Lewin wrote:

> What we are witnessing just now is yet another recasting of the political, social, and economic institutions, but this time, quite probably, with, over an unpredictable time span, the potential to switch to very different historical rails and to produce a renewed and viable urban-industrial policy.[73]

The nature of Stalinism

What then, was Stalinism? First, it was not an extension of Leninism or Bolshevism. Lewin was resolute on this point. There were moments of doubt, but they passed quickly.[74] Stalinism was 'not a direct outgrowth of bolshevism but rather an autonomous and parallel phenomenon and, at the same time, its gravedigger',[75] indeed a 'counterrevolution',[76] a 'systemic aberration'.[77]

Lewin tried out several terms to describe its essence. The first was 'totalitarian', which he used in his first book without too many qualms and without explanation of the term. In *Russian Peasants and Soviet Power* he wrote of 'anti-democratic and even totalitarian practices' of the Bolshevik Left, of the 'totalitarian methods' of Stalin's industrialization drive, the rise of 'a totalitarian bureaucracy' under 'the Stalinist totalitarian dictatorship'.[78] This interpretation was indebted to Trotsky, who had also used the t-word to describe Stalin's regime.[79] 'The Stalinist period', wrote Lewin in *Lenin's Last Struggle*, 'might be defined ... as the substitution of the bureaucracy for the original social basis of the regime, namely, the working class, a section of the poorest peasants and certain strata of the intelligentsia'.[80] Later, he silently dropped the term, but continued to describe the phenomenon: a state which 'substituted itself for society', a state of affairs where 'the whole social structure' was 'sucked into the state mechanism'.[81] In his most successful innovation, he replaced a key term of totalitarianism theory ('atomization') with an alternative ('quicksand society') which described the same empirical state of affairs, but allowed talk about it without reference to the conceptual apparatus of the academic Right.[82] By the early 1980s, he explicitly criticized the term, following the convention among 'revisionists'.[83] Totalitarianism, rather than a descriptor for the Stalinist phase of Soviet history, now was 'an historically inadequate and purely ideological tool'.[84] He also began to critique his earlier Trotskyite interpretation of Stalinism as bureaucracy triumphant, as 'some have theorized', as he wrote in 1991.[85]

With 'totalitarianism' in its Trotskyite version discarded, Lewin began to play with two other terms – 'Asiatic despotism' and 'agrarian despotism'.[86] Eventually, he settled on the latter, developing a line of thought which began with *Russian Peasants*.[87] The 'agrarian nexus', Lewin declared, had been a central aspect of Russian history since pre-modern times. Revolution and civil war had removed the landowning nobility, but strengthened traditional peasant culture. War, revolution and civil war had led to an 'archaization' of the country, which had made a proletarian revolution without a proletariat. Any further expansion of industrial production beyond the levels reached at the end of the 1920s involved in some way forcing peasants to give up their grain, which was needed to feed the cities and to export it to gain capital to pay for industrialization. This line of reasoning could easily lead to a Stalinist conclusion: Stalin's methods had been necessary to break the agrarian nexus. The logic of the argument, then, came into creative tension with the ideological commitment to anti-Stalinism.

Lewin resolved this tension by again introducing alternatives – not to developmental dictatorship and state-led industrialization, but to this particularly cruel version of both.[88] The decision to collectivize was taken in the context of a crisis which was the result of poor prior decisions by the leadership. Had the Soviet leaders managed the NEP better from the middle of the 1920s, this crisis could have been avoided and less radical methods, and more moderate tempos, could have been employed. The result would have been a less brutal dictatorship.[89]

Stalinism, then, was the result of the particular way chosen to deal with the 'agrarian nexus'. Stalin's methods amounted to a war against the majority of the population, which necessarily led to a growth of the repressive apparatus, more and more arrests, executions, deportations. The result was an 'agrarian despotism' reminiscent of, but much more dynamic than, its Tsarist predecessor. A brutal state extracted resources from a recalcitrant peasantry in order to develop industry. Much of what Stalinism was known for – mass repression, a sprawling Gulag, poverty, hunger, and callous administrative methods – were direct results.[90]

The argument about Stalinism as 'agrarian despotism' moved it out of the history of Bolshevism and embedded it squarely into the history of Russia instead: 'Stalinism, a unique agrarian despotism reemerging in the twentieth century', he wrote in 1991, 'is certainly a very Russian phenomenon.'[91] After he had allegedly broken with Bolshevism and killed the old Bolsheviks, Stalin switched 'to a nationalist "great power" ideology, comparable to Tsarism and adopting its attributes', he elaborated in 2005.[92] The system he built 'belonged in the old category of landowning autocracies' and 'adopted the ideological principles of the Tsarist state'.[93]

Here, Lewin took over a central idea of Pipes, without, of course, citing him: Stalinism, Lewin asserted, 'brought back an old trait of the erstwhile Muscovite princes as owners of all the state's lands'.[94] State ownership was 'a continuation of an older noncapitalist Russian political tradition, with its concept of a tsar "owning" a whole state that grew out of a princely estate'.[95] Nothing could be further from socialism.

The 'agrarian nexus' had another aspect – peasant culture, which Lewin probed for a while as an alternative reason for Stalinism: maybe the thick-skulled peasant, the Russian *muzhik*, was to blame? Several essays explored peasant folklore as an origin for Stalinism's culture, by speculating that maybe the Stalin cult and the 'demonization of politics' was a tactical accommodation of peasant culture. He must have felt uneasy enough about such victim blaming, as he immediately added another speculation: 'maybe' it was instead 'a way of appeasing some inner demons that haunted the ruler's soul'?[96] Eventually, he embraced this explanation, which personalized Stalinism in Stalin and let the peasants off the hook.[97]

The Great Terror

This interpretation securely removed Stalinism from the history of Bolshevism. Making Stalinism about the despotism of one man

– Stalin – also helped explain the paradox of how the bureaucracy – the supposed social base of Stalinism – became victimized in the Terror.

Lewin developed two explanations for the Great Purges, both squarely located in political rather than social history, and both centring on Stalin as the mover and shaker of events. The first was that Stalin needed to eradicate 'a whole historical period and rid himself of those who had witnessed it and who knew who had done what in those heroic years'.[98] More often, Lewin evoked a second theory: that Stalin used the Terror to pulverize the bureaucracy his own policies had created, which had become a break on his power.[99] While both explanations allowed him to solve the puzzle his earlier Trotskyite theory of Stalinism had created, they did not explain the events which caused the largest number of deaths in the Great Terror: the so-called 'mass operations', which targeted ordinary Soviet citizens presumed to be enemies either because of their social or their national background.[100] By the end of his career, Lewin was aware of some of these operations, but did not offer an explanation for them.[101]

This avoidance of a central event of Stalinism was quite logical. To explain the mass operations, we need to pay attention to the Bolshevik aspects of Stalinism, in particular its continued ideology of class warfare and its torturous relationship with national minorities. Likewise, 'agrarian despotism' could not explain one central feature of the regime: that it was a developmental dictatorship pushing industrialization at unprecedented speed. It was commitment to force-paced industrialization which had led to the decision to collectivize, and it had been collectivization, as Lewin rightly pointed out, which led to the growth of the repressive apparatus and to a renewed brutalization of Soviet politics (after the first wave of brutalization during war, revolution and civil war).[102] None of this could be explained by 'agrarian despotism' or the idea that Stalin wanted to be a new tsar. Lewin's entire scheme of isolating Stalinism from Leninism required ignoring the entire Leninist legacy. Whenever Stalin used Marxist language, referred to himself as Lenin's pupil, or tried to make sense of the Soviet situation in terms of Marxist–Leninist historical schemes, he must have been lying: 'that was so much empty talk', claimed Lewin.[103]

Teacher of teachers

Essay writing (and teaching undergraduate students) was not the only activity which kept Lewin busy after his move to Philadelphia. He had come to the United States in 1978 'in hopes of developing a group of like-minded specialists in Russian and Soviet history, initially to be formed around a Penn–Princeton axis. In the end, this did not work out', as his friend and colleague Alfred Rieber wrote.[104] An attempt to receive funding for a postdoctoral research school in Philadelphia failed amid scathing reviewer comments.[105] Thus, Rieber and Lewin moved on to plan B: a National Seminar for the Study of Russia in the Twentieth Century, 'Misha's brainchild'.[106]

Organization began in earnest in 1979,[107] and the first Seminar, focusing on methodology, was held in May 1980, with twenty participants.[108] The topics for the next Seminars were set as well, as Lewin reported to his mentor from Birmingham days: the second on the peasantry (1982), the third on bureaucracy, and the fourth on the Civil War.[109] After organizing the first two Seminars, Lewin stepped back from organizational duties. Rieber ran the third one, on bureaucracy, in early 1983, and Bill Rosenberg of the University of Michigan the fourth, on the Civil War, in October 1984.

Under Rosenberg's leadership, two innovations took place. The National Seminar for the first time attracted outside support from the Social Science Research Council (SSRC), a New York-based non-profit organization devoted to furthering social science research. It provided adequate, but not lavish, funding. Moreover, the Seminar for the first time produced a major book, the now classical *Party, State, and Society in the Russian Civil War* (1989).[110] Not that publication had been unimaginable before, but the very rough, discussion-style papers which the first two Seminars had produced were a hard sell. Lewin had sent the entire run from the second conference to a journal, but it only published his introductory remarks – an unfootnoted collection of his thoughts on the Russian peasantry.[111] He then gave up on the other papers, but attempted to publish his own in *The Russian Review*, leading to a remarkable exchange with its editor, who demanded footnotes, which Lewin claimed he was too preoccupied to provide: 'I am so busy now that I cannot return to the files and cards to match all my statement with the sources.'[112] After some back and forth he constructed some footnotes and got it published,[113] nearly in parallel with its reprint in *The Making of the Soviet System* (1985).[114]

With the SSRC providing money, the rules of the game changed. The funding agency wanted to see a publication, and publishers were unwilling to publish unfootnoted discussion papers.[115] Thus, under the dual impact of the expectations of university presses and the funding agency, a pattern was set. The SSRC funded the Seminar for two more rounds: in 1986, a conference on the NEP (originally planned for late 1985) was held at Indiana University; and in 1988, the University of Michigan hosted a Seminar on pre-war Stalinist society in Ann Arbor. Both conferences led to publications following the model of the Civil War volume.[116]

By now, the National Seminar had developed its own dynamic. Originally founded as a group centred around Lewin and his institution it had evolved into an externally funded enterprise which rotated among universities. At the beginning of this process of professionalization stood Lewin's refusal to continue to lead. Rosenberg, after asking for Lewin's help, was left to look after the third Seminar, but at Lewin's institution.[117] He apologized afterwards for the 'anger which flared between the two of us at Al's house', again expressing his hope that 'you will continue to play an active role'.[118] Lewin replied that he could not recall any anger and that any misunderstanding was probably due to 'the fact that the two of us had so few occasions for good conversation over a glass of youknowwhat(ka)'. But he refused to take on further organizational duties.[119]

While Lewin had thus lost interest, his brain-child grew up. From the NEP conference onwards the one-man, relatively ad hoc organization of the first few Seminars was replaced by committee work – replete with formal meetings, minutes, external funding and publications of results.[120] A major innovation occurred at the NEP Seminar: instead of reading papers to each other, they were distributed ahead of time. Participants read them in preparation, which meant the Seminars could be devoted to discussion and critique.[121] This practice remained the standard modus operandi, and Lewin would adopt it for the big conference he would organize himself – the comparative one on Germany and Russia, held in 1991 in Philadelphia.[122]

Unbelievably ambitious in scope and design, with an international cast of historians of Germany, Russia, and the Soviet Union, its organization lacked the professionalism of the National Seminar during the SSRC years. The intellectual work on the conference had started as far back as 1988,[123] and Lewin had merrily invited speakers. However, he only applied for funding in June 1990, less than a year before the original date (April 1991).[124] Predictably, his application was rejected and the conference needed to be postponed to September 1991. As usual, Lewin's ambitions bore no real relationship to the outcome. The conference was designed as a longitudinal study of Germany and Russia from the nineteenth century to the present;[125] it led to a much more modest – and more conventional – comparative volume on Nazism and Stalinism.[126]

Meanwhile, the increasing professionalization of the National Seminar also had its downside. The growing profile of the enterprise made it into a battleground for factions among the American historians of the Soviet Union. Their squabbles contributed to the defunding of the Seminar in 1988, which spelled its end.[127] A conference on the Soviet working class, held at Michigan State University in November 1990, was no longer badged as part of the National Seminar. However, it stood very much in its tradition: a workshop with pre-circulated papers, with a focus on discussion rather than presentation, as the organizers stressed in a circular to the participants.[128] And again, the outcome was a high-quality edited volume setting an agenda for further research in the field.[129]

Lewin, meanwhile, had not lost his ambition to lead the field, and he made one more attempt to gather a group of scholars around himself. To organize a new seminar, he drafted Mark von Hagen (1954–2019), then associate director of Columbia's Harriman Institute, and Frank Wcislo, then assistant professor at Vanderbilt, who had just finished a postdoctoral fellowship at the Institute. The Seminar met at Columbia University in 1989. In the words of Lewin, the meeting was an attempt 'to produce a "research coop" … Not a kolkhoz'.[130] The by now well-established group of revisionists were marked by their absence, as were the usual senior participants in the National Seminar. But the group that gathered was not a new generation, even if the organizers described them as 'Young American Historians in the Field of Twentieth-Century Russian/Soviet History'. Like the 'new cohort' Fitzpatrick had identified in 1986, most of them had completed PhDs in the 1980s, including Ziva Galili (PhD 1980), Jane Burbank (PhD 1981), Alan Ball (PhD 1982), Frank Wcislo (PhD 1984), Doug

Weiner (PhD 1984), David McDonald (PhD 1988), David Shearer (PhD 1988), and Stephen Kotkin (PhD 1988). A few were more senior, including Jeffrey Brooks (PhD 1972), Laura Engelstein (PhD 1976), Neil Weissman (PhD 1976), and Don Raleigh (PhD 1978).[131]

As far as institution-building was concerned, the venture failed, despite the initial enthusiasm of at least some of the participants for 'an umbrella organization for "revitalizing" Russian and Soviet studies in the US'.[132] While all the scholars present would make a mark on the field in the years and decades to come, as a group they did not formulate a research agenda, which would have set it apart from 'the revisionists'. Only one of them – Kotkin – would later make an attempt to replace Lewin as the sage and the guru of the profession (see Chapter 7).

Legacy

In the end, then, Lewin failed as an institution-builder while producing relatively little serious research on Stalinism. The projected big books on the Stalin years – a second volume on collectivization and a social history of Stalinism – never emerged. The collections of essays, chief among them the oft-quoted *Making of the Soviet System* (1985, reissued 1994), were no substitute for the elusive monographs. He was not patient enough to do the research, which he found mind-numbing. He had no stamina to nurture institutions he himself had invented. An ideas man, he got easily annoyed by organizational work or the requirement to provide footnotes in scholarly works. He left editing to others, if at all possible,[133] and handed over organization of the National Seminar as soon as was feasible.

Nevertheless, he was among the most influential historians in the American discussion about Stalinism. His first book, *Russian Peasants*, and his long essay on the *Gorbachev Phenomenon*, have stood the test of time as brilliant pieces of historical analysis, as have a handful of his essays. Many scholars were inspired by the big questions he liked to ask, questions with philosophical and political undercurrents (to use a favourite term). These brought together the ideological influences of his youth with the experience of wartime Stalinism and the quite disparate stimuli of his subsequent stays in Israel, Paris and Birmingham. An original with considerable charisma, Lewin remained in touch with these intellectual ecosystems by both continuing travel and correspondence. His mere presence at conferences and workshops broadened the sometimes insular intellectual world of American academics.

Second, his attempted institution-building had far-reaching consequences. Even as it broke apart over the political bickering between many of its most influential participants, the National Seminar, for nearly a decade, created an important focus for specialists in Russian and Soviet history. The practice of pre-circulated papers, which the Seminar invented, was well ahead of its time. Even today, when it is much more feasible due to electronic distribution systems, it remains the exception rather than the rule. This practice was not Lewin's idea, but part of the process of professionalization after he stood back. To most participants, however, the intellectual experience of these Seminars would be connected to the name of its founder: Moshe Lewin.

And finally, there were his tireless efforts as a patron, corresponding with his clients and talking to them on the phone (late at night), dining them and plying them with vodka, writing letters to get them jobs and promotions, and protesting if these efforts failed. It is no accident that one of his big projects was accomplished by one of his followers who managed to sit down long enough to write a sweeping history of the Soviet experience which brought together social and political history from a distinctly left-wing angle.[134]

Notes

1. Ron Suny's term: Alfred J. Rieber, 'Moshe Lewin: A Reminiscence and Appreciation', *Kritika: Explorations in Russian and Eurasian History* 12, no. 1 (2011): 127–39, here: 131.
2. Moshe Lewin, letter to Michael Hall (3 December 1979), University of Pennsylvania Archives and Records Center, Moshe Lewin Papers (henceforth: MLP) box 1, folder 14.
3. Lewin to Cohen, 25 September 1986, MLP, box 1, folder 17.
4. Lewin to Alec Nove, 1 April 1988, MLP, box 1, folder 18.
5. See his dismissal of Fitzpatrick's work on social mobility as well as on the cultural revolution: Moshe Lewin, *The Making of the Soviet System: Essays in the Social History of the Interwar Years* (New York, 1985), 34, 38–41, 33, 38–41. Later he would reverse course and accept her argument on social mobility and regime support – but without citing her work: Moshe Lewin, 'On Soviet Industrialization', in: *Social Dimensions of Soviet Industrialization*, ed. William Rosenberg and Lewis H. Siegelbaum (Bloomington, 1993), 272–84, here: 274–76; Moshe Lewin, *The Soviet Century* (London, 2005), 290.

6   Cohen to Lewin, 31 July 1986, MLP, box 1, folder 17. Vladimir Andrle, 'Demons and Devil's Advocates: Problems in Historical Writing on the Stalin Era', in: *Stalinism: Its Nature and Aftermath: Essays in Honour of Moshe Lewin*, ed. Nick Lampert and Gabor T. Rittersporn (Armonk, 1992), 25–47, here: 30.
7   Field to Lewin, 8 April 1987, MLP, box 1, folder 18.
8   Lewin to Field, 20 April 1987, MLP, box 1, folder 18.
9   Lewin to Cohen, 25 September 1986, MLP, box 1, folder 17.
10 Numbers according to native language as recorded by census of 1897. See http://demoscope.ru/weekly/ssp/rus_lan_97_uezd.php?reg=91 (accessed 16 March 2017). On Jerusalem of Lithuania, see William Z. Good, 'From "Jerushalayim d'Lita" and back (Wilno, "Jerusalem of Lithuania")', unpublished typescript memoirs, United States Holocaust Memorial Museum (USHMM) RG-02.046.
11 On this history, see Timothy Snyder, *The Reconstruction of Nations: Poland, Ukraine, Lithuania, Belarus, 1569–1999* (New Haven, 2003), 60–65.
12 Dov Levin, 'The Jews of Vilna under Soviet Rule, 19 September – 28 October 1939', *Polin: Studies in Polish Jewry* 9 (1996): 107–37, here: 108.
13 Ronald Grigor Suny, 'Living in the Soviet Century: Moshe Lewin, 1921–2010', *History Workshop Journal* 74, no. 1 (2012): 192–209, here: 193; Omer Bartov, 'Moshe Lewin's Century', *Kritika: Explorations in Russian and Eurasian History* 12, no. 1 (2011): 115–22, here: 117; Rieber, 'Moshe Lewin', 128; Paul Buskovitch, '[Interview with] Moshe Lewin', in: *Visions of History*, ed. Henry Abelove et al. (Manchester, 1983), 281–308.
14 Buskovitch, 'Moshe Lewin', 281–83.
15 Levin, 'The Jews of Vilna'; Mark Edele, 'Soviet Liberations and Occupations, 1939–1949', in: *The Cambridge History of the Second World War*, vol. 2, ed. Richard Bosworth and Joe Maiolo (Cambridge, 2015), 498.
16 Buskovitch, 'Moshe Lewin', 283.
17 Buskovitch, 'Moshe Lewin', 283.
18 Levin, 'The Jews of Vilna', 117–18.
19 Reprinted in *Stalinskie deportatsii 1928–1953: Dokumenty*, ed. N. L. Pobol' and P. M. Polian (Moscow, 2005), 215–17.
20 NKGB report (17 June 1941), reprinted in: *Stalinskie deportatsii*, 222–24.
21 Good, 'From "Jerushalayim d'Lita" and back', 13. On arrests of Zionists in Soviet Lithuania, see also Zorach Warhaftig, *Refugee and Survivor: Rescue Efforts During the Holocaust* (Jerusalem, 1988), 116–17, 145.
22 Lewin to John Higham, 2 April 1986, MLP box 1, folder 17.
23 Buskovitch, 'Moshe Lewin', 284. Lewin's use of the term 'officer' is anachronistic. At the time, they were called 'commanders' in the Red Army.
24 Bartov, 'Moshe Lewin's Century', 117.
25 Buskovitch, 'Moshe Lewin', 284–85, 285.
26 Mark Edele, Sheila Fitzpatrick and Atina Grossmann (eds), *Shelter from the Holocaust: Rethinking Jewish Survival in the Soviet Union* (Detroit, 2017), 72–74, 120–22, 145–48, 202.
27 Bartov, 'Moshe Lewin's Century', 118, 119; Buskovitch, 'Moshe Lewin', 286; Rieber, 'Moshe Lewin', 128; Arfon Rees, 'Moshe Lewin obituary', *Guardian* (28 September 2010), https://www.theguardian.com/society/2010/sep/27/moshe-lewin-obituary (accessed 5 December 2017).

28 This effectively elaborated an idea first developed by Isaac Deutscher. Isaac Deutscher, *Stalin: A Political Biography*. 2nd ed. (London, 1967), 318–19.
29 Moshe Lewin, *Russian Peasants and Soviet Power: A Study of Collectivization* (New York, 1975), 159.
30 Lewin, *Russian Peasants*, 164–65, 159.
31 Moshe Lewin, *Lenin's Last Struggle* (London, 1973).
32 As opposed to Cohen's 'Bukharin alternative' (see Chapter 1).
33 Lewin, *Lenin's Last Struggle*, 137–38.
34 Lewin, *Lenin's Last Struggle*, xiii.
35 Lewin, *Russian Peasants*, 146.
36 Lewin, *Lenin's Last Struggle*, 34. See also Lewin, *Russian Peasants*, 166.
37 Lewin, *Lenin's Last Struggle*, 41.
38 Lewin, *Lenin's Last Struggle*, 133–34.
39 Lewin, *Lenin's Last Struggle*, 41.
40 Lewin, *Lenin's Last Struggle*, 134.
41 Lewin, *Lenin's Last Struggle*, ix.
42 Lewin, *Lenin's Last Struggle*, 136.
43 Moshe Lewin, *Lenin's Last Struggle: With a New Introduction* (Ann Arbor, 2005), xxix.
44 Lewin, *The Soviet Century*, 14, 201.
45 Rees, 'Moshe Lewin obituary'; Bartov, 'Moshe Lewin's Century', 119. On R. W. Davies and the Centre, see Julian Cooper, Maureen Perrie and E. A. Rees, 'Introduction: A Tribute to R. W. Davies', in: *Soviet History, 1917–53: Essays in Honour of R. W. Davies*, ed. Julian Cooper, Maureen Perrie and E. A. Rees (New York, 1995), xii–xxiii.
46 Lewin, *Russian Peasants*, 11.
47 Lewin to Paul Avrich, 24 October 1975, MLP, box 2, folder 26.
48 Lewin to Schiffrin, 1 February 1983, MLP, box 1, folder 15.
49 This was the guiding thought of the mega-conference on Russia and Germany he hosted in September 1991 (see MLP, box 1, folders 5–11).
50 Lewin to Andrea Graziosi, 3 March 1987, MLP, box 2, folder 1.
51 Moshe Lewin, *The Gorbachev Phenomenon: A Historical Interpretation* (Berkeley, 1988); Moshe Lewin, *The Gorbachev Phenomenon: A Historical Interpretation*. Expanded ed. (Berkeley, 1991).
52 Moshe Lewin, *Political Undercurrents in Soviet Economic Debates: From Bukharin to the Modern Reformers* (Princeton, 1974).
53 Sheila Fitzpatrick, *Education and Social Mobility in the Soviet Union 1921–1934* (Cambridge, 1979); Lynne Viola, *The Best Sons of the Fatherland: Workers in the Vanguard of Soviet Collectivization* (Oxford, 1989).
54 Lewin to Paul Avrich, 24 October 1975.
55 Lewin to Dorothy Thompson, 27 January 1976, MLP, box 2, folder 26.
56 The classic work based on this source base is Alex Inkeles and Raymond Bauer, *The Soviet Citizen: Daily Life in a Totalitarian Society* (Cambridge, Mass., 1961).
57 Today, they are available in a searchable database: https://library.harvard.edu/collections/hpsss/index.html (accessed 19 December 2019).
58 Merle Fainsod, *Smolensk under Soviet Rule* (New York, 1958); J. Arch Getty, *Origins of the Great Purges: The Soviet Communist Party Reconsidered*

(Cambridge, 1985); Roberta T. Manning, 'The Great Purges in a Rural District: Belyi "Raion" Revisited', *Russian History* 16, no. 2/4 (1989): 409–33.
59   See Patricia Kennedy Grimsted, 'Spoils of War Returned, Part 3. US Restitution of Nazi-Looted Cultural Treasures to the USSR, 1945–1959', *Prologue Magazine* (Spring 2002), https://www.archives.gov/publications/prologue/2002/spring/spoils-of-war-3.html (accessed 18 January 2018). Today, a copy is also available at the Davis Center at Harvard University: https://daviscenter.fas.harvard.edu/library/research-guides/archival-sources-soviet-history/smolensk-oblast-party-archive-1917-1938 (accessed 18 January 2018).
60   Others did significantly earlier. See Fitzpatrick, *Education and Social Mobility*; and Viola, *Best Sons of the Fatherland*.
61   Andrea Graziosi to Moshe Lewin, 23 January 1988, MLP box 2, folder 1.
62   Lewin to Graziosi, 19 February 1988, MLP, box 2, folder 1. The sources were eventually published by Andrea Graziosi, '"Lettres de Kharkov". La famine en Ukraine et dans le Caucase du Nord à travers les rapports des diplomates italiens, 1932–1934', *Cahiers du Monde russe et soviétique* 30, no. 1/2 (1989): 5–106.
63   Moshe Lewin, 'Swing of the Pendulum: Stalin's Model', in: *Political Undercurrents in Soviet Economic Debates*.
64   Moshe Lewin, '"Taking Grain": Soviet Policies of Agricultural Procurements Before the War', first published in *Essays in Honour of E. H. Carr*, ed. C. Abramsky (London, 1974), reprinted in *The Making of the Soviet System*.
65   Moshe Lewin, 'Who was the Soviet Kulak?', first published in *Soviet Studies* 18, no. 2 (1966), reprinted in *The Making of the Soviet System*.
66   Moshe Lewin, 'The Disappearance of Planning in the Plan', first published in *Slavic Review* 32, no. 2 (1973): 271–87, republished in Moshe Lewin, *Russia/USSR/Russia: The Drive and Drift of a Superstate* (New York, 1995).
67   For an example of ideological polemics to save 'Socialism' from the Soviet Union, see Moshe Lewin, 'USSR from A to Z', and 'Soviet Socialism: A Case of "Mislabeling"', both in *Russia/USSR/Russia*.
68   Of the twelve essays published in *The Making of the Soviet System*, eleven had been previously published elsewhere. The follow-up volume *Russia/USSR/Russia* repeated the pattern: of fifteen essays, seven had previously been published. *Political Undercurrents in Soviet Economic Debates* focused on both the pre-Stalin and the post-Stalin years, but also included one lucid essay on the political economy of Stalinism.
69   Quoted in Suny, 'Living in the Soviet Century', 192.
70   Lewin, 'Preface', in: *The Making of the Soviet System*, 6. This line of inquiry was first developed in *Political Undercurrents*.
71   Lewin, *Russia/USSR/Russia*, xiv.
72   Lewin, *The Gorbachev Phenomenon* (1988), 151. Unchanged in 1991 edition, 151 (which had been finished in June 1990).
73   Moshe Lewin, 'Russia/USSR in Historical Motion: An Essay in Interpretation', *The Russian Review* 50, no. 3 (1991): 265–66. Lewin did not change this statement when reprinting the essay in 1995: *Russia/USSR/Russia*, here: 94. In a new essay in the same collection (not previously published), he also ended with careful optimism about the future of a Russian market economy: 'Soviet Socialism. A Case of "Mislabeling"', 170.

74 In 'The Social Background of Stalinism' (originally published 1977), Lewin acknowledged that Stalinism might have been one of the 'potentials' of Leninism. See Lewin, *The Making of the Soviet System*, 263 (if not otherwise noted, the 1985 and 1994 editions are identical). In 'The Civil War' (first published 1989) he drew lines of continuity between civil war Bolshevism and Stalinism, which also imply that there are continuities between one version of Leninism and Stalinism. (*Russia/USSSR/Russia*, esp. 59, 63–65, 70–71). In 'Soviet Socialim. A Case of "Mislabeling"' (1995), he asserted that the Lenin of 1922, that is, the Lenin of the N.E.P, was the real Leninist legacy (*Russia/USSR/Russia*, 154).
75 Lewin, *The Making of the Soviet System*, 9.
76 Moshe Lewin, 'Stalin in the Mirror of the Other', *Russia/USSR/Russia*, 214.
77 Lewin, *The Soviet Century*, 12.
78 Lewin, *Russian Peasants and Soviet Power*, 146, 374, 517.
79 Leon Trotsky, *The Revolution Betrayed: What is the Soviet Union and Where is it Going?* (New York, 1972).
80 Lewin, *Lenin's Last Struggle*, 124–25.
81 Moshe Lewin, 'Society, State, and Ideology during the First Five-year Plan', in: *The Making of the Soviet System*, 209.
82 Lewin, *The Making of the Soviet System*, 44, 221, 265.
83 Buskovitch, '[Interview with] Moshe Lewin', 294–95. Lewin repeated the charge in 1995: 'Soviet Socialism. A Case of "Mislabeling"', 147. Even the volume which reproduced the old Stalinism–Nazism comparison on which 'totalitarianism' was built, theoretically, dismissed the concept. See Ian Kershaw and Moshe Lewin, 'The Regimes and Their Dictators: Perspectives of Comparison', in: *Stalinism and Nazism: Dictatorships in Comparison*, ed. Ian Kershaw and Moshe Lewin (Cambridge, 1997), 1–25, here: 3–4. See also Lewin, *The Soviet Century*, 273.
84 Lewin, *The Soviet Century*, 378–79.
85 Lewin, 'Russia/USSR in historical motion', in: *Russia/USSR/Russia*, 91.
86 Lewin, 'Bureaucracy and the Stalinist State', in: *Russia/USSR/Russia*, 189, 206; Lewin, 'Russia/USSR in Historical Motion', esp. 82–88.
87 Lewin, *The Soviet Century*, chapter 13.
88 Moshe Lewin, 'The Immediate Background of Soviet Collectivization', in: *The Making of the Soviet System*, 115.
89 Lewin, 'The Immediate Background of Soviet Collectivization', essentially a restatement of much of *Russian Peasants and Soviet Power*.
90 Lewin, '"Taking Grain"'. Lewin, 'The Disappearance of Planning in the Plan', 112.
91 Lewin, 'Russia/USSR in Historical Motion', 93.
92 Lewin, *The Soviet Century*, 143.
93 Lewin, *The Soviet Century*, 381, 382.
94 Moshe Lewin, 'Bureaucracy and the Stalinist State', in: *Russia/USSR/Russia*, 206.
95 Lewin, 'Soviet Socialism. A Case of "Mislabeling"', 167–68.
96 Lewin, *The Making of the Soviet System*, 16–17. See also 'Rural Society in 20th Century Russia', and 'Popular Religion in Twentieth Century Russia', in: *The Making of the Soviet System*. The strongest argument is developed

in 'The Social Background of Stalinism' (1977), in: *The Making of the Soviet System*, esp. 268, 273, 275, but again he retreats to Stalin: 276.
97 Lewin, 'Stalin in the Mirror of the Other', 218.
98 Lewin, *The Soviet Century*, 98.
99 Lewin, 'Bureaucracy and the Stalinist State', 188; Lewin, *The Soviet Century*, 143–44; Lewin, 'The Social Background of Stalinism', 279.
100 Mark Edele, *Stalinist Society 1928–1953* (Oxford, 2011), 48–51.
101 Lewin, *The Soviet Century*, 100–01.
102 Dietrich Beyrau, 'Brutalization Revisited: The Case of Russia', *Journal of Contemporary History* 50, no. 1 (2015): 15–37.
103 Lewin, *The Soviet Century*, 146.
104 Rieber, 'Moshe Lewin', 129.
105 Joseph D. Duffey (National Endowment for the Humanities) to Lewin, rejection letter, 30 November 1979; Harold C. Cannon to Alfred Rieber, 13 December 1979, both MLP, box 1, folder 13.
106 Rieber, 'Moshe Lewin', 130.
107 Letter to Gail Lapidus, 9 April 1979, MLP, box 1, folder 14.
108 Lewin to Terence Emmons, 16 November 1982, MLP, box 1, folder 15.
109 Lewin to R. W. Davies, 24 February 1981, MLP, box 1, folder 15.
110 Diane P. Koenker, William G. Rosenberg and Ronald Grigor Suny (eds), *Party, State, and Society in the Russian Civil War: Explorations in Social History* (Bloomington, 1989).
111 Keith Nield and Janet Blackman to Lewin, 11 November 1983, MLP, box 1, folder 15. Moshe Lewin, 'Rural Society in Twentieth-Century Russia: An Introduction', *Social History* 9, no. 2 (1984): 171–80; reprinted as chapter 1 in *The Making of the Soviet System*.
112 Lewin to Terence Emmons, 16 November 1982, MLP, box 1, folder 15.
113 Moshe Lewin, 'Customary Law and Russian Rural Society in the Post-Reform Era', *The Russian Review* 44, no. 1 (1985): 1–19. On the prehistory, see Daniel Field to Lewin, 4 January 1983 (requesting footnotes), and Lewin's answer, 1 February 1983; Field to Lewin, 16 February 1982; Lewin to Field, 7 March 1983; all MLP, box 1, folder 15.
114 Lewin to Field, 10 January 1985, MLP, box 1, folder 15.
115 Rosenberg to Lewin, 2 January 1985, MLP, box 1, folder 16.
116 Koenker, Rosenberg and Suny, *Party, State, and Society in the Russian Civil War*; Sheila Fitzpatrick, Alexander Rabinowitch and Richard Stites (eds), *Russia in the Era of NEP: Explorations in Soviet Society and Culture* (Bloomington, 1991); William Rosenberg and Lewis H. Siegelbaum (eds), *Social Dimensions of Soviet Industrialization* (Bloomington, 1993).
117 Rosenberg to Lewin, 14 June 1984, MLP, box 1, folder 16.
118 Rosenberg to Lewin, 2 January 1985, MLP, box 1, folder 16.
119 Lewin to Rosenberg, 8 January 1985, MLP, box 1, folder 16.
120 Lewin to Rabinowitch, 27 March 1985, MLP, box 1, folder 16; 'Meeting of the Planning Group for the National Seminar on Social History of Twentieth Century Russia; Conference on the 1930s, SSRC, New York, New York, April 14, 1985', (minutes), MLP, box 2, folder 8; Bailes to Lewin, 1 October 1985, MLP, box 2, folder 8.
121 Rabinowitch to Lewin, 16 July 1986, MLP, box 2, folder 13.

122 MLP, box 1, folders 5–11.
123 Ely to Lewin, 4 December 1988, MLP, box 1, folder 3.
124 Application material to German Marshall Fund, 1990, MLP, box 1, folder 4.
125 This ambition was the guiding thought of the mega-conference on Russia and Germany he hosted in September 1991 (see MLP, box 1, folders 5–11).
126 Ian Kershaw and Moshe Lewin (eds), *Stalinism and Nazism: Dictatorships in Comparison* (Cambridge, 1997).
127 Orlovsky to Lewin, 20 May 1988; Lewin to Orlovsky, 31 May 1988; Orlovsky to Lewin, 2 November 1988; all MLP, box 2, folder 2.
128 Lewis Siegelbaum, Robert Johnson, Ronald Suny to Participants in the Conference: 'The Making of the Soviet Working Class', n.d. (before September 1990), MLP, box 2, folder 16.
129 Lewis H. Siegelbaum and Ronald G. Suny (eds), *Making Workers Soviet: Power, Class, and Identity* (Ithaca and London, 1994).
130 Lewin to Orlovsky, 4 October 1989, MLP, box 2, folder 3.
131 Moshe Lewin, Mark von Hagen and Frank Wcislo, circular letter, 26 September 1989, MLP, box 2, folder 3.
132 David Shearer to Mark von Hagen, 17 October 1989, MLP, box 1, folder 12.
133 See, for example, Lewin to Schiffrin, 14 September 1983; Avrich to Schiffrin, 14 January 1984; Schiffrin to Lewin, 31 January 1984; all in MLP, box 1, folder 15.
134 Ronald G. Suny, *The Soviet Experiment: Russia, the USSR, and the Successor States* (Oxford, 1998); 2nd ed. 2011.

3
The Russian origins of totalitarianism: empire and nation

Among the flat-earthers

Harvard Professor Richard Pipes, like Pennsylvania's Moshe Lewin, remained silent at the time of the 1986–87 debate recounted in Chapter 1.[1] By his own account, he did not read 'revisionists', whom he likened to Holocaust deniers. 'I ignore their work', he noted. 'How do you fight people who deny the Holocaust? It's like somebody who believes the earth is flat.'[2] These flat-earthers were, to Pipes, political zealots. They were 'like the early Bolsheviks': 'broad-minded toward their own kind but ferociously intolerant of outsiders'. They formed a 'party determined to impose control on the teaching of modern Russian history' in the United States. In sinister ways, they 'took over many of the leading university chairs' and 'imposed their views on students and professional organizations ... by means of patronage more appropriate to politics than scholarship'. The results were predictable: 'a stultifying form of "political correctness"' and 'group think'; more, even: 'thought control' unparalleled in history-writing 'save possibly Black studies'.[3]

The feeling of disgust was mutual. Pipes was the social historians' bête noire. A nearly imaginary figure, given that he was infrequently encountered at conferences, he represented all they hated: right-wing politics, unsubtle anti-Sovietness, the totalitarian model, political history. Maybe he was a Russophobe, too, many thought. A Pole, after all. 'You don't give Russia to the Poles', Lewin told a reporter, 'they don't think straight.'[4] As the non-ironic Pipes countered this 'ethnic slur': it was 'ludicrous, given that Professor Lewin happens to be himself a native of Poland'.[5] And indeed, Pipes and Lewin were both Polish Jews who had fled their homeland in the Second World War – one going west, the other east. After they arrived in the United States their work would mark the respectable left and right wing of academic debate on the Soviet Union. Both contributed to the debate on how Stalinism emerged.

Pipes was not a historian of Stalinism itself, but of the Russian and Soviet empires more broadly.[6] Nevertheless, some of his most influential books –*The Formation of the Soviet Union* (1954), *Russia under the Old Regime* (1974), *The Russian Revolution* (1990), and *Russia under the Bolshevik Regime* (1993) – elaborated a coherent vision of the origins of Stalinist totalitarianism out of the traditions of Russian patrimonialism and imperialism.[7] To Pipes, Stalinism was the essence of Bolshevik totalitarianism, a fusion of revolutionary practice with Russian culture. Pipes was also one of the founding fathers of the study of nations in the Soviet context. Finally, Pipes was an anti-Soviet public intellectual, pundit and policy adviser – a part of his career beyond the topic of this book.[8] His public work was an expression of his self-understanding as a teacher, rather than a researcher. He was dedicated to education: teaching undergraduates about Russia and about communism, teaching the wider public about the evils of the Soviet Union, teaching government about the enemy. His books were teaching books: they both came out of his undergraduate teaching and were meant to teach a lesson.

Escape

One and a half years younger than Lewin, Richard Pipes was born on 11 July 1923 at the other end of Poland, in Cieszyn (Teschen), formerly in Austrian Silesia.[9] His family united two parts of the new Polish state's Jewish population. Pipes's father had been born in Lwów, then called Lemberg and located in Austria-Hungary (today it is Lviv in Ukraine). He had thus grown up a Habsburg subject. His mother, by contrast, had been born under the rule of the Russian tsar. She hailed from an affluent business family in Warsaw, then part of the Romanov Empire. In the course of the First World War and its violent aftermath, Mark (Marek) Pipes, Richard's father, helped forge the new Poland: he fought under an assumed Polish name as part of Joseph Piłsudski's Polish Legions.

The new Polish state cobbled together disparate regions housing a multiethnic population previously ruled by the three partitioning powers: the German Empire of the Hohenzollerns in the northwest, the Austro-Hungarian Empire of the Habsburgs in the south, and the Romanov Empire in the centre and east. About a third of the population were not Poles, with significant minorities of Ukrainians (14 per cent), Jews (10 per cent), Belarusians (4 per cent), and Germans (2 per cent). In this situation, nation-building could proceed along two possible axes: either by stressing loyalty to the state or to the Polish ethnos. The former, which was Piłsudski's initial programme, allowed an integration of non-Polish groups into the nation via a version of civic nationalism. The latter, which eventually took over, was exclusionary and required, at best, full assimilation of Ukrainians, Jews and Germans.[10]

The Pipes family was part of the new nationalist establishment attempting, in the early post-war years, to build a multiethnic Polish state. During the war, Mark Pipes had forged strong friendships with Piłsudski's officers 'who subsequently would run the Polish republic'.[11] Thoroughly assimilated and well-educated Jews, the family's politics were deeply patriotic, although the rising anti-Semitism did worry them. Economically, they were well-off businesspeople, part of the 'Jewish middle class'.[12] Their political connections and economic means gave the Pipes family options Lewin did not have.

Pipes senior had few illusions about the fate of Poland's Jews under German occupation. He knew the honorary consul of 'a Latin American country' who was willing to furnish false papers. Earlier preparations for an escape from an increasingly anti-Semitic Poland had resulted in a war chest deposited in a Stockholm bank. False passport in hand, Mark Pipes began negotiating exit visas for his allegedly South American family with the German occupation authorities. Although he was carefully hiding this fact, his fluent German, acquired as a young man in Vienna, would have helped in this quest. Eventually he succeeded, and the family left on the first available train when services had been restored after the fighting. On 27 October 1939, they left Warsaw for Breslau, then continued on to Munich from where they reached Rome. After a sojourn in Mussolini's Italy, Richard and his father escaped in a small hydroplane to Las Palmas, and then on by boat to Barcelona. His mother and their dog travelled separately, with the luggage, via Genoa. On 7 June the family was reunited. On 24 June they continued to Portugal, where with some effort and no small amount of luck they found a ship to America. On 11 July 1940, Richard's seventeenth birthday, they arrived in New Jersey. As they would learn later, very few in their family survived, as attempts to extract other relations had failed.

The Pipes's escape story was extraordinary. Not only did the entire family get away, they were even able to bring their dog along. Only people of considerable means, connections, perseverance, and luck could escape through Nazi Germany and Fascist Italy to the United States. Escape to the Soviet Union was much more frequent, as recent research has pointed out. Given the Pipes's politics and social class, however, such a choice was unlikely, although not impossible.[13]

Thus, Pipes evaded direct experience of Stalinism. Given his escape track from occupied Poland, the future historian of Soviet totalitarianism had known only German Nazism first hand. Stalin's quite different totalitarianism remained an abstraction, but one which had helped to destroy the very Poland which had been the site of Pipes's youthful dreams of education and career. He would never forgive this loss, even as he forged a highly successful career in the United States. His later travels to the Soviet Union would only confirm his notion that the Soviet Union continued to be totalitarian. They did not alert him to the complexities of life under Stalin itself, or how the country might have changed since the death of the dictator.

Career

After Pipes arrived in the United States he wrote to a whole range of colleges explaining his penniless situation as a refugee, and asked for admissions and financial aid. Four institutions replied, and he chose Muskingum College in Ohio, without knowing much about it. It turned out to be 'an excellent choice'. During his time there – from September 1940 to January 1943, when he got drafted into the army – he learned, first of all, 'a command of English'. He applied to join the Army's Specialized Training Program and was sent to Cornell to learn Russian. He graduated in June 1944 and spent the rest of the war in more or less meaningless posts in various parts of the United States. He never saw action and was demobilized in March 1946.[14]

The language-training and the war had awakened his interest in Russian studies. Taking advantage of the GI Bill, he applied to graduate school and enrolled at Harvard, where Michael Karpovich was professor of Russian history. Karpovich was an extraordinary scholar. Never publishing much, he was famous for his polished lectures. He trained important specialists in US Russian studies: Martin Malia and Nicholas Riasanovsky would go to Berkeley, Leopold Haimson and Marc Raeff would build a programme at Columbia, and Pipes would become Karpovich's successor. Karpovich brought the traditions of the liberal Russian intelligentsia to Harvard. Born in 1888 in Tiflis, he had become radicalized in the 1905 Revolution, later drifting from the Socialist Revolutionaries to the liberal Kadets. He studied in Moscow and Paris, worked in the war administration from 1916, and after the February Revolution became secretary to the Provisional Government's ambassador in the United States. As his state disappeared in the Bolshevik revolution, he was stranded in the US and began teaching Russian history at Harvard in 1927.[15]

Pipes was a model doctoral and postdoctoral scholar. His correspondence with Karpovich shows a disciplined and hard-working young man checking in with his mentor, systematically implementing his research plan, and completing every task on time.[16] His stable home life helped with this productivity. Alone among the three scholars whose life is explored in the first part of this book, Pipes was happily married, never got a divorce, and lived in a family with clearly delineated gender roles. Irene Roth, whom he had met while at Cornell, was of a similar background. The families had even 'vaguely' known each other back in Poland. They married in 1946. 'My marriage was for me a continuous source of joy and strength', wrote Pipes later. Irene 'assumed command of the earth, I of the clouds, and between us, kept our little universe in good order'.[17]

Pipes's dissertation topic was Soviet nationality policy, interesting at the time because Russian nationalism had all but eclipsed Bolshevik rhetoric in the Soviet Union. 'I wanted to find out why this had happened.' The thesis was done in early 1950. It would become the basis of his first book, *The Formation of the Soviet Union* (1954). The transformation of the thesis into a book required more and prodigious research, which Pipes conducted at the Hoover Institution in 1950, and in London, Paris and Istanbul in 1951, where he interviewed surviving members of the non-Russian governments of the revolutionary era, an early example of oral history.[18]

All the while, Pipes competed with Malia for the position of the soon-to-be retired Karpovich. In their recollections, both act as if they had nothing to do with the final outcome. Pipes had spent the first half of 1956 on a teaching gig in Berkeley, and after his return to Harvard found the atmosphere 'heated'. He claimed that he escaped, against Karpovich's advice, and spent 1956 and much of 1957 in Paris, the Soviet Union, and Switzerland. He returned to Harvard in September 1957 to find that still no decision had been reached. Malia was the most likely choice, because he was already on an assistant professorship and because his views of Russian history were closer to Karpovich's. It came as a surprise when Pipes learned that he would get the job.

According to Malia, Pipes was much less detached. He was 'campaigning for the job', which involved courting powerful members of the department at a 1955 Rome meeting of the World Historical Association (which Pipes attended, but Malia did not). Whatever the facts of the matter might be, the choice could not have been too hard, given that Pipes had produced a major monograph as well as eight published articles in scholarly journals and collections, while Malia had been too busy talking to intellectuals in Paris and Moscow to finish the footnotes to his unpublished manuscript. He still got a chair in Berkeley, and would clash, much later, with Pipes over whether Soviet totalitarianism was Russian or Marxist, as well as whether or not Lenin had taken German money in 1917.[19]

Pipes would remain in Harvard until his retirement in 1996, interrupted only in 1981 for two years' service on President Ronald Reagan's National Security Council. (He is often credited with inventing the phrase 'evil empire' for the Soviet Union during this time, but when asked in post-Soviet Russia if he was the author, he answered 'Unfortunately, I am not.'[20])

Lessons learned

The odyssey which had brought Pipes from Poland to Harvard began with the German invasion in 1939. The Hitler–Stalin Pact and its consequences – the destruction of the Polish state, the dual occupation of his homeland, and ultimately the Holocaust – were central life shocks. He began his memoirs not with his birth, or with his earliest childhood memories, but with the moment he learned about the Hitler–Stalin Pact. He was, of course, fortunate enough to soon escape, but what he could observe left deep impressions:

> Life in occupied Poland returned with surprising rapidity to normal: it is amazing how quickly the everyday overwhelms the 'historic'. This experience left me with the abiding conviction that the population at large plays only a marginal role in history, or at any rate in political and military history, which is the preserve of small elites; people do not make history – they make a living.[21]

Even deeper sat the terrible experience of surviving genocide. The Holocaust, implemented in Poland after Pipes had left the country, was the trauma that drove him to write what he did about Bolshevism. As he worked on the murder of the imperial family for his *Russian Revolution* (1990) he was 'acutely depressed. I smell a whiff of the Holocaust', he wrote in a notebook. Imagining the burned bodies of the murdered imperial family conjured up 'the smokestacks of Auschwitz'.[22] Indeed, the experience of escape in the last minute informed his entire approach to history. 'I am', he wrote, if not a survivor of the Holocaust, then a fortunate escapee from it.' His good fortune, however, came with survivor's guilt. 'I find it emotionally difficult to accept that the people I knew and the events I have experienced or witnessed have vanished as if they had never existed. I find it especially hard to cope with the fact that I am probably the only custodian of the memory of many people long dead: much of my family and nearly all my school friends, who perished without a trace in the Holocaust. I am depressed by this thought because it seems to make life meaningless.'[23] Thus, he made the memory of the dead his calling. 'I felt and feel to this day that I have been spared ... to spread a moral message by showing, using examples from history, how evil ideas lead to evil consequences.' Much of his *oeuvre* was a displaced discourse on the Holocaust, about which 'enough' had been written already. 'I thought it my mission to demonstrate this truth using the example of communism.'[24]

The teacher

A scholar with this sense of mission is unlikely to become an archive rat. His interest was not in finding evidence to destabilize perceived wisdom. Not that Pipes did not go to the archives or, more frequently, to libraries. He also did oral history well before the term was invented. His research was prodigious, and he preferred citing primary sources over secondary literature. But the role of these sources was different from the way 'revisionists' would use them. Rather than hunting for evidence that would falsify what he already knew, he used primary sources as raw material for his literary practice. As he described this process: 'The art of the historian consists of selecting, according to his own criteria, some evidence from the boundless store of available facts and then weaving them in a convincing and, if possible, aesthetically satisfying narrative.' Writing history was 'an experience akin to the artistic'.[25]

This aesthetic approach worked hand-in-glove with teaching. Pipes was the only one of the three major historians discussed here who was genuinely interested in educating undergraduates. Lewin preferred to 'teach teachers', and Fitzpatrick to train researchers. Pipes also advised over sixty PhD students, including many scholars mentioned in this book (Peter Kenez, William Rosenberg and Daniel Field, for example). But his approach was relatively hands-off and remarkably laissez-faire. He simply was not much interested in the focused topics doctoral research produces. It was intellectual 'brickmaking'. Pipes was much more interested in the intellectual 'architecture' of broad interpretations: an ideal fit for the lecture hall.[26]

Pipes liked lecturing. His memoirs are full of references to teaching, which he 'enjoyed … greatly'.[27] He fondly remembered the 'exhilaration' of teaching his first lecture course. He quickly realized that 1950s students had no longer attention spans than their twenty-first century peers: they 'did not exceed ten to twelve minutes'. Hence, he 'interrupted the lecture at such intervals with stories and anecdotes that had some, even remote, bearing on the subject'. He was gratified when the class responded with laughter.[28] In his correspondence he commented on the students he taught, and how they did in class.[29] He took pride when his enrolments increased, despite his reputation as a hardliner in a liberal university.[30] And when he went on study leave he moved heaven and earth to get a senior scholar as his teaching replacement, if the department tried to hire a cheap, inexperienced junior instructor.[31]

He vigilantly retained control over his classroom. When university bureaucrats tried to impose student evaluations, he refused, pointing out that his courses were popular. 'I prefer my students to vote with their feet, or, more correctly, the seats of their pants.'[32] When proposals were floated to reform teaching because modern students were 'primarily concerned with self-hood' he marked such passages with a fat, red 'NO!' An incensed letter to the inventors of such innovation followed: 'Students may well be "primarily concerned with self-hood"', he wrote, 'but then young men and women always were ... The purpose of education is to get them out of their own shells and to teach them to be concerned with the world outside.'[33]

His writing and his teaching were deeply entwined. When he began thinking about the Russian Revolution book, he first organized a class around the theme to get into the swing of things.[34] And in his books he distilled lessons for his readers. 'The tragic and sordid history of the Russian Revolution', he wrote at the end of *Russia under the Bolshevik Regime*, 'teaches that political authority must never be employed for ideological ends. It is best to let people be.'[35]

These are the words of a teacher, not a researcher. A teacher needs to explain to students why what they learn is significant. Good undergraduate teachers are able to distil such meanings. Pipes always wrote with the classroom in mind. He wrote for a broad public, not for other historians. He was not the only one, of course: Soviet history could teach very different lessons. For example, Ronald Suny, one of Lewin's disciples, had this to offer: 'We learn from the Soviet Union several important lessons. One: There is no socialism without democracy'. But he then moved on to the history of the West, which taught that 'there is no real democracy without socialism'.[36] These are not the lessons you learn from studying archival documents; these are lessons you develop for the lecture hall. No wonder Pipes was cited more often than any other historian of the Soviet experience: his work 'made sense' of it (see Figure 4.2 in the next chapter).

The Polish line

But what was it that Pipes tried to teach? Critics scoffed that it was Russophobia, possibly Polish in origin. And one can read his work as an indictment of what was wrong with Russia: lack of private property, lack of civil liberties, an overbearing police state. We could call this Pipes's 'Polish line' of thought, a notion he confirmed: 'When you live next to these people', he stated in 1991, 'you know some things; for instance, that the Russians can be a brutal people.'[37] These 'Polish attitudes toward Russia' he must have 'absorbed ... from the air', he mused in his memoirs. During his youth in Poland he had no interest in Russia or its history, but his later research 'confirmed me in some of these attitudes'.[38]

Pipes's 'Polish line' originated as a gentle polemic with the Harvard establishment, both his doctoral adviser Karpovich and his competitor for the succession, Malia. Karpovich, the failed Russian liberal, saw pre-revolutionary Russia as part of Europe and on the way to liberal modernity. Even the war, he believed, did not have to derail this normal path to liberalism, had the tsar been more flexible. But things went wrong, and the Bolsheviks stole the Revolution. The rest was not so much history, but an aberration.[39] Malia followed this line fairly closely, and would eventually write a major interpretation of Soviet history as not only the result of Marxism, but even of the Enlightenment.[40]

Pipes would disagree with nearly every one of these statements, save the point that the Bolsheviks had not taken power in a revolution but a coup. The argument was developed over the course of several books. First came *Russia under the Old Regime* (1974). It was a sweeping interpretation of the long stretch of Russian history before the Revolution, which drew strong lines of continuity between the old regime and the Soviet empire. At its heart was Russia's property regime. The princes of Muscovy, and later the tsars of the Russian Empire, lay claim to all land, and would dole it out as reward for service to the state. This system worked well for the autocracy until the challenge of the French and the Industrial Revolution in the nineteenth century. The autocracy was now confronted by intellectuals, alienated from both the regime and the peasant majority, and radicalized under the influence of Western political thought. Unable to mobilize a deeply conservative peasantry, they turned to terrorism, killing state officials. Their most prominent and spectacular victim was Tsar Alexander II. The government reacted by building a fierce police state. Those who fought against it – including Lenin's Bolsheviks – learned its methods, and would eventually replicate them, building an even more systematic repressive apparatus which monopolized property even more successfully. The Soviet regime, then, was politically and economically continuous with the Tsarist patrimonial state. This line was then brought all the way up to the time the Soviet Union had been rebuilt from the rubble of the Tsarist empire. It took two more thick tomes to complete this task: *The Russian Revolution* (1990) and *Russia under the Bolshevik Regime* (1994). The Soviet Union, to Pipes, was a transfiguration of the Russian Empire, of Russian patrimonialism, and the late Tsarist police state.

The 'Polish line' could lend itself to Cold War hawkishness, as it did in the case of Pipes. But it could also lend itself to a defence of Marxism: if the Marxist plant grew differently depending on the cultural soil it was planted in, then an American, a German, a French, or a British Marxism would build different, more liberal states and societies.[41] If what was wrong with the Soviet Union was that it was Russian, Marxists could simply ignore it and go on building their socialism elsewhere. And indeed, the socialist historian Lewin went down just that path. He tended to chalk up to Russian authoritarianism whatever 'went wrong' with socialism: he, too, ran a 'Polish line'.

The conservative line

Pipes's Polish line thus ran into contradiction with his conservatism: Pipes was an anti-Marxist. While he remained a registered Democrat to the end of his life, despite his later support of the Reagan administration, never did he flirt with socialism, as many of his colleagues did.[42] A real caesura for him politically were student protests on Harvard's campus in 1969. They began his alienation from his institution, which he saw meekly giving in to radicals, destroying the Harvard he loved. He was appalled by the violence, by the protesters' lack of refinement, their wilful ignorance, and their contempt for learning, contemplation and scholarship.[43] He associated the uncouth youth he encountered in the protests with the social historians who started to make an impact around the same time. In his memoirs, a section entitled 'historical revisionism' is not about history or revisionism at all, but about the protests. Increasingly, he felt that his university, his field, and his profession was being taken over by the crazies.[44]

It was only a matter of time until Pipes would react to these real-life political sentiments in a scholarly fashion. As he worked through his Polish line from the end of the nineteenth century through the final years of Tsarism, the Revolution, and the building of socialism, the dissonance of his Russocentrism with his anticommunism became stronger and stronger. By the end of the second volume of his revolution-epos – 'the work I was born to do'[45] – it had emerged as a fully-fledged contradiction. *Russia under the Bolshevik Regime* ended in 1924, with Lenin's death, but in a final chapter, entitled 'Reflections on the Russian Revolution', Pipes put the story in its wider context. Stalinist totalitarianism was a particularly heinous instantiation of Russia's special path. It could not be reduced to the one or the other.[46] 'Soviet totalitarianism', he later wrote, in probably his most memorable phrase, 'grew out of Marxist seeds planted on the soil of tsarist patrimonialism.'[47] While he thus still disagreed with Karpovich, he conceded some ground to Malia, whose stress on the Marxist – even the Enlightenment tradition – he partially adopted.[48]

This position, however, could still let socialist historians off the hook; socialism was corrupted by Russia, and could flourish elsewhere. Pipes did not have a clear solution to this problem. For the time being, he joined a smaller fight: the one about continuity and discontinuity from Lenin to Stalin – a preoccupation of socialist historians. First, he pointed out that Lenin had sponsored Stalin. That late in life he had second thoughts 'should not obscure the fact that until that moment he had done everything in his power to promote Stalin's ascendancy'. Even after the break, 'the shortcomings he attributed to him were not very serious – mainly rudeness and impatience – and related more to his managerial qualifications than his personality. There is no indication that he ever saw Stalin as a traitor to his brand of Communism.'[49]

Not only was Lenin a patron of Stalin, Stalin was also a devoted pupil of Lenin. 'Every ingredient of what has come to be known as Stalinism save one – murdering fellow Communists – he had learned from Lenin.'[50] That difference still left the door open for arguments about alternative pasts, as embraced by Lewin or Cohen.

Pipes shut that door as well: In theory, he wrote, one could conceive of Trotsky or Bukharin as alternatives to Stalin, but in practice no other leader had the chance to replace Lenin. And that result was Lenin's fault. 'By throttling democratic impulses in the Party in order to protect his dictatorship, and by imposing on the Party a top-heavy command structure', Pipes continued, 'Lenin ensured that the man who controlled the central party apparatus controlled the Party and through it, the state. And that man was Stalin.'[51]

Resolving the contradiction

By the end of *Russia under the Bolshevik Regime*, then, Pipes had worked himself deep into a contradiction between his Polish and conservative lines.[52] If Marxism became totalitarian only under Russian (or similarly non-Western) conditions, then what was the problem with the student radicals in Harvard Yard and the socialist historians who seemed to take over the field? A teacher and writer had to try resolve this contradiction creatively. Pipes did so in one of his most ambitious books, *Property and Freedom* (1999). But the issue had bugged him at least since 1959, when he sent an essay entitled 'Property and Political Power' to a scholarly journal, only to receive 'crushing criticism' by one reviewer. The piece was rejected, and Pipes wrote to the editor: 'I don't see how your critic's objections could be taken care of without developing the essay into a book.'[53]

Property and Freedom presented an argument about the benefits of private property, not for economic prosperity like in much of liberal thought, but for the attainment and maintenance of individual liberty. In a wide-ranging, philosophical book, he argued that there are two competing ways to allocate resources: through private property or through political power. Where property was widely distributed, it gave property owners the means to combat incursions by the state into their lives; where property was completely held by the state (or by a prince, king, or tsar) individuals lost all ability to resist its power. Russia became a prime example of what happens if property rights are not guaranteed and widely dispersed – despotism at best, totalitarianism at worst. At the same time, however, the tendency of modern welfare states to interfere with property rights had worrying implications for liberty: if liberty is based on property, any restriction on property rights spells the end of freedom. Be careful not to become like Russia, was the message. Hence, the contradiction was resolved: Russian patrimonialism and Stalinist totalitarianism became radical instantiations of a more universal principle.

Pipes and Lewin

Pipes's conservative line seems to make him the ideal representative of the generation of 'totalitarian' scholars who were allegedly replaced by revisionists from the 1970s. However, Pipes and Lewin are patently of the same generation. One became the arch-totalitarian, the other the proto-revisionist. One declared that Lenin had built totalitarianism and that Stalin was his faithful pupil. The other first contained totalitarianism to the Stalinist period, then abandoned the term altogether once he became aware what a powerful tool it was in the hands of the opposition.

Their lives also warn of simplistic analyses which deduce a political or historical position from the background of the historian alone. Two Polish Jews, it turns out, of the same generation, although not the same region or social class, with fairly similar experiences of escaping the Holocaust, can have diametrically opposed appreciations of the same history. Clearly, 'being a native of Poland (even an expatriate one)' does not determine one's 'opinions on Russia', as one author has warned.[54] And yet, the interwar Polish context, the war itself, and the Holocaust, all played their role in structuring their questions and approaches, even if they led them in radically different directions.

Their life-paths, both as men and as scholars, exemplify the extent to which academic history is not the outgrowth of one country or historical context. Like the historians who write them, the gestation of many histories is global. Lewin was influenced by his politics and his experience of the Soviet Union, but also by the many theorists and historians he met along his convoluted scholarly path to Philadelphia: Fernand Braudel and the French *Annales*, British Marxists and social historians. The encounter with Karpovich put Pipes in conversation with the Russian liberal tradition, which sharpened his Polish line considerably. For both, writing during the Cold War was an essential context. Thus, neither of these men was the product of only one place and one time. Their personalities, their politics, and their historical outlooks, as different as they were, were truly transnational. As we shall see in chapters to come, this cosmopolitanism was the norm in the English-language scholarship on Stalinism. Increasingly, it also became widespread in the more self-contained historiographies of Germany, France, and the successor states of the Soviet Union.

Nation-breaking

Maybe the most cosmopolitan subfield of Soviet studies was research on nations and nationalism, a field Pipes more or less founded with his first book. The fact that first Russia, and then the Soviet Union, were multinational empires was 'a stunning discovery' of his doctoral research, he remembered later.[55] Other transnational intellectuals had similar epiphanies at the same time. Already in 1944, Walter Kolarz (1912–62) pointed out that the 'Soviet regime has developed and expanded the aptitude of the Russians for colonizing to an undreamt-of extent.'[56] His path-breaking *Russia and her Colonies* (1952) – published half-way between Pipes's dissertation and the book – portrayed Soviet policy as a failure. There was 'no future for the peoples of Russia in the sense of a genuine political and cultural development'. Like Pipes later, he predicted that the Soviet empire would fall apart once real political change would occur.[57] Pipes read Kolarz soon after the book was published and included it in his bibliography as 'the most thorough ... study on this subject'.[58]

Kolarz was uniquely qualified for studying the national question. Born in Bohemia in what was then the Austro-Hungarian Empire, he spoke five languages 'and read many others'.[59] His father had been a prisoner of war of the Russian Empire in the First World War. Interned in Central Asia, Kolarz senior saw a 'Russia' that was far from Russian. What he told his son about this experience 'perhaps first stimulated the interest in the Soviet minorities which ran through so much of Walter Kolarz's published and broadcast work', as one of his colleagues at the BBC speculated.[60]

Where Kolarz catalogued the state of affairs in Stalinist nationality policy, Pipes was concerned with its origins. In *The Formation of the Soviet Union* (1954), he showed that nationality was a central problem in the making of the new state. Tsarism had been a multinational empire, which broke apart once central power was weakened through war and revolution. The Bolsheviks originally ruled over only the Russian heartland, but would regather the empire under the red flag. According to Pipes, they did this largely through military means, but they also made some tactical concessions to the national question, namely the creation of formally independent union republics (Ukraine, Belarus, etc.) which were fused into the transnational Union of Soviet Socialist Republics. To Pipes, this was an artificial creation based on force. It required a totalitarian state to be held together. Should central authority weaken again, the Union would break apart along the borders established as a result of the regathering of the empire.

The Formation would be the foundational text for an entire sub-discipline within Soviet studies: the study of empire and nationalities. Until fairly late in the game, most of its practitioners came from the right end of academe. Like Kolarz and Pipes, they stressed the repressive aspect of Soviet nationality policy: nation-breaking. Major scholars in this school included Robert Conquest (1917–2015) and Alexander Nekrich (1920–93).

Conquest began his study of Stalinist nationality policy with one of its most gruesome aspects: the deportation of minorities. The title of his first book on this subject was restrained and merely descriptive: *The Soviet Deportation of Nationalities* (1960). Ten years later, however, he added *The Nation Killers* to the title. By 1991, he declared Stalin the 'breaker of nations'.[61] Such escalation, however, masked an underlying continuity. Already in the 1960 book he accused the Soviet Union of genocide. He conceded that the deportation of the Volga Germans, Karachai, Kalmyks, Chechens and Ingush, Balkars, and Crimean Tatars between 1941 and 1944 did not compare 'with the spectacular horrors of the Nazi gas chambers'. Nevertheless, there were 'other ways of destroying a nation':

> To remove it ... from its homeland, and scatter it widely over an alien territory, with a minimum of economic resources, deprived of civil rights, of cultural opportunities and of education in its own tongue is, even leaving aside the high incidence of actual deaths, a sign that the aim can hardly be other than the extinction of the nation, as a nation.[62]

The genocide convention was attached as an appendix to remind readers that the United Nations had defined the term as the 'intent to destroy, in whole or in part, a national, ethnical, racial or religious group'.[63] As we shall see in the final chapter of this book, the question of genocide would become the centrepiece of the polemic around the 1932–33 famine in Ukraine.

Like Pipes, Conquest thus described Soviet nationalities policies in purely negative terms: while the deportation of entire populations under Stalin was the extreme end of this policy, it encapsulated the hostile attitude towards national feelings. Positive policies towards minorities were a 'façade', the attitude of the authorities deeply cynical: 'it wishes to exploit or delude those who feel national sentiment'.[64] Chapter 8 remains a lucid summary of the underlying philosophical assumptions guiding Soviet nationality policy – an essential introduction to the topic, which built on Pipes's earlier work. It formed the foundation for a short but punchy 1962 publication: with *The Last Empire*, Conquest delivered an overall consideration of 'Soviet colonialism'. Stalinism was its essence: 'Stalin's system', he wrote, 'remains in force'. As far as the developmental aspects of Soviet imperialism, such as education and industrialization, were concerned, such claims 'could be, and have been, made by all colonial powers in recent times'. While Western empires were 'going through a process of break up', however, the Soviet one not only defended its colonial holdings, but also 'remains expansionist'.[65]

Eight years after the second edition of Conquest's deportation book had hit the shelves, the exiled Soviet historian, Alexander Nekrich, published *The Punished Peoples*, which covered much of the same ground, but was based on a much broader source base. Nekrich, a Stalingrad veteran turned historian, was part of the brave group of Soviet scholars who attempted to de-Stalinize their country's history in the 1960s. Nekrich, a researcher at the Academy of Sciences and the secretary of the Academy's party cell, took on the holiest of the holies: the Great Patriotic War. His *22 June 1941* (1965) was published the year after the reformer Nikita Khrushchev fell from power (see Chapter 5). Two years later, a Stalinist cabal threw Nekrich, who had joined at the front line, out of the Communist Party. His book was purged from libraries, its copies destroyed or locked away in the poison cabinets of restricted-access special collections. Nekrich, already an internationally renowned historian, was allowed to keep his job and his salary, but his ability to publish, to travel, even to attend conferences within the Soviet Union, was severely circumscribed. Eventually, aged sixty-six, he took the painful step to emigrate, leaving his country in 1976.[66]

The Punished Peoples moved from Stalin's crimes of omission at the start of the war to his crimes of commission later on. Completed in Nekrich's final years in Moscow it was, like his 1941 book, an elaboration of what Khrushchev had said in his Secret Speech of 1956. Smuggled abroad, the book was published in both Russian and English in 1978. Part memoir (Nekrich had served in Crimea during the war), part oral history, part excavation of the available evidence, *The Punished Peoples* was a much richer book than Conquest's. Nekrich's remarkably balanced assessment could draw on sources Conquest did not have. There was oral history and unpublished memoirs of witnesses and survivors, unfootnoted throughout, but informing the account considerably. There were unpublished dissertations by Soviet scholars written during Khrushchev's Thaw, and drawing on archival sources. These were available – to Soviet researchers like Nekrich – in the dissertations reading room of Moscow's Lenin Library (today's Russian State Library). Nekrich seems to have also seen some archival sources himself, albeit again without giving a footnote. Finally, he critically used German scholarship on the war and the occupation, books published after Conquest's studies.[67]

The opening of the archives has confirmed many of Conquest's and Nekrich's conclusions, although researchers now prefer the term 'ethnic cleansing' over 'genocide' to describe these operations.[68] It was not for nothing that the most accomplished post-Soviet Russian historian of forced migration under Stalin, Pavel Polian, dedicated the English translation of his book 'to Robert Conquest and Alexander Nekrich, the first researchers of Soviet deportations'.[69] Even their numbers, deduced from information contained in official Soviet publications, turned out to be reasonably accurate. Conquest's overall tally – 1.2 to 1.3 million in the 1960 edition, 1.6 to 1.7 million in the 1970 edition – was an extremely conservative estimate.[70] As we now know, Soviet Germans alone furnished 1.2 million deportees, Chechens and Ingush 484,000, and Crimean Tatars 182,000, to name only the largest groups. And Conquest did not even know about Koreans in 1937, and likewise missed the removal of Soviet Finns, Greeks, and Italians in 1942.[71] Nekrich's overall guesstimate of 'somewhat more than one million' deported in 1943–44 alone was spot-on. Archival sources report a tally for these years of 1,022,700 deportees.[72]

Nation-making

Within this field, dominated by 'totalitarian' scholars focusing on nation-breaking, there was one outlier: Suny. He was one of the 'revisionists', a self-declared 'Marxist–Lewinist', and a proudly left-wing professor with a 'larger-than-life-size poster of Lenin' on the door of his Oberlin college office.[73] Suny hailed from Philadelphia. His family was left wing and self-consciously Armenian. In seventh grade, he earned the title 'Comrade Suny' after he had given a report 'on the achievements of the Soviet Union'. Armenian-ness and socialism were the two poles of his identity. As a dual obsession with nationality and class in Soviet history they would define his scholarly career. 'Without much self-reflection', he wrote in 1999, 'I wrote about class and nationality, which now seems to have come out of my own experience as a leftist Armenian in America.'[74]

His oeuvre stressed the other aspect of Soviet nationality policy: nation-making. It stretched from *The Baku Commune* (1972), in which nationality issues appeared in the guise of spoilers of a more 'moderate Bolshevism',[75] to studies of post-Stalinist Georgia[76] and Armenia,[77] and on to a series of lectures and articles in 1990 and 1991, which tried to come to terms with the rising nationalism in the Soviet Union. They would evolve into his most influential book: *The Revenge of the Past* (1993), a thinly disguised polemic against Pipes.[78] Together with the works of Yuri Slezkine, a displaced Soviet intellectual and early doctoral student of Fitzpatrick, it would inspire scholars focusing on the productive aspect of nationality policy.[79] Landmarks in this literature include Jeremy Smith's investigation of early Bolshevik nationality policy, an open challenge to Pipes's focus on repression;[80] Kate Brown's poetic *Biography of No Place* (2003), which chronicled the transformation of a multi-ethnic borderland into Ukraine's heartland;[81] and Francine Hirsch's *Empire of Nations* (2005), which focused on the work of experts – economists, statisticians, anthropologists, ethnographers and geographers – in the 'conceptual conquest' of the vast spaces and the many peoples of the Soviet empire.[82]

THE RUSSIAN ORIGINS OF TOTALITARIANISM

From the 1990s, an important shift took place in this nation-making literature: from looking at the problem from the perspective of the centre, as most had done ever since Pipes, to a perspective from the periphery. In practical terms, it meant work in archives outside Moscow: in Central Asia, in Ukraine, or the Transcaucasian republics. Such work paid much more attention to the agency of local and indigenous elites in the making of the Soviet nations, the drawing of the borders, the development of languages and national cultures.[83] Some scholars of this new wave stressed the fact that the Soviet project opened up possibilities for self-advancement and self-realization among non-Russians, even under Stalin.[84] In particular, women could forge alliances with the Soviet state to further their own agendas, be it reform of Islam, liberation from local patriarchy, or both.[85] Others focused on the Soviet Union as an empire and explored the extent to which governmental practices amounted to a kind of colonialism,[86] a surprisingly controversial interpretation, maybe because the notions of Red imperialism and Soviet colonialism had long been monopolized by the academic Right.[87]

Nation-making and nation-breaking would be brought together in the work of Sheila Fitzpatrick's student, Terry Martin, who worked with both central Soviet and republic-level Ukrainian archives. He managed to entwine the two themes in one coherent interpretation, building self-consciously on Pipes.[88] Fittingly, he became a professor at Harvard, where together with Pipes he supervised David Brandenberger, who investigated what had first inspired Pipes to go into this field: the rise of Russian chauvinism in the 1930s.[89]

Reconciliation

Pipes was pleasantly surprised by Martin: 'He seems able and not infected with revisionism', he wrote in 1997.[90] How could that be, given he was a student of one of the most notorious of the revisionists? Over much of the 1980s and 1990s, Pipes had felt beleaguered by this well-organized group of left wingers who had taken over much of the field. His graduate students often defected to this camp. The social historians, on their part, continued to see themselves confronted by an anti-Soviet establishment impersonated by Pipes (like many scholars growing into middle age, some failed to realize that they, now, *were* the establishment). When the Soviet Union reformed under Gorbachev, revisionists celebrated the fact that they had been right: this was not an unchanging totalitarianism which could not evolve. When the Soviet Union collapsed, Pipes celebrated that he had been correct: this system was unreformable, a prison house of nations held together only by force. Together with Malia, he harangued 'the revisionists' to recant.[91]

But the encounter with Martin started a process of rethinking the politics of the field.[92] In 2001, Pipes, the scholar who had likened revisionists to flat-earthers and Holocaust deniers, and who claimed that he did not read them, cited the arch-revisionist Fitzpatrick in his book on communism.[93] In a way, he repaid a courtesy Fitzpatrick had extended by citing Pipes in her 1982 book on the Russian Revolution.[94] Then, in 2004, Fitzpatrick reviewed Pipes's *Vixi. Memoirs of a Non-Belonger* (2003). Besides barbs about Pipes's anti-communism, his dislike of Russia and his scorn for most of his colleagues, she used the occasion to extend an olive branch. She praised him as an iconoclast, 'a trait I have always found attractive'; she noted approvingly that he had 'not acquired the plastic veneer of most public men in America'; and she commended his 'prickly independence of spirit'.[95] In reply, Pipes sent Fitzpatrick a short letter, one of only two communications between the two scholars I could find in their respective archives. It read: 'Dear Sheila Fitzpatrick, Having read your review of *Vixi*, it occurred to me that you may be interested in seeing how *Voprosy Istorii* handled the same subject. Yours sincerely, Richard Pipes'.[96] (The review in the Russian journal, of course, was highly positive.) Then, Fitzpatrick published the first volume of her own memoirs, *My Father's Daughter* (2010), and Pipes, the alleged non-reader of revisionists, read it as well. It clearly impressed him, as did Fitzpatrick's foray into political history in *On Stalin's Team* (2015). When his turn came to write a review of the latter, Pipes sounded nearly gushing. Fitzpatrick's was 'an important book', a 'kind of "revisionism"' that was 'persuasive' and added 'a new dimension to the totalitarian model'. It was to be 'warmly welcomed'.[97]

These were stunning words. Clearly, the Cold War was finally over. Some revisionists and some totalitarians were, if not friends, then at least reconciled enough to respectfully read each other. They might even agree to work on the same project: understanding Stalinism. What a momentous historiographical event that was is hard to understand for those who did not experience the acrimony of the 1970s, 1980s and 1990s.

Notes

1. On Pipes's life and work see his memoirs: Richard Pipes, *Vixi: Memoirs of a Non-Belonger* (New Haven, 2003); and Jonathan Daly, *Pillars of the Profession: The Correspondence of Richard Pipes and Marc Raeff* (Leiden, 2019).
2. Beth Pinsker, 'The Quarrel: Looming Loopiness in Soviet Studies', *Forward* (New York) (9 October 1998): 7.
3. Richard Pipes, '1917 and the Revisionists', *The National Interest*, (Spring 1993): 68–79, here: 68, 69, 77. This polemic was focused on revisionist work on 1917 rather than Stalinism. Pipes, *Vixi*, 222.
4. Mark Munro, 'To Russia with Loathing. What the Soviets call the Anti-Soviet Professor: Comrade Pipes Attacks the Soviet Union – and the Soviets Love it', *The Boston Globe* (18 May 1991): 12,18, here: 18.
5. Pipes, '1917 and the Revisionists', 70 n. 4.
6. For a full bibliography of Pipes's prodigious output, see Daly, *Pillars of the Profession*, 367–86.
7. Richard Pipes, *The Formation of the Soviet Union: Communism and Nationalism, 1917–1923* (Cambridge, 1954); Richard Pipes, *Russia under the Old Regime* (London, 1974); Richard Pipes, *The Russian Revolution* (New York, 1990); id., *Russia under the Bolshevik Regime* (New York, 1993).
8. Jonathan Daly is working on a biography of Pipes.
9. Unless otherwise noted, the following is based on Pipes, *Vixi*. Only direct quotations are footnoted.
10. Historians disagree over the extent to which a civic form of nationalism failed because of Polish disinterest or the non-cooperation of the minorities. Compare the stridently pro-Polish account by Peter D. Stachura, *Poland, 1918–1945: An Interpretive and Documentary History of the Second Republic* (London, 2004), with the more mainstream critical assessment by Andrzej Korbonski, 'Poland: 1918–1990', in: *The Columbia History of Eastern Europe in the Twentieth Century*, ed. Joseph Held (New York, 1992), 229–76.
11. Pipes, *Vixi*, 15.
12. Pipes, *Vixi*, 10.
13. Mark Edele, Sheila Fitzpatrick and Atina Grossmann (eds), *Shelter from the Holocaust: Rethinking Jewish Survival in the Soviet Union* (Detroit, 2017).
14. Pipes, *Vixi*, 41–54.
15. On Karpovich as a lecturer: Martin Edward Malia, 'Historian of Russian and European Intellectual History', an oral history conducted in 2003 by David Engerman. Regional Oral History Office, The Bancroft Library, University of California, Berkeley, 2005, 26–28, 30, 93. On the Karpovich seminar and its influence on Russian studies, see Jonathan Daly, 'The Pleiade: Five Scholars who Founded Russian Historical Studies in the United States', *Kritika: Explorations in Russian and Eurasian History* 18, no. 4 (2017): 785–826.

16 Mikhail Mikhailovich Karpovich, Correspondence, Box 2, Bakhmeteff Archive, Columbia University.
17 Pipes, *Vixi*, 50, 60.
18 Richard Pipes, 'The Genesis of Soviet National Policy', PhD diss., Harvard University, 1950; Pipes, *The Formation of the Soviet Union*; Pipes, *Vixi*, 67, 71–74.
19 Pipes, *Vixi*, 80–90; Malia, 'Historian of Russian and European Intellectual History', 89–90; Daly, 'The Pleiade', 796. In addition to the *Formation*, Pipes's publications at that point were: 'The Russian Military Colonies, 1810–1831', *Journal of Modern History* 22, no. 3 (1950): 205–19; 'The First Experiment in Soviet National Policy: The Bashkir Republic, 1817–20', *Russian Review* 9, no. 4 (1950): 303–19; 'Russian Moslems Before and After the Revolution', in: *Soviet Imperialism: Its Origins and Tactics: A symposium*, ed. Waldemar Gurian (Notre Dame, 1953), 75–89; 'Bolshevik National Theory Before 1917', *Problems of Communism* 2, no. 5 (1953): 22–27; 'The Moslems of Soviet Central Asia: Trends and Prospects', *The Middle East Journal* 9, no. 2 (1955): 147–62; 'Max Weber and Russia', *World Politics* 7, no. 3 (1955): 371–401; 'The Soviet Impact on Central Asia', *Problems of Communism* 6, no. 2 (1957): 27–32; and 'Karamzin's Conception of the Monarchy', in: *Russian Thought and Politics*, ed. Hugh McLean, Martin Malia, and George Fischer (Cambridge, Mass., 1957), 35–58. The clashes occurred in *TLS* (14 February 1997): 17; (7 March 1997): 17; (21 March 1997): 17; and *The New Republic* 220, no. 17/18 (1999): 100–08, 220, no. 23 (1999): 4–5.
20 Andrzej Nowak, 'A "Polish Connection" in American Sovietology. Or: the Old Homeland Enmities in the New Host Country Humanities', in: *East and Central European History Writing in Exile 1939–1989*, ed. Maria Zadencka, Andrejs Plakans and Andreas Lawaty (Leiden, 2015), 375–95, here: 389.
21 Pipes, *Vixi*, 9.
22 Pipes, *Vixi*, 223.
23 Pipes, *Vixi*, xiii.
24 Pipes, *Vixi*, 56.
25 Pipes, *Vixi*, 75.
26 The overwhelming majority was in pre-revolutionary Russian history. Personal communication (email) with Jonathan Daly, 16 December 2018. Pipes himself claimed 'over 70' PhDs: Pipes, *Vixi*, 94. On bricks and architecture: Pipes, '1917 and the Revisionists', 79.
27 Pipes, *Vixi*, 66, also 71.
28 Pipes, *Vixi*, 79–80.
29 For example: Pipes to Karpovich, 26 March 1956, Harvard University Archives, Correspondence of Richard Pipes, box 2. Pipes to Malia, 16 May 1956, Harvard University Archives, Correspondence of Richard Pipes, box 3; Pipes to Shulman, 13 February 1956, Harvard University Archives, Correspondence of Richard Pipes, box 4.
30 Pipes, *Vixi*, 75, 213.
31 Pipes to Ulam, 24 September 1981, Harvard University Archives, Correspondence of Richard Pipes, box 4.
32 Pipes to Robert Kiely, 13 April 1975, Harvard University Archives, Correspondence of Richard Pipes, box 2.

33 Pipes to Whitla, 23 January 1973, Harvard University Archives, Correspondence of Richard Pipes, box 4.
34 Pipes to Walicki, 20 April 1976, Harvard University Archives, Corresondence of Richard Pipes, box. 4.
35 Pipes, *Russia under the Bolshevik Regime*, 512.
36 Sean Guillory, 'Nation, Nationality, and Empire', [interview with Ron Suny], *Sean's Russia Blog Podcast* (2018), https://seansrussiablog.org/2018/08/24/nation-nationality-and-empire/ (accessed 22 September 2018), @1:05:30 to 1:05:46.
37 Munro, 'To Russia with Loathing', 18.
38 Pipes, *Vixi*, 81.
39 Michael Karpovich, *Imperial Russia, 1801–1917* (Hinsdale, 1960); Michael Karpovich, *A Lecture on Russian History* (The Hague, 1972).
40 Martin Malia, *The Soviet Tragedy: A History of Socialism in Russia, 1917–1991* (New York, 1994).
41 This is one possible reading of the first chapter of Richard Pipes, *Communism: A History* (New York, 2001).
42 On being a Democrat: Pipes, *Vixi*, 69. The information that he remained a Democrat to the end is from Daniel Pipes, personal communication (email), 6 February 2019.
43 Pipes, *Vixi*, 107–12.
44 Pipes, *Vixi*, 107–12.
45 Pipes, *Vixi*, 224.
46 Pipes, *Russia under the Bolshevik Regime*, 501.
47 Pipes, *Communism: A History*, 27.
48 Pipes, *Russia under the Bolshevik Regime*, 511.
49 Pipes, *Russia under the Bolshevik Regime*, 507.
50 Pipes, *Russia under the Bolshevik Regime*, 508.
51 Pipes, *Russia under the Bolshevik Regime*, 508.
52 Malia, 'Historian of Russian and European Intellectual History', 205.
53 Pipes to Thrupp, 14 May 1959, Thrupp to Pipes, 21 May 1959, Pipes to Thrupp, 27 May 1959, Harvard University Archives, Correspondence of Richard Pipes, box 4.
54 Nowak, 'A "Polish Connection"', 376.
55 Pipes, *Vixi*, 72.
56 Walter Kolarz, *Stalin and Eternal Russia* (London, 1944), 34.
57 Walter Kolarz, *Russia and Her Colonies* (London, 1952), 316.
58 Pipes, *The Formation of the Soviet Union*, 295.
59 Austin Harrison, 'Dem Andenken an Walter Kolarz (1912–1962)', *Jahrbücher für Geschichte Osteuropas* 11, no. 3 (1963): 467–68.
60 G. H. Gretton, 'Mr. Walter Kolarz', *The Times* (25 July 1962), 15.
61 Robert Conquest, *The Soviet Deportation of Nationalities* (London, 1960); Robert Conquest, *The Nation Killers: The Soviet Deportation of Nationalities* (London, 1970); Robert Conquest, *Stalin: Breaker of Nations* (New York, 1991).
62 Conquest, *The Soviet Deportation of Nationalities*, xii.
63 Conquest, *The Soviet Deportation of Nationalities*, 203.
64 Conquest, *The Soviet Deportation of Nationalities*, 126–27.

65 Robert Conquest, *The Last Empire* (London, 1962), quotations: 8, 9, 123, 125.
66 A. M. Nekrich, *1941, 22 iunia* (Moscow, 1965). On Nekrich's life, see his autobiography: Aleksandr Nekrich, *Foresake Fear: Memoirs of an Historian* (Boston, 1991).
67 Aleksandr Nekrich, *Nakazannye narody* (New York, 1978); Aleksandr Nekrich, *The Punished Peoples: The Deportation and Fate of Soviet Minorities at the End of the Second World War* (New York, 1978). On the gestation of the book: Nekrich, *Forsake Fear*, 274; Nekrich, *The Punished Peoples*, ix.
68 J. Otto Pohl, *Ethnic Cleansing in the USSR, 1937–1949* (Westport, 1999). On Conquest and Nekrich: xiii.
69 Pavel Polian, *Against their Will: The History and Geography of Forced Migrations in the USSR* (Budapest, 2004). The Russian original did not have this dedication, but listed Nekrich as the historian who had established 'the problematic of the "punished peoples" as an independent scholarly pursuit': Pavel Polian, *Ne po svoei vole… istoriia i geografiia prinuditel'nykh migratsii v SSSR* (Moscow, 2001), 16. Conquest, too, was mentioned as a precursor: Polian, *Ne po svoei vole*, 15.
70 Conquest, *The Soviet Deportation of Nationalities*, 51–54; Conquest, *The Nation Killers*, 64–66.
71 Terry Martin, 'Stalinist Forced Relocation Policies: Patterns, Causes, Consequences', in: *Demography and National Security*, ed. Myron Weiner and Sharon Stanton Russell (New York, 2001), 305–37, here: 321–22, 324–25, 330; N. L. Pobol' and P. M. Polian (eds), *Stalinskie deportatsii 1928–1953* (Moscow, 2005), 791–97, 512.
72 Nekrich, *The Punished Peoples*, 105; Mark Edele, 'The Second World War as a History of Displacement. The Soviet Case', *History Australia* 12, no. 2 (2015): 17–40, here: 26, table 2.
73 Ronald G. Suny, *Red Flag Unfurled: History, Historians, and the Russian Revolution* (London, 2017), 2.
74 Ronald G. Suny, 'Confessions', in: *Intellectuals and the Articulation of the Nation*, ed. Ronald G. Suny and Michael D. Kennedy (Ann Arbor, 1999), 52–56, quotations: 52, 55.
75 Ronald G. Suny, *The Baku Commune 1917–1918* (Princeton, 1972) – 'moderate Bolshevism' is on p. xii.
76 Ronald G. Suny, 'Soviet Georgia in the Seventies', Kennan Institute of Advanced Russian Studies, The Wilson Center, Washington, DC, Occasional Paper No. 64 (1979).
77 Ronald Suny, *Armenia in the Twentieth Century* (Chico, 1983).
78 Ronald Suny, 'The Revenge of the Past: Socialism and Ethnic Conflict in Transcaucasia', *New Left Review* I, no. 184 (1990): 5–34; Ronald Suny, 'Incomplete Revolution: National Movements and the Collapse of the Soviet Empire', *New Left Review* I, no. 189 (1991): 111–25; Ronald Suny, *The Revenge of the Past: Nationalism, Revolution, and the Collapse of the Soviet Union* (Stanford, 1993).
79 Yuri Slezkine, 'How I Became Multicultural', in: *Intellectuals and the Articulation of the Nation*, ed. Ronald G. Suny and Michael D. Kennedy (Ann Arbor, 1999), 257–58; Yuri Slezkine, *Arctic Mirrors: Russia and the Small Peoples of*

the North (Ithaca, 1994); Yuri Slezkine, 'The Soviet Union as a Communal Apartment, or How a Socialist State Promoted Ethnic Particularism', *Slavic Review* 53, no. 2 (1994): 415–52.
80 Jeremy Smith, *The Bolsheviks and the National Question, 1917–23* (Basingstoke, 1999).
81 Kate Brown, *A Biography of No Place: From Ethnic Borderland to Soviet Heartland* (Cambridge, Mass., 2003).
82 Francine Hirsch, *Empire of Nations: Ethnographic Knowledge and the Making of the Soviet Union* (Ithaca, 2005).
83 Serhy Yekelchyk, *Stalin's Empire of Memory: Russian–Ukrainian Relations in the Soviet Historical Imagination* (Toronto, 2004); Adrienne Lynn Edgar, *Tribal Nation. The Making of Soviet Turkmenistan* (Princeton, 2004); Adeeb Khalid, *Making Uzbekistan: Nation, Empire, and Revolution in the Early USSR* (Ithaca, 2015).
84 Brigid O'Keeffe, *New Soviet Gypsies: Nationality, Performance, and Selfhood in the Early Soviet Union* (Toronto, 2013); Ali Igmen, *Speaking Soviet with an Accent: Culture and Power in Kyrgyzstan* (Pittsburgh, 2012).
85 Douglas Northrop, *Veiled Empire: Gender and Power in Stalinist Central Asia* (Ithaca, 2004); Marianne Kamp, *The New Woman in Uzbekistan: Islam, Modernity, and Unveiling under Communism* (Seattle, 2006). An influential precursor is: Gregory Massell, *The Surrogate Proletariat: Moslem Women and Revolutionary Strategies in Soviet Central Asia* (Princeton, 1974).
86 Shoshana Keller, *To Moscow, Not Mecca: The Soviet Campaign against Islam in Central Asia, 1917–1941* (Westport, 2001); Jörg Baberowski, *Der Feind ist überall: Stalinismus im Kaukasus* (Munich, 2003); Paula A. Michaels, *Curative Powers: Medicine and Empire in Stalin's Central Asia* (Pittsburgh, 2003).
87 For an introduction to this debate, see Paula A. Michaels, Douglas Northrop, Francine Hirsch and Yuri Slezkine, 'Nationalities in the Soviet Empire', *The Russian Review* 59, no. 2 (2000): 159–234.
88 Terry Martin, 'The Origins of Soviet Ethnic Cleansing', *The Journal of Modern History* 70, no. 4 (1998): 813–61; Terry Martin, *The Affirmative Action Empire: Nations and Nationalism in the Soviet Union, 1923–1939* (Ithaca, 2001).
89 David Brandenberger, 'The "Short Course" to Modernity: Stalinist History Textbooks, Mass Culture and the Formation of Popular Russian National identity, 1934–1956', PhD diss., Harvard University, 1999; David Brandenberger, *National Bolshevism: Stalinist Mass Culture and the Formation of Modern Russian National Identity, 1931–1956* (Cambridge, Mass., 2002); David Brandenberger, *Propaganda State in Crisis: Soviet Ideology, Indoctrination, and Terror under Stalin, 1928–1941* (New Haven, 2011).
90 Pipes to Brandenberger, 11 February 1997, personal archive of David Brandenberger.
91 'They have never explained or apologized for their mistakes': Pipes cited about the revisionists in: Alice Gomstyn, 'Where the Cold War still rages', *The Chronicle of Higher Education* (6 February 2004), A13. For a similar call from Malia: 'To the Editors', *Kritika: Explorations in Russian and Eurasian History* 3, no. 3 (2002): 569–71.
92 This point was suggested to me by David Brandenberger.

93 Pipes, *Communism*, 162 n. 12, 167.
94 Sheila Fitzpatrick, *The Russian Revolution* (Oxford, 1982; 2nd ed. 1994; 3rd ed. 2008).
95 Sheila Fitzpatrick, 'The Rise and Fall of the Baggy-Trousered Barbarians', *London Review of Books* 26, no. 16 (2004): 7–10, quotation: 7.
96 Pipes to Fitzpatrick, 22 August 2004, Sheila Fitzpatrick Papers, Box 33.
97 Richard Pipes, 'Stalin: "He Couldn't Have Done it Without Them"', *The New York Review of Books* (3 December 2015).

4
Unrevisionist revisionism

Australian beginnings

Moshe Lewin and Richard Pipes were refugees from Eastern Europe, both born in the early 1920s, who brought in their luggage the political struggles of interwar Poland, the experience of the Second World War, and the trauma of the Holocaust. By contrast, Sheila Fitzpatrick, the scholar at the centre of *The Russian Review* debate, was the much younger offspring of Australian radicalism.[1] Born in 1941, her father, Brian Fitzpatrick (1905–65), was a bohemian, a civil rights activist, and a journalist. A mainstay of the Melbourne intellectual pub scene, he was also an extremely productive historian of Australia, writing influential interpretations of his country's economic history from an independently Marxist point of view. He managed to accomplish these as a freelancer at the margins of Australian academia. Although his books were listed by the University of Melbourne as essential undergraduate reading, his repeated attempts to land a job at this institution, or at any other, failed. The professoriate balked at the idea of having an opinionated troublemaker as a colleague, a non-conformist who spent his afternoons in Melbourne's Swanston Street Family Hotel, holding forth at the bar, and who also had an eye for young, intelligent women. That one of them, his estranged first wife, Kathleen Fitzpatrick, had become an associate professor in the department also did not help. Finally, professional envy played a part, as his biographer pointed out: 'However much he drank, he had produced a good deal more than most academic researchers.'[2]

Sheila was her 'father's daughter'. Brian looms large in the very sad memoirs she wrote about growing up in Melbourne in the 1940s and 1950s. And while she was frustrated with his drinking, repelled by his affairs with young women, and in rebellion against his politics, she also loved him intensely, internalizing much of his intellectual habits. First of all was non-conformism, a distaste for thought control, intellectual prohibitions, and party lines. Second was contrariness, a delight in upsetting perceived wisdom and 'sticking it' to the establishment, Left or Right. Third was an interest in the Soviet Union. Brian was a prominent fellow traveller, defending the Soviet Union not only because of the romance of the Russian Revolution and because it had saved the world from fascism during the war, but also because he balked at what anti-communism stood for: restrictions on what could be said or thought, narrow-minded celebration of the status quo, philistinism and intellectual laziness. In his daughter's mind, though, such uncritical embrace of the first socialist state would transform into a forensic attempt at understanding this society. But the impulse to stick it to the philistines remained.[3]

The logical rebellion for the daughter of a left-wing maverick, who despised university historians as mediocre time-servers on too large incomes, would have been to become a cold warrior and an academic. Fitzpatrick did the latter, but not the former. 'We did not', as her university boyfriend put it, 'react to our parents as strongly as that!' (Like Fitzpatrick, he was the offspring of 'fathers who exaggerate, drink, and are prone to rhetorical flourishes'.)[4] Her father did not oppose her decision to become an academic. 'Make sure of a First', he advised, 'turn in a meaningless modest MA thesis, get an academic appointment, and then, and only then, associate yourself with real thinking.' Academics, he cautioned, were 'pleasant people, but quite incapable of rethinking or originating an interpretation, and, naturally, suspicious and resentful of anyone better endowed'. Sheila, however, decided to 'become a successful academic *without* … becoming like them. I was not going to swap originality for advancement; I was going to go for both.'[5] This programme was, of course, one her father had tried, too.

The combination of a left-wing socialization with the need to develop a perspective on the world distinct from her overbearing father led to a 'non-committal stance that was a betrayal of both sides', as she scathingly summarized in retrospect.[6] For a long time after leaving Australia her working hypothesis about the Soviet Union was that both the Left (her father and his fellow-travelling friends) and the Right (the people who attacked her father as a presumed communist) were likely to be wrong. This position, which would cause her endless trouble later, was already visible in her first scholarly publication, printed just before she left Australia in 1964 for doctoral study abroad. 'Interpreting Soviet Literary Politics: The Scholar and the Party Line' was a review of recent publications on Soviet literature. 'Typically', Fitzpatrick wrote later, 'my stance was "a plague on all your houses".'[7] The cold warriors were as misguided, she implied, as the fellow travellers (her father). 'Certainly at this comfortable distance', the 22-year-old wrote about the British pro-Soviet celebrities Sidney and Beatrice Webb, 'it is hard to image how the Webbs convinced themselves or anyone else that Stalin was not a dictator.' She listed other examples of left-wing misrepresentations of Stalinism, 'less notorious but as distressing', before moving on to the other side. 'It is almost obligatory', she observed, 'in American works on Soviet literature to surround their text with an introduction and conclusion on the concept of totalitarianism.' Oddly, however, these same scholars seemed to be wedded also to the idea of Russian exceptionalism and continuity with the result that 'more than one scholar has wondered if pre-revolutionary Russian government was not also totalitarian'. Others took cover 'behind the facts and the newspaper files', said very little, and wrote no more than 'academic footnotes to an anti-Party line'. The article also prefigured her later interest in the politics of culture, as had her first work of independent research, her fourth-year honours thesis. And it identified a type of historian she would eventually become – the 'debunker'. 'Debunkers', she wrote, were 'relatively rare in Soviet studies'. In contrast to the moralists, they 'do not take sides in a conflict but point to the invariable futility and meanness of human endeavour'.[8]

This tendency to see the 'futility and meanness of human endeavour' was a somewhat perverse result of the relationship with her father. The constant taunts at school – Brian was rumoured to be a communist, and sometimes showed up drunk, embarrassing his daughter – the miserable home life with an unhappy mother and an alcoholic, unemployed father: these experiences left wounds which 'never have quite disappeared', as Fitzpatrick's second husband noted.[9] They formed a view of human nature which was much less optimistic than her father's had been. People, it seemed, were 'naturally mean': 'people either enjoyed causing each other pain, as at school, or couldn't help it, as at home'.[10] The political attacks she suffered later for the assumed politics of her research, and the nasty politics of academia, did nothing to soften this dark view of human nature, which, as one of her students observed in an insightful interpretive essay, formed the philosophical undercurrent of her historical study of Stalinism.[11] It was this assumption of the fundamental meanness of much of humankind that allowed her to see Stalin as popular with a distinct constituency, without seeing such support as to his credit. 'Stalin's *worst* qualities and values' explained his 'popular support', she wrote, to Daniel Field, in the course of *The Russian Review* melee of 1986–87.[12]

Finally, Fitzpatrick was also the product of the history department of the University of Melbourne. That department's 'emphasis on primary sources and objectivity stayed with me for life', she wrote. The training she received as a historian dovetailed with her father's example: his most influential books were based on substantial and innovative primary research, accomplished with the help of his second wife, Sheila's mother Dorothy.[13] At Melbourne, Fitzpatrick also learned some Russian, which she put to work in her fourth-year honours thesis on Soviet composers and their influence on the public. This work with primary sources had her hooked: 'I couldn't image that there was anything else in the world I would rather do.'[14]

Secondary socialization: Oxford and Moscow

At the time, the custom for up-and-coming Australian academics was to go abroad, to Oxford or Cambridge, to get a degree, often to return to make a career back home. Fitzpatrick followed this pattern, only she did not come back until much later. Her choice was St Antony's College, Oxford, renowned as a spy factory. She arrived there in 1964.

In her memoirs, she remembers her time at St Antony's as miserable: 'I hated Oxford from the start.' There were no historians of the Soviet Union, her supervisor was a literary scholar with intelligence connections, and Oxford was not in the business of teaching its doctoral students anything. 'Go off and write your book', they were told. This recollection is somewhat uncharitable, probably tinged by the personal unhappiness she experienced at the time: the conflict with her father had escalated to non-speaking terms, and her love life was chaotic, to put it mildly. Soon, several deaths clouded her world, including that of her father.[15]

In 1984, she recounted a somewhat different story when agitating for a concerted effort to teach doctoral students about sources on Soviet history. 'When I was at Oxford', she wrote in a memo, 'the Sheldonian bibliographer John Simmons used to teach a Soviet bibliography course in which he would lovingly explain, for example, how the three editions of the *Bol'shaia sovetskaia entsiklopediia* differ, which editions of Lenin's works contain what, and at which letter of the alphabet the various dictionaries of revolutionary biography etc broke off. It was the only thing they taught you at Oxford, but I must say it came in very handy.'[16] Such training dovetailed with the empiricism she had brought from Melbourne. She agreed to teach a summer school along these lines in 1984,[17] and a similar introduction became 'her first graduate course at the University of Chicago'.[18] A clear line thus runs from her Melbourne to her Oxford training and on to her own *oeuvre*, as well as the training of the 'Chicago school' (of which more below).

Fitzpatrick had soon resolved that, in order to do real historical research on the Soviet Union, she would have to go there and get into the archives. Neither was easy, but she accomplished it. She even travelled to Japan quickly to marry a university boyfriend in order to get British citizenship, which made her eligible for a British–Soviet student exchange – the only path to doing research in the Soviet Union. (Needless to say, the marriage did not flourish.) After many trials and tribulations, described in detail in the second volume of her memoirs, she was off to Moscow and the archives.

In an early autobiographical essay, Fitzpatrick remembered her first year in Moscow in 1966. In the Soviet Union, life was 'a struggle' – but it was 'a struggle that often pays off for the foreign students in knowledge and pleasure'. Written in 1982, while she was battling to establish herself in US academia, she presented herself as an unambiguous go-getter who got into the archives by the force of her wits.[19] Later, when she had become 'the great

Establishment historian on the Soviet Union of her generation'[20] she remembered the same episodes somewhat differently: as a combination of her own chutzpah with an academic-political game played by her supervisor, which happened to work in her favour.[21]

The research Fitzpatrick did in this first big project was political history of the Civil War: a study of Anatoly Lunacharsky and his Commissariat of Enlightenment until 1921 (an endpoint chosen because she ran out of space rather than material). Combining archival with informal oral history it was neither social history nor was it on Stalinism – the two fields which would make her notorious as a 'revisionist' later. But she learned several things which pointed to the path ahead. She encountered educational policies which amounted to affirmative action of proletarian cadres; she learned how to work in the Soviet archives, which gave her considerable clout among historians; and she learned something about the complexity of the Soviet political system if seen 'from below', that is, from the perspective of one commissariat rather than from the top of the hierarchy.[22]

But the stay in Moscow in 1966 had another effect: it deepened her alienation from the established positions in the Cold War. In the course of her research she was adopted by Igor Sats, Lunacharsky's one-time secretary and a major player in *Novyi mir*, an important literary journal which, under the determined editorship of Alexander Tvardovsky, tried to push the limits of what could be said about the past and the present. (It was *Novyi mir* which first published the later dissident, Aleksandr Solzhenitsyn.) The *Novyi mir* crew were no dissidents. They were Communist Party members and devoted to the cause of building socialism. Sats was an Old Bolshevik – one who had joined before the Revolution. They saw themselves as something like a loyal opposition: non-Stalinist communists. As Fitzpatrick began to see the Soviet world not only through the eyes of the archival files she encountered, but also through the eyes of Sats and his friends, she again achieved a position normally unavailable in the Cold War. You were either a fellow traveller or an outright communist, forever excusing all Soviet actions; or you were an opponent and a supporter of the dissidents. Sheila was neither. The dissidents reminded her far too much of her father, and her loyalties were to her Moscow friends, who were communists but critics of the regime.[23]

Americanization

Melbourne, Oxford and Moscow were not the last stages of Fitzpatrick's transnational formation. 'By origin you are an Australian. In the past you were English, and now you are an American', began an interview in a Soviet newspaper in 1989.[24] By now, the scholar who had left Melbourne an Australian and entered the Soviet Union British was one of the most prominent 'American Russianists' included in anthologies bringing their research to the attention of Russian-reading audiences.[25] Sometimes, her mysterious origins in the left wing of an incomprehensible country far, far away were remembered and spun into creative accounts explaining her infuriating success. 'Some say I got the archives because my father is a big man in the Australian Communist Party', she wrote to her brother. 'There are many rumours of that kind about me: one student in effect asked me to intercede in his behalf with KGB.'[26] But what was lost to most observers was that the way she saw the world, and her intellectual reflexes were not American at all. They were an idiosyncratic mixture of an upbringing in a marginal political subculture in Australia overlaid by secondary socialization in an, again distinct, Moscow milieu. This individualism augured well for original research, but it also led to political difficulties with all sides.

Fitzpatrick's 'American' identity was acquired haphazardly. After finishing her doctoral thesis, Fitzpatrick spent 1969–71 as a research fellow at the London School of Economics. She could have secured an ongoing teaching-and-research position, but she was so uninterested in the undergraduate classroom that the natural choice was for a postdoc instead. True to her position outside the front lines of the Cold War, she cultivated good relations with both the 'cold warrior' Leonard Schapiro and his nemesis, historian E. H. Carr, of whom she was 'in awe', as she wrote to his biographer.[27] In 1971–72 she obtained a one-year contract with the University of Birmingham, home of the economic history group around R. W. Davies, which then also included her later nemesis, Moshe Lewin. In the following year, it was a contract position in Slavic Languages and Literature at the University of Texas at Austin, followed in 1974–75 by a temporary gig in history at St John's University in New York. Between 1975 and 1980 she worked on a non-tenurable Associate Professor position at one of the major centres for Russian studies in the United States: Columbia University in New York. In 1980, after a failed fight for tenure, she moved back to Austin to take up a full professorship. Seven years later, she was promoted to a named chair, only to leave in 1990 to the University of Chicago.[28]

Revisionist

In the United States, Fitzpatrick began to position herself as a social historian of Stalinism, a field of research that appealed to her sense of historiographical adventure: there was relatively little social history of this period and developing this perspective was likely to be controversial. It could be used to stick it to the establishment. Her first volley was 'Cultural Revolution in Russia', published in 1974, just ahead of a conference later that year which would result in a volume marking this territory. They dealt with the cultural corollary of the First Five-Year Plan and forced collectivization: 'class war on the cultural front'. The cultural revolution was 'the product of grass-roots enthusiasm among local party and Komsomol activists'. The leadership 'did not need to instruct' these activists to go after bourgeois intellectuals and bureaucrats, long an irritation to the radicals. All Stalin needed to do was 'to unleash them'.[29]

These were carefully calibrated provocations. Just when campus radicals embraced Mao's cultural revolution as the latest form of human emancipation, Fitzpatrick assimilated it to Stalinism. But Fitzpatrick thumbed her nose at the academic Right as well by suggesting that Stalin's revolution from above had a popular base. Indeed, she seemed to suggest that it was a revolution from below.[30] Fitzpatrick's argument, then, seemed to repeat for Stalinism what other 'revisionists' did for the Russian Revolution at the same time: deny that it was an (illegitimate) coup and celebrate it as a (legitimate) revolution.[31] Fitzpatrick, it seemed, was a Stalinist. This was a mind-boggling misreading of her position, which careful reading could have dispelled, but it was hard to avoid in an atmosphere where there were only two camps: those against the Soviets and those for them.

These impressions were solidified with the next provocation. *Education and Social Mobility* (1979) was, in one sense, a sequel to her Lunacharsky book: it took up the story of educational policy where the first volume had left it off, and brought it all the way to the end of the cultural revolution in 1932. But it also marked her turn towards social history. In its most controversial passages, she showed that the Bolsheviks instituted a massive affirmative action programme in education which trained an entire generation of new cadres loyal to the regime that had advanced them. Stalin's Great Terror of 1937–38 then catapulted these former proletarians into positions of power, now vacant because of the blood-letting among old Bolsheviks. The implications of this argument raised colleagues' blood pressures. If Stalinism had social support, did this not imply its legitimacy? This pleased neither the Right nor the Left, and the claim that these new Stalinists were old proletarians irritated Marxists intent on loving the working class.[32]

Finally, in 1982, Fitzpatrick published a textbook called *The Russian Revolution*, her only book closely connected to what she otherwise treated as a necessary evil: undergraduate teaching. As she wrote to her editor just before signing a contract in 1979, her teaching the Russian Revolution 'has made me organize my ideas and given me the chance to test them on an undergraduate audience'.[33] *The Russian Revolution* developed her position beyond the front lines in a tightly constructed volume: another provocation in all directions, but in some ways probably more annoying to the Left than the Right. It assimilated the early years of Stalinism to the Revolution, denying the kind of clean break between Lenin and Stalin many were agitating for. In subsequent editions she went even further down that path, treating the Great Terror of 1937–38 as the final upsurge of revolutionary fever. The worst excesses of Stalinism, then, were an integral part of the Russian Revolution. She even used the word 'totalitarian' and cited Richard Pipes approvingly.[34] The latter was confounded. A 'quite conventional and in some respects even un-revisionist' account, he wrote later, not knowing if he should approve or reproach the well-known 'revisionist' for not being one after all.[35]

Power struggles

These intellectual endeavours were embedded in both a struggle to find continuing employment – solved only in 1980 when she became a full professor at Austin – and in a power struggle within the field of Soviet studies more broadly. Here, most opponents were on the academic Left. One was Stephen Cohen, who first thought she might be an ally. In 1972, he invited Fitzpatrick to participate in a panel at the annual convention of the central institution for scholars of the Soviet Union in the United States: The American Association for the Advancement of Slavic Studies (AAASS), the precursor of today's Association for Slavic, East European and Eurasian Studies (ASEEES). The panel tried to prove that the New Economic Policy (NEP) was a viable alternative to Stalin's revolution from above, and Fitzpatrick's assigned role was 'to make this argument with respect to cultural policy'. Her research into the question, however, had unearthed so much evidence to the contrary, that instead Fitzpatrick delivered a paper which argued that the relatively tolerant cultural policies of the NEP 'were actually proving *un*viable, ... because the lower-class, "hard line" majority of the Communist Party ... disliked them'. Typically, Fitzpatrick 'was not displeased with this conclusion, which I saw as an interesting discovery'. To her surprise, however, 'Cohen was'.[36]

The tensions continued to grow. After Fitzpatrick had married the political scientist Jerry Hough, in 1975, she was held responsible for his increasingly controversial opinions, but also for having 'corrupted and radicalized' him.[37] By the mid-1980s, relations between Fitzpatrick and Cohen had broken down. In his 1985 collection of essays rethinking the Soviet experience – which Fitzpatrick pointedly ignored – Cohen criticized her for 'minimizing' and 'obscuring' Stalin's crimes, a charge he would repeat nearly verbatim during *The Russian Review* debate a year later. He left it open if Fitzpatrick was motivated by 'an overreaction to the revelatory zeal of cold-war sovietology, the highly focused nature of social historical research, or an unstated political desire to rehabilitate the entire Stalin era'. He added dismissively: 'such elliptical scholarship is not real scholarly revisionism'. Whatever common ground there had been originally had disappeared completely. 'I thought', Fitzpatrick reminisced two decades later, 'he was whitewashing "original Bolshevism," and he thought I was whitewashing Stalinism.'[38] These mutual suspicions exploded in *The Russian Review* exchange.

The second opponent on the Left was Moshe Lewin. In 1984, Fitzpatrick invited him to the first of three workshops at the Harriman Institute, Columbia University, which, as she wrote to him, would shape the field:

> This will be the first in a series of workshops on the social history of the Stalin period. Their purpose is to identify the community of scholars in the U.S. working in this field, discuss problems of interpretation, methodology and sources, and familiarize ourselves with the work currently in progress. The participants – probably 15–25 scholars, including some recent PhDs and a couple who are still finishing dissertations – will almost all be social historians, most of them actively engaged in research on the Stalin period.[39]

Although this was not Fitzpatrick's intention, to Lewin, these plans must have looked like a takeover of the agenda of his National Seminar, which was going from strength to strength (Chapter 2). More, still: Fitzpatrick's agenda seemed to hijack his own. In *The Making of the Soviet System*, published the year after this invitation was issued, Lewin described himself as 'a historian who tries to practice and promote the study of Russian/Soviet society' and framed the agenda in similar, but chronologically wider, terms: social history of twentieth-century Russia, 'especially the Soviet period'.[40] To add insult to injury, Fitzpatrick arrogated the position of main commentator and agenda-setter to herself: she would set out the 'general problems' and then guide the discussion of 'young scholars' – exactly the kinds of activities Lewin had come to the United States for.[41] Collectivization, rural–urban interconnections, and Soviet labour history, likewise, were what Lewin had explored in both his dissertation book and many of the essays which would appear, a year later, as *The Making of the Soviet System* (1985). Fitzpatrick, meanwhile, was a specialist in the narrower 'field of cultural policies', as he had defined her expertise in 1979.[42] Now he found her playing his role – the role of the generalist who is writing a big-picture book: the never completed *Stalin's Russia: A Social History*.[43] Lewin did not attend the workshop.[44]

Fitzpatrick tried to assert leadership of the community of historians of Stalinism just at the time when Lewin had run out of steam in his own attempt to do so. 'After taking stock of my first five years in the U.S.', he wrote to William Rosenberg in January 1985, 'I had to reorient my work into more research which means much less external and occasional activities.'[45] From now on, his correspondence is full of polite rejections of proposals which would actually have put him into the position he thought he deserved. Leadership, it turned out, was hard work. And hard work was something Fitzpatrick never shied away from. In addition to her research and her teaching, she was engaged actively in what she described as 'field-building'.[46]

The relative backwater of Austin, Texas might not appear like the ideal place to build a Soviet studies centre, but this did not stop Michael Katz, the chairman of the Slavic Department. Fitzpatrick became his co-conspirator. 'UT-Austin is the natural center for Soviet studies in the Southwest', she wrote to a possible patron in the university hierarchy in June 1984. Funding Soviet studies, she argued with no lack of chutzpah, would help UT-Austin 'to combat a lingering reputation for parochialism and practical-technical bias'. Establishing no less than three chairs would put it in the league with 'the Harvards, Columbias and Princetons' which have 'always stressed Soviet Studies'.[47] In the same year, Fitzpatrick helped found the programme for Soviet and East European Studies at UT-Austin, which subsequently grew through the new appointments she consistently lobbied for.[48] A major journal, *The Slavic Review*, organ of the AAASS, moved to Austin, and funding was secured from government and private sources.[49] By 1988, the Soviet Center had received US government ('Title VI') funding, an 'important breakthrough'.[50]

Her field-building activities during those years also included editing a handbook on sources on social history, which would allow doctoral students to orient themselves about the source base, even without expert supervision;[51] and service on the National Council for Soviet and East European Research, as well as the Subcommittee on Soviet History of the Joint Committee on Soviet Studies (JCSS) of the Social Science Research Council Joint Committee which, from 1984, funded the activities of the National Seminar.[52] These activities embroiled her in conflicts with Cohen, who chaired the Subcommittee on Soviet History.[53] Her work on the organizing committees for the National Seminar on the NEP, and the next one on the 1930s, and her more and more prominent role in these, furthered her conflict with Lewin.[54]

Brouhaha

Her struggle to establish herself as a politically independent scholar and a leader in her field thus took place on a range of levels. It was a struggle to displace Cohen and Lewin and assert her own leadership in the quickly growing field of the social history of the Soviet Union in general, and Stalinism in particular. Eventually, the various resentments which had accumulated as a result of this power struggle exploded in *The Russian Review* affair of 1986–87.

The paper which sparked the debate originated as Fitzpatrick's agenda-setting piece at her first Columbia workshop in February 1985. The original was less confrontational than the final result, quoting, for example, the totalitarian model as a fairly good fit for the Stalin years and referring to Lewin's writings as 'profitably' combining Trotsky's view of the ruling class with the 'state-against-society model'. Lewin, she wrote, provided 'a plausible explanation of socio-political dynamics in the Stalin era' – albeit only of some phenomena, not of others.[55] The argument got a little sharper in a paper for the Third World Congress for Soviet and East European Studies in Washington at the end of the year.[56] But the reactions were positive. Stalin biographer Robert Tucker, who was on the panel, thought it was 'interesting and useful'.[57] Already, before she could deliver the paper, *The Russian Review* editor Daniel Field asked Fitzpatrick for a copy.[58] Soon he sent it out to reviewers, with an eye to publication.

The reactions were negative. One thought it was a 'rather self-serving hodge-podge'. It was 'evasive', not pointing out that the new social historians had not just methodological but also 'direct ideological differences with their predecessors'. The account of the older literature was '*very* sketchy', and there was not enough detail about the new historians either. 'I don't think that this should be published in its present form.' Another reviewer was unhappy with the conciliatory tone. 'The basic thrust of the article seems to be an attempt to reconcile everyone (with the possible exception of the "young Turks"), to argue that social history is not a threat to pre-existing viewpoints.' This would sound like a repudiation of her own work – especially the cultural revolution argument – as 'people seldom bother over nuance'. Completely missing the point Fitzpatrick was trying to make – that social history might find social processes relatively independent of the political process – the reviewer felt that the claim to the importance of social history contradicted the claim that it did not invalidate the idea of revolution from above (and, hence, totalitarianism). Field, however, accepted the essay with some suggestions for amendments, adding optimistically: 'I think this is a fine piece and, especially if the commentators do their job properly, will do real good for the field.'[59]

Fitzpatrick reacted to some of these criticisms, but ignored many others. Following Field's recommendation, she added a footnote noting that some 'revisionist' themes had already been discussed by Merle Fainsod – an admission which would not save her from accusations that she had ignored his work.[60] And she deleted a self-critical section, which described how the sources had falsified her initial hypothesis about the cultural revolution: 'I wanted to make the case for "revolution from below" but could not find a way round the fact that my narrative began with signals from above.'[61] In the published version she instead rehearsed, in a footnote, her careful formulations in the *Cultural Revolution* volume ('elements of "revolution from below"'), while conceding that she now accepted the importance of initiative 'from above'.[62]

No doubt, both Field and Fitzpatrick did expect controversy. 'Bearing in mind your reader's appropriate comments on evasiveness', Fitzpatrick wrote, 'I have changed a few of the offending passages. But one danger of not being evasive is that you may end up saying more about yourself than people need or want to know.'[63] She was right to be apprehensive, but what came her way clearly took her and Field aback, as we have seen in Chapter 1.

Meanwhile, her original point got lost in the storm. Her research tactic was misread as an interpretation of Stalinism 'from below'.[64] As Fitzpatrick wrote to Roberta Manning in early 1987:

> What struck me in this debate is that I really am much more of a relativist on historical explanation than most of you. I am interested in getting new angles on things, putting things together in a new way. When I dislike an interpretation, it is often because I think it is boringly familiar, overworked to the point of sterility. ... I currently want to downplay the state because I think that is the only way to get a new perspective on Soviet society in the 1930s. ... It is a research strategy, not a substantive intellectual position.[65]

The book that never was

Although she failed in promoting this tactic, in the long-term the controversy boosted Fitzpatrick's reputation as the *enfant terrible* of the social history of Stalinism. Ultimately, it helped her career. From 1994, Fitzpatrick was cited more often than Lewin (Figure 4.1), although never as often as Pipes (Figure 4.2).

In the short-term, however, the debate had negative consequences. 'My skin is temporarily a bit thinner than normal', wrote Fitzpatrick in October 1987, 'though I trust this is not evident to readers of R[ussian] R[eview].'[66] This was an understatement. Sometime in March, she had got into a shouting match on the phone with her friend and long-term supporter at the University of Texas at Austin, Sidney Monas, a 'shameful spectacle' and clearly unprecedented. 'Please let us not do that sort of thing', he wrote shortly thereafter in an attempt at mending fences. 'I realize you were upset.'[67]

Short-term loss of temper fed into longer-term psychological fallout. When the storm broke, Fitzpatrick had been working on a book entitled *Stalin's Russia: A Social History of the 1930s*. Back then she had announced, optimistically, that the volume 'should be finished in 1986'.[68] She had just sent a proposal to Oxford University Press and soon signed a contract.[69] Four chapters had been ready since early 1984, and bits and pieces of other chapters were written as articles which, with one exception, were all subsequently published.[70] Another chapter – on peasants after collectivization – had been drafted for a workshop in 1985.[71] But the book itself would never be completed. 'It was the viciousness of the subsequent debate I think', Fitzpatrick wrote to me in 2017, when I inquired why the book project was dropped, 'or perhaps just the general viciousness of the time. I became very depressed and for several years couldn't write or even do research, and when that was over I had lost the thread of that book.'[72]

The plans for the book evolved over the course of the 1980s until it merged into three other projects. At first, it was an ambitious, chronological history of the entire Stalin years, including war and post-war. Then, the 1940s and 1950s were amputated and the book concentrated on the 1930s. By 1988, the project had grown out of proportion despite no longer covering the 1940s and 1950s. Now, she thought about a two-volume version. Volume one would

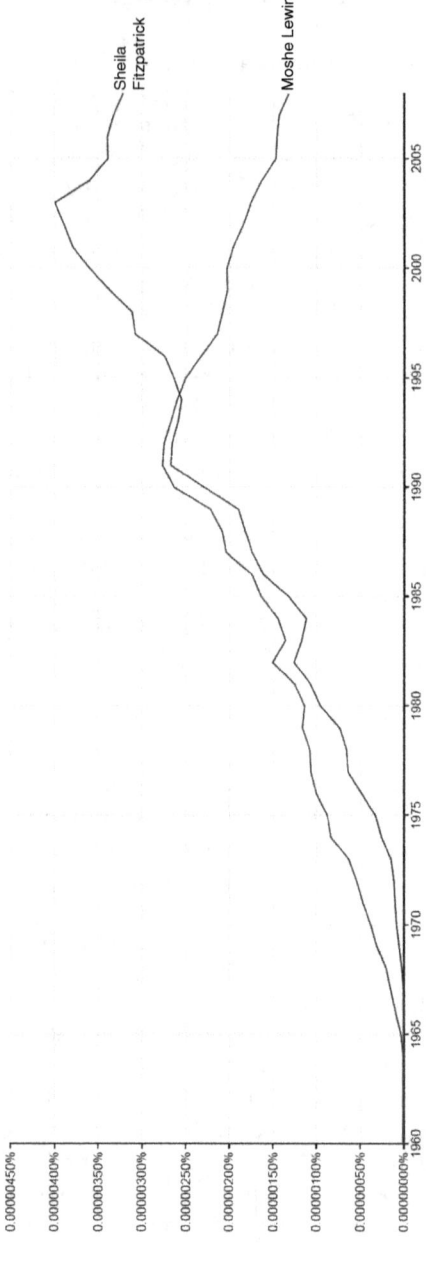

Figure 4.1 Google Ngram for 'Sheila Fitzpatrick' and 'Moshe Lewin'. At the time of the *Russian Review* debate, Lewin was still cited more often. By the mid-1990s, Fitzpatrick would surge ahead.

UNREVISIONIST REVISIONISM

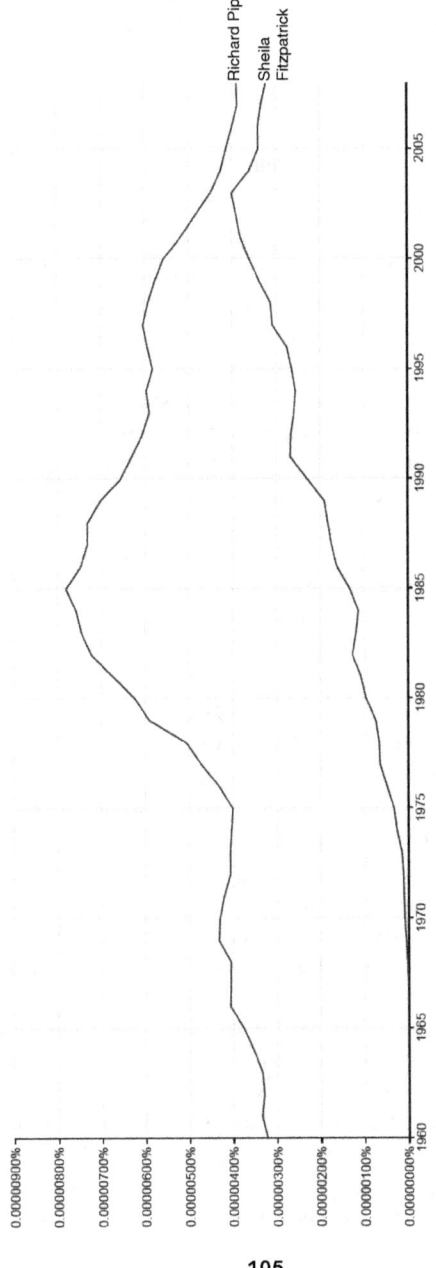

Figure 4.2 Google Ngram for 'Sheila Fitzpatrick' and 'Richard Pipes'. Pipes reached his maximum popularity in the years following his service on the National Security Council. Thereafter, his citations decreased. Fitzpatrick, meanwhile, went from strength to strength, nearly reaching Pipes's popularity by the early 2000s.

cover the collectivized village (later written as *Stalin's Peasants*). Volume two would be concerned with 'classes of enemies' (it would lead to two books: *The Cultural Front*, and *Tear Off the Masks*).[73]

Establishment historian

The recovery from depression was aided by a new marriage – this time a happy one – to the physicist Michael Danos, and a relocation to the University of Chicago in 1990, which also marked Fitzpatrick's final acceptance as part of the historical establishment in the United States. This new status was confirmed when she served, in 1997, as President of AAASS. Intellectually, the end point of the process was a reconceptualization of the social history of Stalinism as the history of everyday life. What was originally one book became three. First was *Stalin's Peasants*, which built on one of the completed chapters of the original book, much additional research, and material from the newly opened archives. She had envisioned this work already in 1986, although then as part of the larger book on Stalin's Russia. 'Will we add more to our present understanding of the impact of collectivization', she asked rhetorically in her riposte, 'by continuing to focus exclusively on state intervention and response, or by trying an "anthropological" study of the post-collectivization village?'[74] In 1989, she announced publicly that she was in the process of finishing the book,[75] although she still feared controversy. 'You already can't stand Lewin', Hough wrote to her, 'so it is not clear to me why you just don't go ahead and write it in broad enough terms to be readable. I guess you don't want the controversy, but other than scars from your childhood, I don't see what you have to lose.'[76]

In *Stalin's Peasants*, Fitzpatrick's world view found its perfect expression. The peasants were victims of the regime, but victimization did not ennoble them. The Russian village, like the intellectual village of the revisionists, was riven by strife, resentment and jealousy. The peasants were smart, to be sure, making the best of a terrible situation, working the system to their least disadvantage. Indeed, when given the chance, they worked it for their own ends: during the Great Terror, when asked from up high to identify 'enemies of the people' among local officials, they did so with relish, denouncing the former collectivizers, who often lost their lives as a result. Thus, they had their revenge, which for a moment satisfied their resentments. But it would not ease their lot.[77]

Having dealt with the village, Fitzpatrick moved on to the city, applying the same approach: the history of everyday life. Essentially, this was social history without a focus on structure and devoid of class analysis – which she found too contaminated by Marxism to be useful. Informed by what she had learned about Soviet life from Sats and other Moscow friends, and drawing on both her own research and that of her doctoral students, the book documented in detail the trials and tribulations of the average Soviet citizen who tried to make a living in Russia's cities of the 1930s. Remarkably, for a major critic of totalitarianism, the Soviet person emerging from these pages was extremely isolated – atomized, to use the words the totalitarians would use. Fitzpatrick had abandoned the idea of writing social history with the state left out that she had promoted in 1986.[78]

The final book in the series was a collection of essays circling around the theme of social identity, which had interested her for a while. It was published at a time when the most fashionable approach to studying the 1930s was to focus on subjectivity (see Chapter 7), but Fitzpatrick dealt with the phenomenon with the tools of the social historian and from the perspective of everyday life. *Tear off the Masks* explored the way in which social categories were ascribed by authority, accepted, negotiated and reworked by individuals, and contested by their peers. The book also returned to the post-war years, which were now possible to research thanks to the open archives.[79]

The 'Chicago school'

The unwritten *Stalin's Russia* had an afterlife not only in the three main books Fitzpatrick would publish in the decade between 1994 and 2005. It also became a framework for an entire group of researchers flocking to Fitzpatrick during her Chicago years. During her tenure at the University of Texas at Austin (1980–89) she advised the dissertations of Yuri Slezkine (1989) and Roger Reese (1990), which resulted in the first two important books of the new school.[80] Since moving to the University of Chicago in 1990 she established this institution as the largest doctoral programme in Soviet history outside the successor states: the 'Chicago school'.

The first generation of Chicago graduate students largely produced studies on the formative years of Soviet society, from the First to the Second World War: James Andrews on science and technology in revolutionary Russia; John McCannon on the 'Red Arctic' (both 1994); Matthew Payne on the Turksib (1995); Golfo Alexopoulos on outcasts and citizenship; James Harris on the influence of the Soviet provinces on the making of the Soviet system; Terry Martin on nationalities policy; Steven Richmond on theatre censorship (all 1996); Matthew Lenoe on journalism; Emily Pyle on veterans' policies and their impact on village social relations (both 1997); Joshua Sanborn on military conscription (1998); Jonathan Bone on the Soviet Far East (2003); and Michael David on tuberculosis (2007). Of this first cohort, Julie Hessler (1996), Christopher Burton (1999), Stephen Bittner (2000) and Kiril Tomoff (2003) reached out into the war and post-war years.[81]

The tendency to gravitate to the 1940s and 1950s became stronger in the next cohorts of *Chicagtsy*, as they came to call themselves in a Russified self-identification. Now, most worked on the war and post-war years, for which new archives as well as other sources were now freely available: Steven Harris on housing under Khrushchev (2003); myself on Second World War veterans (2004); Charles Hachten on property relations (2005); Rachel Green on war orphans; Brian Lapierre on hooliganism under Khrushchev (both 2006); Edward Cohn on the Communist Party in the late Stalin years (2007); Alan Barenberg on Vorkuta (2007); Mie Nakachi on reproductive policies during and after the war (2008); Benjamin Zajicek on psychiatry (2009); Kyung Deok Roh on the institute of world economy (2010); Michael Westren on deportees (2012); Andrew Janco on refugees (2012); Rachel Applebaum on Soviet–Czechoslovak contact (2012); Natalie Belsky on evacuees (2014); Kristy Ironside on price policies (2014); Leah Goldman on Soviet composers (2015); and Flora Roberts on Central Asia (2016).[82] Only two of this latest cohort worked exclusively on the interwar years.[83] One particularly adventurous student ventured into economic history, covering not only the Stalin years but also the post-Stalin decades.[84]

These scholars form a relatively dense network of shared information, shared stories and shared loyalties, an esprit de corps sometimes perceived as cliquish by outsiders. More important, however, is another commonality: a style of doing history clearly inspired by Fitzpatrick's example. Members of this school are, as a rule, archive rats – or 'archival fetishists', as critics say. A lot of pride is taken in knowing the archives well and mastering a large number of primary sources, often from multiple locations. Projects are usually driven by an open-ended question and a set of sources, rather than by a clearly articulated theory. Theorizing happens as part of the process of making sense of data; it is not seen as an end in itself. The theories employed tend to come from the social sciences rather than the humanities: classical anthropology, the rethinking of modernization theory as 'neo-traditionalism', neo-totalitarianism, welfare state theory, anthropology and sociology of property, sociology of group formation and disintegration, or political economy. This orientation, together with a strong empiricism – critics would say 'positivism' – created a literature with a particular flavour and style distinctive to this school.

Return to political history

While thus training an entire school of socio-cultural historians, Fitzpatrick looked for new frontiers. And she also faced a new set of critics. As we shall see in Chapter 7, by the 1990s a new cohort of scholars had emerged. They were inspired by new cultural history and the linguistic turn, and began to focus on Fitzpatrick's old topic of regime support – but this time not grounded in social mobility, but in ideas. Self-indoctrination led to regime support, they argued, not the self-interest of cynical social climbers, as in Fitzpatrick's work. A parallel critique targeted the fact that Fitzpatrick's *Everyday Stalinism* focused on ordinary city folk and their struggles to survive. Did the political elite not also have an everyday life? Did Fitzpatrick again commit her old sin and leave the politics out?

The establishment historian countered such criticism by writing the history of everyday life of the dictator's entourage, now possible because of archival access, oral histories, and new, uncensored memoir literature. An early manifesto pointed out that the fashion of social and cultural history (which she herself had helped to promote) predisposed scholars not to do the most obvious history the open archives now allowed: political history.[85] A decade later she followed suit herself with a study of the Politburo, published just at a time when writing biographies of Stalin had suddenly become à la mode again (Chapter 5). Rather than follow this trend, however, Fitzpatrick chose the perspective of Stalin's closest collaborators to write a new history of the highest levels of Soviet society: team Stalin. This book was both a return to her earlier interest in political history and an extension of her everyday-life approach to the realm of high politics.[86]

The consequences of iconoclasms

Fitzpatrick, then, forged an impressive transnational career relying on her wits and her ambition, hard work and considerable mental toughness. A pioneer in archival history of the Soviet period and a school builder, she became an influential player not only in the English-language literature on Stalinism but also in a transnational discourse encompassing the former Soviet space. She was a major driver of the professionalization of the field. Along the way, she also contributed to a narrative about the historiography of Stalinism which we have critiqued in the first chapter and will dismantle further in chapters to come. It told the history of the field as a succession of generations, each with its own paradigm: totalitarians, revisionists, and post-revisionists. As we shall see in the remainder of this book, this story required those who recounted it to forget a lot of what had been written earlier.

Both Fitzpatrick and Hough, for example, believed that she had 'discovered' affirmative action, social mobility, and their role in Stalinism.[87] This claim was widely accepted,[88] but in fact, Fitzpatrick's most controversial book developed a theme the Marxist Isaac Deutscher had first touched upon: a new cohort of Bolsheviks of working-class or peasant extraction, he explained, had made dizzying careers in the wake of the Great Terror, which opened up positions and allowed an extraordinary cadres exchange unseen before or after. These, Deutscher wrote, were Stalin's constituents who had 'a vested interest in his rule'. In a nutshell, then, we find the thesis of *Education and Social Mobility* in Deutscher's 1949 Stalin biography.[89] Other instances of forgetting about predecessors sometimes led to vigorous protests during *The Russian Review* debate (Chapter 1), and I shall list more in future chapters.

Partially, this forgetfulness was a function of the rudimentary formation of the field when Fitzpatrick entered it. Soviet history was not taught at the University of Melbourne when Fitzpatrick was a student.[90] There was no established curriculum, no reading lists, no historiographical narratives like this book to guide students engaged in self-education. At St Anthony's, she was basically told to go and write her book. Her adviser was a literary specialist ignorant of primary sources, archives, and historical methodology. When she went to Russia for the first time, her knowledge of Soviet history was so shaky that she did not know who the great purger Nikolai Yezhov was.[91] Thus she learned on the job, and her 'discovery' that there was affirmative action for proletarians in Soviet society was exactly that: an archival finding. Had she had the kind of doctoral adviser she would become herself, she might have learned that this insight was not so new. But no such adviser existed in her life.

But the forgetfulness was also part of the intellectual sensibilities she had absorbed from her father: iconoclasm, an essentially negative approach to those who came before. This tendency was already well-established during her Melbourne University days. 'It was more my style', she later wrote of her student self, 'to criticise or deny any intellectual influence', generally only admitting 'to negative stimulus from lectures and tutorials, keeping positive reactions largely to myself'.[92] This very same style was evident in her contributions to *The Russian Review* brouhaha in 1986–87, and explains at least some of the negative reactions she received.

The iconoclasm also explains another aspect of Fitzpatrick's career. While she became a prolific adviser of doctoral students and a patron for young scholars, she was never much interested in undergraduate teaching – an activity much more reliant on the work of others and thus more likely to foster a consciousness of one's own indebtedness to precursors. A physically small, short-sighted, and shy young woman she was glad of the authority academic gowns bestowed on tutors when she first forayed into the university classroom at Melbourne in 1962–64.[93] Unlike her self-confident, charismatic father she was not a born university teacher; what interested her was research – 'doing' history. 'Just reading and teaching it', she noted in her memoirs, 'always interested me less.'[94] She was interested in learning new things, not teaching what she already knew.

This focus on research rather than teaching occasionally led to odd career choices. When, in 1969, the London School of Slavonic Studies asked her to choose between 'a teaching position with prospects of permanency' and a one-year research fellowship with no teaching obligations, she indicated her preference for the latter. 'Looking back, it's hard to imagine how I could have been so stupid', she later wrote 'with astonishment'.[95] Thus began a string of temporary positions. This life, together with the controversies she courted, created considerable stress, often triggering depression.[96] It was only in 1980, after two path-breaking monographs, that she managed to secure an ongoing teaching-and-research position at the University of Texas. And it was only after her move to the University of Chicago in 1990 that she was able to realize her second calling: to become a school builder.

Notes

1 On Fitzpatrick's life and work see Golfo Alexopoulos, Julie Hessler and Kiril Tomoff (eds), *Writing the Stalin Era: Sheila Fitzpatrick and Soviet Historiography* (New York, 2011); as well as her autobiographical writings: Sheila Fitzpatrick, *My Father's Daughter: Memories of an Australian Childhood* (Melbourne, 2010); Sheila Fitzpatrick, *A Spy in the Archives: A Memoir of Cold War Russia* (London, 2014); Sheila Fitzpatrick, 'Revisionism in Soviet History', *History and Theory* 46, no. 4 (2007): 77–91; Sheila Fitzpatrick, 'Revisionism in Retrospect: A Personal View', *Slavic Review* 67, no. 3 (2008): 682–704. For a basic biography, see: Sharon M. Harrison, 'Fitzpatrick, Sheila Mary (1941–)', *The Encyclopedia of Women & Leadership in Twentieth-Century Australia*, http://www.womenaustralia.info/leaders/biogs/WLE0468b.htm (accessed 22 November 2018).
2 Don Watson, *Brian Fitzpatrick: A Radical Life* (Sydney, 1979), quotation: 276.
3 Watson, *Brian Fitzpatrick*, xvii, 121, 213; Sheila Fitzpatrick, 'Brian Fitzpatrick and the World Outside Australia', in: *Against the Grain: Brian Fitzpatrick and Manning Clark in Australian History and Politics*, ed. Stuart Macintyre and Sheila Fitzpatrick (Melbourne, 2007), 37–69, here: 54–59.
4 Peter Nicholls, 'Sheila Fitzpatrick as an Australian Teenager', in: *Writing the Stalin Era*, 197–202, here: 199.
5 Fitzpatrick, *My Father's Daughter*, 149, 150.
6 Fitzpatrick, *My Father's Daughter*, 184.
7 Fitzpatrick, *My Father's Daughter*, 185.
8 Sheila Fitzpatrick, 'Interpreting Soviet Literary Politics. The Scholar and the Anti-Party Line', *Dissent* (Melbourne) 4, no. 3 (1964): 13–16; Sheila Fitzpatrick, 'Soviet Music: The Composer, the State, and the Public', Honours thesis, University of Melbourne, 1961.
9 Jerry F. Hough, 'Reminiscences', in: *Writing the Stalin Era*, 212–16, here: 212.
10 Sheila Fitzpatrick, 'My Father's Daughter: A Memoir', in: *Against the Grain*, 163, 164.

11 Julie Hessler, 'Sheila Fitzpatrick: An Interpretive Essay', in: *Writing the Stalin Era*, 21–35, here: 27–28. Jonathan Steinberg made a similar observation: letter to Fitzpatrick, 19 July 2009, Sheila Fitzpatrick Papers (henceforth: SFP), The University of Chicago Special Collections, box 34.
12 Fitzpatrick to Field, 8 October 1987, SFP, box 30.
13 Fay Anderson and Stuart Macintyre (eds), *The Life of the Past: The Discipline of History at the University of Melbourne, 1855–2005* (Melbourne, 2006). On the research by Dorothy, see Fitzpatrick, *My Father's Daughter*, 104. On the influence: 151 (quotation).
14 Fitzpatrick, *A Spy in the Archives*, 9.
15 Fitzpatrick, *My Father's Daughter*, 198–231.
16 Sheila Fitzpatrick, 'Memo to JCSS on Soviet Sources Workshop' (7 February 1984), SFP, box 3.
17 16 March 1984 meeting of the JCSS Subcommittee on History (minutes), SFP, box 3.
18 Hessler, 'Sheila Fitzpatrick: An Interpretive Essay', 30.
19 Sheila Fitzpatrick, 'A Student in Moscow, 1966', *The Wilson Quarterly* (Summer 1982): 132–41, here: 132.
20 Hough, 'Reminiscences', 212.
21 Fitzpatrick, *A Spy in the Archives*, chapter 5.
22 Sheila Fitzpatrick, *The Commissariat of Enlightenment: Soviet Organization of Education and the Arts under Lunacharsky, October 1917–1921* (Cambridge, 1970).
23 Fitzpatrick, *A Spy in the Archives*, chapters 4 and 6.
24 'Kreslo gostia. Sheila Fittspatrik: "mne udalos' popast' v arkhivy"', *Moskovskii komsomolets* (26 January 1989), SFP, box 8.
25 Michael David-Fox (ed.), *Amerikanskaia rusistika: vekhi istoriografii poslednikh let, sovetskii period: antologiia* (Samara, 2001).
26 David Fitzpatrick, 'But Louder Sang that Ghost, "What Then?": Letters from Sheila Fitzpatrick, 1968–1979', in: *Writing the Stalin Era*, 203–09, here: 207.
27 Fitzpatrick, *A Spy in the Archives*, 287–89. Correspondence with E. H. Carr, 1969–76, SFP, box 22. Fitzpatrick to Haslam, 25 January 1994, SFP, box 31.
28 'Sheila Fitzpatrick. Curriculum vitae. March 1990', SFP, box 7.
29 Sheila Fitzpatrick, 'Cultural Revolution in Russia 1928–32', *Journal of Contemporary History* 9, no. 1 (1974): 33–52, quotation: 35. Sheila Fitzpatrick (ed.), *Cultural Revolution in Russia, 1928–1931* (Bloomington, 1978).
30 Fitzpatrick, *Cultural Revolution in Russia*, 6–7.
31 Ronald G. Suny, 'Toward a Social History of the October Revolution', *The American Historical Review* 88, no. 1 (1983): 31–52.
32 Sheila Fitzpatrick, *Education and Social Mobility in the Soviet Union, 1921–1932* (Cambridge, 1979); Sheila Fitzpatrick, 'Stalin and the Making of a New Elite, 1928–1939', *Slavic Review* 38, no. 3 (1979): 377–402.
33 Fitzpatrick to David Attwooll, 2 March 1979, SFP, box 28.
34 Sheila Fitzpatrick, *The Russian Revolution* (Oxford, 1982; 2nd ed. 1994; 3rd ed. 2008).
35 Richard Pipes, '1917 and the Revisionists', *The National Interest* (Spring 1993): 68–79, here: 78.
36 Fitzpatrick, 'Revisionism in Retrospect: A Personal View', 686–87.

37 Hough to Fitzpatrick, 26 July 1989, SFP, box 23 (quotation). Also: Cohen to Lewin, 8 February 1976, MLP, box 2, folder 26; Hough, 'Reminiscences', 215–16; Martin Peretz, 'Cambridge Diarist', *The New Republic* (8 May 1989), 43.
38 Stephen F. Cohen, *Rethinking the Soviet Experience: Politics and History Since 1917* (New York, 1985), 33–34; Fitzpatrick, 'Revisionism in Retrospect: A Personal View', 687–88.
39 Sheila Fitzpatrick and Seweryn Bialer to Moshe Lewin, 18 December 1984, MLP, box 1, folder 16.
40 Moshe Lewin, *The Making of the Soviet System: Essays in the Social History of Interwar Russia* (New York, 1985), 3.
41 Sheila Fitzpatrick and Seweryn Bialer to Moshe Lewin, 18 December 1984, MLP, box 1, folder 16.
42 Moshe Lewin to Michael Hall, 3 December 1979, MLP, box 1, folder 14.
43 Sheila Fitzpatrick and Seweryn Bialer to Moshe Lewin, 18 December 1984, MLP, box 1, folder 16.
44 Workshop participants: Alexander Babyonyshev, Robert Beattie, Seweryn Bialer, William Chase, Linda Cook, Patrick Dale, Sheila Fitzpatrick, J. Arch Getty, Mark von Hagen, Robert Johnson, Herbert Kelien, Diane Koenker, Hiroaki Kuromiya, George Liber, Jim Millar, Jonathan Sanders, Nobuaki Shiokawa, Lewis Siegelbaum, Gerald Suhr, Ron Suny, Lynne Viola. SFP, box 9.
45 Moshe Lewin to William Rosenberg, 8 January 1985, MLP, box 1, folder 16.
46 Soviet and East European Program, University of Texas at Austin, Proposal to the McArthur Foundation: 'Inter-Area and inter-Disciplinary Approaches to Soviet and East European Studies: Eight Projects', SFP, box 3.
47 Fitzpatrick to Newton, 8 June 1984, SFP, box 28.
48 Michael Katz, 'Expansion of Russian/Soviet and East European Studies at the University of Texas at Austin, 1985–6' (1986), SFP, box 3.
49 'The University of Texas at Austin. Center for Soviet and East European Studies' (pamphlet, c.1988), SFP, box 6.
50 John Higley to Fitzpatrick, 5 May 1988, SFP, box 22.
51 Sheila Fitzpatrick and Lynne Viola (eds), 'Sources on the Soviet History of the Prewar Stalin Period: A Special Issue', *Russian History/Histoire Russe* 12, no. 2 (1985); Sheila Fitzpatrick and Lynne Viola (eds), *A Researcher's Guide to Sources on Soviet Social History in the 1930s* (Armonk, 1990).
52 Sheila Fitzpatrick, Vita, February 1986, SFP, box 7.
53 On the conflicts on the Subcommittee: Joint Committee on Soviet Studies, Agenda for April 1989 meeting, pp. 10–11, SFP, box 3.
54 See Chapter 2.
55 Sheila Fitzpatrick, 'Towards a Social History of the Stalin Period', paper for the First Workshop on the Social History of the Stalin period, Harriman Institute for the Advanced Study of the Soviet Union, Columbia University, 15 February 1985, 1, 5–6, SFP, box 9.
56 Sheila Fitzpatrick, 'New Perspectives on Stalinism: The View from Social History', paper for the panel on Stalinism at III World Congress for Soviet and East European Studies, 2 November 1985, SFP, box 8.
57 Tucker to Fitzpatrick, 8 October 1985, SFP, box 26.

58 Field to Fitzpatrick, 29 September 1985, SFP, box 30.
59 Reader reviews; Field to Fitzpatrick, 29 March 1986, SFP, box 8.
60 Field to Fitzpatrick, 29 March 1986, SFP, box 8; Sheila Fitzpatrick, 'New Perspectives on Stalinism', *Russian Review* 45, no. 4 (1986): 357–73, 369 n. 19.
61 Fitzpatrick, 'New Perspectives on Stalinism: The View from Social History', 25.
62 Fitzpatrick, 'New Perspectives on Stalinism', 371 n. 36.
63 Fitzpatrick to Field, 8 April 1986, SFP, box 8.
64 There were exceptions, who understood. For example: Nobuaki Shiokawa to Fitzpatrick, 7 September 1988, SFP, box 34.
65 Fitzpatrick to Manning, 6 March 1987, SFP, box 32.
66 Fitzpatrick to Daniel Field, 8 October 1987, SFP, box 30.
67 Monas to Fitzpatrick, 17 March 1987, SFP, box 32.
68 Fitzpatrick, 'New Perspectives on Stalinism', 360 n. 6.
69 Fitzpatrick to Bialer, 15 April 1986; Fitzpatrick to OUP, 11 February 1987; both SFP, box 28. An earlier contract with Allen & Unwin had by then lapsed. Michael Holdsworth (Allen & Unwin) to Fitzpatrick, 9 November 1978, SFP, box 26.
70 See book proposals from 1984 (January 1984 and Spring 1984), SFP, box 1. The finished chapters were chapters 1–4, entitled 'Soviet Society in the 1920s', 'The Bolsheviks' Analysis of Society', 'The Great Break, 1929–1932' and 'Urban Upheavals: Cultural Revolution: Liquidation of NEP'. Articles connected to the project, which were written by 1984 and subsequently published, included Sheila Fitzpatrick, 'After NEP: The Fate of NEP Entrepreneurs, Small Traders, and Artisans in the "Socialist Russia" of the 1930s', *Russian History* 13, no. 2/3 (1986): 187–233; Sheila Fitzpatrick, 'Everyday Life and "Middleclass Values" in Stalin's Russia', in: *Soviet Society and Culture: Essays in Honor of Vera S. Dunham* (Boulder, 1988); Sheila Fitzpatrick, 'Postwar Soviet Society: The "Return to Normalcy," 1945–1953', in: *The Impact of World War II on the Soviet Union*, ed. Susan J. Linz (Totowa, N.J, 1985), 129–56; and an unpublished 1978 paper which would later attain something of a cult status among historians working on the social history after the war: Sheila Fitzpatrick, 'Social Mobility in the Late Stalin Period: Recruitment into the Intelligentsia and Access to Higher Education, 1945–1953'.
71 Sheila Fitzpatrick, 'Peasant Society after Collectivization', paper for the Second Workshop on the Social History of the Stalin Period, Harriman Institute, Columbia University, 15 April 1985, SFP, box 1.
72 Sheila Fitzpatrick, personal communication with the author (email, 20 March 2017). For a slightly different recollection, see Fitzpatrick, 'Revisionism in Retrospect', 695–96.
73 Outline '2 (3) volume version of *Stalin's Peasants*' (1988), SFP, box 19.
74 Sheila Fitzpatrick, 'Afterword: Revisionism Revisited', *The Russian Review* 45, no. 4 (1986): 409–13, here 412.
75 'Kreslo gostia. Sheila Fittspatrik'.
76 Hough to Fitzpatrick, 9 May 1989, SFP, box 31.
77 Sheila Fitzpatrick, *Stalin's Peasants: Resistance and Survival in the Russian Village after Collectivization* (Oxford, 1994).

78 Sheila Fitzpatrick, *Everyday Stalinism: Ordinary Life in Extraordinary Times: Soviet Russia in the 1930s* (Oxford, 1999).
79 Sheila Fitzpatrick, *Tear Off the Masks!: Identity and Imposture in Twentieth-Century Russia* (Princeton, Mass., 2005). The central essay was 'Ascribing Class: The Construction of Social Identity in Soviet Russia', first published in *Journal of Modern History* 65, no. 4 (1993): 745–70.
80 Roger R. Reese, *Stalin's Reluctant Soldiers: A Social History of the Red Army 1925–1941* (Lawrence, Kansas, 1996); Yuri Slezkine, *Arctic Mirrors: Russia and the Small Peoples of the North* (Ithaca, 1994).
81 The books resulting from these dissertations are James T. Andrews, *Science for the Masses: The Bolshevik State, Public Science, and the Popular Imagination in Soviet Russia, 1917–1934* (College Station, Texas, 2003); John McCannon, *Red Arctic: Polar Exploration and the Myth of the North in the Soviet Union, 1932–1939* (Oxford, 1998); Matthew J. Payne, *Stalin's Railroad: Turksib and the Building of Socialism* (Pittsburgh, 2001); Golfo Alexopoulos, *Stalin's Outcasts: Aliens, Citizens, and the Soviet State, 1926–1936* (Ithaca, 2003); James R. Harris, *The Great Urals: Regionalism and the Evolution of the Soviet System* (Ithaca, 1996); Terry Martin, *The Affirmative Action Empire: Nations and Nationalism in the Soviet Union, 1923–1939* (Ithaca, 2001); Matthew Lenoe, *Closer to the Masses: Stalinist Culture, Social Revolution, and Soviet Newspapers* (Cambridge, Mass., 2004); Joshua Sanborn, *Drafting the Russian Nation: Military Conscription, Total War, and Mass Politics 1905–1925* (DeKalb, 2003); Julie Hessler, *A Social History of Soviet Trade: Trade Policy, Retail Practices, and Consumption, 1917–1953* (Princeton, 2004); and Kiril Tomoff, *Creative Union: The Professional Organization of Soviet Composers, 1939–1953* (Ithaca, 2006).
82 Books resulting from this second wave include: Mark Edele, *Soviet Veterans of the Second World War: A Popular Movement in an Authoritarian Society, 1941–1991* (Oxford, 2008); Stephen Bittner, *The Many Lives of Khrushchev's Thaw: Experience and Memory in Moscow's Arbat* (Ithaca, 2008); Brian LaPierre, *Hooligans in Khrushchev's Russia: Defining, Policing, and Producing Devience during the Thaw* (Madison, 2012); Alan Barenberg, *Gulag Town, Company Town: Forced Labor and its Legacy in Vorkuta* (New Haven, 2014); and Edward Cohn, *The High Title of a Communist: Postwar Party Discipline and the Values of the Soviet Regime* (DeKalb, 2015).
83 Andrew Sloin (2009) and Julia Fein (2012).
84 Oscar Sanchez-Sibony, *Red Globalization: The Political Economy of the Soviet Cold War from Stalin to Khrushchev* (Cambridge, 2014).
85 Sheila Fitzpatrick, 'Politics as Practice: Thoughts on a New Soviet Political History', *Kritika: Explorations in Russian and Eurasian History* 5, no. 1 (2004): 27–54.
86 Sheila Fitzpatrick, *On Stalin's Team: The Years of Living Dangerously in Soviet Politics* (Melbourne, 2015). For a more extensive discussion of this book, see Mark Edele, 'Unrevisionist Revisionism: Stalin's Team Reconsidered', *Australian Book Review* (April 2016): 9–11.
87 Fitzpatrick, *My Father's Daughter*, 244; Fitzpatrick, *A Spy in the Archives*, 331; Hough, 'Reminiscences', 213.

88 For example: Peter Kenez, 'Stalinism as Humdrum Politics', *The Russian Review* 45, no. 4 (1986): 395–400, here: 395.
89 Isaac Deutscher, *Stalin: A Political Biography*. 2nd ed. (London, 1967), 383–84.
90 Fitzpatrick, *A Spy in the Archives*, 4.
91 Fitzpatrick, *A Spy in the Archives*, 161–62.
92 Fitzpatrick, *My Father's Daughter*, 150, 130.
93 On the gowns: Fitzpatrick, *My Father's Daughter*, 161.
94 Fitzpatrick, *My Father's Daughter*, 181.
95 Fitzpatrick, *A Spy in the Archives*, 280.
96 On anxiety and depression during the Columbia years, see Barbara Gillam, 'Sheila Fitzpatrick in New York', in: *Writing the Stalin Era*, 210–11, here: 211.

Part II
Cold War debates

5
Stalinism with Stalin left in

Epiphany

Sheila Fitzpatrick was a geeky ten-year-old Melbournian when, on a Saturday afternoon in 1951, Robert C. Tucker had an epiphany. He was in Moscow.

> I had been browsing in the Academy of Sciences bookstore and was walking down Gorky Street toward the U.S. embassy on Mokhovaia. In full view below was the Red Square and, off to its right, the Kremlin. ... Suddenly I had ... a momentous thought ...: What if the idealized image of Stalin, appearing day after day in the party-controlled, party-supervised Soviet press, were *an idealized self in Horney's sense*? If so, Stalin must be a neurotic ... [with] political power unprecedented in history. ... The Stalin cult must reflect Stalin's own monstrously inflated vision of himself as the greatest genius of Russian and world history. ... Finding out what was most important about him would not require getting him onto a couch; one could do it by reading *Pravda*, while reading Horney![1]

Tucker was a hostage of Stalin. Born in Missouri in 1918, he now worked at the American embassy in Moscow. He had married a Russian just before such liaisons had become illegal after the war. An exit visa for his wife, Evgenia Pestretsova, was not forthcoming. Tucker was thus stuck in Stalin's capital, reading Soviet newspapers for a daily bulletin of translations for the embassy, and watching the Stalin cult grow ever more grotesque. In his spare time he read and re-read Karen Horney, a feminist psychoanalyst who had liberated her field from the notion of 'penis envy'. Her final book, *Neurosis and Human Growth*, had arrived in the diplomatic mail in 1950. Tucker would make use of her idea of a dialectic between a person's 'ideal self' and his or her 'real self', the tension between our view of who we would like to be with who we empirically are – a possible cause for neurosis.[2]

Tucker's 1951 epiphany was intellectually satisfying. The idea of the neurotic in the Kremlin who created the cult around his own person to meet his psychological needs not only explained what Tucker read day in and day out, and what he could observe on the streets of Moscow. It also helped make sense of his own situation. Why would the Soviet government not allow the handful of Soviet subjects who had married Westerners to leave the country? Clearly, it was not in the interest of the Soviet government 'to allow such a trivial matter to fester in relations with our own and other foreign governments'. So why do it? Horney's theory provided the answer: Stalin's neurotically over-inflated view of himself extended to his state and to the people manning it. The women who slept with foreigners implied that the local men were not good enough. Hence that the state was weak. Hence Stalin was emasculated.[3]

Tucker's Saturday afternoon epiphany was a transnational moment, bringing together central European psychological thought in its New York elaboration with Soviet sources, Tucker's own personal situation, and his observations of Soviet reality. The long-term results of this fusion would be two landmark studies of Stalin's life: *Stalin as Revolutionary* (1973) covered his youth and rise to power; *Stalin in Power* (1990) continued the story to 1941. A planned third volume on the war and post-war years was never finished.[4] This chapter explores these volumes in the larger context of biographical writings on Stalin. It shows the centrality of this literature to the study of Stalinism and further expands on two themes raised in earlier chapters: transnationalism and scholarly forgetfulness.

Marxist decades

Tucker's psychoanalytical volumes built on decades of Marxist scholarship. Three books in this tradition stand out. The disillusioned French communist Boris Souvarine (1895–1984) set the pattern in his hostile 1935 biography of Stalin. It established the basic storyline later work would follow. Because of a sluggish translator, the English edition only hit the bookshops in 1939, just when the Hitler–Stalin pact made many sympathetic to this reading. It disappeared from the shelves again after Stalin had become 'Uncle Joe' to Americans from 1941: a man fighting the good fight against Hitler. Souvarine presented Stalin as presiding over a 'counter-revolution' leading to a 'new sort of capitalism'.[5] The book anticipated many later interpretations, such as the notion that the Civil War had transformed Bolsheviks into proto-Stalinists,[6] or the idea that in Stalin's First Five-Year Plan, planning 'disappeared in the plan'.[7] Souvarine was adamant that the Great Terror was directed by Stalin personally, an interpretation which has stood the test of the archives.[8] He hated Stalin, whom he portrayed as 'lazy and intriguing', without foresight, 'except on the vulgar plane of personal relationships when the preservation of his power was at stake'. He was without political vision, a lacuna forcing him to 'adopt a day-to-day policy by borrowing from right and left'.[9]

Leon Trotsky further built on Souvarine's sketch. Writing in exile, after he had lost the power struggle, he portrayed Stalin as a practical worker without theoretical understanding who played no role in the heroic October of 1917. He later became the counter-revolutionary leader of the new class of Soviet bureaucrats, an interpretation later inspiring the left wing of the social historians of Stalinism.[10] Trotsky's Stalin biography, meanwhile, was 'subverted by the bile and hatred that motivated him', as his own biographer remarked.[11] Stalin was an 'Asiatic' with a 'jaundiced glint' in his eyes, 'a clever schemer, a cynic, a person capable of the lowest sort of conniving', Trotsky wrote. He had 'neither theoretical imagination nor historical intuition nor the gift of foresight' and his intellect 'always remained immeasurably inferior to his will'.[12] Stalin did not take such slights lightly. He sent a man with an ice axe and Trotsky's blood was splattered across his unfinished manuscript.[13]

More cold-blooded was Isaac Deutscher's account. Of nearly the same generation and of a similar political background as Souvarine, Deutscher was born in 1907. He hailed from Galicia, then part of Austria-Hungary. Brought up in an observant Jewish family, he lost his faith early and became an atheist as a young man. Soon, he was converted to Marxism, and in 1927 joined the Communist Party, an illegal organization in Poland. A trip to the Soviet Union followed in 1931. Deutscher returned to Poland and formed an anti-Stalinist group, leading to his exclusion from the

Communist Party. Deutscher's crime: he had called for a united front against Nazism. In April 1939, less than half a year before Hitler's troops attacked Poland, Deutscher moved to London to work for a newspaper. The move saved his life. His family was murdered by the Nazis. London would remain his home, where he made a living as a freelance journalist and historian. *Stalin. A Political Biography* (1949, second edition 1967) made his name, followed by a three-volume biography of Trotsky.[14]

While Deutscher clearly did not like Stalin, he did appreciate his achievements. Writing after the Soviet victory in the Second World War, he described Stalin as an unsympathetic lower-class brute whose despotism was historically necessary to drag Russia out of its backwardness and win the war against fascism. Perusing all the – then still rather scarce – sources on Stalin's life, the former communist tried as hard as he could to overcome his anti-Stalinist biases and write what he saw as a balanced history of the Soviet Union from the Revolution to the end of the Second World War.[15] Unlike Trotsky, he did not minimize Stalin's role in the pre-revolutionary Bolshevik Party, or the Civil War. Like Souvarine, he did not separate Stalinism from Bolshevism. Instead, he saw Stalin as one legitimate and logical heir of Lenin – a line the vast majority of subsequent biographies would follow. Collectivization and the First Five-Year Plan were not 'revolution betrayed', as Trotsky and his followers would have it. Stalin did not lead a 'counter-revolution', as Souvarine had claimed. Instead, he led a 'second revolution'. The communization of Eastern Europe after the war, likewise, was not Red imperialism but a 'revolution from above'.

These concepts would have a long history. Tucker would adjust the scheme, uniting the 'second revolution' (1928–32) and the Great Terror (1936–38) as two stages of the 'revolution from above' – today a standard way to read the history of Stalinism.[16] Deutscher's notion that conquered Eastern Europe was subjected to a 'revolution from above' would be reconfigured by Jan Gross, who used the term 'revolution from abroad' instead.[17]

Deutscher's narrative was grounded in his Marxism, which taught him that history was deterministic. Stalinism had happened. Hence it was necessary. Hence the historian had to show that this was so.[18] The only time this commitment broke down was in the chapter on the Hitler–Stalin Pact, among the most scathing indictments of Stalin's diplomacy.[19] Here, the former activist was unable to transform himself into the dialectical fatalist he believed the historian had to be. Instead, Deutscher diagnosed mistake after mistake. After all, it had been Soviet policies towards Nazism which had most estranged the young communist Deutscher from his party. And it had been the results of these policies which had enabled the Nazis to kill his family.

The Thaw

Between the first and the second edition of Deutscher's *Stalin*, a momentous event took place: in 1956, at the 20th Party Congress, Nikita Khrushchev, First Secretary of the Communist Party of the Soviet Union (CPSU), spoke about the dead boss. In the worst kept 'secret speech' of history, Khrushchev denounced the 'Cult of Personality', Stalin's rudeness, and his egocentric brutality. In particular, the destruction of communists in the Great Terror and his various failings as a military leader in the run up to and during the Second World War, fired Khruschev's ire. Miraculously, however, all of Stalin's policies, apart from the destruction of communist cadres and the wartime deportation of nationalities, turned out to be correct: the sidelining of the oppositions, collectivization and dekulakization, and the Five-Year Plans. Such half-heartedness was unsurprising: Khrushchev had been one of Stalin's closest associates.[20]

Nevertheless, the Secret Speech was a major event. Communists all over the world suffered a 'collective nervous breakdown', according to a less than sympathetic observer.[21] Although cringeworthy hagiographies of the dear leader continued to be written,[22] leftists in the capitalist world became more likely to exorcise Stalin from Leninism, to declare him an aberration or a wrong turn, as we have seen in the examples of Stephen Cohen (Chapter 1) and Moshe Lewin (Chapter 2).

The 22nd Party Congress of 1961 marked a deepening of the 'shift towards shaming and disgrace' of the dead leader, culminating in the removal of his body from the Lenin Mausoleum on Red Square on the night of 31 October. A new edition of the history of the CPSU increased criticism of Stalin by a notch, and biographies of prominent victims were published 'in unprecedented quantity'. Moreover, 'terror literature' appeared in print, a canon far exceeding

Aleksandr Solzhenitsyn's famous Gulag novella, *One Day in the Life of Ivan Denisovich* (1962).[23]

Meanwhile, professional historians were kept on a short leash. Already in 1957, the journal *Questions of History* was slapped down by the Party leadership, its editor-in-chief reprimanded and her deputy relieved of his duties. Their error had been 'revisionism' of the early history of the Party. A group of historians from Moscow State University were sentenced in early 1958 to labour camp sentences of up to a decade for 'counter-revolutionary revisionism'. They had been foolish enough to point out that Khrushchev – the First Secretary of the Party – had been an accomplice of Stalin and his crimes.[24]

More careful was a group of researchers who reconsidered the history of collectivization. This topic did not directly indict Khrushchev, but certainly would be critical of Stalinism: still a risky bet. The key historian was Victor Danilov at the Institute of History of the country's central research institution: the Soviet Academy of Sciences. From 1956 he published on various aspects of this problematic past, although his research on the topic preceded the Secret Speech by years. In 1958, he became the head of a research team on the history of collectivization, which gained access to formerly closed archives. A major conference followed in 1961, and in 1964 the Danilovites presented a massive tome of nearly 800 pages, the first professional, archive-based Soviet history of this cataclysmic event. A second volume was planned, supposedly bringing the story to 1937. The proofs were with the publisher when Khrushchev was dismissed in a coup by his closest associates and sent to his dacha into retirement. 'Within 24 hours', writes a historian of Soviet historiography, the proofs were withdrawn, 'never to see the light of day.' Soon, the manuscript began to circulate as *samizdat* – unauthorized, typed-up copies passed from hand to hand between trusted friends.[25]

Soon, bolder minds ignored what could be published altogether. Roy Medvedev, a Communist Party member, convinced Leninist, and a friend of Danilov, authored one of the most damning pieces of historical writing on Stalin. Drawing on unpublished memoirs and oral history from survivors, this book was not meant to be a biography, but a study of Stalinism's crimes. Inevitably, though, it spent quite some time on biographical issues, painting a scathing portrait: Stalin as an evil and immoral mediocrity of great ambition, a vain, malicious, envious man who compensated his inferiority complex with ruthless brutality against his intellectual, political, or military betters.[26]

Finished in 1968, four years after Khrushchev's fall and during a period of Leonid Brezhnev's conservative retrenchment, the book had no chance of publication. Too radical was the dissonance of Medvedev's vision with the official Soviet view: he criticized 'mistakes' during collectivization, mentioned the man-made famine of 1932–33, acknowledged that the Great Terror victimized many ordinary citizens (not just communists), indicted the entire Stalinist leadership for complicity in the dictator's crimes, and even compared the Gulag with Nazi extermination camps. Medvedev was excluded from the Communist Party. Smuggled abroad, the manuscript was published in English in 1972, followed by German, French, Italian, Japanese, Russian and Chinese editions. It provided an alternative to Deutscher as the standard Marxist interpretation of the Stalin years.[27]

Putting Stalin on the couch

This was the situation when Tucker began writing. There was no lack of literature on the dictator, but Souvarine's, Deutscher's and Medvedev's Stalin had remained a social type – the son of the freed serf, the brutal lower-class activist, the half-educated upwardly mobile proletarian, forever insecure and resentful of his social and intellectual betters. This roughly hewn image was a result of the approach. To Marxists, people were – at least 'in the final instance' – expressions of social forces, not complex individuals. This sociological reductionism was one of the great strengths of Marxism: it made it possible to ignore the white noise of complexity and hear only the clear harmonies of the historical dialectic. But as far as understanding people was concerned, this was never a successful strategy.

The twentieth century's other great guru was more obliging. Sigmund Freud's movement never tried to make a revolution or take over a state. But as far as influence among the thinking elites of Europe and the Americas was concerned, psychoanalysis was as successful as Marxism. It was only a matter of time until it would turn to the problem of Stalin. Indeed, some pedestrian attempts were made early on to explain Stalinism through childhood beatings and anxieties over fused toes.[28] But it would only be with Tucker's first volume that a serious attempt would be made to put Stalin on the couch.

After Stalin's death and the granting of the long-coveted exit visa for his wife, Tucker returned to the United States to become an academic. Here, he read all the available biographies. Deutscher, Souvarine and Trotsky, he wrote, had provided 'very penetrating passages of psychological characterization'.[29] Tucker read Khrushchev's speech, published in the *New York Times* on 5 June 1956, as portraying 'a neurotic personality precisely in Horney's sense, an example of the "arrogant-vindictive" type'. This Stalin was 'a self-idealizer, insatiably hungry for the glorification that the public cult provided'. He was 'easily aroused to vindictive hostility by whatever appeared to detract from his inflated vision of himself as a leader and teacher of genius. His aggressions ... were the other side of his self-glorification.'[30] Tucker latched on to Khrushchev's description of how Stalin edited his official biography. Stalin, it turned out, had written it himself! Khrushchev's report thus confirmed Tucker's hypothesis of 'an organic link between the cult of Stalin and the official idealization of Stalin's Russia'.[31] This slightly tendentious, if plausible, reading was supported by other new evidence. Tucker read with relish the new publications made possible by Khrushchev's Thaw and by the continued trickle of dissidents and defectors to the West.[32]

The resulting image was complex. Tucker's Stalin might have been a neurotic, but he was also a major player among the Bolsheviks, one of Lenin's most faithful lieutenants, a major contender for the leadership and, eventually, the dictator: the centre of 'Stalinism'. Tucker broke with the habit of historians sympathetic to Bolshevism to see Stalin as essentially a tactician without a vision, driven only by his will to power and his resentments. Instead, Tucker's Stalin was one of the best political strategists among the Bolsheviks. He did have a political position: the revolution from above, which Tucker saw as prefigured in the positions he took in the leadership struggle. Far from simply copying Bukharin or Trotsky, he had his own line all along. This position remains original – and controversial – in the political history of Stalinism.[33]

Tucker also provided a subtle version of the thesis of a logical evolution from Leninism to Stalinism. While Stalinism was not the same as Leninism, it was one legitimate heir of the Bolshevik tradition. Tucker stressed Lenin's long-term support of Stalin, which only gave way at the very end to a shocked appreciation of the monster he had created. Stalin, in turn, was a 'heavy-handed professor of Leninism with complete command of the texts in his field'. He was the 'systematizer' of Lenin's thought, an intellectual contribution many in the Bolshevik party appreciated, who had neither the time nor the ability to immerse themselves in Lenin's writings. They needed, not Trotsky's 'rarified interpretation of Leninism', but 'a textbook'.[34]

If Tucker's appreciation of Stalin's Leninism was closer to 'totalitarian' interpretations of the continuity from Lenin to Stalin[35] than to the later Lewin–Cohen version of 'revisionism', it also prefigured subsequent work on 'Stalin as Marxist'.[36] Moreover, it pointed the way to newer interpretations of the rise of Stalin, who do not see him as simply manipulating the levers of power at his command as the General Secretary of the Party.[37] Instead, Tucker stressed that Stalin succeeded because of his 'extraordinary skill as a political strategist', who managed to convince strong forces in the Bolshevik Party that he was the leader they needed, 'an uncommonly gifted man' who knew how 'to navigate the treacherous waters of Bolshevik politics with skill', a 'master politician'.[38] That this talented man was also a neurotic with a vindictive streak, a man who suffered from terrible inner turmoil because his idealized self-image could not be reconciled with what others saw, and what the dictator himself at times suspected was true – these psychological 'trifles' (as Bolsheviks would call the role of personalities in history) would matter once he was in power: in the Great Terror, 'untold thousands of loyal party members and other Soviet citizens would have to be condemned as covert enemies of the people so that Djugashvili could prove to himself and Russia that he really was Stalin'.[39]

The evil spirit of Bolshevism

If Tucker had hoped to write the definitive biography of Stalin, he was scooped. Adam B. Ulam (1922–2000) worked in parallel and drew on the same source base. His engagingly written, often scathing, and at times darkly funny *Stalin: The Man and His Era* was published in the same year as Tucker's first volume: 1973.[40] Ulam started from the other end of the continuum of politics and psychology than his psychoanalytical colleague, but arrived at strikingly similar conclusions. If Tucker had been unable to separate the neurotic Stalin from the politician, Ulam found it impossible to divorce the Bolshevik from the psychopath, no matter how hard he tried. The two were just too closely entwined.

Ulam was yet another of the many Polish Jews who would make such a deep impact on Soviet studies in the United States.[41] Like Lewin, Deutscher and Richard Pipes, he got away from Poland just in time, in 1939. Of the entire family, only Adam and his brother survived the Second World War.[42] By the time he wrote his *Stalin*, he was a tenured academic at Harvard, a 'Russia watcher' and 'Kremlinologist' with a historical bent. *Stalin* was his ninth book, which built on previous studies of Marxism, Bolshevism, and the history of Soviet foreign policy.[43]

His analysis was premised on the assumption that Stalin was a typical Bolshevik and that the pathologies of his person reflected those of Bolshevik ideology, revolutionary political culture and Soviet politics.[44] The deeper he got into his study, however, the more he had to concede that Stalin was an extreme case. His Stalin, like Tucker's, was vindictive, suspicious and cruel. At times, he teetered at the brink of madness. What Ulam set out to show was the method of this insanity: 'Stalin epitomized the Communist mind.'[45] It was the madness of Bolshevism in power, but also the lunacy of dictatorship more generally: a solitary and risky business. The more powerful Stalin became, the more vulnerable he felt, and the more vulnerable he felt, the more vindictive he became.[46]

Ulam's Stalin was a complex personality, a sociopath and an extremely intelligent politician, who could control his violent emotions and temper his pathological suspiciousness if it was in his own self-interest (which he equated with the interest of both the Soviet Union and the Bolshevik revolution). Most importantly to Ulam, he was a Marxist, 'a man for whom power was a mandate to build and transform'. He lusted for power not for its own sake (or in order to stabilize his inflated image of himself, as Tucker had it), but for the sake of the cause. Stalin, Ulam declared, 'was not a hypocrite'.[47]

Over wide stretches, the book was a confident presentation of what Stalin supposedly felt and thought as much as what he did. Like Tucker, then, Ulam tried to get into Stalin's head, and like Tucker he did so through a close reading of Stalin's public utterances as well as by interpreting the descriptions left by witnesses. Unlike Tucker, however, Ulam did not employ any explicit psychological theory. His method consisted in 'cold empathy' – the attempt to think oneself into the context and the mind of a historical actor one does not identify with.[48] This non-theoretical approach had the advantage of saving Ulam's prose from psychoanalytical jargon. As theoretical fashions come and go, this lack of sophistication made Ulam's *Stalin* age better than Tucker's.

Despite an infuriating lack of footnotes, *Stalin: The Man and His Era* was a major scholarly achievement. Read four and a half decades later, with access to much more archival information on Stalin and Stalinism and entire libraries of specialized scholarly studies on all aspects of this society, it is striking how little Ulam got wrong. Whenever he engaged in the numbers game (*How many people did Stalin kill?*), he was strikingly modest for a 'totalitarian'. Once archival tallies became available, he was surprised at these 'grim statistics' which showed that 'the victims of Stalinism were much more numerous than I dared to assume'.[49] He demonstrated that social and political history of the 1930s and 1940s could be reconstructed on the basis of a careful reading of published, samizdat and émigré sources – a project Lewin had abandoned as too complicated (Chapter 2), and Fitzpatrick was in the process of reconstructing (Chapter 4). Ulam's conceptualization of collectivization and dekulakization as a 'War against the Nation'[50] would re-emerge in archive-based research of the 1990s as the 'Great Soviet Peasant War' and the 'War against the Peasantry'.[51] The Great Famine of 1932–33 was treated with a differentiation many contemporary historians might want to emulate (Chapter 9). Ulam's deductions about the Kirov murder stood the test of archival research: it was committed by a lone and deranged gunman, not, as Stalin would claim, by an enemy conspiracy, or, as many anti-Stalinists continue to imagine, by Stalin himself.[52] Finally, Ulam also anticipated Fitzpatrick's idea of 'dosage': the thesis that Stalin was 'a master in the art of timing' when it came to destroying political enemies.[53]

Learning from the enemy

Ulam's book demonstrated how much one could learn from political adversaries – in this case, Deutscher. The enmity between the two men was overdetermined. A scion of a solidly bourgeois family, Ulam was not tempted by Marxism, let alone communism. During the initial phase of the Second World War, he had been as worried about his father's fate under Stalin – the Ulams hailed from Lwów, then occupied by the Soviets – as he would later be for their survival under Nazi rule. Ulam thus quite logically embraced the idea of totalitarianism, which was a label he affixed not only to Stalin's regime, but also to pre-Stalinist Bolshevism.[54] De-Stalinization did not change his mind about the Soviet Union, which now simply presented a 'new face of totalitarianism'.[55] This conceptualization stood in glaring contrast to Deutscher's Marxist–Hegelian developmental approach, where a democratic Leninism was replaced by a necessary phase of totalitarian despotism, only to give way to a more humane state socialism once the conditions were ripe.

The theoretical confrontation was exacerbated by personal ties. Ulam was a friend of anti-communist *Survey* editor Leo Labedz, who had been threatened with legal action over a hard-hitting review of Deutscher's work. This 'most vehemently relentless assault of anyone in the annals of Cold War historical scholarship'[56] chronicled each and every instance where Deutscher, the analyst of current affairs, had made a wrong (and tendentious) prediction. Labedz was picking an easy target, given that political punditry makes the weather forecast seem like an exact science. The ensuing legal wrangle with the lawyers of the enraged Deutscher delayed the publication of a second piece, written in late 1962, on Deutscher's *Stalin*. It denounced the book as a 'hagiography', which had not spent nearly enough time on Stalin's crimes, used primary sources selectively, ignored much of the extant historiography, and was unbearably Hegelian in its apologetics. Such 'historiographical liabilities' were hidden because of Deutscher's seductive style. The man could write. This backhanded comment was published only decades later, in 1978. Labedz had visited Ulam in the middle of the entire brouhaha, in October 1962, and surely mentioned the issue.[57] Finally, Deutscher and Ulam also crossed swords on at least one occasion at the Russian Research Center at Harvard University.[58]

In 1988, Ulam summarized his view of Deutscher's book by reiterating Labedz's devastating critique of 1978,[59] which had just been republished.[60] Ulam took the opportunity to rub it in. 'Isaac

Deutscher', he repeated Labedz's claim, did not pass 'the basic test' any Soviet expert has to pass. He played 'fast and loose with evidence', ignored all facts reflecting 'too adversely on the Soviet experiment', and disregarded 'almost completely Western sources and writings which are not strongly sympathetic to the Soviet Union'. His Stalin biography was 'flawed' and 'quite uncritical'.[61]

This was an ungenerous reading of Deutscher's *Stalin* and a broad-ranging dismissal of the entire 'revisionist segment of the Sovietological tribe'.[62] Focusing on mistakes rather than contributions, it illustrated what deep enmities the Cold War fuelled between scholars. This hostility was reflected in the way Ulam treated his precursor in his own Stalin book. Whenever he cited Deutscher, it was to dismiss or to ridicule his work. Deutscher's capitulation to Stalinism clearly irritated him, especially the insistence that Stalinism was necessary to win the Second World War.[63]

And yet, Ulam accepted Deutscher's idea that Stalin was inevitable. Given the Bolshevik victory in 1917–21, and given the situation of the Bolshevik version of the Russian Empire by the late 1920s, something like the Stalin revolution was the only alternative to doom: 'under Communist rule Stalin's inhumanity was instrumental in the Soviet Union emerging from World War II as an awesome giant'. He even elaborated upon one of Deutscher's more adventurous interpretations: the thesis that the Great Terror was motivated by an attempt to root out all possible resistance which, in case of war, could wage a coup or make a revolution. Other 'Deutscherisms' in Ulam's work include the idea that the Stalin revolution was born of ignorance, obsession and chance, or the notion that in Stalin, his parents' serf-past reasserted itself. Of course, he never quoted the origins of these ideas, behaviour the reader will recognize from previous chapters, and a treatment, indeed, which Ulam's work would receive at the hand of subsequent historians as well.[64]

Information revolution

After Tucker and Ulam had explored the new evidence which had become available under Khrushchev, there was a long silence on the biographical front. Biography was out of favour with historians, who worked themselves through a succession of fashions – economic, social, and eventually cultural history. In the 1980s, scholars could obsess about how to write a history of Stalinism – with the state left in or left out, from above or from below, with or without Marxism. Lewin and Pipes could disagree over the relationship between Lenin's revolution and Stalin's state, and Fitzpatrick could work to establish social history methodology for the study of the 1930s. Few, however, thought that a new biography of the dictator was desirable. One who tried concluded, somewhat dejectedly, that he could say nothing new: 'Almost thirty-five years after his death we know the official file number of the Stalin papers in the Central Party Archive (*fond* 558), but that is all we know about this presumably vast store of information.'[65]

This state of affairs would change radically with the breakdown of the Soviet Union. But even before then, one historian got spectacular access to the archives: Dmitri Volkogonov (1928–95). The publication of his Stalin biography was a sensation.[66] Volkogonov was 'an improbable candidate for launching the first full-scale, documented Soviet assault on the Stalinist system', as his translator pointed out. The book was one moment in the three-star general's gradual disillusionment with Lenin's cause, which would eventually lead him to embrace Christianity instead. But at the time he produced his Stalin biography he was still a Leninist.

Volkogonov grew up in a communist family. His father was shot during the Great Terror and he and his mother were exiled to Western Siberia, where she died. Nevertheless, Volkogonov would join the Party in 1951 and remain a member until 1991. He began his working life as a school teacher in 1946, but joined the army in 1949 and made a career. Once Khrushchev's de-Stalinization drive removed barriers for children of repressed communists, Volkogonov was able to enter a military academy in 1961. Ten years later he landed a job in the propaganda administration of the armed forces – a sign of his ideological steadfastness. His doubts about Stalinism and worries about its ongoing deformation of Soviet society emerged in stages. Reading party journals from the 1920s showed how free debate had once been. Khrushchev's 1956 revelations inspired Volkogonov, as they did his contemporary Medvedev, to collect materials on Stalin. His position in the army's propaganda arm gave him access to archives, in particular the secretive Ministry of Defence archive, which would form the basis of his chapters on the Second World War. Volkogonov began writing in 1978 and had nearly finished when Gorbachev became General

Secretary in 1985. At this point, his double life as an ideological functionary burying himself in the archives for critical purposes had come to the attention of his superiors. He was ordered to stop or lose his job. Volkogonov instead managed to secure the position of Director of the Institute of Military History in 1988, which allowed him to continue, publishing his bombshell biography at the end of the decade. He lost his job in the conservative onslaught against Gorbachev's liberalizations in 1991, just before the fall of the Soviet Union, a dismissal which seems to have only further radicalized him: after being baptized in the early 1990s, he published a scathing biography of Lenin.[67]

Triumph and Tragedy was the first Stalin biography which could draw on secret Soviet archives. In addition to the already mentioned military archive, Volkogonov also accessed the Stalin *fond 558* in the Party archive, as well as other collections, some of which – like the Foreign Ministry archive – remain very hard to work in. He also read the memoir literature which had grown since Khrushchev's Thaw, and which despite self-censorship did include useful information, already exploited by Tucker and Ulam. Going beyond these carefully selective accounts he also interviewed survivors of Stalinism. Volkogonov used this unprecedentedly large source base to argue simultaneously against two representations of Stalin's life. The first was the official *Short Biography* of 1939 and 1947.[68] His other target was Trotsky's dismissal of Stalin as a mediocrity.

Increased interaction

Shortly after Volkogonov, in 1990, Tucker finally published the sequel to his earlier Stalin volume, bringing the story to the German attack in 1941. He laid out his scheme of the revolution from above in detail, with the initial onslaught on the peasantry and forced collectivization forming the 'first phase' and the Great Terror the 'second phase'. His account remains among the best written and influential political histories of the 1930s. He again grappled with the relationship of Stalinism to Bolshevism on one hand, and to fascism on the other – a preoccupation of the totalitarian theory. By now, Tucker had moved further away from his earlier argument that Stalinism was a legitimate heir of Bolshevism. In *Stalin in Power*, the dictator was still a Bolshevik, but a Bolshevik 'of the radical right. As such it was wayward, deeply deviationist, and questionably Bolshevist save insofar as it could and did lay claim to all that was harsh, repressive, and terrorist in Lenin's legacy.' Stalin was closer to Hitler than to Lenin: 'As a Bolshevism of the radical right, Stalin's Russian national Bolshevism was akin to Hitler's German National Socialism.'[69]

Tucker's second volume was among the first biographies which quoted Volkogonov's magnum opus and other Soviet publications of the 1980s; and it was among the last not to use Russian state and party archives.[70] From now on, archival access became more even, and Russian and non-Russian scholarship increasingly cited each other. Even textbook accounts would draw on the odd archival source.[71] Such entanglement of Western and Soviet historiography was, of course, not completely new: Western scholars had always read Soviet historiography – and cited it either critically or for sources unavailable to outsiders. This exchange now intensified.

Volkogonov's *Triumph and Tragedy* marked one moment of increased interaction between Soviet and Western historiography. Western scholarship was not freely available in the Soviet Union. Only particularly privileged scholars could get access to closed special collections in research libraries. Most had to 'stew' in their 'own juice'.[72] Historians of Bolshevism and of the Soviet Union rarely cited Western literature, unless their job was to debunk it. Volkogonov, meanwhile, had read widely, even if he did not always understand the authors' politics. Thus he dismissed not only the card-carrying 'totalitarians' Leonard Schapiro and Robert Conquest as attempting to 'discredit – with Stalin's "help" – the very notion of socialism', but he also included Tucker and even Deutscher in this list. On the positive side, he cited the Italian scholar of the Russian Revolution, Giuseppe Boffa, as providing a 'fairly accurate picture', but also cited Ulam, Cohen and Pipes for their contribution to his knowledge. The German arch-conservative military historian, Joachim Hoffmann, meanwhile, got a well-deserved treatment as a falsifier of the history of the Second World War.[73]

Medvedev went further. In the second, fundamentally revised edition of *Let History Judge* (1989), he cited Western literature extensively. He particularly highlighted his reading of Tucker, Cohen, Boffa, Robert V. Daniels and Ulam, whom he all met at one point or another in person while they visited Moscow. Other Western authors who shaped his views included Souvarine, Schapiro and Lewin.[74] Such interactions only grew in the years following the breakdown of the Soviet Union. From 1991, Western and Russian scholarship began to be integrated to an extent unthinkable before. In the 1990s and 2000s, major works of Western scholarship would be translated into Russian, and thus became available even to scholars without foreign languages. Meanwhile, the best of Russian scholarship was routinely translated into English, and to a lesser extent German or French, allowing undergraduate students in Melbourne, Berlin or Toronto to read it. The fact that a growing cohort of scholars from the former Soviet Union received training in the West, or migrated there to take up better paid academic positions, further blurred the once clear boundaries of the scholarly cold war.

Stalin's penis

This interaction soon also extended to Stalin's private life. As we have seen, much of the biographical literature on Stalin focused on the public man: the revolutionary, the politician, the dictator. In extremis, this Stalin had no private life, as in Deutscher's account, where the only indication that he must have had, occasionally, sex, was the existence of his children. The Bolshevik activist, the follower of Lenin, and the dictator seemed to have no fears or hopes outside of politics. This absence of the private was partially a result of the approach: this was a 'political biography', after all. It was also a function of the sources, as little information was available on Stalin's personal life. Most importantly, however, it was part of the interpretation. For Deutscher, Stalin was a political being through and through. He had no time for romance, sex, or family life: 'the existence of a professional revolutionary', he opined, 'left only the narrowest margin for "private life".'[75] Volkogonov followed the same line in a chapter concluding that the dictator was a terrible husband and 'utterly useless as a father'.[76]

Tucker filled in some of the blanks, but the psycho-historian's interest was largely in what Stalin's relationships with women could tell us about his neurosis. The first marriage with Ekaterina Svanidze was 'indicative of the mother-attachment' which formed the core of Stalin's elevated self-image.[77] He also knew about rumours that Stalin, in Siberian exile, had shacked up with 'a local peasant woman' and had a child with her,[78] and he provided a fairly chaste description of the romance with Nadya Alliluyeva, the revolutionary teenager who would become his second wife in 1919.[79] Ulam, too, added a few details largely based on the memoirs of Stalin's daughter's, published in emigration in 1967,[80] and another historian followed suit, claiming that Stalin had grown bored with skinny intellectuals and slept with his more substantial peasant-housekeeper instead.[81]

A real step forward was Edvard Radzinsky's 1997 volume. A historian by training and playwright by profession, Radzinksy had once been a Stalinist boy who broke into his school to correct a grammatical mistake in a letter he had written to the dear leader. By the end of Stalin's life, however, he had inherited his father's pre-revolutionary liberalism, hated Stalin, and felt lonely among the crowds of mourners. After the breakdown of the Soviet Union, he would write one of the strongest anti-Leninist – indeed, anti-Marxist – biographies. Part memoir, part oral history, part archival investigation, his *Stalin* was deeply steeped in Moscow's intelligentsia gossip, but also impeccably researched. Full of conspiracy theories, some of which it debunked, others which it embraced, the book paid particular attention to the women who had slept with Stalin.[82]

Soon, a Westerner strengthened this emerging focus on Stalin's penis. In Simon Sebag Montefiore's two volumes, the dictator's sex life moved to the centre of attention. They provide lurid tales of the moral degeneracy of Stalin and his surroundings, but no analysis. 'Stalin had a penis and he used it', scoffed one critic, not without reason.[83] So what?

Two answers might be given. One is that this kind of history sells. Radzinsky and Montefiore are freelancers without the guaranteed income of tenured professors. They cannot disregard sales figures. The other answer is political. In the 1990s and 2000s, political identities have become focused on sexual politics. The flipside of this obsession, as Masha Gessen has pointed out, is that sexual behaviour easily becomes an index for politics and morals more generally.[84] Stalinism was bad, such reasoning goes, hence the Stalinists must have been bad people. And you know bad people when you observe their promiscuity.

This approach harks back to Trotsky, whose demonology had found Stalin's sex life 'all the more precious for the light it shed on him as a man'.[85] At stake here was, again, the first marriage to a profoundly religious and traditional woman. That a revolutionary could love such a person Trotsky found scandalous: a transgression of revolutionary morality. After all, this was not 'a bourgeois environment in which the husband regards himself as an agnostic or amuses himself with Masonic rites, while his wife, having consummated her latest adultery, duly kneels in the confession box before her priest'. Among revolutionaries, matters of the heart (and of the penis) were 'immeasurably more important', and that Stalin, that 'tyrannical nature' could be 'indulgently tolerant of his intimate companion's beliefs' just showed that he was no Marxist. His sex life revealed him as a backward provincial who 'required no more of his wife than his father had found in the long-suffering Keke', Stalin's mother.[86] If, in Trotsky's account, thus, Stalin's intimate life revealed the real man behind the revolutionary mask, in Montefiore's the indictment was spread across the beds of all the Bolsheviks. Their sexuality became an index for the depravity of their cause.

The return of political biography

Meanwhile, 'ascetic academic historians' remained focused on the political side of this history, 'bashfully toning down the truth'.[87] Outside the successor states of the Soviet Union, three academics wrote biographies of Stalin after the archival revolution: one British, one German, and one American. All three stood in Deutscher's tradition of political biography, although Stalin's sexuality makes the occasional appearance. First off the block was the British scholar Robert Service, like Deutscher also a biographer of Trotsky. Second came Jörg Baberowski, a German professor who had made his name as a historian of the Caucasus.[88] And third was Stephen Kotkin, an American historian with an excellent turn of phrase.[89]

These were three very different accounts. Service provided a competent one-volume assessment of Stalin, which would remain the standard scholarly treatment until replaced by Oleg Khlevniuk's. It somewhat lost steam once Service reached the Second World War – that is, territory not covered by Tucker's classic. He emphatically reasserted Deutscher's, Tucker's, and Ulam's view that Stalin was a major Bolshevik and a disciple of Lenin, but otherwise simply brought the biography of Stalin up to date by citing newer research and perusing now available archival sources.[90]

Baberowski's book, by contrast, really came into its own once it reached the war, which it recounted as an unmitigated disaster: a poorly prepared bloodletting full of miscalculations, callous disregard of human life, terror and brutality. An expanded rewriting of his youthful *Red Terror* (2002), *Scorched Earth* constantly teetered at the brink of demonology. Originally, Baberowski had seen Stalinism as a result of the modern impulse to order society and make it 'legible' – a position he now described as 'nonsense'. Instead, he drove home a new thesis: *No Stalin – no Stalinism*. Other communist rulers, Baberowski asserted, without quoting a single example, also 'professed to be communists without deducing a license to mass murder from this ideology'. Dismissing all attempts to understand Stalin's behaviour with reference to ideology, geopolitics or modern statecraft, Baberowski asserted that Stalin was a 'psychopath' who loved the state of exception 'because it redefined normality and made "normal" people do what they would not under other circumstances'. At the centre of this history, then, was the Great Terror, planned and implemented by Stalin, a history of violence which also structured the way the Second World War was narrated: as totalitarian, terroristic warfare. The ups and downs of violence under Stalin, and the evolution of state repression from the 1930s to the 1940s and beyond, all but disappeared.[91]

Kotkin's three-volume magnum opus, meanwhile, was less an attempt to write a biography of Stalin than a history of modern Russia in the world from the late nineteenth century to the end of Stalin's life. Unlike Baberowski, but very much like Service, or before him Ulam, Tucker and Deutscher, he stressed Stalin's Leninism. He went as far as embracing the empirically shaky thesis that Lenin's 'Testament' was a forgery. As one of his critics pointed out, this discredited position is otherwise embraced only by Russian neo-Stalinists.[92] For Kotkin, however, it served the purpose of removing any gap between Leninism and Stalinism. If Lewin had embraced 'Lenin's Last Struggle' as a means to separate Lenin from Stalin, Kotkin – who had encountered Lewin's neo-Leninism as a young historian participating in the National Seminars – felt compelled to dismiss the rift between the two Bolsheviks, making Stalinism no more than consequently implemented Leninism.

Somewhat contradictorily, Kotkin then asserted at the end of the first volume that, had Stalin died, his revolution from above would not have happened. Here, he got caught between his commitment to the centrality of ideology for the course of Soviet history on the one hand, and of personal agency of historical actors on the other. Kotkin also re-emphasized Deutscher's point that the way Stalin rose to power was essential to understanding his brutality. Rather than looking for clues to Stalin's behaviour in his childhood or youth (Tucker), or in a generalized psychopathic streak (Baberowski), he located the origins of his brutality in the bruising experience of the succession struggle after Lenin's death. He combined this Deutscherism with restating Ulam's argument regarding the good fit of Stalin's personality and the Bolshevik political ecosystem. Stalin's paranoia was the 'structural paranoia' of the Bolsheviks, aggravated by the bitter political fights of the 1920s.

This interpretation cannot explain why it was only Stalin who was turned into a Stalinist. Both his opponents in the 1920s and his comrades in the 1930s and 1940s were exposed to the same 'structural paranoia'. Yet, it was only Stalin who succumbed to it: neither Bukharin nor Trotsky did, and after Stalin's death his closest associates could not wait to dismantle his rule of terror and replace it by a more measured form of dictatorship.[93] In volume two, then, Kotkin changed tack, focusing both on unexplained but pre-existing psychological traits and on the corrupting influence of absolute power, which 'shapes absolutely'. The revolution from above would be 'deeply reinforcing of his hypersuspicious, vindictive disposition'.[94]

Despite the obvious differences between the works of Service, Baberowski and Kotkin, they shared two traits: rather than obsessing about Stalin's sex life or his psychology, they focused on the politics, which 'subsumed' personal life.[95] Standing thus in Deutscher's tradition, they could not be further from his convoluted Marxist politics. Two of the three authors were public intellectuals with explicitly conservative profiles. Baberowski became extremely controversial in Germany once he publicly opposed the immigration policies of the Merkel government.[96] Kotkin, meanwhile, did not hide that he thought that any type of welfare state was a fateful step on the road to serfdom.[97] And Service had made himself *persona non grata* among the well-organized and vocal remnants of Trotskyism by committing an act of sacrilege: he had dared to write a biography of the saint, which did not cast him a hero.[98] But the point here is not about Trotsky, but about the consensus among recent scholars writing about Stalin in what used to be 'the West': outside Russia, no serious scholar was left who would find anything positive about Stalin and Stalinism. Even those who continued to embrace the glorious Bolshevik revolution could do so only by separating it clearly from Stalinism, as left-wing historians had done ever since Trotsky.[99]

Culmination point

Vladimir Putin's Russia, meanwhile, saw a rising tide of pro-Stalinist writings. These ranged from returns to hagiography in neo-Stalinist celebrations of the dead leader as a great statesman, to more nuanced approaches which read very much like an updated version of Deutscher's diagnosis. The latter position was taken by the President himself, at pains to embrace Stalin as the competent wartime leader in order to claim the singular achievement of victory over Nazism as part of a positive history of Russia. The corollary to these panegyrics to Stalin was a commitment to a strong, authoritarian state, a dismissal of civil liberties and democracy, and an aggressive foreign policy (Chapter 8).

Oleg Khlevniuk's *Stalin*, released in both Russian and English in 2015, was a reaction to this neo-Stalinism.[100] A senior research fellow at the Russian State Archive and at the Higher School of Economics in Moscow, Khlevniuk made his name as the leading historian of high politics under Stalin.[101] Despite his unparalleled mastery of the archives, he acknowledged those who came before him. In particular, he stressed the huge contributions Ulam and Tucker had made to the biographical literature on Stalin. Volkogonov, Radzinsky and Montefiore also got honourable mentions for their archival digging. He was critical of revisionists who tried to find the origins of the Terror 'from below', which he saw as involuntarily helping neo-Stalinist apologetics.[102] And Khlevniuk was not only intellectually part of both the Russian and the Western literature; he was also embedded in a transnational network of amazing reach. His acknowledgments read like a who's who in Soviet history, with major scholars from Germany, the United Kingdom, North America and Russia.[103]

Khlevniuk marshalled all the new evidence from the archives to present a Stalin who was formed by 'traditional Russian authoritarianism and imperialism, European revolutionary traditions, and Leninist Bolshevism'. He was ideologically driven by 'extreme anti-capitalism'. But he was also creative, adapting ideological doctrines 'to the interests of his own dictatorship and emerging superpower'. His mind was 'repellent' but 'ideally suited to holding onto power'. His personality – 'cruel by temperament and devoid of compassion', 'stubborn and inflexible', with a preference for solving problems by force – was decisive for the political choices he made. 'He made limited and half-hearted reforms only when socioeconomic crises were reaching breaking point and the stability of the system was imperilled. His theoretical dogmatism lay at the root of the violence that defined his regime'. His goal was building a socialist economy, by which he meant 'a money-free powerhouse where people would work as ordered by the state and receive in exchange the natural goods that the state decided they needed' – an authoritarian twist to Marx's utopia, where each received according to need and worked according to ability.[104]

Khlevniuk mounted a tightly organized assault on unsubstantiated theories. The future dictator's childhood was quite typical for his place and time, and thus psychoanalytical obsessions with early experiences explained little; he was a senior Bolshevik in 1917, not some nobody as in the Trotsky version of events; he was a loyal Leninist and a close collaborator of the Bolshevik leader, and Lenin only turned against him late in his life. The final confrontation between Lenin and Stalin was not a fundamental ideological rift, but a disagreement over tactics, a 'bureaucratic squabble'. It only became a major fight because 'an ailing Lenin' felt power slip from his hands and elevated the issue as 'a pretext for attacking his ambitious associates', in particular the General Secretary.[105] Lenin's 'testament' was written in this context – and the letter was real. Khlevniuk sounds exasperated at what he sees as ignorant nonsense when writing about doubts about the authenticity of Lenin's final writings, which all of Lenin's comrades-in-arms accepted as the words of the leader. 'With no real evidence beyond an assumption of Stalin's infallibility, some revisionists have proposed that evidence of Lenin's doubts about Stalin were manufactured and placed in Lenin's archives by followers of Trotsky!'[106] Once in power, Stalin was not a 'weak dictator'. The documentary record contains not 'a single decision of major consequence taken by anyone other than Stalin'.[107]

DEBATES ON STALINISM

Khlevniuk's unparalleled mastery of sources and secondary literature, his innovative storytelling, which combined narrative with structural analysis centred around Stalin's last days, his careful analysis and forceful arguments regarding major controversies surrounding Stalin's rule, make his book the apotheosis of the many attempts to write a history of Stalin's life and times. It will remain the standard biography for some time, not least because Khlevniuk put in the effort required to keep it short – less than 400 pages, including the apparatus. 'I regret the omission of many telling facts and quotes', he wrote about this labour of compression, 'but I am glad for the reader. I know how it feels to gaze wistfully at stacks of fat tomes that will never be conquered.'[108]

Notes

1. Robert C. Tucker, 'A Stalin Biographer's Memoir', in: *Psychology and Historical Interpretation*, ed. William McKinley Runyan (Oxford, 1988), 63–81, here: 65.
2. Karen Horney, *Neurosis and Human Growth: The Struggle Toward Self-Realization* (New York, 1950).
3. Slightly paraphrased from Tucker, 'A Stalin Biographer's Memoir', 70.
4. Robert C. Tucker, *Stalin as Revolutionary: A Study in History and Personality* (New York, 1973); Robert C. Tucker, *Stalin in Power: The Revolution from Above, 1928–1941* (New York, 1990).
5. Boris Souvarine, *Staline, aperçu historique du bolchévisme* (Paris, 1935); *Stalin: A Critical Survey of Bolshevism* (New York, 1939). The 1940 edition was republished in 1985: *Staline, aperçu historique du bolchévisme* (Paris, 1985). It includes an interesting 1977 preface on the gestation and publication history: 10–17. On this issue see also: Fredric Warburg, *An Occupation for Gentlemen* (London, 1959), 270–71. Unless indicated otherwise, I cite from the US edition of 1939. On counter-revolution: Souvarine, *Stalin*, 513, 558–66, 597–676.
6. Souvarine, *Stalin*, 188–254, esp. 254.
7. Souvarine, *Stalin*, 547. Moshe Lewin, 'The Disappearance of Planning in the Plan', first published in *Slavic Review* 32, no. 2 (1973).
8. Souvarine, *Stalin*, 627. Oleg Khlevniuk, *Master of the House: Stalin and His Inner Circle* (New Haven and London, 2009).
9. Souvarine, *Stalin*, 231, 599.
10. Leon Trotsky, *The Revolution Betrayed: What is the Soviet Union and Where is it Going?* (New York, 1972). A free e-book is available at: https://www.marxists.org/archive/trotsky/1936/revbet/ (accessed 6 March 2018).
11. Dmitri Volkogonov, *Trotsky: The Eternal Revolutionary* (London, 1997), 421.
12. Leon Trotsky, *Stalin: An Appraisal of the Man and His Influence*, ed. and trans. Charles Malamuth, introduction by Bertram D. Wolfe, new ed. (New York, 1967), 1, 18, 30, 51, 54, 83–84, 177.

13 Volkogonov, *Trotsky*, 464–69.
14 Isaac Deutscher, *Trotsky: The Prophet Armed* (1954); *The Prophet Unarmed* (1959); *The Prophet Outcast* (1963). On Deutscher's life, see David Horowitz (ed.), *Isaac Deutscher: The Man and His Work* (London, 1971); Richard Bosworth, *Explaining Auschwitz and Hiroshima: History Writing and the Second World War 1945–1990* (London and New York, 1993), 156–58; and David Caute, *Isaac & Isaiah: The Covert Punishment of a Cold War Heretic* (New York, 2013), 19–35.
15 I quote here from the second edition, which had an additional preface and a final chapter on Stalin's last years, which the original did not include. Isaac Deutscher, *Stalin: A Political Biography*. 2nd ed. (London, 1967).
16 Tucker, *Stalin in Power*. Robert C. Tucker, 'Stalinism as Revolution from Above', in: *Stalinism: Essays in Historical Interpretation*, ed. Robert C. Tucker (New York, 1977), 77–108, here: 84–85. He was critical of Deutscher's interpretation of what caused this revolution, but accepted that it constituted a revolutionary upheaval completing the October revolution. Tucker, 'Stalinism as Revolution from Above', 84–89.
17 Jan T. Gross, *Revolution from Abroad: The Soviet Conquest of Poland's Western Ukraine and Western Belorussia*. expanded ed. (Princeton, 2002).
18 Deutscher, *Stalin*, xiii.
19 Deutscher, *Stalin*, chapter XI.
20 Nikita Khrushchev, 'On the Cult of Personality and its Consequences', speech to the 20th Congress of the CPSU, 24–25 February 1956, https://www.marxists.org/archive/khrushchev/1956/02/24.htm (accessed 30 January 2018).
21 Adam Ulam, *Understanding the Cold War: A Historian's Personal Reflections* (New Brunswick, 2008), 134.
22 For example: Maurice Thorez, 'Stalin' (1960), in: *Fils du Peuple* (Paris, 1970), English translation (2004) at: https://www.marxists.org/reference/archive/thorez/1960/stalin.htm (accessed 27 January 2018).
23 Polly Jones, *Myth, Memory, Trauma: Rethinking the Stalinist Past in the Soviet Union, 1953–70* (New York, 2013), 1, 102–04, 108–09, 124, 146–47, and chapter 1; Leonard Schapiro, 'A New History – a New Mythology', *Problems of Communism* 9, no. 1 (1960): 58–60. 'I. V. Stalin (k 80-letiiu so dnia rozhdeniia)', *Kommunist* no. 18 (December 1959): 47–56, quotations: 47, 48, 49, 50.
24 'XX s"ezd KPSS i zadachi issledovaniia istorii partii', *Voprosy istorii* no. 3 (1956): 3–12, esp. 4, 9–10; E. N. Burdzhalov, 'O taktike bol'shevikov v marte -aprele 1917 goda', *Voprosy istorii* no. 4 (1956): 38–56; Schapiro, 'A New History – a New Mythology', 58; Roger D. Markwick, *Rewriting History in Soviet Russia: The Politics of Revisionist Historiography, 1956–1974* (Basingstoke, 2001), 47–62; Jones, *Myth, Memory, Trauma*, 58, 90–96.
25 Markwick, *Rewriting History*, 111–54.
26 Roy Medvedev, *Let History Judge: The Origins and Consequences of Stalinism*, ed. David Joravsky and Georges Haupt (New York, 1971). On the connection between Medvedev and Danilov, see Markwick, *Rewriting History*, 125.
27 The original edition (New York, 1971) – despite the copyright imprint, it was released in 1972. A revised edition (with a useful new preface and with

reference now to works by Western Soviet Union specialists) was published during perestroika: Roy Medvedev, *Let History Judge: The Origins and Consequences of Stalinism*, 2nd rev. ed. (Oxford, 1989).

28 Louis Fischer, *The Life and Death of Stalin* (New York, 1952).
29 Robert C. Tucker, 'The Dictator and Totalitarianism', *World Politics* 17, no. 4 (1965): 555–83, here: 556.
30 Tucker, 'A Stalin Biographer's Memoir', 73–74.
31 Tucker, 'A Stalin Biographer's Memoir', 73–74. The reality of the writing of the biography was somewhat more complicated: David Brandenberger, 'Stalin as Symbol: A Case Study of the Personality Cult and its Construction', in: *Stalin: A New History*, ed. Sarah Davies and James Harris (Cambridge, 2005), 249–70.
32 Tucker, *Stalin as Revolutionary*, xiii–xiv.
33 Tucker, *Stalin as Revolutionary*, chapter 11.
34 Tucker, *Stalin as Revolutionary*, chapters 7 and 8, quotations: 318, 321, 323, 324.
35 See, for example, Leszek Kolakowski, 'Marxist Roots of Stalinism', in: *Stalinism: Essays in Historical Interpretation*, ed. Robert C. Tucker (New York, 1977), 283–98; and Leszek Kolakowski, *Main Currents of Marxism: Its Rise, Growth, and Dissolution*, 3 vols (Oxford, 1978).
36 Eric van Ree, 'Stalin as Marxist: The Western Roots of Stalin's Russification of Marxism', in: *Stalin: A New History*, ed. Sarah Davies and James Harris (Cambridge, 2005), 159–180; and Eric van Ree, *The Political Thought of Joseph Stalin: A Study in Twentieth-Century Revolutionary Patriotism* (London, 2002).
37 James Harris, for example, sets up his reconsideration of Stalin's rise to power as a revision of Tucker, among others. He concludes that rather than through manipulation of the secretariat, Stalin 'largely carried the Central Committee on the basis of his policies' – a direct reformulation of Tucker's point. 'Stalin as General Secretary: The Appointments Process and the Nature of Stalin's Power', in: *Stalin: A New History*, 63–82, here: 63, 78–79 (quotation).
38 Tucker, *Stalin as Revolutionary*, chapters 8 and 10, quotations: 300, 392, 393.
39 Tucker, *Stalin as Revolutionary*, 493.
40 Adam B. Ulam, *Stalin: The Man and His Era* (New York, 1973). 2nd, expanded edition with a new introduction: Boston, 1989. I quote from the 1989 edition, which is identical with the exception of the new introduction.
41 See Andrzej Nowak, 'A "Polish Connection" in American Sovietology, Or: The Old Homeland Enmities in the New Host Country Humanities', in: *East and Central European History Writing in Exile 1939–1989*, ed. Maria Zadencka, Andrejs Plakans and Andreas Lawaty (Leiden, 2015): 375–95.
42 On Ulam's life, see his memoirs: *Understanding the Cold War*. On the decision to leave early: 30–32, 43.
43 Adam B. Ulam, *Philosophical Foundations of English Socialism* (Cambridge, 1951); *Titoism and the Cominform* (Cambridge, 1952); *The Unfinished Revolution: An Essay on the Sources of Influence of Marxism and Communism* (New York, 1960); *The New Face of Soviet Totalitarianism* (Cambridge, 1963); *The Bolsheviks: The Intellectual and Political History of the Triumph of Communism in Russia* (New York, 1965); *Expansion and Coexistence:*

The History of Soviet Foreign Policy, 1917–67 (New York, 1968); The Rivals: America and Russia since World War II (New York, 1971); The Fall of the American University (New York, 1972).
44 Ulam, Stalin, 288.
45 Ulam, Stalin, 362.
46 For example: Ulam, Stalin, 259, 261, 286, 288.
47 Ulam, Stalin, 301.
48 Robert Gerwarth, 'Cold Empathy: Perpetrator Studies and the Challenges in Writing a Life of Reinhard Heydrich', in: *Totalitarian Dictatorship: New Histories*, ed. Daniela Baratieri, Mark Edele and Giuseppe Finaldi (New York, 2014), 21–38.
49 Ulam, Understanding the Cold War, 198.
50 Ulam, Stalin, chapter 8.
51 Andrea Graziosi, *The Great Soviet Peasant War: Bolsheviks and Peasants, 1917–1933* (Cambridge, Mass., 1996).
52 Ulam, Stalin, 380–88; Matthew E. Lenoe, 'Did Stalin Kill Kirov and Does it Matter?', *The Journal of Modern History* 74, no. 6 (2002): 352–80; and Matthew E. Lenoe, *The Kirov Murder and Soviet History* (New Haven and London, 2010).
53 Ulam, Stalin, 282. Sheila Fitzpatrick, *On Stalin's Team: The Years of Living Dangerously in Soviet Politics* (Melbourne, 2015).
54 In his earlier book on Lenin (originally published in 1965), Ulam described Bolshevism as a 'totalitarian movement' which by the end of 1917 had not yet built 'the administrative machinery of a full-blown totalitarian state'. Adam B. Ulam, *The Bolsheviks: The Intellectual and Political History of the Triumph of Communism in Russia* (Cambridge, Mass., 1998), xi, 395.
55 See Adam B. Ulam, 'The New Face of Soviet Totalitarianism', *World Politics* 12, no. 3 (1960): 391–412; as well as Ulam, *The New Face of Soviet Totalitarianism*.
56 Caute, *Isaac & Isaiah*, 166.
57 On the friendship and the timing of the visit: Ulam, *Understanding the Cold War*, 153–54. On the threatened legal action: Edward A. Shils, ' Leopold Labedz', in: *Portraits: A Gallery of Intellectuals*, ed. Joseph Epstein (Chicago, 1997), 155–77, here: 159; Caute, *Isaac & Isaiah*, 166–69. The essays in question were Leopold Labedz, 'Deutscher as Historian and Prophet', *Survey: A Journal of Soviet and East European Studies* 41 (April 1962), and Leopold Labedz, 'Isaac Deutscher's "Stalin"', *Encounter* 52, no. 1 (1979): 65–82, both reprinted in *Survey* 30, nos 1–2 (1988): 33–93 (on 'hagiography': 70; assets and liabilities: 80). The 1979 essay also includes Labedz's version of events with regards to the legal threat.
58 Caute, *Isaac & Isaiah*, 190.
59 Labedz, 'Deutscher as Historian and Prophet'.
60 Leopold Labedz, *The Use and Abuse of Sovietology* (New Brunswick, 1988).
61 Adam Ulam, 'Keeping Them Honest: A Tribute to Leo Labedz', *The National Interest*, no. 14 (1988): 108–11, here: 109.
62 Ulam, 'Keeping Them Honest', 110.
63 Ulam, *Understanding the Cold War*, 197.
64 Ulam, *Understanding the Cold War*, 198; Ulam, *Stalin*, 264, 290, 294–95, 300.

65 Robert H. McNeal, *Stalin: Man and Ruler* (Basingstoke, 1988), xi.
66 Dmitri Volkogonov, *Triumf i tragediia: Politicheskii portret I. V. Stalina*, 2 vols (Moscow, 1989); abridged translation: *Stalin: Triumph and Tragedy*, ed. and trans. Harold Shukman (London, 1991).
67 Harold Shukman, 'Editor's Preface', in Dmitri Volkogonov, *The Rise and Fall of the Soviet Empire: Political Leaders from Lenin to Gorbachev* (London, 1998), ix–xvi.; 'Volkogonov Dmitrii Antonovich', *Kto est' Kto v Rossii i v blizhnem zarubezh'e. Spravochnik* (Moscow, 1993), 144–45. The Lenin biography is Dmitri Volkogonov, *Lenin: Politicheskii portret*, 2 vols (Moscow, 1994); English translation: *Lenin: A New Biography* (New York, 1994).
68 Marx-Engels-Lenin Institute, *Stalin* (Moscow, 1947), https://www.marxists.org/reference/archive/stalin/biographies/1947/stalin/01.htm (accessed 29 January 2018). This was the authorized translation of the second, revised edition of the original 1939 full version of this canonical text. See *Iosif Vissarionovich Stalin: Kratkaia biografiia* (1st ed.: Moscow, 1939; 2nd rev. ed.: Moscow, 1947).
69 Tucker, *Stalin in Power*, 591.
70 Other examples were Walter Laqueur, *Stalin: The Glasnost Revelations* (London, 1990); and Robert Conquest, *Stalin: Breaker of Nations* (New York, 1991).
71 For two examples see Hiroaki Kuromiya, *Stalin: Profiles in Power* (Harlow, 2005); and Kevin McDermott, *Stalin: European History in Perspective* (Basingstoke, 2006).
72 Efim Iosifovich Pivovar, 'Reminiscences', in: *Writing the Stalin Era: Sheila Fitzpatrick and Soviet Historiography*, ed. Golfo Alexopoulos, Julie Hessler and Kiril Tomoff (New York, 2011), 221.
73 Volkogonov, *Triumph and Tragedy*, xxii, 445, 591–615.
74 Medvedev, *Let History Judge*, 2nd rev. ed., xiv.
75 Deutscher, *Stalin*, 127.
76 Volkogonov, *Triumph and Tragedy*, 144–56, 153.
77 Tucker, *Stalin as Revolutionary*, 107.
78 Tucker, *Stalin as Revolutionary*, 160.
79 Tucker, *Stalin as Revolutionary*, 172–73, 223.
80 Svetlana Alliluyeva, *20 Letters to a Friend*, trans. Priscilla Johnson (London, 1967).
81 McNeal, *Stalin*, 161–68.
82 Edvard S. Radzinskii, *Stalin* (Moscow, 1996); English translation: Edvard Radzinsky, *Stalin: The First In-Depth Biography Based on Explosive New Documents from Russia's Secret Archives* (New York, 1996).
83 Stephen Kotkin, *Stalin. Vol. 1: Paradoxes of Power, 1878–1928* (London, 2014), 8.
84 Masha Gessen, 'Al Franken's Resignation and the Selective Force of #METOO', *New Yorker* (7 December 2017) https://www.newyorker.com/news/our-columnists/al-franken-resignation-and-the-selective-force-of-metoo (accessed 19 March 2018).
85 Trotsky, *Stalin*, 85.
86 Trotsky, *Stalin*, 85, 86.

87 Montefiore's judgement on his academic colleagues in his sex-and-crime version of the history of the tsars, a sequel of sorts to his Stalin books. Simon Sebag Montefiore, *The Romanovs 1613–1918* (London, 2016), xx.
88 Jörg Baberowski, *Der Feind ist Überall: Stalinismus im Kaukasus* (Munich, 2003).
89 On Kotkin, see Chapter 7. I disregard here Sarah Davies and James Harris, *Stalin's World: Dictating the Soviet Order* (New Haven, 2014), which explored the Stalin archive and what it can tell us about how Stalin viewed the world around him. Sheila Fitzpatrick's history of Stalin's team is explored in Chapter 4.
90 Robert Service, *Stalin: A Biography* (Cambridge, Mass., 2005).
91 Jörg Baberowski, *Verbrannte Erde: Stalins Herrschaft der Gewalt*. 2nd ed. (Munich, 2012), 16, 218. For more, see my review in *Jahrbücher für Geschichte Osteuropas* 62, no. 2 (2014): 313–16.
92 David Brandenberger in *American Historical Review* (February 2016): 333–34, here: 334. Such critique did not change Kotkin's mind. See Stephen Kotkin, *Stalin: Waiting for Hitler, 1929–1941* (New York, 2017), 67, 302–3.
93 A point made strongly by Sheila Fitzpatrick, *On Stalin's Team*, which appeared in parallel with Kotkin's first volume.
94 Kotkin, *Stalin: Waiting for Hitler*, 6 (quotation), 303.
95 Kotkin, *Stalin: Waiting for Hitler*, 3.
96 For a particularly scathing report on Baberowski's legal fights, see Andreas Fischer-Lescano, 'Jörg Baberowski. Die Selbstinszenierung eines Rechten', *Frankfurter Rundschau* (11 June 2017).
97 Stephen Kotkin, 'Communism's Bloody Century', *Wall Street Journal* (3 November 2017).
98 Robert Service, *Trotsky: A Biography* (Basingstoke, 2009).
99 Mark Edele, 'A Century after 1917: Why Should You Care about the Russian Revolution?', *Australian Book Review* (October 2017): 10–15.
100 Oleg V. Khlevniuk, *Stalin: Zhizn' odnogo vozhdia* (Moscow, 2015); English translation: *Stalin: New Biography of a Dictator* (New Haven, 2015).
101 O. V. Khlevniuk, *Stalin i Ordzhonikidze: Konflikty v politbiuro v 30-e gody* (Moscow, 1993), translated as *In Stalin's Shadow: The Career of 'Sergo' Ordzhonikidze* (Armonk, 1995); O. V. Khlevniuk, *Politbiuro: Mekhanizmy politicheskoi vlasti v 1930–3 gody* (Moscow, 1996), revised edition translated as *Master of the House: Stalin and his Inner Circle* (New Haven, 2009). Also: Yoram Gorlizki and Oleg Khlevniuk, *Cold Peace: Stalin and the Soviet Ruling Circle, 1945–1953* (Oxford, 2004).
102 Khlevniuk, *Stalin: New Biography of a Dictator*, ix–x.
103 Khlevniuk, *Stalin: New Biography of a Dictator*, 379–80.
104 He thus agreed with Eric van Ree's image of Stalin the Marxist, which he quotes as the scholarly consensus. Khlevniuk, *Stalin*, 7, 98. On van Ree, see fn. 36 above.
105 Khlevniuk, *Stalin*, 13, 53, 67–73.
106 Khlevniuk, *Stalin*, 73.
107 Khlevniuk, *Stalin*, 37.
108 Khlevniuk, *Stalin*, xv–xvi.

6

Totalitarianism and revisionism

Eternal life

Again and again in this book, the term 'totalitarianism' has served as a historiographical beacon. We have seen how 'revisionism' was construed as totalitarianism's other in the historiographical fights of the 1980s. We encountered Moshe Lewin's flirtation with the term, and his groping for alternatives, before exploring the work of Richard Pipes, a major proponent of understanding the Soviet Union as 'totalitarian'. We demonstrated how the unrevisionist revisionist, Sheila Fitzpatrick, used the concept, while arguing against the model. The term reappeared repeatedly in the chapter on Stalin biographies. Leon Trotsky, Robert Tucker and Adam Ulam all asserted that Stalinism was 'totalitarian'.

The prominence of the term might surprise, given how often it has been declared dead. A 'defunct' theory, we read, even if the word might still be 'useful'.[1] Such utility, declare others, is restricted for propaganda purposes, which invalidate any analytical use.[2] The term conflates Nazi Germany and Stalinist Russia, reads a common complaint. It irons out crucial differences. It assumes 'total control' of the population, while in reality such penetration of everyday life 'was never that total'. The very fact that the Soviet Union 'did change over time' further falsifies its central assumption.[3] A cultural artefact of the Cold War, it deserves to be buried 'once and for all'.[4]

And yet, the term keeps creeping out of its conceptual grave. The reason for this longevity is that it does important analytical work. Dictatorships, as Lewin was wont to stress, come in all shapes and sizes. None are pleasant, but some are more intrusive than others. József Piłsudski 's 'guided democracy' or Vladimir Putin's 'managed' variant can only be categorized as authoritarian states. But living in them was a far cry from the mobilizational regimes of Adolf Hitler or Iosif Stalin.[5] It was easier to arrange oneself with the dictatorship of Saddam Hussein than with the regime of terror of the so-called Islamic State. Totalitarianisms form extreme cases: dictatorships which aim at the total reconstruction of society, albeit with a variety of different utopian end goals: communism, a post-genocidal racial utopia, a pure Islamic califate.

The theory of 'totalitarianism' thus captures an essential aspect of Stalinism and links it closer to certain extreme forms of dictatorship. It can integrate the political, social, economic and cultural aspects of this society, which anti-totalitarian scholars have investigated. The original idea did not assume total control or total knowledge, and later 'revisions' added further complications but did not falsify the overall framework. The concept also had a political edge, which originally was democratic in its thrust, even if it could be exploited for anti-democratic ends. Together, these theoretical and political strengths continued to attract scholars to this productive approach to Stalinism.

The origins of 'totalitarianism'

The term 'totalitarianism' originated in Italy. The anti-fascist journalist Giovanni Amendola used 'totalitarian system' (*sistema totalitarian*) 1923 to distinguish fascist rule as a new political form different from earlier 'majoritarian' or 'minoritarian' types of government. Mussolini's fascists were rather pleased by this elevation of their improvisations to the status of complete novelty. After beating Amendola to death, they adopted the term as a positive self-description, an aspiration, which would define the idea of 'totalitarianism' for supporters as well as critics. In this notion, as an entry under Mussolini's name in a 1923 encyclopaedia suggested, the state was 'all-embracing; outside of it no human or spiritual value can exist, much less have value. Thus understood', the article written by the philosopher Giovanni Gentile continued, 'fascism is totalitarian, and the fascist state ... interprets, develops and potentiates the whole life of a people.' Soon, German right-wing intellectuals – Carl Schmitt and Ernst Jünger, to name the most prominent – took up the term. Opposed to the democracy of the

Weimar Republic, they embraced what seemed to express their own political ambition for a complete break with liberalism. This transfer away from Italy explains why Trotsky could write, in 1937, that 'this word arrived from Germany'. It fitted the Soviet Union under Stalin well, he thought.[6]

Given later mystifications, this point bears repeating: in the 1930s, 1940s, and 1950s 'totalitarianism' as a phenomenon linking Nazism and Stalinism was a concept used by left-wing anti-Stalinists like Trotsky, Louis Fischer, Victor Serge and George Orwell (alongside liberal mavericks like Hannah Arendt). It transitioned only slowly from the Left to the Right, a process that sped up during the Cold War.[7]

A key moment in this transition was Stalin's pact with Hitler, the subsequent outbreak of the Second World War in Europe, the Soviet takeover of parts of Poland, Finland, and Romania, and the annexation of all three Baltic republics. 'What makes an external policy totalitarian?' became a question more and more intellectuals asked from September 1939, after the Soviets had joined the Nazis in their attack on Poland.[8] Comparisons of Nazism and communism now abounded in the American press.[9] Soon, academics followed suit. In November 1939, the first conference on totalitarianism was held in Philadelphia. Participants discussed anything from totalitarian politics, education, philosophy of war, the relationship between totalitarian policies and the international economic system, and 'the novelty of totalitarianism in the history of western civilization'[10]

Left-wing anti-totalitarians, however, also received a boost. Trotsky, still alive, weighed in soon after the start of the war, asserting that both Hitler's and Stalin's regimes were totalitarian, but stressing that their foreign policy goals were fundamentally different: Hitler was aggressive, Stalin defensive.[11] In a lengthy article written in late September 1939, he reaffirmed his earlier analysis of Stalinism as totalitarian,[12] and elsewhere, too, he noted that the Soviet dictatorship had taken on 'monstrous totalitarian forms'.[13] This dictatorship would 'pitilessly crush the workers and peasants' in the newly acquired formerly Polish territories 'in order to bring them into subjection to the totalitarian bureaucracy'.[14] The popular acclamations of the Soviet annexation in these regions amounted to a 'totalitarian plebiscite' which gave the subjected populations no choice.[15] The Stalin biography he was in the process of writing when he was murdered in 1940 further developed the theme of 'the totalitarian era', the 'totalitarian concentration of all the means of oral and printed propaganda', and 'Stalin's totalitarian regime'.[16]

Trotsky was far from alone at the time in his left-wing anti-totalitarianism. The English translation of Boris Souvarine's Stalin biography hit the bookshops just after the outbreak of the war in Europe, vastly increasing its impact.[17] The bulk of it had been written between 1930 and 1935, when Souvarine tried out the term, still putting it in quotation marks.[18] By the time he wrote the chapter which would bring the story to the start of 1939, he had grown more confident, calling Mussolini's Italy and Stalin's Soviet Union both 'totalitarian regimes' and pointing out 'the affinities between left and right wing totalitarianisms'.[19] He now formulated the credo of the idea of 'totalitarianism':

> The new terms, Bolshevism and fascism ... were necessary to describe hitherto unknown social movements and their empirical ideology. In the final analysis, these movements show so many similarities, and are open to so many mutual plagiarisms, they borrow and exchange so many things from one another, that the same word, 'totalitarian', another addition to the modern vocabulary, becomes them both perfectly.[20]

Other anti-Stalinist leftists were also quickly off the block. In December 1939, the exiled Austrian-German ex-communist Franz Borkenau, a one-time affiliate of the Frankfurt School renowned for his reporting on the Spanish Civil War, signed the introduction to his own reaction to the pact. Written in exile in London, *The Totalitarian Enemy* was published the following March, and contributed the term 'Red Fascism' to the debate, which would have an illustrious career. The Hitler–Stalin Pact 'brought out the essential similarity between the German and the Russian systems'.[21]

Borkenau's book marks the beginning transfer of the term 'totalitarianism' from the Marxist Left. Already in 1936, he had explored the similarities between fascism and Bolshevism – 'slightly different specimens of the same species of dictatorship'.[22] He now built on this analysis, repeating that 'the Nazi and the Bolshevist revolutions were only two specimens of one and the same movement'. Both were leadership-centric systems, based on 'boundless obedience to the Führer, with complete disregard for any rules of truth and morality'. Both relied on parties staffed by 'classless' or '*déclassé* elements', and both reacted to a crisis of capitalism. They watched and copied each other. And while Borkenau, the exile from Nazism, spent many more pages on the German variant, the former communist saw communism as 'the purest and most logical form of totalitarianism'. It had taken over the entire economic system and thoroughly broken the pre-revolutionary class system in a way Nazi Germany had not.[23]

In 1936, Borkenau had argued as a critical Marxist. The Hitler–Stalin Pact did not mark a break with this tradition, although politically he now embraced liberalism as the only alternative. The war, as he saw it, revealed a division of the world, which 'could not be more clear-cut: liberal powers here, totalitarian powers there'. At stake was the defence of liberty, democracy, even the very 'foundations of Western civilization'. Nazism and communism represented a totalitarian world revolution with apocalyptic consequences, threatening 'all the values which have been handed down from Athens and Jerusalem, through the Rome of the Emperors and the Rome of the Popes, to the Reformation, the age of enlightenment, and the present age'. Liberty could 'only win by overcoming the challenge of totalitarianism'.[24]

Notwithstanding such liberal pieties, *The Totalitarian Enemy* was still underwritten by a Marxist, albeit unorthodox, interpretation. And it did not argue for the restoration of economic liberalism. Instead, the book concluded with a plea against the 'extremists of the Liberal bourgeoisie' and for a 'mixed system' which would combine political liberty with 'those features of the totalitarian revolution which are inevitable results of the conditions of modern life'.[25] In the economic sphere, totalitarianism marked 'the transition from an economic system run by individual property owners ... to a centralized and planned economy', a change which he thought was 'inevitable'. Any post-totalitarian settlement would have to combine political liberty with 'a certain loss of wealth and influence on the part of that capitalist bourgeoisie which had been the ruling class of all industrial nations in the nineteenth century'. The New Deal showed the way to a democratic form of economic planning which would overcome both totalitarianism and nineteenth-century liberalism. Borkenau, in essence, argued for a more expansive form of what would become the post-war democratic welfare states.²⁶

Vulgarization and sophistication

Once the Germans attacked the Soviets in 1941 and Stalin became 'Uncle Joe', the reliable 'Russian' ally to Britain and the US, the emerging consensus on totalitarianism was suppressed. But it was not entirely forgotten. Once the war was won, the Soviets had expanded into Eastern Europe and Asia, and a new confrontation between the United States and the Soviet Union became more and more likely, the pre-war ideas about Stalinism as totalitarian were remembered. By the time the Cold War was in full swing, the old left-wing concept of totalitarianism had entered the mainstream.²⁷

At this point, we can observe two processes running in parallel. The first was vulgarization. Like many theories which become part of the common intellectual currency of an epoch, totalitarianism began to suffer from unsophisticated use. It could simply be added, like a conceptual sauce, to any historiographical dish. Thus, Louis Fischer, in his demonology of Stalin, used the term as part of an entire barrage of concepts, which in the process lost all meaning. Stalin's Soviet Union, he claimed, in a quick succession of contradictory labels, was totalitarian, feudal, modern super-feudal, medieval ('the Middle Ages with tractors'), or maybe just terrifyingly modern. Stalin, the feudal totalitarian primitive, was 'the machine age at its ugliest', who mechanized 'politics and men', and thus represented 'the dual danger of the machine and the machine state' which 'hangs over the entire world'. Building 'feudalism in one country', the 'Robot-in-Chief' was 'a model cynic', whose political system was no more than 'political banditry'.²⁸ Such crude term-dropping would become standard in the decades to come, particularly in political polemics and punditry.

Thus, by the late 1940s, Borkenau's term 'Red Fascism' had become mainstream in the United States. The Chairman of the Republican National Committee, B. Carroll Reece, used it to denounce the Truman administration in 1946, J. Edgar Hoover to warn of subversives at home in 1947, and the socialist leader Norman Thomas to argue for his own form of social democracy in 1948.²⁹ As a landmark study has it, the 'nightmare of "Red Fascism" terrified a generation of Americans and left its mark on the events of the cold war and its warriors'.[30] It was this vulgar totalitarianism which would dominate the public sphere during the Cold War; and it was opposition to this vulgate which inspired revisionist historians to continually attack the term.

In parallel with this process of vulgarization, however, the concept of totalitarianism saw careful elaboration by scholars. Most famous is the book by the philosopher Hannah Arendt, an exile from Nazi Germany, who built on Borkenau's analysis. Her 1951 magnum opus, *The Origins of Totalitarianism*, was more often cited than read, but became a landmark for supporters and critics alike. Like Borkenau's earlier work, it had much more to say about Nazism than Stalinism, and was much more interested in where totalitarianism came from (as the title implied) than how it functioned once in power. It did not provide a generalized model and did not, as critics sometimes wrote, assume total control of the state over the population. In Arendt's view, totalitarianism in power did the opposite: it destroyed the state and replaced it by an ever-radicalizing movement. The only places where total control was more or less realized were the concentration camps. The majority of the population was not brainwashed by propaganda, but instead shielded from the radicalism of the inner circle of the totalitarian rulers by dynamic layers of radicalism. Arendt's totalitarianism was a complex and dynamic force and its claims at total transformation and total mobilization were aspirations, albeit lethal ones.[31]

Empiricism

Arendt's book was a philosophical attempt to grapple with the new phenomenon of ideological mass mobilization dictatorships. It was strikingly ignorant about the realities of life under Stalinism. Other scholars would put the term to use in empirical work, with much more promising results. For the debate on Stalinism, two main contributions stand out: one sociological, the other historical.

The first was the Harvard Interview Project, or as it was originally termed, the Harvard Project on the Soviet Social System (HPSS). Funded by the United States Air Force, which hoped to gain sociological input for the planning of strategic bombing raids, it brought together excellent scholars from anthropology, sociology and psychology with an army of interviewers sent out to talk to recent emigres from the Soviet Union – the so-called 'displaced persons' of the Second World War.[32] The result of these efforts was a small library of high-quality, specialized monographs on many aspects of Soviet society, reflecting the situation in the 1930s and 1940s, the time the interviewees had experienced Stalin's country. Together with the transcripts, now digitized and available online, they continue to form a treasure trove for historians of Stalinist society. Two volumes stand out: *How the Soviet System Works* (1956) summarized the view 'from above', an attempt to conceptualize the Soviet social system in its totality. *The Soviet Citizen* (1961) was destined to be quoted more by historians, because of the unique view it provided from below. It tried to understand what daily life was like in this 'totalitarian society'.[33]

Neither volume claimed that the state exerted total control; neither thought that everybody was brainwashed by propaganda; and neither believed that there was no dynamism in this society. Soviet citizens were intelligent and understandable actors living in a complex political, economic and social system. The state loomed large, but so did the family, or the workplace. The overall thrust of HPSS was an implicit, and at times explicit, comparison with the United States under the umbrella term 'industrial society'. The social organization of the Soviet Union was 'in many respects' the result of this industrialism, rather than of the totalitarian political structure.[34]

As far as 'totalitarianism' was concerned, it referred to the aspirations of those in power. The political leaders 'attempt to coordinate for the attainment of their goals all the material and human resources of their society, extending even to the private feelings and sentiments of the populace'. Attempts, of course, are not the same as results, and the outcomes of the mobilizational regime's actions formed the 'soviet system', a complex of traditional and new institutions, values and patterns of behaviour manifesting themselves on the territory of the Soviet Union.[35]

A second major contribution to the empirical study of Stalinism as a totalitarian society was Merle Fainsod's *Smolensk under Soviet Rule*, a book several contributors to the 1986–87 debate cited as the definitive social history of Stalinism. Jerry Hough sounded exasperated when he wrote about social history attacks on this 'really top-notch scholar' and his 'sophisticated work'. 'God knows', he wrote, 'why the young historians have to keep misrepresenting

Fainsod's work to make their points.' Surely they could find other and 'far more deserving' objects of derision.[36]

The answer was that Fainsod had done what allegedly still needed to be developed: a social history of Stalinism. And an archival-based one, at that. Fainsod, of course, had no access to archives held in the Soviet Union. Instead, he relied on the Smolensk Party Archive which had been displaced by the Second World War from western Russia to the United States. Like many political scientists of his generation, Fainsod worked historically, if that was where the empirical evidence was. And with the Soviet political system inaccessible and secretive, archival work on the relatively recent past was much more satisfying than the usual Kremlin-watching guesswork of 'Kremlinology'.

The Smolensk archive gave unique insight into the workings of the Stalinist system of governance at a provincial level – a window into an otherwise closed world. What he found was a 'totalitarian façade' which 'concealed a host of inner contradictions'. This society was 'totalitarian' because of the state's far-reaching aspirations to completely mobilize the population for all-encompassing social transformation; it exerted a lot of effort to monitor, control and mobilize; but the state's abilities did not match its ambitions. The society Fainsod found refracted through the archival records was one of 'infinite complexity'. Terror went hand in hand with social mobility, which he saw as most important for regime support.[37]

Model building

In parallel with such empirical use of the concept, theoretical work also continued. In 1956, Arendt's friend Carl J. Friedrich, who had teamed up with the younger Zbigniew Brzezinski, destined to a brilliant career as a policy adviser in Washington, published *Totalitarian Dictatorship and Autocracy*. The book updated Arendt's theory, which really had been a post-mortem of Nazism. Reflecting the new context of the Cold War, now Stalinism, only recently deceased itself, became the main source for the abstraction. Compared to Arendt's philosophical and literary brilliance, the exhaustive empiricism of the Harvard Project, or Brzezinski's PhD adviser Fainsod's careful archival study, theirs was a relatively crude model. It lent itself to transformation into a straw man.

Like all other theorists of totalitarianism, Friedrich and Brzezisnki saw this type of dictatorship as a modern phenomenon ('there has never been anything quite like it before'). Established in both Nazi Germany and Stalin's Russia, the 'totalitarian syndrome' was defined by six aspects: (1) an official ideology 'covering all aspects of man's existence, to which everyone living in that society is supposed to adhere at least passively'; (2) a 'single mass party led typically by one man, the "dictator"'; (3) a 'system of terroristic police control'; (4) 'near-complete monopoly of control ... of all means of effective mass communication'; (5) a 'near-complete monopoly of control ... of all means of effective armed combat'; and (6) 'central control and direction of the entire economy through the bureaucratic co-ordination of its formerly independent corporate entities'.[38]

This model was relatively easily attacked. What society did not have an official ideology? Was the effective control of the means of violence not a basic definition of the state, at least as conceptualized by Max Weber? Did the Soviet government really control the entire economy? Did the Nazis? And what was 'near-complete control' as opposed to 'control' and lack thereof? Most damaging to their cause was the prediction that 'the totalitarian dictatorships will continue to become more total' – a sentence published in a year when Nikita Khrushchev gave his anti-Stalinist Secret Speech. Quite obviously, the Soviet Union was on a different trajectory than it should be, and critics of totalitarianism pointed to this fact again and again as a major argument against the concept.[39]

Other critiques, however, missed their mark. Friedrich and Brzezinski were not as naive as their critics sometimes believed. The 'totalitarian syndrome' was a theory of totalitarian government, not totalitarian society. The book included an entire part on 'islands of separateness': first of all the family, which provided 'a true oasis in the sea of totalitarian atomization'.[40] Like all serious scholars, they knew that totalitarian aspirations were incompletely realized and often had unintended consequences.

Mystification

Critics quickly forgot such complications. It would be the 'T-model', to use Ron Suny's term, that would become the main target of attacks on 'the totalitarian model': a version of Friedrich and

Brzezinski's relatively crude six-point 'syndrome', but purged of its complications and residual sophistications. However, such critique had less the Stalin years in view than the Soviet Union of the 1960s and 1970s, which the critics had experienced themselves. As the influential self-declared Marxist–Lewinist described the process:

> From the mid-1960s a younger generation of historians ... were travelling to the Soviet Union through expanded academic exchange programmes. The luckiest among them were privileged to work in heavily restricted archives, but all of them saw at first hand the intricacies, complexities and contradictions of everyday Soviet life that fitted poorly with the totalitarian image of ubiquitous fear and rigid conformity. ... the totalitarian approach neglected to note that in the actual experience of these societies the regime was unable to achieve the full expectation of the totalitarian model, that is, the absolute and total control over the whole of society and the atomisation of the population.

This critique confused both the vulgarized straw man with the social science concept, and the Soviet Union in the 1930s and 1940s with the Soviet Union in the much more 'vegetarian' 1960s. To further augment the temporal and conceptual muddle, these same scholars also encountered the then increasingly fashionable ideas of the Freudian-Hegelian-Marxists of the Frankfurt School, who cheerfully proclaimed that 'enlightenment is totalitarian'. The continental gravitas of such statements and the convoluted language of such 'high theory' led to deep rethinking of their own situation. Maybe US society was, really, totalitarian behind its liberal mask? Maybe Stalinism wasn't? Because the '"totalitarian" effects of modernity more generally were excluded from the original model?'[41]

The increasing resistance to the application of the term to Stalin's Soviet Union obscured the relatively recent origin of such opposition. Well into the 1970s, scholars on the academic Left embraced the concept wholeheartedly, at least as far as Stalinism was concerned. Robert Tucker, who by the 1986–87 *The Russian Review* debate presented himself as an early critic of the concept,[42] had originally used it affirmatively. In 1961, in one of the essays he cited in the 1980s as critiques of the term, he had written: 'The fact is that Stalinism was essentially identical with Hitlerism and the other expressions of fascism.'[43] Rather than a critique of the totalitarianism approach, this 1961 essay was an extreme formulation of one of its central theses – and it would reappear in his second volume on *Stalin in Power*.[44] In another essay in the same year – a response to Brzezinski – he restated the case, adding that a clearly defined concept of totalitarianism was 'virtually indispensable in today's political discourse'.[45] A few years later, in 1965, he then set out to define the 'authentic totalitarian dictator'. Again, this essay was an extension and a refinement of the approach, not its negation.[46]

Likewise, Stephen Cohen's work, as Hough pointed out in the debate, was hyper-totalitarian when it came to the Stalinist decades. Cohen was resistant 'even to the thought of studying phenomena in the Stalin period that might introduce subtleties into the analysis'.[47] At stake, for both Cohen and Tucker, was not if Stalinism was totalitarian, but if there was a generic link with Leninism. The critique of 'totalitarianism' referred to the periods prior to and following Stalinism, not the 1930s and 1940s. 'The theory of totalitarianism', wrote Tucker, 'has tended to equate not Stalinism and fascism but communism and fascism, and this is a mistake'.[48]

Both sides of the debate, thus, were engaged in a type of time switch, a version of synchronic history: the 'totalitarians' thought about the Stalin years when speaking about the present, and the 'revisionists' thought about the present when speaking about the Stalinist past. Paradoxically, this double shift made political scientists like Ulam the better historians of Stalinism, while 'revisionist' historians turned out to be the better analysts of contemporaneous Soviet politics.

Moshe Lewin was one of the latter. Like everybody else, he was drawn into this time warp caused by the turbulences of Cold War politics. Originally, he had employed the term affirmatively in the 1960s and 1970s to describe Stalinism.[49] But in the 1980s he began to lead the chorus of critics, claiming that it allegedly disregarded 'the social dimension'. No matter that Lewin had himself used the 'tool for the ideological battle produced by the cold war' in his earlier writing. Now he denounced it.[50] What changed his mind was the increasing realization of what kind of ideological work the term did in American domestic as well as foreign politics. From the early 1970s, American scholars began to argue that this concept was misleading, simplistic and emotional. It led to the idea that because 'appeasement' had failed with Hitler, it would do so again with the Soviet Union – a typical fallacy of thinking in analogies. It thus had right-wing implications domestically and opposed détente internationally. Hence, it needed to be resisted.[51]

Soon, this political logic captured the arguments about the historiography of Stalinism. After *The Russian Review* debate of 1986–87, a narrative established itself, which inscribed the totalitarian straw man constructed by Lewin into a narrative of generational succession. This narrative was proposed in Fitzpatrick's original essay, but was further refined by Roberta Manning in her response. First came the 'totalitarianists' – crude political scientists who denied any social dimension to Stalinism. Then came the 'first generation revisionists', to use Manning's term. They included Cohen, Lewin and Tucker. Although not mentioned by Manning, Fitzpatrick would classify herself in this generation as well. Her own cohort, Manning continued, constituted 'second generation revisionism' now moving from the 1920s into Stalinism proper.[52]

This narrative of a generational development of the study of Stalinism became widely accepted. It started to form something of a myth of origin – a story historians of Stalinism told themselves about their own past. It allowed them to understand their own work as part of an upward historical movement, from the darkness of totalitarianism to the light of revisionism.[53] This narrative was so strong that when members of the next cohort of scholars tried to define who or what they were, they called themselves 'post-revisionists' (Chapter 7).

Totalitarian social history

The narrative of social-science totalitarianism giving way to historical revisionism only to find its Hegelian synthesis in Foucaultian post-revisionism flattened out the complex history of the field. It required ignoring major scholars who did not fit the mould. Richard Pipes (1923–2018) and Robert Conquest (1917–2015) could probably be accommodated into a generational model as representatives of the older totalitarians, although they were historians not social scientists. Lewin did not fit, as he was of the 'totalitarian' generation but a revisionist before the term was invented. Geoffrey Hosking posed another challenge to the story. A social historian of Fitzpatrick's generation (she was born in 1941, he in 1942) he should have been a first-wave revisionist. Instead, he was an explicit and outspoken defender of the term 'totalitarianism'.

Part of this disconnect was geographic. Hosking was a London-based scholar and the totalitarian-revisionist paradigm was a deeply American story. In the United Kingdom, the situation was at times reversed: here 'the "nuanced" establishment' with a distinctly social history bent could be confronted by younger 'totalitarians' interested in political history.[54]

Hosking's scholarship was completely out of step with the American discussion. In chapter eight of his 1985 *History of the Soviet Union*, he combined what, according to the American polemic happening at the same time, were opposed approaches: totalitarianism and social history. Entitled 'Stalinist Society', it began with recounting the emergence of the totalitarian model. 'During Stalin's lifetime', he wrote,

> contemporary Western observers sought an explanation for the bizarre and horrifying phenomena of the late thirties by concentrating on the situation of the leader. In the absence of a vigilant press or parliamentary opposition, they hypothesized that he needed to combat corruption, sloth and incipient independence among his subordinates by instituting a 'permanent purge' in their ranks, periodically removing those who had taken root too comfortably, and replacing them with fresh appointees totally dependent on him personally. This 'permanent purge' was held to be the cardinal feature of a new kind of political system, 'totalitarianism'.[55]

After listing the six features of Friedrich and Brzezinski's 'syndrome', he asserted that 'in most respects' the model 'seems to me convincing', although incomplete: the totalitarian model 'did not describe the society as a whole', but only the centre of political rule. Not only assuming, erroneously, that 'workers, peasants and intelligentsia were passive objects of the terror', it 'did not even examine at all closely the kind of ruling stratum the leader would need to exercise his power'. Expressing what would be seen by most as a central revisionist thesis, he continued to stress that these 'various social strata were not simply passive'. They had 'their input, their goals and aspirations' and 'profoundly influenced the evolution of the system'. As a result of the permanent purge and the economic turmoil created by Stalin's policies, 'a new kind of society was taking shape, and one which proved in the long run not to be "permanently purgeable".[56] While his colleagues across the Atlantic were about to sharpen their pencils for heated polemics about whether or not there was a society in the Soviet Union, if the state should be left in or left out, or whether or not social history was an alternative to 'the totalitarian model', Hosking had already, quietly and carefully, inscribed social history into a totalitarian framework.

What did Hosking mean, in 1985, by 'Stalinist society'? At its core were the *vydvizhentsy*, or what he described as 'the technological graduates of the first Five Year Plan'. In an analysis reminiscent of Deutscher's *Stalin* (1949) and elaborated fully in Fitzpatrick's *Education and Social Mobility* (1979), Hosking stressed that these men, who 'formed a key role in the subsequent leadership of the Communist Party, right up to the very recent past', were to a considerable degree 'of working-class origin'.[57] After an extensive sketch of this 'embryonic ruling class', its culture and everyday life, Hosking moved on to family policy, education and ideology, implying a connection between the rise of the elite and the retrenchment in these spheres.[58]

For Hosking, 'Stalinist society' did not denote the social formation extant during the years of Stalin's dominance over it, but those structures that lent support to the dictatorship. His later thought remained consistent with this basic idea. In an article published in 2000, he described the *nomenklatura*, which regulated the level of each member of the elite within the state structure, as 'the backbone of society'. From each position on this list, the tentacles of patron–client relations spread throughout the population. Rather than relying on the well-worn distinction between a 'state' and a 'society', then, Hosking began to describe the Soviet social formation as a system of patronage networks originating in government and party, but extending far beyond them, blurring clear distinctions, but also leaving spaces and social relations outside this network of power.[59] Again, we can note affinities with Fitzpatrick's work.[60]

Scholars enmeshed in the US debate often did not notice such convergence. Lynne Viola, reviewing the American edition of the book,[61] focused on (minor) factual mistakes and omissions – both relatively easy targets in a work of this nature. She criticized the 'inordinate amount of space ... devoted to the history of any and all opposition movements..., the persecution of the Church and ethnic minorities, and government repression'. Ten and more years later Viola herself would make major contributions to these histories of repression and resistance, but in 1986 she ended scathingly: 'The book perpetuates cold-war views of the Soviet Union that counterpose an alien, oppressive state to a repressed, atomized populace. It fails to fulfil the great need of the profession for a balanced, thorough, and readable textbook on Soviet history.'[62] Others, however, disagreed. Mark von Hagen, by his own account part of the revisionists simply by matter of cohort,[63] proclaimed the book to be 'the best ... of the new offerings', an account 'refreshingly free of the obfuscating rhetoric of most Soviet and anti-Soviet sources', demonstrating 'how to write a political history that elevates society to an important role'.[64]

Hosking, too, remained unapologetic. While he would later avoid the term, as we shall see below, in 1990 he returned to the concept in *The Awakening of the Soviet Union*. Questioning the widespread notion that Soviet citizens were simply not sophisticated enough for democracy, he located the impediment to democratic reform in the Stalinist past: 'The obstacle ... is the political system handed down from Stalin, which has proved remarkably tenacious and resistant to change.' He again offered to call this system 'totalitarian' and again recounted the six points of Friedrich and Brzezinski, only to spend over a page listing the various critiques which have been levelled against the concept. None of these, however, convinced him. 'For a totalitarian society is neither demonic, nor unchanging, nor totally manipulated from above', he wrote, and the model was 'capable of affording us a more complete view of Soviet society than any alternative yet propounded'.[65]

Similarly, the 'final edition' of the *History of the Soviet Union* (1992) adopted the 1985 chapter unchanged, with only an updated bibliography. Its basic ideas re-emerged, in slightly revised form, in the history of the Russians within the Soviet Union. Here, the central chapter, as far as Stalinism is concerned, was entitled 'Two Russias Collide'. It focused on the 1930s and the emergence of the new society. While other English language historians had meanwhile picked up the term 'totalitarianism', Hosking replaced it with 'the surveillance state', a tip of the hat, maybe, to the rise of this term in studies of modern societies more generally.[66] Such

DEBATES ON STALINISM

linguistic niceties notwithstanding, the substance of the argument remained.

Revisionist totalitarianism

Hosking, then, a scholar of Fitzpatrick's generation, was anything but a 'first generation revisionist'. A 'totalitarian', he nevertheless wrote a history which did not ignore forces outside the state, did not believe that the state had total control, and did not assume that this society was unchanging. In essence, he wrote a sociopolitical history of a totalitarian society – something of a contradiction in terms, if the terms are those of the generational narrative established in the mid-1980s. The closer one looks, then, the more this story falls apart.

To begin with Fitzpatrick's work: we have already seen in Chapter 5 how some of her themes were foreshadowed in Stalin biographies, often in those working under a 'totalitarian' framework. Education, social mobility and regime support were also themes the Harvard Project investigated.[67] Fainsod, too, had stressed the importance of 'the creation of a new class of beneficiaries' for regime stability and regime support.[68] No wonder, then, that Fitzpatrick cited the term 'totalitarianism' affirmatively in her textbook. Her later interest in the mechanics of everyday life was also a theme prefigured here. And the work of the 'cohort' of younger scholars she identified can also be understood within the framework of a sophisticated version of totalitarianism, as represented by the HPSS scholars or Fainsod's Smolensk volume.[69] Viola moved from a study of those who supported the regime's onslaught on the peasantry to the peasant victims themselves, followed by Stalin's executioners. Arch Getty revised his views on the Great Terror, an interpretation much more in line with totalitarian views. Like Viola, he began to study the perpetrators of the Terror. His interest in informal practices within the Stalinist political system, explored in his 2013 book on *Practicing Stalinism*, elaborated a central theme of the Harvard Interview Project: how the Soviet system really worked.[70]

As far as the Great Terror was concerned, nobody found an empirically viable alternative to the thesis that it came from above and was directed by Stalin personally. Once unleashed, it developed its own dynamic. Workers denounced their bosses, collective farmers those who had collectivized them, and everybody who was arrested (and often tortured) fingered anybody around them, casting the net wider and wider.[71] The searchlight the investigations of the Terror trained on local circumstances uncovered all kinds of mutual protection networks, which looked like conspiracies, but in reality were necessary to run the country. Dynamics between the centre and the periphery thus played a role in the widening of the Terror, as did the recognition of how widespread hostility to the regime was. This threat was magnified by Stalin's information-gathering mechanism and the institutionalized paranoia of the system of surveillance and control.[72] So while the widening of the purge was fuelled by social and cultural dynamics, these could only unfold because the Terror was decreed from above in the first place. Once Stalin decided that enough was enough, he ordered the purge ended. The violence stopped.

Looking away from the state, and focusing on the level of the everyday life of ordinary citizens, also revealed the centrality of the state's total ambitions. Fitzpatrick's book on ordinary life under Stalin was about the interactions between the state and individual citizens.[73] Labour history of Stalinism – another potentially 'revisionist' approach – also showed the clash between the state and the life-world of its citizens. Forced industrialization led to resistance not just by peasants, but also by workers.[74] However, in the long-term, Stalinist policing destroyed the ability of workers to act in concert. As a result, they switched to individual acts of resistance and accommodation: shifting workplaces frequently, pilfering, slowing down the pace of production. Their bosses could try to lessen these through incentive schemes, better housing, increased pay, but given the severe scarcity of everything in Stalin's economy, these could only be applied to a small aristocracy, the shock workers and Stakhanovites. In the end, the only way to react to the various means by which the workers tried to make do in the Stalinist system of production was more of the same: tighter regulations, increasingly severe property laws – an escalation of state repression of the working class, which was only lessened after Stalin's death. These social dynamics were effects of the top-down, state-led, non-market-driven dynamics of Stalinist industrialization which suppressed civilian consumption in order to push the building of heavy industry and, ultimately, armaments. These empirical facts can be understood easily within the frame of the totalitarian approach of the Harvard Project or Fainsod's Smolensk book.[75]

The Thurston Affair

How strongly revisionist work on Stalinism was furthering the framework drawn up by totalitarianism scholars was demonstrated when one historian broke ranks and tried to deliver a truly 'revisionist' work. Drawing on newly available archival materials, Robert Thurston argued for a radical rethinking of the 1930s: Stalin did not have a plan for the Terror, but reacted in ad hoc ways to events; the Terror was not a mass phenomenon, and the majority of the population was not afraid; most ordinary Soviets loved Stalin because they benefited from his rule; and the mass heroism in the Great Patriotic War demonstrated that this was all so.[76]

The reaction was swift and brutal. The liberal anti-communist *New Leader* compared Thurston to Holocaust denier David Irving;[77] the *Times Literary Supplement* unleashed Robert Conquest, who diagnosed a typical case of revisionism, a 'school of thought that has accepted falsification, dismissed established evidence and misinterpreted newer materials'. The totalitarian war horse trampled all over the argument, its factual mistakes and the 'honest naivity' of the author.[78] The *New York Times* followed suit, in the process getting the history of revisionism spectacularly wrong.[79]

Few Soviet Union specialists were intrigued. At best, the book set up 'a straw man' but could be 'commended' for the 'attempt to account for the agonizing paradoxes of the Stalinist state'.[80] Another friendly critique called the book 'unusual', 'unconventional' and 'iconoclastic', raising 'ample food for thought'.[81] Others were more direct. 'An apology for Stalin', was the curt summary of one colleague.[82] A 'fundamentally flawed' book, wrote another. Thurston had gone 'overboard' in his 'revision of received wisdom' and argued against a straw man: 'No scholarly proponents of the "totalitarianism" model would confuse the regimes' desire to control their subjects with what actually occurred.'[83]

And this confusion was indeed the problem: Thurston – who had been trained by William G. Rosenberg at the University of Michigan, had discussed his earlier work for years with Manning,[84] and had corresponded with Suny, Getty and Gabor Rittersporn about this new project[85] – had taken the mythologized 'totalitarian model' as his starting point. This model was a 'composite opponent', as one reviewer termed it, a nemesis to be opposed at all costs. This confrontational approach to an inexistent historiographical other corrupted the entire book, despite its wide-ranging research and often interesting material.[86]

The historiographical chimera of the 'totalitarian model' was, of course, not Thurston's invention. It was the collective fantasy social historians had developed about the enemy for decades, prior to this affair. Thurston's mistake was that he took this fantasy seriously, rather than taking it for what it was: a story one told friends and doctoral students about the past to explain one's position in the present.

Given how deeply rooted his work was in 'revisionist' mythology, Thurston probably had a right to imagine that fellow revisionists would leap to his defence. With a few exceptions, however, they sat on their hands.[87] Many were clearly embarrassed by the book. The only major 'revisionist' scholar working in the United States who stood up for Thurston's tome was Fitzpatrick. But she made it quite clear that she was doing so on principle (academic freedom of inquiry and scholarly free speech). Like nearly everybody else, she disagreed fundamentally with the conclusions of the book, which came close to whitewashing Stalin's regime.[88]

Thus ostracized from all sides, Thurston eventually left the field. Maybe in order to deal with his experiences he wrote, first, a book on witch-hunts, then a volume on lynching and mob murder.[89] When, as a doctoral student at the University of Chicago in the early 2000s, I attended a Russian history workshop he hosted, I met an embittered man who felt betrayed by his comrades. Eventually he retreated to drinking coffee and writing about it, a fulfilling empirical quest: 'Just when you think you know something about coffee', he described his new pursuit, 'you become aware of how much else you might explore.'[90]

Notes

1 John Connelly, 'Defunct Theory, Useful Word', *Kritika: Explorations in Russian and Eurasian History* 11, no. 4 (2010): 819–35.
2 Herbert J. Spiro, 'Totalitarianism', in: *International Encyclopedia of the Social Sciences*, ed. David L. Sills, vol. 16 (New York, 1968), 112.
3 Ronald G. Suny, *The Soviet Experiment: Russia, the USSR, and the Successor States*. 2nd ed. (Oxford, 2011), 395.

4   Wendy Goldman in *The American Historical Review* 116, no. 3 (2011): 758–61, quotation: 761.
5   Ivan Krastev and Stephen Holmes, 'An Autopsy of Managed Democracy', *Journal of Democracy* 23, no. 3 (2012): 33–45. On Piłsudski's Poland as 'guided democracy', see Antony Polonsky, *Politics in Independent Poland 1921–1939: The Crisis of Constitutional Government* (Oxford, 1972), vii. On Putin's Russia, inter alia: Timothy J. Colton, *Russia: What Everyone Needs to Know* (Oxford, 2016), 145–50; Łukasz Kondraciuk, 'Is Putinism Sustainable?', *New Eastern Europe* (March–April 2018): 21–26, here: 23.
6   Abbott Gleason, *Totalitarianism: The Inner History of the Cold War* (Oxford, 1995), 13–30, quotations: 14, 19. Leon Trotsky, *The Revolution Betrayed: What is the Soviet Union and Where is it going?* (New York, 1972 [original: 1937]), 95.
7   For Victor Serge, see his *From Lenin to Stalin* (New York, 1937), e.g. 51. On the forgotten history of German socialist anti-totalitarianists, see William David Jones, *The Lost Debate: German Socialist Intellectuals and Totalitarianism* (Urbana, 1999). On Hannah Arendt as 'a maverick thinker of considerable creativity who feared that the United States might itself move in a totalitarian direction', see Alan M. Wald, *The New York Intellectuals: The Rise and Decline of the Anti-Stalinist Left from the 1930s to the 1980s* (Chapel Hill, 1987), 269. Outside of this left-wing anti-totalitarian discourse, in 1930s America the term 'totalitarianism' referred to Germany and at times Fascist Italy, rather than to Stalin's Soviet Union. See Benjamin L. Alpers, *Dictators, Democracy, and American Public Culture: Envisioning the Totalitarian Enemy, 1920s–1950s* (Chapel Hill, 2003), 64–73. On the emerging inclusion of the Soviet Union see Alpers, *Dictators, Democracy, and American Public Culture*, 73–76.
8   My discussion builds on Sabine Dullin, 'How to Wage Warfare without Going to War? Stalin's 1939 War in the Light of Other Contemporary Aggressions', *Cahiers du Monde russe* 52, no. 2–3 (2011): 221–43, here: 223–26.
9   Les K. Adler and Thomas G. Paterson, 'Red Fascism: The Merger of Nazi Germany and Soviet Russia in the American Image of Totalitarianism, 1930's–1950's', *The American Historical Review* 75, no. 4 (1970): 1046–64, here: 1049–50. See also Gleason, *Totalitarianism*, 51–54.
10 The papers were published as 'Symposium on the Totalitarian State', *Proceedings of the American Philosophical Society* 82, no. 1 (1940). Carlton J. H. Hayes, 'The Novelty of Totalitarianism in the History of Western Civilization', *Proceedings of the American Philosophical Society* 82, no. 1 (1940), 91–102.
11 See, in particular: 'Stalin – Hitler's Quartermaster' (2 September 1939), in: *Writings of Leon Trotsky (1939–40)*. 2nd ed. (New York, 1973), 76–80; 'The German–Soviet Alliance', (4 September 1939), in: *Writings of Leon Trotsky (1939–40)*, 81–83.
12 Leon Trotsky, 'The USSR in War' (written 25 September 1939), https://www.marxists.org/archive/trotsky/1939/09/ussr-war.htm (accessed 24 May 2018). He had already denounced Stalin's regime as totalitarian in his 1937 book: Trotsky, *The Revolution Betrayed*, 95, 102, 251. He ran a similar line in other writings in 1937 and 1938, for example: 'It is high time to launch a world offensive against Stalinism. An Open Letter to All Workers' Organizations' (2

November 1937); 'Statement to Journalists on the Dewey Verdict' (13 December 1937); 'Eight Ministers' (1 March 1938); 'Four Doctors Knew too Much' (3 March 1938); 'Stalin's Article on World Revolution' (9 March 1938); 'A Key to the Russian Trials' (10 March 1938); or 'Hitler's Austria coup aided by Moscow Trial' (12 March 1938); all in: *Writings of Leon Trotsky (1937–38)*. 2nd ed. (New York, 1976), 28–33, 95–103, 189–90, 206–09, 241–45, 247–52, 262–64.
13   Trotsky, 'Why I consented to appear before the Dies committee' (11 December 1939), *Writings of Leon Trotsky (1939–40)*, 132–35, here: 133.
14   *Writings of Leon Trotsky (1939–40)*, 96.
15   *Writings of Leon Trotsky (1939–40)*, 122.
16   Leon Trotsky, *Stalin: An Appraisal of the Man and His Influence* (New York, 1967), 115, 284, 421; also: 378, 421.
17   Fredric Warburg, *An Occupation for Gentlemen* (London, 1959), 270–71.
18   Boris Souvarine, *Stalin: A Critical Survey of Bolshevism* (New York, 1939), 512, 557.
19   Souvarine, *Stalin*, 616, 671.
20   Souvarine, *Stalin*, 673.
21   Franz Borkenau, *The Totalitarian Enemy* (London, 1940), 13. Other German émigrés also played with the notion of 'red and brown fascism' at the same time. See Jones, *The Lost Debate*, 109–14.
22   Franz Borkenau, *Pareto* (London, 1936), 196.
23   Borkenau, *The Totalitarian Enemy*, passim, quotations: 197, 198, 209, 229.
24   Borkenau, *The Totalitarian Enemy*, 11, 13–14, 15, 17. Cf. also Mario Kessler, 'Between Communism and Anti-Communism. Franz Borkenau', in: *German Scholars in Exile*, ed. Axel Fair-Schulz and Mario Kessler (Plymouth, 2011); William David Jones, 'Toward a Theory of Totalitarianism: Franz Borkenau's Pareto', *Journal of the History of Ideas* 53, no. 3 (1992): 455–66; and William David Jones, 'The Path from Weimar Communism to the Cold War. Franz Borkenau and "The Totalitarian Enemy"', in: *Totalitatismus: Eine Ideenge-schichte des 20. Jahrhunderts*, ed. Alfons Söllner, Ralf Walkenhaus and Karin Wieland (Berlin, 1997), 35–52.
25   Borkenau, *The Totalitarian Enemy*, 240, 241.
26   Borkenau, *The Totalitarian Enemy*, 243–44. For a recent reassessment of the ideological links between fascism, Stalinism and the New Deal, see Wolfgang Schivelbusch, *Three New Deals: Reflections on Roosevelt's America, Mussolini's Italy, and Hitler's Germany, 1933–1939* (New York, 2006).
27   See Adler and Paterson, 'Red Fascism', 1051–57; on 'Uncle Joe', 1060. Also: Gleason, *Totalitarianism*, 54–71, and Alpers, *Dictators, Democracy, and American Public Culture*.
28   Louis Fischer, *The Life and Death of Stalin* (New York, 1952), 31, 33, 49, 41–44, 47, 61, 76, 78.
29   Adler and Paterson, 'Red Fascism', 1046.
30   Adler and Paterson, 'Red Fascism', 1064.
31   Hannah Arendt, *The Origins of Totalitarianism* (New York, 1951). Borkenau made it into the bibliography: 442.
32   For more on HPSS, see Mark Edele, 'Soviet Society, Social Structure, and Everyday Life. Major Frameworks Reconsidered', *Kritika: Explorations in*

Russian and Eurasian History 8, no. 2 (2007): 349–73, here: 352–58. On the history of the project, see David C. Engerman, *Know Your Enemy: The Rise and Fall of America's Soviet Experts* (Oxford, 2009), chapter 2.

33 For bibliographies of these specialized studies, see A. Bauer, Alex Inkeles and Clyde Kuckhohn, *How the Soviet System Works: Cultural, Psychological, and Social Themes* (Cambridge, Mass., 1956), 252–56; and Alex Inkeles and Raymond Bauer, *The Soviet Citizen: Daily Life in a Totalitarian Society* (Cambridge, Mass., 1961), 252–56. The transcripts are available at https://library.harvard.edu/collections/hpsss/index.html (accessed 19 December 2019).

34 Bauer, Inkeles and Kluckhohn, *How the Soviet System Works*, 26.

35 Bauer, Inkeles and Kluckhohn, *How the Soviet System Works*, 20.

36 Jerry F. Hough, 'The "Dark Forces," the Totalitarian Model, and Soviet History', *The Russian Review* 46, no. 4, 1987, 397–403, here: 398.

37 Merle Fainsod, *Smolensk under Soviet Rule* (New York, 1958), 447, 452, 454 and passim.

38 Carl J. Friedrich and Zbigniew K. Brzezinski, *Totalitarian Dictatorship and Autocracy* (Cambridge, Mass., 1956), 7, 9–10. On Brzezinski, see David C. Engerman, 'The Fall of Totalitarianism and the Rise of Zbigniew Brzezinski', and Stephen F. Szabo, 'The Professor', both in: *Zbig: The Strategy and Statecraft of Zbigniew Brzezinski*, ed. Charles Gati (Baltimore, 2013), 27–41 and 207–14.

39 Friedrich and Brzezinski, *Totalitarian Dictatorship*, 300.

40 Friedrich and Brzezinski, *Totalitarian Dictatorship*, 239–89, quotation: 247.

41 Ronald G. Suny, 'Reading Russia and the Soviet Union in the Twentieth Century: How the "West" Wrote its History of the USSR', in: *The Cambridge History of Russia*, ed. Ronald G. Suny (Cambridge, 2006), 5–64, here: 27–28. On the alleged totalitarianism of the Enlightenment ('Aufklärung ist totalitär'), see Max Horkheimer and Theodor W. Adorno, *Dialektik der Aufklärung: Philosophische Fragmente* (Frankfurt a. M., 1995), 12. This point of view was made particularly popular by Herbert Marcuse, *One-Dimensional Man: Studies in the Ideology of Advanced Industrial Society* (Boston, 1991), originally published in 1964.

42 Robert C. Tucker, 'The Stalin Period as an Historical Problem', *The Russian Review* 46, no. 4 (1987): 424–27, here: 424.

43 Robert C. Tucker, 'Towards a Comparative Politics of Movement-Regimes', *The American Political Science Review* 55, no. 2 (1961): 281–89, here: 282.

44 Robert C. Tucker, *Stalin in Power: The Revolution from Above, 1928–1941* (New York, 1990), 581. See also Chapter 5.

45 Robert C. Tucker, 'The Question of Totalitarianism', *Slavic Review* 20, no. 3 (1961): 377–82, here: 379.

46 Robert C. Tucker, 'The Dictator and Totalitarianism', *World Politics* 17, no. 4 (1965): 555–83.

47 Hough, 'The "Dark Forces"', 398.

48 Tucker, 'Towards a Comparative Politics', 282.

49 See Chapter 2.

50 Paul Buskovitch, '[Interview with] Moshe Lewin', in: *Visions of History*, ed. Henry Abelove et al. (Manchester, 1983), 281–308, here: 293–94; Moshe Lewin, *The Soviet Century* (London, 2005), 273–74.

TOTALITARIANISM AND REVISIONISM

51 See Adler and Paterson, 'Red Fascism' for a particularly strong example of this argument. On the dangers of analogous historical thinking, see Yuen Foong Khong, *Analogies at War: Korea, Munich, Dien Bien Phu, and the Vietnam Decisions of 1965* (Princeton, 1992).
52 Roberta T. Manning, 'State and Society in Stalinist Russia', *The Russian Review* 46, no. 4 (1987): 407–411, here: 407. For Fitzpatrick's self-location in the 'middle-aged cohort' of Cohen, see Sheila Fitzpatrick, 'Afterword: Revisionism Revisited', *The Russian Review* 45, no. 4 (1986): 409–13, here: 409.
53 For an intelligent version of such a history see Suny, 'Reading Russia'.
54 Mark Edele, *Stalinist Society 1928–1953* (Oxford, 2011), 231.
55 Geoffrey Hosking, *A History of the Soviet Union* (London, 1985), 205.
56 Hosking, *A History of the Soviet Union*, 205–06.
57 The bibliography to this chapter – the book has no notes – lists Fitzpatrick's edited volume *Cultural Revolution in Russia* (1978) as further reading and *Education and Social Mobility* (1979) as 'a particularly thorough and comprehensive treatment of the subject'. Hosking, *A History of the Soviet Union*, 206, 207, 489, 498, 499.
58 Hosking, *A History of the Soviet Union*, 209–12.
59 Geoffrey Hosking, 'Patronage and the Russian State', *Slavonic and East European Review* 78, no. 2 (2000): 301–20, quotation: 314.
60 Sheila Fitzpatrick, 'Intelligentsia and Power. Client–Patron Relations in Stalin's Russia', in: *Stalinismus vor dem Zweiten Weltkrieg: Neue Wege der Forschung*, ed. Manfred Hildermeier (Munich, 1998), 35–53; and Sheila Fitzpatrick, '*Blat* in Stalin's Time', in: *Bribery and Blat in Russia: Negotiating Reciprocity from the Middle Ages to the 1990s*, ed. Stephen Lovell, Alena Ledeneva and Andrei Rogachevskii (New York, 2000), 166–82.
61 In the United States, the book was marketed under the title *The First Socialist Society: A History of the Soviet Union from Within* (Cambridge, Mass., 1985).
62 Lynne Viola in *Russian Review* 45, 3 (1986): 340–41.
63 'I was caught up in the graduate school cohort that was witness to the revisionist fight.' Mark von Hagen, 'War, Peace and Cold War Area Studies', *NewsNet: News of the Association for Slavic, East European and Eurasian Studies* 51, no. 1 (2011): 1–6, here: 3.
64 Mark von Hagen in *Slavic Review* 46, no. 1 (1987): 118–22, here: 119.
65 Geoffrey Hosking, *The Awakening of the Soviet Union* (Cambridge, Mass., 1990), 5–7, quotation: 7.
66 Geoffrey A. Hosking, *Rulers and Victims: The Russians in the Soviet Union* (Cambridge, Mass., 2006), 117.
67 See Edele, 'Soviet Society, Social Structure, and Everyday Life', 355–56.
68 Fainsod, *Smolensk under Soviet Rule*, 452–54 – this is what the book concluded on!
69 See Chapter 3.
70 See Chapter 2.
71 Sheila Fitzpatrick, *Everyday Stalinism: Ordinary Life in Extraordinary Times: Soviet Russia in the 1930s* (New York and Oxford, 1999), chapter 8; Sheila Fitzpatrick, *Stalin's Peasants: Resistance and Survival in the Russian Village*

after Collectivization (Oxford, 1994), chapter 11; Wendy Z. Goldman, *Terror and Democracy in the Age of Stalin: The Social Dynamics of Repression* (Cambridge, 2007).
72 James R. Harris, *The Great Urals: Regionalism and the Evolution of the Soviet System* (Ithaca, 1996); Paul Hagenloh, *Stalin's Police: Public Order and Mass Repression in the USSR, 1926–1941* (Baltimore, 2009); David R. Shearer, *Policing Stalin's Socialism: Repression and Social Order in the Soviet Union, 1924–1953* (New Haven, 2009); Edele, *Stalinist Society*, 114–19; James Harris, *The Great Fear: Stalin's Terror of the 1930s* (Oxford, 2016).
73 Fitzpatrick, *Everyday Stalinism*.
74 Lynne Viola, *Peasant Rebels under Stalin: Collectivization and the Culture of Peasant Resistance* (Oxford, 1999); Jeffrey J. Rossman, *Worker Resistance under Stalin: Class and Revolution on the Shop Floor* (Cambridge, 2005).
75 Donald Filtzer, *Soviet Workers and Stalinist Industrialization: The Formation of Modern Soviet Production Relations, 1928–1941* (Armonk, 1986); Hiroaki Kuromiya, *Stalin's Industrial Revolution: Politics and Workers, 1928–1932* (Cambridge, 1988); Lewis H. Siegelbaum, *Stakhanovism and the Politics of Productivity in the USSR, 1935–1941* (Cambridge, 1988); Donald Filtzer, *Soviet Workers and Late Stalinism: Labour and the Restoration of the Stalinist System after World War II* (Cambridge, 2002); Donald Filtzer, 'Atomization, "Molecularization", and Attenuated Solidarity: Workers' Responses to State Repression under Stalin', in: *Stalinist Subjects: Individual and System in the Soviet Union and the Comintern, 1929–1953*, ed. Brigitte Studer (Zürich, 2006), 99–116.
76 Robert W. Thurston, *Life and Terror in Stalin's Russia 1934–1941* (New Haven, 1996).
77 Roger Draper, 'Spring time for Hitler – and Stalin', *The New Leader* 79, no. 5 (1996): 3.
78 Robert Conquest, 'Small Terror, Few Dead', *Times Literary Supplement* (31 May 1996): 3ff. Conquest republished the same piece in *National Review* (15 July 1996), 45–48.
79 Adam Hochschild, 'Cleaning Up Stalin's Act', *New York Times* (8 May 1996): A23.
80 Nellie H. Ohr on *H-Russia* (April 1998) http://www.h-net.org/reviews/showrev.php?id=1880 (accessed 29 May 2018).
81 Andrea Chandler, *Political Science Quarterly* 112, no. 4 (1997): 725–26.
82 Vladimir Andrle, in *The Russian Review* 57, no. 1 (1998): 144–45.
83 Kees Boterbloem, *Canadian Journal of History* 32, no. 2 (1997): 274–75. A similar critique about knocking down a straw man of one's own making came from Geoffrey Hosking, in *The Journal of Modern History* 69, no. 4 (1997): 897–98.
84 See the acknowledgments in his dissertation book: Robert W. Thurston, *Liberal City, Conservative State: Moscow and Russia's Urban Crisis, 1906–1914* (Oxford, 1987), vii.
85 Thurston, *Life and Terror*, xi–xii.
86 Abbott Gleason in *The Journal of Interdisciplinary History* 28, no. 1 (1997): 133–35.

87 Positive reviews came nearly exclusively from the UK. See Chris Ward in *Slavic Review* 56, no. 1 (1997): 150–51; Alan Wood in *Labour History Review* 62, no. 1 (1997): 83–85.
88 Sheila Fitzpatrick in *American Historical Review* 102, no. 4 (1997): 1193–94.
89 Robert W. Thurston, *Witch, Wicce, Mother Goose: The Rise and Fall of Witch Hunts in Europe and North America* (London, 2001); Robert W. Thurston, *Lynching: American Mob Murder in Global Perspective* (Farnham, 2011).
90 Robert W. Thurston, Jonathan Morris and Shawn Steiman (eds), *Coffee: A Comprehensive Guide to the Bean, the Beverage, and the Industry* (Lanham, 2018), xv. Thurston's personal web page describes him now as 'coffee entrepreneur and historian', https://robertwthurston.wordpress.com (accessed 29 May 2018).

7
After revisionism

If revisionism did not break the original frame built by the totalitarian pioneers of the study of Stalinism, neither did subsequent scholarship. In the 1990s, historians became interested in the subjective aspect of Stalinism: how was it experienced by individuals? A related group explored a comparative angle: how different was Stalinism to other modern societies? Others moved into the post-war years and soon the Second World War. Finally, 'totalitarianism' was reinvented as a term, a revival which was eased by the compatibility of most 'revisionist' and 'post-revisionist' scholarship with the original approach, a phenomenon sketched in the previous chapter.

Waiting for Foucault

In 1995, Stephen Kotkin published a revised version of his doctoral thesis. We have met Kotkin already as a younger scholar in Chapter 2, where he participated in Moshe-Lewin-inspired Seminars, and in Chapter 5 as an elder statesman who authored a recent Stalin biography. His dissertation book was an exercise in urban history, bringing together the perspectives from above and from below in an intriguing portrait of the building of the largest steel plant in the world in the middle of nowhere. Kotkin had managed to get access to some archival files already in the 1980s, and augmented this source base for the book version. He could not consult the archive of the Communist Party of Magnitogorsk or NKVD files, however. This 'failure' he found 'especially regrettable', together with 'the failure to uncover any diaries or personal letters'. But such holes in the source base would not matter much in the reception of the book, whose greatest achievement was not new empirical evidence but the perspective it brought to its topic. *Magnetic Mountain* established Kotkin as the founder of a movement of self-consciously 'post-revisionist' historians of Stalinism.[1]

Kotkin was an outsider in the field. Born in 1959, he was too young for either the totalitarian or the revisionist school of thought. He was not part of any discernible cohort and did not partake in any of the transnational displacements which had animated much of the earlier historiography. Hailing from New Jersey, his trajectory was unconvoluted. After completing his BA at the University of Rochester in 1981 he moved on to Berkeley, where he received an MA in 1983 and a PhD in 1988. During his Californian years, Russian history was taught at Berkeley by the Marxian labour historian Reginald E. Zelnik (1936–2004) and the conservative Martin Malia (1924–2004). Zelnik's teaching had lured Kotkin into Russian history, Malia's into the Soviet period.[2]

Both teachers left their marks. Zelnik's influence showed in the interest in the living conditions of the workers in Magnitogorsk and the ways they made do. Kotkin's politics, however, were much closer to Malia, who would have felt little to quibble with the claim that the crisis of the post-Soviet state was axiomatic for all welfare states. This thesis was a variant of Malia's argument that Soviet history showed what happened if you let the Enlightenment run amok.[3]

As important was another encounter Kotkin had at Berkeley: with French philosopher Michel Foucault, whom he met as a graduate student in 1982–83. A one-time member of the French Communist Party who had left in disgust over the anti-Semitic campaign of late Stalinism, Foucault had become famous for his work on the histories of madness, the prison, and other institutions asserting discipline over individuals and punishing dissenting bodies. In the early 1980s, Foucault filled Californian lecture halls to the brim, with overflow crowds clamouring to get in to hear the visiting Parisian sage utter esoteric sentences about pleasure and power, bodies and knowledge. Intellectually obscure, Foucault was nevertheless an immensely accessible professor, holding open office hours and taking his brighter students to lunch, coffee or dinner. Like many others, Kotkin was impressed by Foucault's personality and smitten by his work. Part of a group of students closely interacting with Foucault, he was among the editors of a Berkeley-based publication entirely devoted to the philosopher. While most historians reserve the final sentence of their acknowledgments to parents and lovers, partners and children, Kotkin ended on thanking the philosopher. *Magnetic Mountain* was thus dedicated 'To M. F'.[4]

A philosopher to whom the Gulag had 'remained a paradox' was an odd choice for theoretical guidance in the study of Stalinism. What he provided beyond sheer force of personality was the chance to assume a position outside the established squabbles of American Sovietology. Power, to Foucault, was not something that came 'from above' or bubbled up 'from below'. Disseminated through discourses, practices and institutions, constituting itself inside individuals and between them, it was everywhere. Diffuse, enacted and fluctuating, power was productive as well as coercive. Hence, to the student of Foucault, posing the questions in the way revisionists and totalitarians had done just showed their lack of sophistication.[5]

Kotkin also mobilized two other then-fashionable French theorists: Michel de Certeau and Pierre Bourdieu. The latter's interest in how constraining social, economic or cultural structures become the basis of individual agency, and how individual action in turn reproduces (and partially changes) the overall structure, resonated strongly with Kotkin's own preoccupations. De Certeau's distinction between 'the grand strategies of the state' and the 'little tactics of the habitat' structured the overall book: the state would draw up the field of power within which the individuals moved tactically. The 'intentions, programs, and policies' of the Soviet state, wrote Kotkin, 'were responsible for the fields of action within which the behaviour of individuals took place'. It was 'within these fields of action that we must look to see how the intentions were played, how the programs were implemented, and what their consequences were'. Only within the context of the state's strategies was it possible to understand 'what kinds of lives people were able to lead, and how they understood their lives'. So far, so 'totalitarian'. But the interaction between the state and the individual was not just repressive. While the available options of Magnitogorsk's workers were constrained by the overall attempt to build both socialism and a huge steel plant, they were also enabled by them to build their own lives. The state, in turn, relied on the actions of a multitude of individual citizens to exist and persist, a rather 'revisionist' thesis. The result of this dialectic of strategies and tactics was 'Stalinist civilization': a distinct form of life which combined the state plans with individual and group improvisation.[6]

Chapter five of *Magnetic Mountain* was a stroke of genius. Entitled 'Speaking Bolshevik' it coined a phrase which would be the most-cited legacy of the book. It denoted the process by which Soviet citizens used the official language, often to their own ends. In order to get ahead in the socialist city, they needed to learn how to use the official jargon, whether they believed in it or not. This phenomenon had been described before. But with 'speaking Bolshevik' it acquired a snappy label. Moreover, it could be used by all sides of the debate about whether or not Soviet citizens believed in official discourse: Kotkin left the answer open. While the standard totalitarian notion pointed to the force of official propaganda to shape people's world view; while the Harvard Project had concluded that those Soviet citizens who made a career in the official structure eventually began to internalize the words and concepts they had to use on a daily basis, while those exploited by it remained critical; and while Deutscher, Fitzpatrick and Hosking assumed that those who benefited from Stalinist affirmative action and the purges came to reciprocate for their careers with loyalty to Stalin and his regime, Kotkin declared the question moot. Whether or not Soviet citizens believed what they said did not matter. The mere practice of speaking Bolshevik reproduced Bolshevism.

The heroic pose of assuming a position outside established historical discourse on Stalinism required a concerted effort at forgetting one's predecessors. As we have seen in Chapter 1, many of the revisionists had a fairly Foucaultian vision of power, without using the philosopher's jargon.[7] Conversely, Kotkin's notion that it was the state which set out the parameters of everyday life and that individuals could only react with 'tactics' to this great strategy; the notion that political action began 'from above' but would be changed when implemented 'below', was reminiscent not only of revisionist work of the earlier decade, but also of the earlier totalitarians. Scraping away the latest theoretical sauce revealed a dish not unlike the one the old 'totalitarian' Merle Fainsod had cooked decades earlier. The main difference was the focus of interest: Fainsod was more interested in the extent to which state control worked, while Kotkin was intrigued by the possibility that state action created the precondition for individual agency.[8]

Compared to the work of both the Harvard Interview Project and revisionist social history, Kotkin's book had a remarkably impoverished theory of society. State power was everywhere. Individuals simply reacted. Their only meaningful relationship was with the state. That in real life the inhabitants of Magnitogorsk also had ties to other citizens, bonds to their spouses and children, and emotional links to their families back in the villages they came from; that they brought with them to the building site in the Urals their preconceptions, beliefs, and experiences which originated in long and complex histories independent of the Soviet state's; and that they had notions of themselves as gendered beings with an ethnic, regional and local identity, forced Kotkin to introduce residual categories into his analysis: the categories of social history his adviser Zelnik had taught him about. These, of course, were also the categories of the 'revisionism' he tried to overcome with the help of Malia and Foucault.[9]

Post-Kotkinism

Kotkin's book, then, was a reformulation of earlier approaches in a new language. But recasting old debates in different words can help engender novel ideas. Kotkin's book opened important avenues for 'post-revisionist' work. The term he had coined – 'speaking Bolshevik' – became a starting point for a younger group of scholars who radicalized his approach into a field of research known as 'Stalinist subjectivity'.[10]

The most outstanding scholar of this trend was Jochen Hellbeck. His discovery of unpublished diaries from the 1930s allowed work on how Stalinism felt from the inside.[11] In what amounted to a foundational manifesto of the new research trend, Hellbeck and his co-author Igal Halfin pointed to inconsistencies in Kotkin's framework and argued that it needed to be purified to become internally consistent. Attention had to shift from the overall system to the experience of ordinary Soviets. To re-establish 'the Stalinist subject' as 'an ideological agent in its own right' became the mission of this new research.[12] If successful, it would have liberated Kotkin's approach from its inconsistencies, but stripped his account of life in Magnitogorsk of its empirical richness. As an overall framework to rethink Stalinism, this project failed. Along the way, however, it produced some of the most exciting histories written in the 1990s and early 2000s.

Starting with the manifesto he had penned with Halfin, Hellbeck produced a series of essays, and eventually a book on diary writing in the 1930s. His assumptions evolved as he learned more and more about life in pre-war Stalinism. At first he assumed that the cultural universe available to Soviet citizens was restricted to official discourse, which surrounded the subject and hence became internalized – a process he understood as an active struggle to remake the own self. Soviet citizens, Hellbeck maintained, even those who were victimized by the regime, believed deeply in Soviet socialism; they worked hard to 'fashion' their 'Stalinist souls' in attempting to belong to the revolutionary polity on its march to the future. The private was political and the regime inscribed in the individual psyche. There was no place to retreat, no possibility to oppose or resist this order, which worked through language as much as through coercion.[13]

Empirical challenges to Hellbeck's assumptions abounded after the opening of the archives. Colleagues took delight in pointing them out. Reacting to such evidence, Hellbeck shifted his explanation from the cultural to the social. Now it became social pressure and the threat of atomization, rather than the monolithic structure of the cultural universe, that enforced conformity to, and internalization of, Stalinist ideology. Effectively, he acted as if all social relations under Stalin followed the logic of those in the Communist Party. And archival evidence showed that people could think and say things they really better should not have. Thus nudged, Hellbeck eventually avoided arguing about impossibilities to think, and developed a more limited thesis about the internalization of regime discourse and its use as a basis for agency.[14]

Hellbeck's monograph, published a decade after his initial essay, was one of the most compelling accounts of how hard it was to be a communist. The demands on purity of thought and standards of behaviour rivalled those of the most exacting religious orders, and the constantly changing party line required individuals to again and again 'remake themselves', to undergo gruelling public sessions of 'criticism and self-criticism', and to struggle to reform the self and cleanse one's soul of impure thoughts. While this was a widespread struggle in Stalin's country, it was not ubiquitous, a fact Hellbeck now conceded but did not stress in his narrative. He made remarkably short shrift of diaries which did not fit his interpretive scheme, quickly moving on to examples of those struggling to become part of the revolutionary collective.[15]

Hellbeck never seemed entirely convinced by his own change of heart. It had been enforced from the outside by peer review and the sustained public critique. The reluctance to abandon the original scheme was demonstrated in his next book. It consisted of a selection of transcripts of oral history interviews Soviet historians had conducted right after the Battle of Stalingrad. In a lengthy introduction, Hellbeck restated the original thesis of Stalinism as a regime deeply rooted in the ideological conviction of masses of rank-and-file Stalinists. After renewed empirical challenges to this thesis – supported in part by the transcripts Hellbeck had published himself – he somewhat softened the interpretation in the English translation of the originally German book, but overall stuck to his guns. By now, however, the discussion about Stalinist subjectivity had gone on so long that people had lost interest. Hellbeck's Stalingrad book did make it into airport bookshops, but it failed to create the same type of debate his work on the 1930s had done. The field had moved on.[16]

Resistance and the mood of the population

Before it moved, however, it became embroiled in a heated polemic driven by the propositions of Hellbeck and some of his closest comrades, scholars often described as the 'Columbia school' to distinguish them from the Fitzpatrick-trained Chicago school (Chapter 4). Its origin was a graduate seminar Kotkin had taught as a visiting professor in New York in 1990.[17] This group eventually coalesced around a new journal some of them had helped create. Its first issue staged what would become known as the 'resistance debate'. Most important were Hellbeck's essay which retreated from a cultural to a social explanation of why people believed in Soviet rhetoric, and an essay by Anna Krylova on the history of thinking about subjectivity in Soviet studies. These two combined to accuse other historians of projecting their own liberal subjectivity on to fundamentally different historical subjects.[18]

The accused did not always take such critique passively, but their protests were ignored.[19] More successful were counter-attacks.

Jeffrey Rossman led one of the most successful charges. Like Kotkin, he was Berkeley-trained, but in his approach much closer to Zelnik. He brought the disciplined study of labour history, in which his mentor had excelled, to the study of the early Stalinist years, showing remarkable continuity of worker radicalism with the revolutionary period.[20] Others conceded that the word 'resistance' might be too broad, opting for 'recalcitrance', 'disobedience', or multiple 'resistances' instead.[21] A parallel debate among historians of national minorities pitted those interested in Soviet colonialism and the resistance it encountered against others stressing nation-making and the potential for personal growth under Soviet rule.[22]

Closely linked to these debates was a polemic about a newly discovered archival source, which threatened to undermine assumptions about the deep roots of Stalinist ideology in the subjectivities of rank-and-file Soviets. These were the reports (*svodki*) about the mood of the population, already used in Fainsod's classic study.[23] They came in two versions: one collected by the secret police, the other by the Communist Party. They abounded in critical, often cutting, remarks about life under Stalin.[24] The question was: could they be trusted? Kotkin originally thought they might. In his *Note on Sources* in *Magnetic Mountain* he regretted his 'failure to gain access to the NKVD archive', especially to the *svodki*, materials which 'would have been valuable in the analysis of popular attitudes, made with considerable difficulty in this monograph'.[25] Once a different scholar did find a large trove of such reports and wrote a book about them, however, he changed his mind. In her study of popular opinion in the 1930s, Sarah Davies had written that the new archival evidence 'undermined' Kotkin's conclusions. He overemphasized the tendency to speak Bolshevik and ignored that 'ordinary people were adept at defeating the censor, seeking out alternative sources of information and ideas in the form of rumours, personal letters, leaflets …, and inscriptions…'. Far from being surrounded by regime discourse, they 'continued to draw on a variety of rival discourses, including those of nationalism, anti-Semitism, and populism, which proved tenacious despite concerted attempts to eradicate them'.[26]

Setting the tone for the polemic to follow, Kotkin hit back in a review of Davies's book. Its aggression showed how thin the evidentiary base was on which was built the entire edifice of 'Stalinist civilization' and 'Stalinist subjectivity'. He now asserted that all these reports showed was 'the play of bureaucratic interest, the mentality of recorders, the bustle of toadies, and ... the deepest fears, even paranoia, of the authorities'. No more mention that they might be useful for assessing what they actually reported on – high levels of discontent even in the cities, let alone the countryside. Davies's careful listing of alternative sources of information and world views he brushed aside with an impatient 'What sources? From where?' Ignoring all the evidence on dissent the *svodki* contain, he offered a different reading, which would have only focused on the extent to which critique of the system implied accepting its legitimacy – a possible, but one-sided, interpretation. What Davies had failed to show, because the woman was 'insufficiently analytical', was that people living in the 1930s did not have 'the mental equipment ... for positing an alternative to Soviet socialism'.[27] This would remain the party line among the faithful, but despite everything did not convince the sceptics. If anything it did the opposite, encouraging more research into mass political culture under Stalin. These works showed diversity of popular opinions throughout the 1930s, 1940s and 1950s.[28]

Modernity

Kotkin's work also opened up the notion of 'modernity' as an avenue of research. It picked up on the thought of Malia. A much more radical conservative than Pipes, Malia did not think that Russia was the cause of Bolshevik totalitarianism. He did not even follow those who thought it was Marxism in action.[29] It was the entire Enlightenment tradition which accounted for the 'Soviet tragedy'.[30] Kotkin developed this line of thought into a thesis about the dead end of the welfare state. [31] Stalinism, in this version, was just one variant of a larger problem of modernity – that is, societies marked by mass production, mass consumption, mass culture and mass politics. In his 1990 Columbia seminar, Kotkin taught 'only monographs that were not about the Soviet Union'. This gesture drove home the point that many Soviet, Stalinist or even totalitarian phenomena observable in the Soviet Union were shared by modern societies more generally.[32]

The scholar who followed Kotkin down this path with most rigour was David L. Hoffmann, like Halfin and Hellbeck a graduate of Columbia University.[33] Originally, he was steeped in revisionist social history, graduating in 1990 with a PhD on social identities in 1930s Moscow. The thesis, and the book which emerged from it, explored the effects of peasant mass migration to the cities during the First Five-Year Plan, picking up a topic both Lewin[34] and Fitzpatrick had explored.[35] Hoffmann argued that while the migration of some 23 million peasants to the cities could not be controlled by the state, and looked chaotic to outsiders, it was guided by existing peasant traditions, established migration paths, and networks of people from the same region. This was a classical revisionist argument, showing that while state control failed, social self-regulation continued.[36] It was a transposition into the context of Stalinism of themes and approaches which had interested scholars of the late Tsarist and revolutionary years. Both labour history and urban history had long been interested in 'peasant-workers', their networks and identities.[37]

Under the impact of Kotkin's thought, however, Hoffmann changed tack. In a series of books, he explored what the notion of 'modernity' could teach about Stalinism. After an exploratory collective volume of essays set the agenda in 2000,[38] two major monographs followed. The first approached the issue from a cultural angle, exploring the values propagated to the Soviet citizenry and reinterpreting the ideological shifts taking place in the Stalinist 1930s.[39] The follow-up volume was originally meant to be co-written with Peter Holquist, another prominent member of the Columbia school, whose fingerprints were still visible in the final product. The basic argument could already be found in Holquist's influential first monograph on war, revolution and civil war: that the Soviet state emerged from the continuum of violence of the First World War and civil war, that it took over and systematized techniques developed during the war, and that it then employed these to its own ideological ends. Hoffmann pushed this argument into the 1930s, focusing on five main areas, each developed in its own chapter: social welfare, public health, reproductive policies, surveillance and propaganda, and state violence.[40]

The book's argument was a carefully calibrated balancing act. On the one hand, Hoffmann argued against views attributing 'all aspects of Soviet social intervention to socialist ideology'.[41] On the other hand, he was at pains not to declare Stalinism the essence of 'modernity'. Instead, it was a historically contingent outcome of the interaction of local and transnational processes. When it came to the key question, however – explaining the immense violence of Stalin's state – the recourse to modernity fell flat. Instead, Hoffmann retreated to the well-trodden paths others had marched before him: the existence of an ideologically driven dictatorship, operating within a hostile domestic and international environment, was decisive for the most distinctive feature of Stalinism: its violence. The various elements of 'modernity' – state interference in social organization via public health, reproductive policies, surveillance and propaganda – were relegated from 'direct causes' to 'conditions of possibility'.[42]

Hoffmann thus updated the thesis that Stalinism was a new form of dictatorship – one which reacted to twentieth-century concerns and used twentieth-century technologies of rule – by integrating the latest comparative literature. This contribution could well be seen as furthering the agenda of the old totalitarian framework, which, after all, had also insisted on the modernity of the phenomenon without declaring it the essence of modernity. Totalitarianism was one possible form of modernity, but modernity was not totalitarian. 'My study of Stalinist culture', he wrote in the first of his modernity monographs, 'is not directed against the impulse to rationalize and improve society.' Like conservatives and liberals before him, he endorsed 'gradual and consensual' change and provided 'a cautionary tale regarding the uncritical application of purportedly scientific social reform'.[43] He hesitated to denounce as totalitarian the modern phenomena of social science, the welfare state, public health and education, interest in the opinions of the population, or attempts to ensure the health of mother and child. Still, they seemed to be diseases, which assumed 'a particularly virulent form' in Stalinism.[44]

Revisionist post-revisionism

Hoffmann's unease with any type of interventionist state, and the Stalinist subjectivity approach's apparent puzzlement that anybody could be a believing communist, resonated widely in a period when neo-liberalism seemed triumphant. The fall of the Berlin Wall in 1989, and the breakdown of the Soviet Union in 1991, ushered in a period where intellectuals would celebrate capitalism as history's endpoint. Together with political liberalism, it seemed the fulfilment of human development.[45] In 1992, Malia published a book which equated any type of 'socialism' with the 'Soviet tragedy' and constructed unregulated capitalism as Stalinism's other.[46]

The widespread conviction that the West had won the Cold War, and that any type of state regulation was detrimental to freedom and prosperity, shielded post-revisionists from the more brutal forms of attack academics trying out new approaches had received in earlier decades. In the mid-1990s, the claim that some people lived fulfilling lives under Stalin was still seen as the height of either naivety or apologetics.[47] By the 2000s, the notion that people deeply believed in Stalinism and acted accordingly, that they felt their lives were exciting, and that this explained Soviet victory in the Second World War, led to no howls from the commentariat. To claim that Stalinism was 'modern' just affirmed its deep otherness in times of 'post-modernity'.[48]

The paradoxes of the old in the new went further. Claiming to form a new cohort which had overcome both totalitarianism and revisionism in a new synthesis, many 'post-revisionists' accepted their predecessors mythologized history of the field. To them, the historiography of Stalinism developed like an argument: the totalitarian thesis was 'in many ways compelling' but 'reduced Soviet society to a victim of the regime's utopian aspirations'; the revisionist antithesis 'deideologized the workings of the Soviet system, explaining its durability in terms of the "interests" of those groups in society that were identified as its beneficiaries'; Kotkin's 'brilliant intervention', finally, was the synthesis integrating 'the disparate strands of intellectual and social history'.[49] Even where they stressed continuities and uniting trends, the academic opinion leaders of the cohort beginning to make their mark in the late 1990s and early 2000s embraced the history of the field as organized in 'three primary generations': the 'totalitarian "fathers"', the 'revisionist "sons"', and the 'post-revisionist "grandchildren"'.[50]

This position can be traced back to Kotkin, who described the development of the field in the following familiar terms: first came totalitarianism, which amounted to 'a replication of Stalinism's self-presentation (with the values inverted)'.[51] Next came a 'subsequent generation of self-proclaimed revisionists, who were led by an outsider, the transplanted Australian Sheila Fitzpatrick'. These scholars 'came of age during the Vietnam War and the domestic convulsions that shook America's post-war sense of complacency and superiority'. Using a wider source base than the totalitarians, they 'plausibly asserted' that 'many people had accepted the values and ideals of the Stalin revolution'.[52] Meanwhile, 'another outsider' worked 'in parallel' with Fitzpatrick: Moshe Lewin. After discussing Lewin's scheme in some detail, Kotkin concluded that all these revisionist approaches 'converged on the bottom-line proposition that the Stalinist state was permeated throughout by social influences', as well as in the notion that Stalinism spelled the end of the Revolution.[53] 'In the end', he concluded, 'the turn to social history has led to the replacement of the manifestly flawed totalitarian thesis by the basic perspective laid down by Leon Trotsky, the Revolution's greatest loser'.[54]

Kotkin and his post-revisionist followers, then, had bought the narrative of subsequent generations, which had been established in the battles of the 1980s, lock, stock and barrel. As we have seen in previous chapters, this story was misleading. Nearly all 'revisionists' had protested the notion that Fitzpatrick was their leader; Lewin, Fitzpatrick and Lynne Viola were not of one, but of three different generations; neither Lewin, nor Fitzpatrick, had 'come of age' during the Vietnam War or in the United States; other 'totalitarianists' (like Hosking) also broke the neat division of the profession into two generations; and the growth of the source base was much more evolutionary than Kotkin described it, with a much broader fund of shared information between the 'generations' of scholarship. We have also seen how the historiography was intensely transnational, with 'transplanted scholars' the norm rather than the exception (and on all sides of the debate: the totalitarians Kenez and Pipes were also transplants). Implicitly taking his own experience of an entirely American education as normal, Kotkin told a US-centred story, relegated British scholarship to the footnotes, and declared the leading scholars in the debate of the 1980s to be 'outsiders'.[55]

Neo-totalitarianism

Meanwhile, the allegedly overcome totalitarian approach was resurrected by scholars from a variety of backgrounds and political positions. Some of the new scholars had been trained by revisionists, others by totalitarians, and still others by neither. All of them assimilated at least part of both revisionist and totalitarian scholarship. But they were not just an extension of the story of revisionism. Indeed, they did not emerge from this internally North American debate. Rather, this neo-totalitarian wave found its inspiration in a complex transnational reconsideration of the term, which began in the 1970s – that is, just at the time when the standard narrative sees revisionism gather its forces.

Four independent traditions interacted and eventually converged in this totalitarian renewal. In Eastern Europe, dissidents like Václav Havel began to think about their own societies in terms of totalitarian oppression, a strain of thought which eventually blossomed in post-Soviet Russia in the 1990s. In Italy and Germany, Right-leaning historians of fascism and National Socialism, most prominently Emilio Gentile and Ernst Nolte, caused considerable controversy by what seemed like attempts to relativize their societies' own dark pasts by gesturing towards communist precedents or parallels. Partially inspired by the East European renaissance, partially by the German discussion, French intellectuals also used the term more and more frequently, mostly with reference to non-democratic forms of socialism. The historian of the French Revolution, François Furet, was a central figure in this process of adapting both Havel and Nolte to French conditions. This literature then infiltrated the United States via the Francophile Malia, who is sometimes credited with resurrecting the term. In effect, he imported the French discussion. Meanwhile, back in Germany, the defeat of totalitarianism in the *Historikerstreit* ('controversy of the historians') was undone once the same French literature, together with Nolte's ghost, seeped back in.[56]

Today, the term is everywhere. As the Soviet system turned from a possible alternative to a historical dead end, which has left Eurasia economically broken and ecologically devastated, the old reflexes against assimilating it to Nazism and fascism have slowed. In Germany, Jörg Baberowski has established himself as the leading neo-totalitarian scholar of Stalinism, while in the United Kingdom Robert Service and Orlando Figes have taken the lead.[57] In France, the trendsetter was Nicolas Werth,[58] while in the United States, historians of the Soviet experience who found the term useful include Matthew Payne, Peter Holquist, Alexander Prusin, Timothy Snyder, Jochen Hellbeck and Amir Weiner.[59] The German and French discussion merged with the American revival, as well as with 'revisionist' scholarship, in a landmark comparative study of Stalinism and Nazism, published in 2009. *Beyond Totalitarianism* was subsequently translated into Russian as well as Czech, which brought this wave of totalitarianism scholarship back to two of its places of origin.[60] In Russia, Ukraine, and elsewhere in the post-Soviet lands, the study of totalitarianism continues to flourish, often treating the entire Soviet period as totalitarian.[61] Like in the case of scholarly Stalin biographies, the historical development of the history of Stalinist totalitarianism thus represents a transnational merging of several scholarly traditions.

We can also see a third, now already familiar, process at work: the assimilation of insights of earlier scholarship one otherwise argues against. Boris Souvarine's basic outline of the story of Stalin's life was absorbed by his successors, if they shared his politics or not; Adam Ulam would polemicize strenuously against Isaac Deutscher, but reproduced many of his best conclusions. The 'revisionists' had of course read the work of the Harvard Interview Project, as well as Fainsod's landmark study of Smolensk. They worked their way through the available Stalin biographies and learned from them. And then they forgot where they had learned it, worked out their own position in dialogue with both the past they studied and the present they lived in, and argued against their 'totalitarian' predecessors.[62]

The post-revisionists, too, assimilated totalitarian and revisionist scholarship before they began to argue against both. 'Speaking Bolshevik' and 'Stalinist subjectivity' were post-modern reformulations of the idea of regime support, which some revisionists – and before them some of the totalitarians – had explored with a more social-science vocabulary. And with state socialism presumably safely discarded on history's trash heap, post-revisionists no longer had to contend with accusations of treason, Stalinism, and whitewashing the enemy.

Meanwhile, totalitarianism was reinvented by historians on the Left as well as on the Right, who could draw on the complex ideological predecessors who had gathered under this term ever since the 1930s, and again from the 1970s. Totalitarianism can still figure as the 'other' of the society we want to live in. The main difference between contemporary versions of anti-totalitarianism is that the Left focuses more on civil liberties, while neo-conservatives stress the importance of economic freedoms. Given that both remain under threat, the concept of totalitarianism is not likely to die any time soon.

Neo-traditionalism

For a while, a third paradigm competed with neo-totalitarianism and the modernity approach: 'neo-traditionalism'. This trend took its terms from the work of Berkeley political scientist, Ken Jowitt. In a seminal 1983 article, he coined the term to describe 'the political corruption' of Leninist regimes. Taking the Harvard Project's attention to 'informal practices pervading the Soviet polity and economy' as his starting point, Jowitt argued that what originally were contributing factors to achieving the 'formal tasks' the Communist Party regime had set itself, later became 'corrupt practices' which 'directly threatened the party's organizational integrity'. For Jowitt, this process took place not under Stalin, but after his death. Stalinism was not 'neo-traditionalist'. It was 'charismatic'.[63]

Three years later, another social scientist, Andrew G. Walder, further explored the concept in a book about life and work in communist China. He opposed the 'neo-traditional image of communist society' to two failed alternatives: totalitarianism and interest-group theory. Neo-traditionalism, like totalitarianism, did stress the centrality of the state in the allocation of life chances and the organization of society; but it also explored systematically and akin to interest-group theory the personalistic ties ubiquitous in real-life communist systems. These ties were not pre-existing or separate from the official structure. They were systematic results of it and thus not likely to lead to 'convergence', as some had predicted.[64]

Drawing on both Jowitt and Walder, the label was taken up in 2000 by Terry Martin.[65] In an essay published simultaneously in two collections of essays, he applied the idea of neo-traditionalism to Stalinism. To Martin, the neo-traditionalist turn took place in the 1930s, not in the post-Stalin years, as Jowitt had it. To the historian of nationality policy, the turning point was the shift in the middle of the pre-war decade, when the original Marxist thought of nations as 'fundamentally modern constructs' was replaced by 'an emphasis on the deep primordial roots of modern nations'.[66]

Martin's engagement with the concept of neo-traditionalism was not conceived as an alternative to 'modernity'. The volume it was written for did not single it out as a counterpoint, but treated it as one example of the new focus. Indeed, his own opposition was not between 'modernity' and 'neo-traditionalism', but between the latter and 'modernization', which referred to the process of forming an industrial civilization. 'Neo-traditionalism' was an alternative modernity resulting from an extremely state-centred form of doing so. 'Modernization', he asserted, 'is the theory of Soviet intentions; neo-traditionalism, the theory of the unintended consequences'.[67]

In the hands of his doctoral supervisor and editor, however, the idea was deployed in a fundamentally different manner. Fitzpatrick republished the essay at the end of her collection on 'new directions' in the study of Stalinism. This position implied that it was the most recent approach, and it served as something of a conclusion to the volume. Even more explicitly, in her introduction she promoted 'neo-traditionalism' not as one branch of the modernity approach, but as a competitor to what she now identified explicitly with the Columbia school. In principle, the two supposed 'paradigms' were quite compatible, as Fitzpatrick noted. But compatible or not, they were in competition. To some of the participants, this news might have come as something of a surprise. In the collection of essays on *Russian Modernity*, which appeared in the same year, Martin's contribution was one of many, and the collection included both 'Columbians' and 'Chicagoans', and many non-aligned scholars. If anything, this was a generational cohort in search of a new way to think about Russian and Soviet history in an international context. Fitzpatrick, instead, elevated Martin to one representative of one group – the 'neo-traditionalists' who were 'sometimes referred to as the Chicago group'. This group was opposed to the Columbia scholars. Thus, Fitzpatrick set up a competition between scholars who originally cooperated.[68]

In constructing a confrontation between Chicagoans and Columbians, Fitzpatrick also promoted the work of another of her doctoral students: Matthew Lenoe. And again she refocused and sharpened an approach which originally had not developed in competition with 'modernity'. His 1997 doctoral thesis, instead, had opposed neo-traditionalism to both totalitarianism and modernization theory.[69] By the time the dissertation had become a book, Lenoe had embraced the opposition of his version of neo-totalitarianism to 'the post-modern emphasis on an overarching "modernity" common to Leninist and liberal states'. This stance also had a political edge. It was opposed to the implications of an approach which assumed 'that the Soviet Union, Imperial Russia, and the liberal democracies of the "West" share or shared something called "modernity" with many nefarious consequences'. What the modernity literature did, in this reading, was to damn liberal democracies by associating them with Stalinism.[70] His opposition to 'modernity', then, was 'a reaction to implied comparisons between liberalism and communism'.[71]

The idea that there was a 'modernist/Columbia school' and a 'neo-traditionalist/Chicago school' became an established narrative in Soviet studies. Six years after the initial introduction of the historiographical split in the younger generation, Michael David-Fox – the non-aligned editor of *Kritika* – responded with an attempt to transcend it with the notion of 'multiple modernities' – an idea implicit in the original contributions, but never fully worked out. He accepted Fitzpatrick's characterization of the historiography as divided into two groups, although he did point out that, in reality, things were a bit more complicated: neither did the 'modernists' all mean the same when they used the term, nor were all modernists Columbia graduates; moreover, there was not an extensive literature on 'neo-traditionalism' which could qualify as a school or a paradigm.[72]

In fact, the unifying potential for the Chicagoans of neo-traditionalism was never realized. There was no consensus about this term among them, and few closed ranks around the new neo-traditionalist flag – quite typical for a 'school' which forever quibbled about whether or not it was, indeed, a school at all.[73] In a certain way, this recalcitrance just honoured the iconoclasm of the school's mentor, but it also did not lend itself to presenting a united front. And the Chicago school itself was not monolithic, including different generations, research interests, countries of origin, and politics. 'Neo-traditionalism' had too many paradoxical resonances with modernization theory, where 'modernity' emerged from 'tradition' in a more or less predetermined upward movement reminiscent of the historical scheme of the German idealist philosopher, Hegel. 'Neo-traditionalism', of course, tried to break with this Hegelianism, but the attempt to describe phenomena as 'new' (neo) despite the fact that they looked 'old' (traditional) only reified the dichotomy the scheme tried to overcome. It also remained unclear what the theoretical, political or historiographical purchase of using the term was. And while there were certainly members of the group who cherished a bit of historiographical sparring, others were much less keen on conflict with their colleagues, and in some cases friends, from the Columbia group. As a result, whatever there was of a debate quietly died down by the second half of the 2000s. Today, few if any still use the term, although the past 'debate' between 'neo-traditionalists' and 'modernists' gets an occasional mention in historiographical overviews.[74]

Creative disorder

In parallel and partially entangled with the developments described above, another innovation took place more quietly: from the early 1990s, the study of post-war Stalinism became a field of study in its own right.[75] Once described as 'an oddly shapeless period',[76] the archival revolution after the Soviet Union's breakdown suddenly allowed pioneering excursions into this unknown terrain.[77] This new literature was transnational from the start; it combined cultural, social and political history, and was driven by scholars of all generations. It mined the opened archives, but also used newly available memoirs, diaries, as well as the press, novels and film. It was inclusive and eclectic to a degree the literature of the 1930s was not. And it was marred less by polemics and controversy: everybody was too busy assimilating the mass of new data now available to fill in the blank spots on the historical map.

The pioneer was a young Russian scholar, Elena Zubkova, whose work provided an indispensable outline of the period.[78] By the 2000s, she had flanked her important studies with the publication of a share of the archival sources underlying them.[79] In Zubkova's footsteps came others and from a variety of backgrounds. Landmark studies were written by the Marxist labour historian Donald Filtzer – an American in self-imposed British exile – which closed the gap his pre-archival studies of the Soviet working class had left in the 1940s. Soon he added an equally important volume on public health in Stalin's final decade, before moving on to work on the war years.[80] David Shearer, a former student of Moshe Lewin's who had made his name as historian of Stalin's industrial revolution, produced an examination of Stalinist policing, which included the post-war years.[81] And James Heinzen, another Lewin student, wrote a landmark study of corruption in later Stalinism.[82] Younger scholars added monographs on the re-Sovietization of Ukraine,[83] the reconstruction of Rostov[84] and Sevastopol,[85] the repopulation of Kyiv,[86] and life and death in Kalinin province.[87] Others worked on housing construction,[88] demobilization and the Soviet veterans' movement,[89] youth,[90] rumour,[91] even the Union of Soviet Composers.[92] A whole literature developed on the late-Stalinist science wars.[93] Russian researchers opened up a new political history, sometimes on their own, sometimes in collaboration with Westerners.[94]

The growing literature on post-war Stalinism was relatively unaffected by the polemics about subjectivity, modernity or neo-traditionalism that marked the parallel scholarship on the 1930s. The reconstruction of what had happened, the archival digging, and the laborious process of making sense of the data kept most scholars who worked on the less well-known 1940s and 1950s busy. With few exceptions, these historians were remarkably collegial, sharing information and documents, reading each other's work, and refraining from trying to declare themselves the exponents of new paradigms. While there were some shared assumptions, the approaches, politics and research methods of this group were as diverse as the scholars themselves. It is for the new literature on the 1940s and 1950s where the judgement of one historian is most apt: that the field had entered a period of 'creative disorder' in methodological choice.[95]

Despite all diversity, however, an important trend in this new literature on the post-war did emerge: a tendency to break down the barriers earlier scholarship had erected between Stalinism and what came after it.[96] Readers will remember from earlier chapters that the notion of Stalinism itself was a means of isolating the terrible years of the 1930s, in particular, from what came before and what would come later. Anti-Soviet scholars turned this logic on its head, declaring Stalinism the essence of Bolshevism rather than its aberration. Their approach was less focused on drawing a clear line between Stalinism and what came after it – in fact, they often struggled to make sense of the 'new face of totalitarianism' after Stalin had died.

Much of the newer scholarship embraced the blurriness of the line marked by Stalin's death, but again changed the logic of this ambiguity. Rather than denying a discontinuity, it showed how in the fields of veterans politics,[97] bureaucratic organization[98] and the political system,[99] housing and house ownership,[100] disability policy,[101] even in hardline sectors such as ideology, the economy or the Gulag, later reforms had been thought about, talked about, and at times experimented with in the years of post-war reconstruction.[102] As long as Stalin was alive, such reforms could not flourish, and were shelved without implementation, but all kinds of reforms did gather momentum under the surface of apparently monolithic 'late Stalinism'. In uncovering the Stalin-era roots of later transformations, this literature subverted the notion of 'Stalinism' itself, together with the neat chronology which tied all changes to the names of the General Secretary in power. In showing how these reforms had widespread support within the bureaucracy, and often well beyond the state structures, however, they also demonstrated yet again how important the person of Stalin was for what could and could not be done in the Soviet Union under his leadership.

Notes

1 Stephen Kotkin, *Magnetic Mountain: Stalinism as a Civilization* (Berkeley, 1995), 373.
2 Kotkin, *Magnetic Mountain*, xv; and 'Kotkin, Stephen 1959–', in: *Contemporary Authors, New Revision Series*, vol. 292, ed. Mary Ruby (Andover, 2016), pp. 225–29; Gale Virtual Reference Library, http://link.galegroup.com/apps/doc/CX3794500064/GVRL (accessed 19 July 2018); as well as his personal website, http://stephenkotkin.com/bio-2/ (accessed 23 July 2018).
3 Kotkin, *Magnetic Mountain*, 6–9, 364, 366.
4 Kotkin, *Magnetic Mountain*, xviii. Keith Gandal and Stephen Kotkin, 'Foucault in Berkeley', *History of the Present* 1 no. 1 (1985): 6, 15. On Foucault in Berkeley, see also James Miller, *The Passion of Michel Foucault* (New York, 1993), 321–25, 344–53; and Didier Eribon, *Michel Foucault* (Cambridge, 1991), 311–16. On his communist phase: Miller, *The Passion*, 57–59, 291. Foucault had influenced cultural historians for a while before he reached Soviet studies. See Patricia O'Brien, 'Michel Foucault's History of Culture', in: *The New Cultural History*, ed. Lynn Hunt (Berkeley, 1989), 25–46. Among the first to apply Foucault to Stalinism was Richard J. Brody, 'Ideology and Political Mobilization: The Soviet Home Front During World War II', *Carl Beck Papers in Russian and East European Studies*, no. 1104 (Pittsburgh, 1994).
5 Jan Plamper, 'Foucault's Gulag', *Kritika* 3, no. 2 (2002): 255–80, here: 256. Among historians, Michel Foucault's most influential books (cited here in their English translation) were *Madness and Civilization: A History of Insanity in the Age of Reason* (London, 1977); *Discipline and Punish: The Birth*

of the Prison (New York, 1977); and *The History of Sexuality, Vol. 1: An Introduction* (London, 1979). An influential introduction is Hubert L. Dreyfus and Paul Rabinow, *Michel Foucault: Beyond Structuralism and Hermeneutics*. 3rd ed. (London, 2013). Cult status among the initiated has been given to *Power/Knowledge: Selected Interviews & Other Writings 1972–1977*, ed. Colin Gordon (New York, 1980).

6 Pierre Bourdieu, *Outline of a Theory of Practice*, trans. Richard Nice (Cambridge, 1997); Pierre Bourdieu, *Practical Reason: On the Theory of Action*, trans. Randal Johnson et al. (Stanford, 1998). On how the Soviet state relied on the practices of its citizens, see Stephen Kotkin, 'The State – Is It Us? Memoirs, Archives, and Kremlinologists', *The Russian Review* 61, January (2002): 35–51. Quotation: Kotkin, *Magnetic Mountain*, 21.

7 Hence, Arch Getty quickly cited Foucault once he discovered his writings. See, for example, J. Arch Getty and Oleg V. Naumov, *The Road to Terror: Stalin and the Self-Destruction of the Bolsheviks, 1932–1939* (New Haven and London, 1999), 19, 58; J. Arch Getty, 'Samokritika Rituals in the Stalinist Central Committee, 1933–38', *The Russian Review* 58, no. 1 (1999): 49–70, here: 52.

8 Merle Fainsod, *Smolensk under Soviet Rule* (New York, 1958).

9 See Kotkin, *Magnetic Mountain*, 221 and the entire second part of the book.

10 A good introduction is Choi Chatterjee and Karen Petrone, 'Models of Selfhood and Subjectivity: The Soviet Case in Historical Perspective', *Slavic Review* 67, no. 4 (2008): 967–86.

11 He was not alone in discovering and analysing these sources. See Veronique Garros, Natalia Korenevskaya and Thomas Lahusen (eds), *Intimacy and Terror: Soviet Diaries of the 1930s* (New York, 1995); and Thomas Lahusen, *How Life Writes the Book: Real Socialism and Socialist Realism in Stalin's Russia* (Ithaca, 1997).

12 Igal Halfin and Jochen Hellbeck, 'Rethinking the Stalinist Subject: Stephen Kotkin's "Magnetic Mountain" and the State of Soviet Historical Studies', *Jahrbücher für Geschichte Osteuropas* 44, no. 3 (1996): 456–63, here: 457, 459.

13 Jochen Hellbeck, 'Fashioning the Stalinist Soul: The Diary of Stepan Podlubnyi (1931–1939)', *Jahrbücher für Geschichte Osteuropas* 44 no. 3 (1996): 344–75.

14 Jochen Hellbeck, 'Speaking Out: Languages of Affirmation and Dissent in Stalinist Russia', *Kritika: Explorations in Russian and Eurasian History* 1, no. 1 (2000): 71–96; Jochen Hellbeck, 'Working, Struggling, Becoming: Stalin-Era Autobiographical Texts', *The Russian Review* 60, July (2001): 340–59. For a summary of empirical challenges: Mark Edele, *Stalinist Society 1928–1953* (Oxford, 2011), chapter 6.

15 Jochen Hellbeck, *Revolution on My Mind: Writing a Diary under Stalin* (Cambridge, Mass., 2006), quotation: xi.

16 Jochen Hellbeck, *Die Stalingrad Protokolle: Sowjetische Augenzeugen berichten aus der Schlacht* (Frankfurt a. M., 2012); Jochen Hellbeck, *Stalingrad: The City That Defeated the Third Reich* (New York, 2015). For a discussion of the changes between the two volumes, see Mark Edele, *Stalin's Defectors: How Red Army Soldiers Became Hitler's Collaborators, 1941–1945* (Oxford, 2017), 167–71.

17 On the 1990 seminar, see Stephen Kotkin, 'Modern Times: The Soviet Union and the Interwar Conjuncture', *Kritika: Explorations in Russian and Eurasian History* 2, no. 1 (2001): 111–64, here: note on p. 111. On the Columbia school: Edele, *Stalinist Society*, 228–29.
18 Hellbeck, 'Speaking Out', esp. 73–74; Anna Krylova, 'The Tenacious Liberal Subject in Soviet Studies', *Kritika: Explorations in Russian and Eurasian History* 1, no. 1 (2000): 119–46.
19 Sarah Davies, 'To the Editors', *Kritika: Explorations in Russian and Eurasian History* 1, no. 2 (2000): 437–39.
20 Jeffrey J. Rossman, *Worker Resistance under Stalin: Class and Revolution on the Shop Floor* (Cambridge, Mass., 2005).
21 Michael David-Fox, 'Wither Resistance?', *Kritika: Explorations in Russian and Eurasian History* 1, no. 1 (2000): 161–65; Lewis Siegelbaum and Andrei Sokolov (eds), *Stalinism as a Way of Life: A Narrative in Documents* (New Haven, 2000), 11–17; Lynne Viola (ed.), *Contending with Stalinism: Soviet Power and Popular Resistance in the 1930s* (Ithaca and London, 2002), 2.
22 See Chapter 3.
23 Fainsod, *Smolensk under Soviet Rule*, e.g. 307.
24 Lesley A. Rimmel, '*Svodki* and Popular Opinion in Stalinist Leningrad', *Cahiers du Monde Russe* 40, no. 1–2 (1999): 217–34.
25 Kotkin, *Magnetic Mountain*, 371.
26 Sarah Davies, *Popular Opinion in Stalin's Russia: Terror, Propaganda, and Dissent, 1934–1941* (Cambridge, 1997), 6–7.
27 Stephen Kotkin in *Europe–Asia Studies* 50, no. 4 (1998): 739–42.
28 Juliane Fürst, 'Prisoners of the Soviet Self? – Political Youth Opposition in Late Stalinism', *Europe–Asia Studies* 54, no. 3 (2002): 353–75; Mark Edele, 'More Than Just Stalinists: The Political Sentiments of Victors 1945–1953', in: *Late Stalinist Russia: Society between Reconstruction and Reinvention*, ed. Juliane Fürst (London, 2006), 167–91; and Edele, *Stalinist Society*, 238–40; David Brandenberger, '"Simplistic, Pseudosocialist Racism": Debates over the Direction of Soviet Ideology within Stalin's Creative Intelligentsia, 1936–39', *Kritika: Explorations in Russian and Eurasian History* 13, no. 2 (2012): 365–93; Olga Velikanova, *Mass Political Culture under Stalinism: Popular Discussion of the Constitution of 1936* (Cham, 2018).
29 Leszek Kolakowski, 'Marxist Roots of Stalinism', in: *Stalinism: Essays in Historical Interpretation*, ed. Robert C. Tucker (New York, 1977), 283–98.; Leszek Kolakowski, *Main Currents of Marxism: Its Rise, Growth, and Dissolution*, 3 vols (Oxford, 1978).
30 See Chapter 3.
31 Kotkin, *Magnetic Mountain*, 366.
32 Kotkin, 'Modern Times', 111.
33 Other examples from a different generation and graduate training include Stephen A. Barnes, *Death and Redemption: The Gulag and the Shaping of Soviet Society* (Princeton, 2011); and Tarik Cyril Amar, *The Paradox of Ukrainian Lviv: A Borderland City between Stalinists, Nazis, and Nationalists* (Ithaca, 2015).
34 Moshe Lewin, *The Making of the Soviet System: Essays in the Social History of Interwar Russia* (New York, 1994), 218–21, 303–04.

35 Sheila Fitzpatrick, 'The Great Departure. Rural–urban migration in the Soviet Union, 1929–33', in: *Social Dimensions of Soviet Industrialization*, ed. William Rosenberg and Lewis Siegelbaum (Bloomington, 1993), 15–40.
36 David L. Hoffmann, *Peasant Metropolis: Social Identities in Moscow, 1929–1941* (Ithaca and London, 1994).
37 James H. Bater, *St Petersburg, Industrialization and Change* (London, 1976); James H. Bater, 'Transience, Residential Persistence, and Mobility in Moscow and St Petersburg, 1900–1914', *Slavic Review* 39, no. 2 (1980): 239–54; or Reginald Zelnik (ed.), *A Radical Worker in Tsarist Russia: The Autobiography of Semen Ivanovich Kanatchikov* (Stanford, 1986).
38 David L.Hoffmann and Yanni Kotsonis (eds), *Russian Modernity: Politics, Knowledge, Practices* (New York, 2000).
39 David L. Hoffmann, *Stalinist Values: The Cultural Norms of Soviet Modernity, 1917–1941* (Ithaca, 2003).
40 Peter Holquist, *Making War, Forging Revolution: Russia's Continuum of Crisis, 1914–1921* (Cambridge, Mass., 2002); David L. Hoffmann, *Cultivating the Masses: Modern State Practices and Soviet Socialism, 1914–1939* (Ithaca, 2011).
41 Hoffmann, *Cultivating the Masses*, 306.
42 Hoffmann, *Cultivating the Masses*, 304–05.
43 Hoffmann, *Stalinist Values*, 187–88. On liberal and conservative precursors: Edele, *Stalinist Society*, 225.
44 Hoffmann, *Cultivating the Masses*, 4. The argument was repeated, for an undergraduate audience, in a narrative textbook which also tried to grapple with the war and post-war years: David Hoffmann, *The Stalinist Era* (Cambridge, 2018).
45 Francis Fukuyama, 'The End of History?', *The National Interest* 16 (1989): 3–18; Francis Fukuyama, *The End of History and the Last Man* (New York, 1992).
46 Martin Malia, *The Soviet Tragedy: A History of Socialism in Russia, 1917–1991* (New York, 1994); Yanni Kotsonis, 'The Ideology of Martin Malia', *The Russian Review* 58, no. 1 (1999): 124–30.
47 See the Thurston Affair, Chapter 6.
48 A similar point has been made by Sheila Fitzpatrick, 'Revisionism in Soviet History', *History and Theory* 46 no. 4 (2007): 77–91, here: 87–89.
49 Halfin and Hellbeck, 'Rethinking the Stalinist Subject', 456.
50 'From the Editors: Really-Existing Revisionism?', *Kritika: Explorations in Russian and Eurasian History* 2, no. 4 (2001): 707–11, here: 709.
51 Kotkin, *Magnetic Mountain*, 2, 376 n. 4–5. Puzzlingly, he cited Merle Fainsod's Smolensk book and the work of the Harvard Interview Project, which cannot be described in these terms – see Chapter 6. In a footnote, he further noted that 'the totalitarian school was far more sophisticated and diverse than generally portrayed', only to dismiss this claim in the next sentence with the (incorrect) statement that 'almost the only social data these scholars consulted were interviews with émigrés' (376 n. 6).
52 Kotkin, *Magnetic Mountain*, 3. Again, he uses a footnote to point to the fact that 'totalitarian' scholars had already done the same, only to imply that this was irrelevant to the narrative. Kotkin, *Magnetic Mountain*, 377 n. 9.

DEBATES ON STALINISM

53　Kotkin, *Magnetic Mountain*, 4–6.
54　Kotkin, *Magnetic Mountain*, 6.
55　Kotkin, *Magnetic Mountain*, 376–77 n. 7.
56　Daniela Baratieri, Giuseppe Finaldi and Mark Edele, 'Beyond the Delusion: New Histories of Totalitarian Dictatorship', in: *Totalitarian Dictatorship: New Histories*, ed. Daniela Baratieri, Mark Edele and Giuseppe Finaldi (New York, 2014), 1–5.
57　Robert Service, *Comrades: A World History of Communism* (London, 2007); Jörg Baberowski, *Der Rote Terror: Die Geschichte des Stalinismus* (Frankfurt, 2007); Orlando Figes, *The Whisperers: Private Life in Stalin's Russia* (New York, 2007).
58　S. Courtois, N. Werth, et al., *Le Livre noir du communisme: Crime, terreur, repression* (Paris, 1997), translated as *the Black Book of Communism: Crimes, Terror, Repression* (Cambridge, Mass., 1999).
59　Matthew J. Payne, *Stalin's Railroad: Turksib and the Building of Socialism* (Pittsburgh, 2001); Amir Weiner, *Making Sense of War: The Second World War and the Fate of the Bolshevik Revolution* (Princeton, 2001); Peter Holquist, 'State Violence as Technique. The Logic of Violence in Soviet Totalitarianism', in: *Landscaping the Human Garden: Twentieth-Century Population Management in a Comparative Framework* (Stanford, 2003); Alexander V. Prusin, *The Lands Between: Conflict in the East European Borderlands, 1870–1992* (Oxford, 2010); Timothy Snyder, *Bloodlands: Europe between Hitler and Stalin* (London, 2010);Hellbeck, *Revolution on My Mind*, xi. My own work also belongs in this context.
60　Michael Geyer and Sheila Fitzpatrick (eds), *Beyond Totalitarianism: Stalinism and Nazism Compared* (Cambridge, 2009). The Russian edition was: *Za ramkami totalitarizma: Sravnitel'nye issledovaniia stalinizma i natsizma* (Moscow, 2011); the Czech translation: *Za obzor totalitarismu: Srovnání stalinismu na nacismu* (Prague, 2012).
61　For Russia see, for example, G. Kurskova, *Totalitarnaia sistema v SSSR: istoki i puti preodeleniia* (Moscow, 2000). For Ukraine: Volodimir Litvin (ed.), *Ukraina: politichna istoriia xx-pochatik xxi stolittia* (Kyiv, 2007).
62　For the revisionist critique of totalitarianism, this point has been made by Abbott Gleason, '"Totalitarianism" in 1984', *The Russian Review* 43, no. 2 (1984): 145–59. Some revisionists today accept their debt to Fainsod, at times citing him as if he were a 'revisionist'. Siegelbaum and Sokolov, *Stalinism as a Way of Life*, 4, 426 n. 6.
63　Ken Jowitt, 'Soviet Neotraditionalism: The Political Corruption of a Leninist Regime', *Soviet Studies* 35, no. 3 (1983): 275–97, quotations: 275, 284; reprinted as chapter 4 in Ken Jowitt, *The New World Disorder: The Leninist Extinction* (Berkeley, 1992).
64　Andrew G. Walder, *Communist Neo-Traditionalism: Work and Authority in Chinese Industry* (Berkeley, 1986).
65　See chapters 3, 4 and 9.
66　Terry Martin, 'Modernization or Neo-Traditionalism? Ascribed Nationality and Soviet Primordialism', in: *Stalinism: New Directions*, ed. Sheila Fitzpatrick (London and New York, 2000), 348–67; published in the same year as chapter

8 of Hoffmann and Kotsonis, *Russian Modernity*. I quote here from the Fitzpatrick volume.
67 Martin, 'Modernization or Neo-Traditionalism', 360, 361.
68 Sheila Fitzpatrick, 'Introduction', in: *Stalinism: New Directions*, 1–14, here: 11 and 14 n. 29.
69 Matthew Edward Lenoe, 'Stalinist Mass Journalism and the Transformation of Soviet Newspapers, 1926–1932', PhD diss., The University of Chicago, 1997, 936–54.
70 Matthew Edward Lenoe, *Closer to the Masses: Stalinist Culture, Social Revolution, and Soviet Newspapers* (Cambridge, Mass. and London, 2004), 251, 4–5. Lenoe singled out two essays in particular: Peter Holquist, '"Information is the Alpha and Omega of Our Work": Bolshevik Surveillance in its Pan-European Context', *The Journal of Modern History* 69, no. 3 (1997): 415–50; and Kate Brown, 'Gridded Lives: Why Kazakhstan and Montana are Nearly the Same Place', *The American Historical Review* 106, no. 1 (2001): 17–48.
71 Michael David-Fox, 'Multiple Modernities vs. Neo-Traditionalism: On Recent Debates in Russian and Soviet History', *Jahrbücher für Geschichte Osteuropas* 54, no. 4 (2006): 535–55, here: 545.
72 David-Fox, 'Multiple Modernities'.
73 David Wolff, Jonathan Bone, Mark Edele, Matthew Lenoe and Ron Suny, 'Roundtable: What Is a School? Is There a Fitzpatrick School of Soviet History?' *Acta Slavica Iaponica* 24 (2007): 229–41.
74 Larissa Zakharova, 'Le quotidien du communisme: pratiques et objets', *Annales: Histoire, Sciences Sociales* 68, no. 2 (2013): 303–14, here: 309; Amar, *Paradox of Ukrainian Lviv*, 9.
75 For a collective manifesto, see Juliane Fürst (ed.), *Late Stalinist Russia: Society between Reconstruction and Reinvention* (London, 2006).
76 Alec Nove, *An Economic History of the USSR, 1917–1991*. 3rd and final ed. (London, 1992), 294.
77 Important pre-archival precursors were Vera S. Dunham, *In Stalin's Time: Middleclass Values in Soviet Fiction*. Enlarged and updated ed. (Durham, 1990 [first edition: 1976]). Zhores A. Medvedev, *The Rise and Fall of T. D. Lysenko*, trans. I. Michael Lerner (New York, 1969); David Joravsky, *The Lysenko Affair* (Cambridge, Mass., 1970); and Loren R. Graham, *Science and Philosophy in the Soviet Union* (New York, 1972).
78 Elena Zubkova, 'Obshchestvennaia atmosfera posle voiny (1948–1952)', *Svobodnaia mysl'*, no. 9 (1992): 79–88; Elena Zubkova, *Obshchestvo i reformy, 1945–1964* (Moscow, 1993); Elena Zubkova, 'Obshchestvo, vyshedshee iz voiny: russkie i nemtsy v 1945 godu', *Otechestvennaia istoriia*, no. 3 (1995): 90–100; Elena Zubkova, *Russia after the War: Hopes, Illusions, and Disappointments, 1945–1957*, trans. Hugh Ragsdale (Armonk and London, 1998); Elena Zubkova, *Poslevoennoe sovetskoe obshchestvo: politika i povsednevnost' 1945–1953* (Moscow, 2000); Elena Zubkova, 'The Soviet Regime and Soviet Society in the Postwar Years: Innovations and Conservatism, 1945–1953', *Journal of Modern European History* 2, no. 1 (2004): 134–52; Elena Zubkova, 'S protianutoi rukoi. Nishchie i nishchenstvo v poslevoennom SSSR', *Cahiers*

du Monde russe 49, no. 2–3 (2008): 441–74; and Elena Zubkova, *Pribaltika i Kreml'. 1940–1953* (Moscow, 2008).

79 E. Iu. Zubkova, L. P. Kosheleva, G. A. Kuznetsova, A. I. Miniuk and L. A. Rogovaia (eds), *Sovetskaia zhizn' 1945–1953* (Moscow, 2003); E. Iu. Zubkova and T. Iu. Zhukova (eds), *Na 'kraiu' sovetskogo obshchestva: Sotsial'nye marginaly kak ob"ekt gosudarstvennoi politiki 1945–1960-e gg* (Moscow, 2010).

80 Donald Filtzer, *Soviet Workers and Late Stalinism: Labour and the Restoration of the Stalinist System after World War II* (Cambridge, 2002); Donald Filtzer, *The Hazards of Urban Life in Late Stalinist Russia: Health, Hygiene, and Living Standards, 1943–1953* (Cambridge, 2010); Wendy Goldman and Donald Filtzer (eds), *Hunger and War: Food Provisioning in the Soviet Union during World War II* (Bloomington, 2015).

81 David R. Shearer, *Policing Stalin's Socialism: Repression and Social Order in the Soviet Union, 1924–1953* (New Haven, 2009). His dissertation book was: *Industry, State, and Society in Stalin's Russia, 1926–1934* (Ithaca, 1996).

82 James Heinzen, *The Art of the Bribe: Corruption under Stalin, 1943–1953* (Stanford, 2016).

83 Weiner, *Making Sense of War*.

84 Jeffrey W. Jones, *Everyday Life and the 'Reconstruction' of Soviet Russia During and After the Great Patriotic War, 1943–1948* (Bloomington, 2008).

85 Karl Qualls, *From Ruins to Reconstruction: Urban Identity in Soviet Sevastopol after World War II* (Ithaca, 2009).

86 Martin J. Blackwell, *Kyiv as a Regime City: The Return of Soviet Power after Nazi Occupation* (Rochester, 2016).

87 Kees Boterbloem, *Life and Death under Stalin: Kalinin Province* (Montreal, 1999).

88 Mark B. Smith, *Property of Communists: The Urban Housing Program from Stalin to Khrushchev* (DeKalb, 2010).

89 Mark Edele, *Soviet Veterans of the Second World War: A Popular Movement in an Authoritarian Society, 1941–1991* (Oxford, 2008); Robert Dale, *Demobilized Veterans in Late Stalinist Leningrad: Soldiers to Civilians* (London, 2015).

90 Juliane Fürst, *Stalin's Last Generation: Soviet Post-War Youth and the Emergence of Mature Socialism* (Oxford, 2010).

91 Timothy Johnston, *Being Soviet: Identity, Rumour, and Everyday Life under Stalin 1939–1953* (Oxford, 2011).

92 Kiril Tomoff, *Creative Union: The Professional Organization of Soviet Composers, 1939–1953* (Ithaca, 2006).

93 Nikolai Krementsov, *Stalinist Science* (Princeton, 1997); Alexei B. Kojevnikov, *Stalin's Great Science: The Times and Adventures of Soviet Physicists* (London, 2004); and Ethan Pollock, *Stalin and the Soviet Science Wars* (Princeton, 2006).

94 R. G. Pikhoia, *Sovetskii Soiuz: Istoriia vlasti 1945–1991* (Novosibirsk, 2000); Yoram Gorlizki and Oleg Khlevniuk, *Cold Peace: Stalin and the Soviet Ruling Circle, 1945–1953* (Oxford, 2004); Oleg Khlevniuk, *Stalin: New Biography of a Dictator* (New Haven, 2015).

95 David R. Shearer, 'From Divided Consensus to Creative Disorder. Soviet History in Britain and North America', *Cahiers du Monde russe* 39, no. 4 (1998): 559–92.
96 Stephen Lovell, *The Shadow of War: Russia and the USSR 1941 to the Present* (Oxford, 2010).
97 Edele, *Soviet Veterans*.
98 Yoram Gorlitzki, 'Ordinary Stalinism: The Council of Ministers and the Soviet Neopatrimonial State, 1946–1953', *The Journal of Modern History* 74, no. 4 (2002): 699–736.
99 Sheila Fitzpatrick, *On Stalin's Team: The Years of Living Dangerously in Soviet Politics* (Melbourne, 2015).
100 Mark B. Smith, 'Individual Forms of Ownership in the Urban Housing Fund of the USSR, 1944–64', *Slavonic and East European Review* 86, no. 2 (2008): 283–305; Stephen Lovell, *Summerfolk: A History of the Dacha, 1719–2000* (Ithaca, 2003).
101 Maria C. Galmarini-Kabala, *The Right to Be Helped: Deviance, Entitlement, and the Soviet Moral Order* (DeKalb, 2016); Claire L. Shaw, *Deaf in the USSR: Marginality, Community, and Soviet Identity, 1917–1991* (Ithaca, 2017).
102 Julie Hessler, 'A Postwar Perestroika? Toward a History of Private Trade Enterprise in the USSR', *Slavic Review* 57, no. 3 (1998): 516–42; Julie Hessler, *A Social History of Soviet Trade: Trade Policy, Retail Practices, and Consumption, 1917–1953* (Princeton, 2004); Aleksandr Vladimirovich Pyzhikov, 'Sovetskoe poslevoennoe obshchestvo i predposylki khrushchevskikh reform', *Voprosy istorii*, no. 2 (2002): 33–43; Zubkova, 'The Soviet Regime and Soviet Society in the Postwar Years', 134–52.

Part III
Contemporary debates

8
Fighting Russia's history wars

History and memory

On 24 December 2014, Vladimir Luzgin failed a history exam with fairly high stakes. The resident of Perm in the Urals did so, unknowingly, by sharing an article entitled '15 Facts about the Supporters of Bandera (*Banderovtsy*), or: What the Kremlin is Silent About'. The article countered what its author perceived as Russian misconceptions about the Ukrainian independence movement in the Second World War, in particular the followers of one of its leaders.[1]

Stepan Bandera (1909–59) was born in Galicia, then part of the Austro-Hungarian Empire. In interwar Poland he became a prominent Ukrainian nationalist, incarcerated in the mid-1930s. He escaped prison between the German invasion of Poland on 1 September and the Soviet one on 17 September 1939, taking up residence in the German-occupied zone. There, he led the Bandera faction of the Organization of Ukrainian Nationalists (OUN-B, or *Banderovtsy*) after a split of the organization in 1940. OUN-B actively collaborated with German counterintelligence units on formerly Polish territory and helped set up two Ukrainian battalions, which participated in the invasion of the Soviet Union. Bandera himself was not allowed onto Soviet territory by the Germans, so the declaration of an independent Ukrainian state in late June 1941 was left to his associates. This step, however, sealed the fate of OUN-B in the German-controlled areas. Hitler was unwilling to accept independent nationalist movements of non-Germans on Soviet territory. The organization was outlawed and Bandera arrested. He languished as a somewhat privileged prisoner in Sachsenhausen concentration camp, and was released at the eleventh hour, in 1944, when the Germans finally tried to instrumentalize anti-Soviet and nationalist sentiments of former Soviet citizens in their fight against the Red Army. An extreme nationalist, Bandera was no friend of Poles, Russians or Jews. His followers were involved both in the ethnic cleansing of Poles and in the Holocaust. He was assassinated by a Soviet agent in post-war Munich, where he had found refuge.[2]

During the 2013–14 Euromaidan protests in Kyiv, and the following 2014 Russian occupation of Crimea, as well as the armed conflict over eastern Ukraine, the memory of Bandera became entangled with Ukrainian and Russian nationalisms. Ukrainians had long celebrated him as a freedom fighter, while the Russian media portrayed him as a fascist and a Nazi collaborator. It is in this context that the '15 facts' were written and distributed, and Luzgin prosecuted for this act.[3]

The Luzgin case was a first high-point in the repoliticization of the Second World War, and with it of Stalinism, in Russia. To many Russians, the war against Nazism remains sacred. Such emotional memorialization is not surprising, given the devastation of this war: some 25–27 million Soviet citizens paid with their lives; thousands of towns, tens of thousands of villages, and millions of buildings were destroyed.[4] But in the end, the Soviets won. This victory is hard to remember without Stalin, the leader of the war effort. This chapter recounts recent struggles to enforce a positive history of this war. It is about the tension between history and memory, about the continuing attractions of Stalinism, about the fate of its critics in the largest successor states of the Soviet Union, and about the renationalization of the history of Stalinism, which continues in parallel with the internationalization recounted in other chapters.

A failed history exam

On that fateful day in December 2014, then, Luzgin shared the anti-Kremlin defence of Bandera and his followers on *VKontakte*, a Russian version of Facebook. While only twenty other users saw his post, one of them was employed by the State Prosecutor's office of Perm District. The procuracy soon investigated a charge of public dissemination of 'lies about the activities of the

Soviet Union in the Second World War', a crime that, since early 2014, was punishable by up to five years' imprisonment under article 354.1 of the criminal code ('rehabilitation of fascism'). The charge was brought to prosecution, and in June 2016 the Perm District Court made history when sentencing Luzgin as charged.[5]

The court had to find that Luzgin's re-post was historically inaccurate, and that he could have known that it was. The historical inaccuracy was fairly easily established. Part of the offending paragraph read as follows:

> In contrast to the communists, who actively collaborated with the Germans and divided Europe with the Molotov-Ribbentrop pact, the UPA [Ukrainian Insurgent Army] and OUN-B did not collaborate either with the German occupation government or with the communist occupation government. In their turn, the communists [and the Germans] learned from each other, cooperated in repressions, held parades together, exchanged weapons, etc. THE COMMUNISTS AND GERMANY TOGETHER ATTACKED POLAND, UNLEASHING THE SECOND WORLD WAR on 1 September 1939. That is, communism and Nazism cooperated closely while Bandera sat in a German concentration camp Auschwitz for the declaration of independence of Ukraine.

There are so many tendentious mistakes in this paragraph that it is hard to decide where to start unravelling them. First, OUN-B did collaborate with the Germans. It was not Bandera but Hitler who ended the cooperation. Second, during the period when the Soviets and the Germans 'cooperated closely' – that is in 1939–1941 – Bandera was not in a concentration camp. He was only arrested after the declaration of Ukrainian independence, which happened not during the period of German–Soviet collaboration but after it had ended with the attack on the Soviet Union. Third, he did not sit in Auschwitz, but in Sachsenhausen.

The prosecution focused instead on a final inaccuracy, the statement that 'the communists and Germany together attacked Poland, unleashing the Second World War on 1 September 1939. As witness for the prosecution, Aleksandr Vertinskii, Dean of the Faculty of History of *Perm State Humanitarian-Pedagogical University*, put it: this formulation did 'not conform to positions recognized internationally'.[6] And, as mentioned, on 1 September only the Germans attacked Poland, unleashing the Second World War. The Red Army did not invade Poland until 17 September.

While the first part of the prosecution's case relied on a confrontation between an amateur with a hazy knowledge of history, and the dean of a faculty of history, the second required showing that Luzgin did not simply make a mistake but knowingly distributed lies. This charge he strenuously denied. He claimed, probably accurately, that he had never read the Nuremberg trial records, and hence did not know what an international court had established about Germany's singular war guilt; he also claimed that he had learned in school that 'on 1 September 1939, fascist Germany attacked Poland, while Soviet forces moved into the eastern part of Poland'. The court dismissed this defence with reference to Luzgin's high-school diploma, which showed that he had passed history with a 'B' (*'good'*), and could thus be presumed to know the basic facts. Thus his dissemination of a document full of silly mistakes was judged the propagation of a historical lie. Luzgin was given a 200,000 rouble fine, quite a significant sum in a country where the average monthly wage was 36,525 roubles.[7] And Luzgin was lucky: he could have ended up behind bars.

Luzgin's prosecution marked a new level of escalation in the ongoing struggle over Russia's past. After the breakdown of the Soviet Union in 1991, the question of what were the historical foundations of contemporary Russia became acute. While the victory over Nazism was not the only useable past available, a sanitized version of 'Russia's' Second World War became a heritage both leaders and led could agree on. It developed into a cornerstone of a positive narrative about the nation. It was popular, not least because it could build on the ideological work done since 1945, when the Great Patriotic War increasingly eclipsed the Bolshevik revolution as the foundational moment of the Soviet polity.[8] The new Russian 'positive nationalism', however, was challenged by critical historians within, and foreign scholars and politicians without.[9]

In the context of the Ukraine crisis, these confrontations came to a head, leading to the passing of a law threatening prison for unspecified 'lies' about the Soviet Union's Second World War.[10] This chapter explores this law in the context of several presidential interventions into the controversy about how to properly remember this war. They make clear that the Memory Law was part of the historiographical front of what has been called Putin's 'preventive counterrevolution': an attempt to immunize Russian society against the virus of 'velvet revolution', the largely unbloody democratic uprisings Eastern Europe had experienced since the late 1980s.[11]

The President of the Russian Federation, of course, did not (re)construct the Russian past single-handedly. There were a variety of other players, the most prominent among them being the Minister of Culture, Vladimir Medinskii (born 1970), a maverick historian who had long argued for the development of a useful past.[12] Putin at times followed Medinskii's lead, but there were also moments of divergence. The President's style of argument, for one, was much more old-fashioned than his minister's. The younger man openly stated that 'facts alone do not mean very much' and that he wanted to 'modernize' the 'Soviet war myth' to create a 'positive mythology' as a foundation of the 'moral imperatives of the people'. His writings were openly imperialist: 'What kind of a myth do we need?' he asked rhetorically in 2011. 'Very easy', he answered. Russia needed a myth stressing 'the unified historical fate of the peoples of the former Russian empire'.[13]

Putin, by contrast, presented himself as the defender of objective historical truth pure and simple. He was more careful and guarded than Medinskii, whose line he did not follow on every subject. Instead, he developed his own personal take on the past.[14] In the struggle over history, as elsewhere in the complex game of Russian politics, Putin, the 'history man', was an independent actor.[15]

The Memory Law and the history of history

On 5 May 2014, the history man in the Kremlin signed a new law, which had been passed by both houses of parliament on 23 and 29 April respectively.[16] Largely ignored by a Western media too busy keeping an eye on fast-moving events in Ukraine, what was popularly known as the 'Memory Law' criminalized the expression of certain opinions about the Soviet past. Article 1 threatened either up to a 300,000-rouble fine (or the equivalent of up to two years' salary), or three years of forced labour or a three-year prison term for the following offences:

- public denial of facts established by the international criminal tribunal for the punishment of the major European war criminals of the Axis powers;

- public approval of said crimes;
- public distribution of lies about the activities of the Soviet Union in the Second World War, if the offender is aware of the false character of these statements.

The penalties increased to 100,000–500,000 roubles (or the equivalent of one to three years' salary), or forced labour or prison for up to five years, if the above offences took place while performing a public office or using mass media or while falsifying evidence.[17] In these cases, the perpetrators would also lose the right to perform their position or job for up to three years.

On the face of it, the Memory Law seemed innocent. Who would deny war crimes judged at the Nuremberg trials? The devil was in the detail, in particular in what would constitute a 'lie' about the Soviet past. In order to better understand the question of truth and lies about Stalin's war, we need to remember the deeper history of the Russian history wars about the Second World War. In the Soviet Union, the Second World War was remembered largely as the Great Patriotic War. This war began when the Germans attacked the Soviet Union on 22 June 1941, rather than when Japan and China went to war in 1937, as historians with their eye to Asia now advocate, or when Germany, backed by the Soviet Union through the Hitler–Stalin Pact, made short work of Poland in 1939, as the more conventional, European narrative has it.[18]

The Great Patriotic War was a defensive war of good against evil, as Stalin stressed in his first wartime address to the population on 3 July 1941, which would set the tone for both wartime propaganda and the post-war war cult. It had been 'forced upon' the Soviets by their 'bitterest and most cunning enemy – German fascism'. The Red Army was 'displaying unexampled valor' fighting this foe. And the military was not alone: 'the entire Soviet people' was 'rising in defense of our native land'. This 'patriotic war of liberation against the fascist enslavers' was a struggle not only for the 'life and death of the Soviet state' and all the peoples of the USSR, but for the liberation of Europe and the world from fascism.[19]

The Great Patriotic War narrative had several strongpoints. For one, the Soviet Union was a clear victim in this story. It was attacked by the most brutal dictatorship in the twentieth century, was threatened with genocidal policies, and became a major player in the anti-Hitler coalition. At great cost and involving enormous suffering, the Soviet Union managed to win this war and hence save Europe, and maybe the world, from Nazi barbarism.[20] Thus, as a positive story of victimization and valour, the myth of the Great Patriotic War had the advantage that much of it reflected historical reality.

Other starting points were less useful for a self-righteous national narrative. If the war started in 1937, the Soviets' role was much more ambiguous. Scared of a two-front war with Germany and Japan, unwilling to commit troops and fight the Asian imperialists on the side of the Chinese victims, Stalin committed weapons, military advisers, and some airmen, but refused to join the fight with all the might of the Red Army. The plan was to help enough to bog down Japan in China and thus neutralize the threat to the eastern flank of Stalin's empire. And this strategy worked. After an undeclared border war in 1938–39 demonstrated to the Japanese that the Red Army was a tough adversary, Japan abandoned plans to attack the Soviets and oriented itself south instead, eventually clashing with the United States. The rest, as they say, is history.[21]

If in the war in Asia the Soviet Union's role was ambiguous, in the European war from 1939 it was problematic. Hitler attacked Poland after the pact with Stalin of 23 August 1939 assured him that the Soviets would keep out of the war, as long as he would let them take control of their 'sphere of influence' in Eastern Europe. Despite such collusion between dictators, few historians blame the outbreak of war in equal parts on Stalin and Hitler.[22] Hitler's decision to attack Poland had been reached well before the neutrality of the Soviet Union had been guaranteed; Soviet neutrality eased, rather than caused, German aggression; it is unlikely that even a broad anti-Hitler coalition would have avoided war, given the German dictator's determination to have one.[23] The real disagreement is over Stalin's intentions in 1939, a discussion that cannot be reduced to a confrontation between 'Russophiles' and 'Russophobes', or their proxies. Positions on all sides of the scholarly front lines are taken by historians of a wide variety of backgrounds, and all serious contenders in this debate marshal considerable evidence in support of their claims. Given the focus on intentions – a notoriously tricky field of historical inquiry – it is unlikely that a consensus will be reached through simple reference to the factual record.

On the one side of the argument are scholars who see Stalin's aims as essentially defensive: his actions were driven by a desire to stay out of the war.[24] They are opposed by others who see Stalin's manoeuvres as the expression of a complex strategy to advance the Soviet system westward: an essentially aggressive, even imperialist venture. Far from intending to prevent a war, these scholars argue, Stalin tried to exploit it. The plan was to keep the Soviet Union out of a new world war as long as possible, and to let the capitalists bloody each other, before joining in to push Soviet boundaries westward. The end goal was either the re-gathering of lands subject to Russian rule before 1917, or an export of the Revolution to the West more generally.[25] Another disagreement is over whether or not Stalin had a choice in 1939, another debate where it is easy to find Westerners who view the course taken as completely understandable, and Russians who do not.[26]

Wherever one stands in these arguments about the origins of the Molotov–Ribbentrop Pact, it is hard to deny that what followed was more than just a violation of the sovereignty of independent states. After the annexation of parts of Poland, 21,857 former Polish citizens were shot for nothing more than being part of the ruling elite of the old regime.[27] In 1940 and 1941, not counting those arrested and sent to prison or concentration camps, 383,000 civilians were deported as class enemies from the incorporated Polish and Baltic territories to remote regions of the Soviet Union. Many died in the process.[28] If the ultimate goal of Stalin's 1939–40 westward expansion was defensive, this was active, forward defence, underwritten by utterly ruthless revolutionary violence on the ground.[29]

Real history is full of moral and political ambiguities. The history of a communist dictatorship surrounded by hostile capitalist countries, and ultimately confronted by an even worse totalitarianism, is no exception to this rule. Ambiguities, however, do not make for good myth-making, and hence are best avoided. The story of the Great Patriotic War did just that: it constructed a victory not only the Soviet state but also much of the Soviet population could be proud of. The basic evolution of the story was the following: under Stalin, the united Soviet people, in particular the Russians, under the leadership of the Communist Party, led by the wise Comrade Stalin, defeated the fascist invaders and saved world civilization; under Khrushchev (1953/56–64), the dictator was removed, and the Communist Party alone, sometimes despite rather than because of Stalin, led the people in this war; under Brezhnev (1964–82), Stalin was carefully reinserted as a competent manager of the war effort. Then came perestroika, followed by crisis and the breakdown of the Soviet Union (1986–91). This war came under attack from all sides: 1939 was remembered, as was the catastrophe of 1941; repression, executions, blocking detachments and penal battalions became a matter of public debate; the anti-Bolshevik feelings of many, the mass surrenders and the positive reception the Nazi troops received in some areas were documented; the campaign in eastern Prussia and the behaviour of Soviet troops there became a matter of the public record. The list could go on.[30]

Indeed, a full-blown counter-myth to the Great Patriotic War emerged, one where the Soviet people were driven on by gun-wielding commissars and where nothing but the worst assumptions about Soviet conduct was admissible. This counter-myth was never dominant and always highly controversial, but it was also likely to lead to a backlash, once the conditions were right. In today's Russia, the old story has evolved into one where the Russian people stood united against not only the German but also the Ukrainian fascists (indeed, a Europe unified under the swastika), a further Russification and de-Bolshevization of the old Soviet master narrative.[31]

Putin's war in 2007

Putin had a personal stake in the Second World War: his father had been severely wounded at the start of the war and his brother, Vitia, died in the siege of Leningrad in 1942, ten years before the later president was born.[32] In power, Putin took an active role in the ebb and flow of public debate about a complex and terrible past, intervening repeatedly in the history wars. Of particular interest are two meetings the President held with historians, one in 2007, the other in 2014. Originally invitation-only events, they became also part of the public record by dissemination of their transcripts via the Kremlin's website. They are thus significant both as a source for Putin's direct interaction with the particular professionals who attended the meetings, and as 'signals' to the wider community of scholars and teachers. A 2015 press conference shortly after Victory Day (8 May in much of the West, 9 May in Russia) allowed the President to repeat many of his convictions, this time directed to an international as well as a domestic audience.

The President's position on the Second World War evolved over time, while exhibiting important continuities. In the 2007 meeting, Putin articulated what at first sight might seem like a contradictory position.[33] On the one hand, he stressed the ideological function of humanities in general and history in particular for his project of a positive Russian nationalism. Addressing the scholars present as 'colleagues', he asserted the importance of the humanities as the 'foundation of foundations', in particular in the education and cultivation of children. What was needed, he claimed, was the transmission of the 'best traditions and values of [our] national culture' to the younger generation. The task of humanities education was to teach young minds what was common and positive about Russia. This would help 'to decide the common tasks, which our country will face in the future'. Teachers, students and the public at large had too much 'mush in their heads'. Nobody could 'teach us' anything about history, in particular foreigners, whose scholarship was no more than an 'instrument to influence our country'. This accusation of cultural imperialism also encompassed Russian scholars who provided critical histories: they were in the pay of foreign grant agencies and hence just wrote what their masters demanded.

On the other hand, the President warned against thought control and advocated plurality of views on historical events: 'I speak about standards of education, not the standardization of thought ... as this was at some time in the past under the rule of one ideology. Of course, textbooks should lay out a variety of views on the problem of social and state development.' Pressed by some in the audience to intervene directly in the history wars, he refused to pronounce an official position on this or that historical question.

Putin did not perceive the contradiction between the ideological function of history and the insistence that a plurality of views should be expressed. Like many nationalists, he embraced a positivist view of history, both in the sense of looking at positive aspects, and in the sense that there is a historical reality, which can be known through self-evident facts. People were allowed an 'opinion' as long as they reproduced the 'facts', which spoke for themselves. The 'results of the Second World War' were a case in point. If the facts were laid out before students, they would 'come to their own understanding of the role and importance of our country in the victory over fascism' and develop a 'feeling of pride' in their country.

Victory over 'fascism' was not the only positive aspect of Russia's past. There were many positive Russian traditions of very long standing, which others should emulate. First of all, there was the long history of a multiethnic and multiconfessional state, which balanced the aspirations of majority and minorities alike. 'Tolerance', the President claimed, 'is in our blood'.

For the Putin of 2007, then, the point was not to imprint one particular position on the minds of students. Rather, his assumption was that the real history of Russia was a positive one, and hence it would, all 'opinion' aside, inspire devotion in those who knew it. While Medinskii would soon argue that if you love your country you will write positive history because facts do not matter, Putin claimed that the factual record was positive and that therefore you should love your country.[34] The unstated corollary to this position is that critical approaches to the Soviet past are either 'opinions' or, worse, 'lies'.

Like any positive nationalist, the President eschewed the difficult questions. If Russian history was one of tolerance toward minorities, why was it that so many thought of the Tsarist empire as a prison house of nations? Why the disintegration of the empire along national lines in the First World War? Why did Finland, the Baltics, Poland, Ukraine and the Transcaucasian republics break away if they were so well integrated? Why the persistent fight with 'bourgeois nationalism' under the Soviets? Why the mass deportations of minorities under Stalin? And why the nearly immediate break-up into national republics in 1991, once central power was weakened? Such facts do not fit into the positive history of national tolerance and multiculturalism the President claimed for his country. Of course there were positive aspects to the Soviet 'affirmative action empire'; but affirmative action and ethnic cleansing were so deeply intertwined that constructing an unequivocally positive narrative required willing amnesia.[35]

Likewise, the Second World War was much messier than Putin presented it. True, as a little army of Western scholars (often equipped with money from foreign grant agencies) pointed out, the Soviets took the brunt of the German onslaught and suffered most for victory over Nazism.[36] Indeed, the appreciation of the

Soviet contribution to victory over Nazism is so well-established in Western literature that a counter-attack intent on highlighting Britain's role has begun.[37] But acknowledging Soviet suffering is just the starting point of the discussion. How much of the catastrophic population loss was due to German policies, and how much to Stalin's? What influence did the Great Terror have on the readiness of the Soviet Union? Was the catastrophe of 1941 avoidable? Were the wartime deportations legitimate defence against treason, crimes against humanity, or even attempted genocide? Most troublingly of all, what role did the Hitler–Stalin Pact play in the early stages of the Second World War? Did the Soviets act as aggressors and de facto allies of Hitler in 1939–41 (in Poland, Bessarabia, the Baltics and Finland), before themselves falling victim to Nazi aggression? These are all difficult questions, and one would expect historians (and readers of history) to disagree over their answers. They simply cannot be solved with reference to unmediated 'facts'. More troublingly, they all stand in the way of an unequivocally positive history of Russia.[38]

In 2007, the president-historian did not completely eschew such hard questions. Yes, he asserted, there were 'problematic pages' in his country's history, in particular the Terror year of 1937. However, these horrors were not unique. 'Every country' had them, he proclaimed. The United States were much worse, to say nothing of the trump card in comparative atrocity:

> In any case, we did not use atomic bombs against civilian populations. We did not, let's say, pour chemicals over thousands of kilometres and we did not drop seven times more bombs on a small country than had been used in the entire Great Patriotic War, as happened in Vietnam. We did not have other black pages, such as Nazism, for example.

The Holocaust, Hiroshima, carpet-bombing and Agent Orange taken together, then, showed that 'every country' had its terrible past, and that Russian history was nothing special.

Putin's war in 2014

After signing the Memory Law in May 2014, the president-historian addressed his 'colleagues' again in November, this time early career historians and history teachers.³⁹ His basic position on history had remained the same since 2007, showing fundamental continuity between the more liberal early 'Putin 1.0' and 'Putin 2.0', his more repressive incarnation from 2012.⁴⁰ Again he displayed a nineteenth-century sense of knowledge generation: history was a science (*nauka*) and hence could not be 'rewritten' (as if scientific theories never change, are not subject to challenge, falsification by new evidence, and revision). Real historians were 'objective', and hence would write the truth. Objective historians, on the basis of their study of the documentation, would arrive at the same conclusions.

Like in 2007, Putin presented himself as a moderate believer in enlightenment. Nothing should be forbidden, 'with the exception of things with criminal character'. Instead, false views of the past should be fought with argument and research. (He did not mention that, earlier that year, he had signed a law potentially criminalizing a whole range of statements about the Soviet Union's Second World War). As in 2007, he asserted that behind the writing of foreign historians lurked the 'geopolitical interests' of their countries. Again he stressed the multinational character of the Russian people; and again he noted the importance of the Eastern Front in the subjugation of Hitler (he did not deny the contribution of the Allies).

The President also added some more details on his view of the war. He now directly addressed some of the more complex questions he had eschewed in 2007. He admitted that there was 'brutality' towards the population, and he suggested, without saying it outright, that this brutality was historically necessary in order to survive the Nazi onslaught (as if the Stalinist regime became brutal only on 22 June 1941):

> It is simply hard to say, if we could have won the war, had the state [*vlast'*] been less brutal, maybe as it had been under Nicholas II [who of course had lost against the Germans in World War I]. This is very hard to say. But what would the results have been, had we lost? The results would have been simply catastrophic. We are speaking about the physical extermination of the Slavic peoples, and not only the Russians, but many others: the Jews, and the Gypsies, and the Poles. This means, that once we put everything on the scales, it is not clear what outweighs what. One has to study this and make judgments, but they should be objective to an extreme degree.

In a very smart polemic, then, Putin suggested that whatever had happened was probably historically necessary because it had happened; and he used the comparison with Adolf Hitler, the all-time winner in any contest of evil, to make the Stalinist war look better than it otherwise would. He used a similar tactic – combining moral equivalencies with the notion that what happened had been necessary because it happened – when dealing with the division of Poland in 1939, and the question of whether the Soviet Union had sided with Hitler and divided up the spoils.

First, Putin invoked Munich 1938, when Great Britain, France and Italy had allowed Hitler to annex part of Czechoslovakia. Putin saw this major moment of the failed policy of 'appeasement' as the equivalent of the Hitler–Stalin Pact: it was a diplomatic agreement with Hitler, which led to the violation of the sovereignty of a third country not present at the occasion. (Of those at the table, of course, only Hitler would annex the Czech lands, Bohemia and Moravia, while in the Hitler–Stalin Pact, both dictators profited.) He claimed that the Munich agreement was being 'hushed up by your colleagues in the West'. He then drew a second moral equivalency: Poland got its just deserts. After all, the Poles had 'taken part of Czechoslovakia' in the aftermath of Munich. After this pseudo-contextualization of the Hitler–Stalin Pact, the President declared it a normal political move, further barricading this position against critique by appeals to objectivity: 'serious research should show that these were the methods of foreign policy at the time'.[41]

These were breathtaking claims about what historians outside of Russia had written. The Munich Agreement has become *the* 'lesson' of the Second World War, oft-invoked when discussing the dangers of 'appeasement' and the necessity of military action against dictators.[42] No head of state in the entire post-war period had ever claimed that Munich had been a good idea or a 'normal' interaction with a dictatorship. Most historians see the politics of appeasement, which led to Munich, as a 'diplomatic catastrophe' and an essential step towards the Second World War.[43]

Putin's exposé of the reasons for the 1939 pact elaborated a line his Minister of Culture had taken in 2011.[44] It is probably a correct reconstruction of part of the thought processes of the Soviet leadership at the time.[45] If, therefore, they need to be embraced by the current Russian leadership is a different question altogether. After all, they alienate many neighbours in Eastern

Europe. Moreover, alternative interpretations of Stalin's conundrum in 1939 are available which are also consistent with the factual record. Stalin did have a choice in 1939. Notwithstanding the glacial speed of negotiations, the British government was ready to ally itself with the Soviets. British negotiations might have been inept, but they were not insincere. The anti-Hitler alliance that came into being in 1941 could have fought the Germans together since 1939. Stalin might not have understood this context; or he might have simply taken the better offer the Nazis made. Neither interpretation is cause for celebration.[46]

Putin's war in 2015

By 2015, then, Putin had developed a fairly consistent line about the history of the Soviet Second World War as part of a positive, nationalist narrative for today's Russia: the Soviet war was an achievement, as it was a war against fascism; Russia played the central role in this war; all negative aspects were historically necessary, 'normal' in the context of the times, and relatively insignificant if compared with other atrocities. Russia could be proud of its past, and whoever said otherwise was either a foreigner (and hence by definition furthering foreign interests) or a hireling of the foreigners. Armed with this basic narrative, Russia began the commemoration of the seventieth anniversary of the victory over Nazi Germany in 2015.

The commemoration should have given Putin a platform to shine as a politician of world renown, but the annexation of Crimea and the Ukraine crisis more generally turned it into a show of defiance against 'the West'. Instead of a celebration of the common past of struggle against Nazism, the commemorations turned into a demonstration of Russia's isolation, as many heads of state declined the invitation to the Victory Day parade.[47] German Chancellor Angela Merkel settled on a compromise, not attending the parade but laying a wreath the day after Victory Day. The following joint press conference achieved some notoriety because the Russian translation published on the Kremlin's website omitted Merkel's characterization of the annexation of Crimea as 'criminal'.[48]

More important for our context here, Putin was asked directly about the Molotov–Ribbentrop Pact and the fears its re-evaluation in Russia engendered elsewhere in Eastern Europe. He first dismissed such anxieties as an 'internal condition of those who are afraid', and hence no concern of his. The sufferers of such nervous conditions should make an effort and forget about 'the phobias of the past'. As far as the pact was concerned, he retraced the well-trodden path that it was not Stalin's but the Western Allies' fault. The Soviet Union had tried hard to establish a system of collective security against Nazism, but failed. After 1938, it was clear to many that war was inevitable. Churchill understood that. The Soviet Union understood that too, and it understood that it would have to face Hitler's Germany alone. The pact was signed in order to escape a direct confrontation with Hitler. Putin then again equated the Polish annexations of parts of Czechoslovakia after Munich with the Soviet annexations, implying that it served the Poles right: 'And it so happened that after the Molotov-Ribbentrop Pact and the division of Poland' the country found itself 'a victim of the same politics' it had tried to engage in itself.[49]

Riding the wave or shaping it?

Since 2007, then, Putin has developed a sophisticated polemical view about the Second World War, which skilfully combines historical facts with omission, relativization and contextualization. This view of history is not easily dismissed. While doubtless dangerous both domestically and internationally, it is intelligent, informed and complex. If engaged, it requires argumentation on a fairly high empirical and historiographical level. It is also very popular within today's Russia. For one, it 'binds together the Russian political leadership and its supporting elites', in particular among the military and security services.[50] It also has significant support among the nonliberal intelligentsia. Critical historians notwithstanding, many Russian colleagues – professionals as well as popular writers – are engaged in what amounts to a conservative counter-stroke in the Russian history wars over the Second World War.[51] Moreover, the sentiments Putin's version of the war reflects have wider resonance. In the 2000s, Russian popular culture has indulged in heroic war fantasies, drawing directly on Soviet myth-making.[52] By the end of the first two decades of the new millennium, 87 per cent of Russians were proud of their country's victory in the Second World War.[53] The old Soviet holiday of Victory Day remains immensely popular, and grassroots projects to commemorate the war started spontaneously 'from below' and only later gained state support.⁵⁴ To a significant extent, then, Putin was riding a wave not of his own making.

In fact, the President's position was in many ways more sophisticated and more informed than those held by many in Russian society at large. He did not deny basic facts, but simply relativized them.⁵⁵ Meanwhile, many of his compatriots held much more extreme views, as opinion surveys consistently showed. A poll conducted by the independent Levada Center in 2005, 2009, 2010 and 2014 asked respondents: 'Have you heard about the secret protocols to the nonaggression pact between Fascist Germany and the USSR (the Molotov-Ribbentrop Pact, providing for the division of Poland and the division of spheres of influence in Europe)?' In 2005, 43 per cent answered: 'I heard about them and believe that they did exist.' In 2014, this share was down to 39 per cent. Meanwhile, those who answered 'I heard about them, but think that they are a falsification' had risen from 9 to 14 per cent. The percentage of those who supported the Hitler–Stalin Pact rose from 40 (2005) to 45 per cent (2014); while the proportion of those who opposed it declined from 24 to 18 in a hundred.⁵⁶ The President was also in accord with many of his voters when he put his pen to the draft of the Memory Law, which had been approved by popular opinion much earlier: in a 2009 poll, 60 per cent endorsed the idea of passing a law criminalizing 'denying victory'.⁵⁷

Clearly, the Kremlin's propaganda campaign – embedded as it was in wider currents of popular as well as high culture – was both sophisticated rhetorically and fell on fertile ground culturally. As one historian put it in an insightful article, 'the prevalent attitudes towards history and memory' cannot be explained with a top-down, the-Kremlin-brainwashing-the-hapless-population model. Rather, we find a 'meeting of minds between the rulers and the ruled in Eurasia'.⁵⁸ Nevertheless, the Levada poll also contained some surprises. For example, those who believed that the 1940 occupation of the Baltic States can be described as an occupation remained at a constant 20 per cent between 2007 and 2014, but the view that 'occupation' was a misleading appellation lost support, declining from 63 to 53 per cent. Today, 27 per cent find this question 'hard to answer'. The voices from Eastern Europe and those of critical Russian historians clearly did not go unheard. Likewise, while a majority of Russians in 2010 (63 per cent) believed that the Soviet

Union could have won without Allied support, this share was down from 71 per cent nine years earlier.[59] Perhaps it is this infiltration of critical voices that encouraged Putin to step up his campaign to rescue the past from those who want to criticize it?

The reasons for the Memory Law

The Memory Law was long in the making. A first draft law was presented to the Duma on 6 May 2009, and subsequently lingered in several versions in the corridors of power. There had originally been resistance to it from the highest echelons of power, which could explain why it was not passed for five years.[60] Given this backstory, the question becomes: Why did Putin decide to sign this law in the spring of 2014? The timing just before Victory Day was one factor. Maybe, then, it was simply the logical solution to the 'memory war' that had been going on in Eastern Europe since perestroika and where Russia was 'on the defensive': in many newly independent states – Latvia, Estonia, Georgia and Ukraine, Soviet history began to be remembered as one of occupation by an alien totalitarian regime akin to the Nazis. Wartime resistance, even where implicated in Nazi crimes, was celebrated as heroic attempts at national liberation and the Soviet Union (i.e., Russia) is routinely accused of genocide.[61]

Indeed, some of the Russian state's initiatives can be seen as direct counter-attacks in this international 'memory war'. The May 2009 announcement of the creation of a presidential commission to suppress the 'falsification of history' was one such event.[62] But the flanking legislation, which would have given that commission some teeth, was at the time judged still too controversial, and hence was shelved. Its return in 2014 had more to do with real-life politics than their symbolic equivalent. The year 2014 was not a major anniversary, nor was there a major assault of East Europeans on Russian historical memory. If this decision had been shaped only by the politics of memory, we should have expected this law to be passed in 2015 (seventy years since the victory over Nazi Germany) or 2016 (seventy-five years since the German attack on the Soviet Union), not 2014.

More important was the immediate political context. Much like the annexation of Crimea, the signing of the Memory Law was an ad hoc decision by a government that increasingly felt embattled and under threat from enemies within and without (witness Putin's persistent attacks on foreign historians and grant agencies).[63] History was part of the ideological front in this struggle, a battlefield in Putin's 'preventive counterrevolution'. Critical historians within Russia had long hoped that a different kind of national historical consciousness would aid the democratization of the country. As 'negative nationalists', they attempted to critique the past to build a better future. President Putin shared their conviction about the centrality of historical memory in the political process, albeit with reversed value judgements. For this 'positive nationalist', a monolithic, triumphalist narrative underwrote an authoritarian state as much as a critical, complex and nuanced one safeguarded, in the minds of liberal Russians, a democratic polity. The popular appeal of the authoritarian version of historical consciousness shows that Putin's counter-revolution was not just a top-down affair, but rather an active mobilization of one sector of society against another.

Implications for histories of the Soviet Second World War

Thus, just when scholarly discourse began to lose some of its Cold War polemical edge, and scholars in Russia, the United States, Europe and elsewhere started to become increasingly integrated in a transnational scholarly community, in Russia (as in other successor states of the Soviet Union) the history of Stalinism was both re-nationalized and re-politicized. With the law of 5 May 2014, the exploitation of the popularity of Great Patriotic War nostalgia for purposes of national mobilization became armed with the full might of the Russian legal-repressive system. A mystified history became part of the state apparatus.[64] While there was considerable popular support for this law and the kind of history it was supposed to preserve, there were also critics, both within the population and among professional historians, who embraced a very different version of the past. It was this section of the population – a minority, no doubt, but a significant one – that was supposed to be silenced by this law.

The Luzgin case revolved around an actual inaccuracy – the timing of the Soviet invasion of Poland. If prosecutions had continued this pattern, the Russian law would have followed a similar track as its Holocaust denial counterparts elsewhere in the world.[65] However, other courts took a broader view. A test case involved Kirill Mikhailovich Aleksandrov, the pre-eminent Russian expert on the Vlasov movement – the most well-known military collaborators with the Germans.[66] His doctoral defence, at the St Petersburg Institute of History of the Russian Academy of Sciences on 1 March 2016, became a cause célèbre in Russian historical circles. Some of the most respected historians of Stalinism – such as Oleg Khlevniuk – submitted favourable reviews of Aleksandrov's work on Vlasov's officer corps. Other historians spoke harshly against the candidate, as did representatives of war veteran organizations. The Institute of History closed ranks and passed the dissertation anyway. Among the crowd of more than ninety attendees – defences are public events in Russia, but usually draw much smaller audiences – were not only historians; both sides of the argument had brought priests of the Russian Orthodox Church; veterans had turned out in force, one of them leaving the room with the words, 'Where would you be, had we not won? Would you be able to sit here [and talk]?'[67]

A right-wing NGO, Narodnyi Sobor (the People's Council, which can also be translated as the People's Church), which describes its goal as 'the rebuilding of Russia on the basis of traditional spiritual-moral values of Russian civilization', went further.[68] It asked the public prosecutor to investigate if the new Memory Law had been broken. Ahead of the defence, the director of the Institute of History was summoned to the prosecutor's office for a 'prophylactic conversation'. This intimidation was part of an incredible amount of pressure 'from above, from below, from the side' to cancel the proceedings, as the director told a journalist: 'They asked me to think about the fate of the institute.'[69] Historians hostile to Aleksandrov also tried to substantiate the case against him in a scholarly journal.[70]

A year later, the affair took a more ominous turn. The Highest Attestation Commission (VAK), in charge of approving all higher degrees in the Russian Federation, sent the offending work to the examination council of the General Staff Military Academy for another opinion. Predictably, the military scholars voted against granting the title.[71] VAK's Council of Experts followed this recommendation on 29 May 2017.[72] After losing his title, Aleksandrov was also dragged in front of the courts to defend himself against charges under the Memory Law.[73] As one historian reported, the

City Court of St Petersburg declared that an article on the OUN Aleksandrov had published in a newspaper was 'extremist'. The basis of this decision: 'The article makes a negative psychological impression.'[74]

Despite such mounting pressure, Aleksandrov decided to continue his work in Russia.[75] Others, too, refused to be intimidated. One central debate which might well fall victim of the Memory Law is what is known as the 'Icebreaker Controversy': historians who claim that Stalin planned to attack Germany in 1941. The majority of historians, both in Russia and elsewhere, believe that the weight of evidence is on the side of those who think that there was no plan to attack, at any rate not in 1941.[76] However, this is an opinion arrived at on the basis of an open and controversial debate, and on the basis of evidence that requires contextualization and interpretation. In Russia, it has continued despite the threat of the Memory Law.[77] Luzgin, by contrast, refused to pay his fine and fled Putin's historical politics. He now lives in exile, the first victim of a repoliticization of the Second World War.[78]

Notes

1 '15 faktov pro "Banderovtsev", ili o chem molchit Kreml', http://saracinua.livejournal.com/2147939.html (accessed 22 August 2016).
2 Timothy Snyder, 'The Causes of Ukrainian-Polish Ethnic Cleansing 1943', *Past and Present* 179 (2003): 197–234; Grzegorz Rossolinski-Liebe, *Stepan Bandera: The Life and Afterlife of a Ukrainian Nationalist: Fascism, Genocide, and Cult* (Stuttgart, 2014); Jared McBride, 'Peasants into Perpetrators: The OUN-UPA and the Ethnic Cleansing of Volhynia, 1943–1944', *Slavic Review* 75, no. 3 (2016): 630–54.
3 David R. Marples, *Heroes and Villains: Creating a National History in Contemporary Ukraine* (Budapest, 2007); Per A. Rudling, 'The OUN, the UPA and the Holocaust: A Study in the Manufacturing of Historical Myths', *The Carl Beck Papers in Russian & East European Studies* 2107 (2011); Eleanora Narvselius, 'The "Bandera Debate": The Contentious Legacy of World War II and Liberalization of Collective Memory in Western Ukraine', *Canadian Slavonic Papers* 54, nos 3–4 (2012): 470–90; Serhy Yekelchyk, *The Conflict in Ukraine: What Everyone Needs to Know* (Oxford, 2015); and Andreas Umland, 'Bad History Doesn't Make Friends', *FP* website (25 October 2016), http://foreignpolicy.com/2016/10/25/bad-history-doesnt-make-friends-kiev-ukraine-stepan-bandera/ (accessed 7 April 2017).
4 Mark Edele, 'The Impact of War and the Costs of Superpower Status', *The Oxford Handbook of Modern Russian History* (online version), ed. Simon Dixon (Oxford, 2015), doi: 10.1093/oxfordhb/9780199236701.013.028.

DEBATES ON STALINISM

5   The most detailed reporting about the case is Maksim Strugov, 'Ssylka v Niurnberg: Zhitel' Permi oshtrafovan za repost materiala ob uchastii SSSR v okkupatsii Pol'shi v 1939 godu', *Kommersant.ru* (30 June 2016), http://kommersant.ru/doc/3026212 (accessed 23 August 2016). For a short English-language summary, see: 'Man in Russia's Perm Fined for "Nazism Rehabilitation"', *Moscow Times* (23 August 2016), https://themoscowtimes.com/news/man-in-russias-perm-fined-for-nazism-rehabilitation-53543 (accessed 23 August 2016). On the legal implications: M. Trutnev, 'Judgment in the Luzgin Case and its Implications for Freedom of Historical Discussion', *Legal Dialogue/Pravovoi dialog* (June 2017), http://legal-dialogue.org/judgment-luzgin-case (accessed 14 February 2018). The materials from the court case can be accessed at: http://new.prpc.ru/news/predlagaem-vashemu-vnimaniyu-materialy-dela-luzgina.html (accessed 14 February 2018).
6   Strugov, 'Ssylka v Niurnberg'.
7   Strugov, 'Ssylka v Niurnberg'. Wage data are for July 2015. 'Russia Average Monthly Wages 1992–2016', http://www.tradingeconomics.com/russia/wages (accessed 23 August 2016).
8   Nina Tumarkin, *The Living and the Dead: The Rise and Fall of the Cult of World War II in Russia* (New York, 1994); Amir Weiner, *Making Sense of War: The Second World War and the Fate of the Bolshevik Revolution* (Princeton, 2001); Stephen Lovell, *The Shadow of War: Russia and the USSR 1941 to the Present* (Oxford, 2010).
9   By 'positive nationalism' I mean the opposite of the critical embrace of one's heritage often found among intellectuals, particularly in Germany and Russia.
10 On historical and historiographical aspects of the Ukraine crisis see the forums 'Ukraine and the Crisis of "Russian Studies": Participant Observation of History in the Making', *Ab Imperio* 3 (2014): 22–228; and 'The Ukrainian Crisis: Past and Present', in *Kritika: Explorations in Russian and Eurasian History* 16, no. 1 (2015): 121–55.
11 Robert Horvath, 'Putin's "Preventive Counter-Revolution": Post-Soviet Authoritarianism and the Spectre of Velvet Revolution', *Europe–Asia Studies* 63, no. 1 (2011): 1–25; and Robert Horvath, *Putin's Preventive Counter-Revolution: Post-Soviet Authoritarianism and the Spectre of Velvet Revolution* (London, 2013).
12 Vladimir Medinskii, *Voina: Mify SSSR 1939–1945* (Moscow, 2011).
13 Medinskii, *Voina*, 116, 642, 643, 76.
14 For subtle differences in the line taken on the revolutions of 1917, see Mark Edele, 'Putin, Memory Wars and the 100th Anniversary of the Russian Revolution', *The Conversation* (10 February 2017), https://theconversation.com/friday-essay-putin-memory-wars-and-the-100th-anniversary-of-the-russian-revolution-72477 (accessed 7 April 2017).
15 See Mikhail Zygar, *All the Kremlin's Men: Inside the Court of Vladimir Putin* (New York, 2016). On Putin as 'history man', see Fiona Hill and Clifford G. Gaddy, *Mr Putin: Operative in the Kremlin* (Washington, 2013), chapter 4. See also Putin's thoroughly Soviet 'reading list' on the Second World War: Vladimir Putin, 'The Reading List' (2011), http://www.historynet.com/vladimir-putins-world-war-ii-reading-list.htm (accessed 13 April 2017).

16 The text of the law is available at http://kremlin.ru/acts/20912 (accessed 22 January 2015).
17 The law also punishes any display of lack of respect for military honour and dates of commemoration, but this point is less central to the argument made here.
18 For the Asian perspective, see Evan Mawdsley, *World War II: A New History* (Cambridge, 2009); for the European equivalent: Gerhard L. Weinberg, *A World at Arms: A Global History of World War II*. 2nd ed. (New York, 2005).
19 The Russian text of Stalin's radio address is reprinted in I. Stalin, *O Velikoi Otechestvennoi voine Sovetskogo Soiuza* (Moscow, 2002), 11–16; an English translation can be found at: https://www.marxists.org/reference/archive/stalin/works/1941/07/03.htm (accessed 12 April 2017). On wartime propaganda, see Karel C. Berkhoff, *Motherland in Danger: Soviet Propaganda during World War II* (Cambridge, Mass., 2012).
20 The best introductions to this history remain John Barber and Mark Harrison, *The Soviet Home Front, 1941–1945: A Social and Economic History of the USSR in World War II* (London, 1991); and Evan Mawdsley, *Thunder in the East: The Nazi–Soviet War 1941–1945* (London, 2005; rev. 2nd ed., London, 2015). For the definitive military history from below, see Roger Reese, *Why Stalin's Soldiers Fought: The Red Army's Military Effectiveness in World War II* (Lawrence, 2011). For life and death at the home front, see also Wendy Z. Goldman and Donald Filtzer (eds), *Hunger and War: Food Provisioning in the Soviet Union during World War II* (Bloomington, 2015).
21 For two sketches of such a history, see Mark Harrison, 'World War II', in: *Encyclopedia of Russian History*, ed. James R. Millar (New York, 2004), 4: 1683–92; and Mark Edele, 'A Long Second World War (1937–1949)', in: *The Soviet Union: A short History* (Hoboken, 2019), 123–43. See also Jonathan Haslam, *The Soviet Union and the Threat from the East, 1933–1941: Moscow, Tokyo, and the Prelude to the Pacific War* (Pittsburgh, 1992); Zhang Baijia, 'China's Quest for Foreign Military Aid', in: *The Battle for China: Essays on the Military History of the Sino-Japanese War of 1937–1945*, ed. Mark Peattie, Edward Drea and Hans van de Ven (Stanford, 2011), 283–307.
22 An exception is Timothy Snyder, *Bloodlands: Europe between Hitler and Stalin* (London, 2010), 116; Timothy Snyder, 'Putin's New Nostalgia', *New York Review of Books* (10 November 2014), http://www.nybooks.com/daily/2014/11/10/putin-nostalgia-stalin-hitler/ (accessed 12 April 2017).
23 Sergei Sluch, 'Warum brauchte Hitler einen Nichtangriffspakt mit Stalin?', in: *'Unternehmen Barbarossa': Zum historischen Ort der deutsch-sowjetischen Beziehungen von 1933 bis Herbst 1941*, ed. Roland G. Foerster (Munich, 1993), 69–87; Mawdsley, *World War II*, 95; Gerhard L. Weinberg, 'How a Second World War Happened', in: *A Companion to World War II*, ed. Roland G. Foerster (Oxford, 2013), 1: 13–28; Peter Jackson, 'Europe: The Failure of Diplomacy, 1933–1940', in: *The Cambridge History of the Second World War*, vol. 2, *Politics and Ideology*, ed. Richard Bosworth and Joseph Maiolo (Cambridge, 2015), 217–52, esp. 241, 252.
24 For example, Jonathan Haslam, *The Soviet Union and the Struggle for Collective Security in Europe, 1933–39* (New York, 1984); Geoffrey Roberts's

books, *The Unholy Alliance: Stalin's Pact with Hitler* (Bloomington, 1989); *The Soviet Union and the Origins of the Second World War: Russo-German Relations and the Road to War, 1933–1941* (New York, 1995); and *Stalin's Wars: From World War to Cold War, 1939–1953* (New Haven, 2006), chapter 2; M. I. Mel'tiukhov, *17 sentiabria 1939: Sovetsko-pol'skie konflikty 1918–1939* (Moscow, 2009). For a broader perspective: Alfred Rieber, 'Stalin as Foreign Policy-Maker: Avoiding War, 1927–1953', in: *Stalin: A New History*, ed. Sarah Davies and James Harris (Cambridge, 2005), 140–58.

25 For three versions – by Russian, Ukrainian and North American scholars – see S. Sluch, 'Germano-sovetskie otnosheniia v 1918–1941 godakh: Motivy i posledstviia vneshnepoliticheskikh reshenii', *Slavianovedenie*, no. 3 (1996): 101–13; V. M. Litvin et al., *Ukraina: Politichna istoriia XX-pochatok XXI stolittia* (Kiev, 2007), 665–69; Robert Gellately, *Stalin's Curse: Battling for Communism in War and Cold War* (Oxford, 2013), 46–49.

26 For the latter, see M. I. Semiriaga, *Tainy stalinskoi diplomatii. 1939–1941* (Moscow, 1992), 57–58. For the former, see the all-time classic of revisionist historiography: A. J. P. Taylor, *The Origins of the Second World War* (New York 1996), 263; similarly, P. M. H. Bell, *The Origins of the Second World War in Europe*. 3rd ed. (Harlow, 2007), 305. For a re-evaluation of Taylor's provocations, see Gordon Martel (ed.), *The Origins of the Second World War Reconsidered*. 2nd ed. (London, 2002).

27 A. Shelepin to Khrushchev, 3 March 1959, reprinted in Anna M. Cienciala, Natalia S. Lebedeva and Wojciech Materski (eds), *Katyn: A Crime without Punishment* (New Haven, 2007), 332.

28 Mark Edele, 'World War II as a History of Displacement: The Soviet Case', *History Australia* 12, no. 2 (2015): 24. That these deportations were less lethal than the organized genocide the Germans implemented against the Jews is a fact worth considering. See Mark Edele, Sheila Fitzpatrick and Atina Grossmann (eds), *Shelter from the Holocaust: Rethinking Jewish Survival in the Soviet Union* (Detroit, 2017).

29 Dietrich Beyrau, *Schlachtfeld der Diktatoren: Osteuropa im Schatten von Hitler und Stalin* (Göttingen, 2000); Alexander V. Prusin, *The Lands Between: Conflict in the East European Borderlands, 1870–1992* (Oxford, 2010).

30 Lisa Kirschenbaum, *The Legacy of the Siege of Leningrad, 1941–1995: Myth, Memories, and Monuments* (Cambridge, 2006); Denise J. Youngblood, *Russian War Films: On the Cinema Front, 1914–2005* (Lawrence, 2007); Thomas Sherlock, *Historical Narratives in the Soviet Union and Post-Soviet Russia: Destroying the Settled Past, Creating an Uncertain Future* (New York, 2007); Stephen Norris, *Blockbuster History in the New Russia: Movies, Memory, Patriotism* (Bloomington, 2012), chapter 6; Mark Edele, 'The Soviet Culture of Victory', *Journal of Contemporary History* 54, no. 4 (2019): 780–98.

31 Teddy J. Uldricks, 'War, Politics and Memory: Russian Historians Reevaluate the Origins of World War II', *History and Memory* 21, no. 2 (2009): 60–82.

32 Elizabeth A. Wood, 'Performing Memory: Vladimir Putin and the Celebration of World War II in Russia', *Soviet and Post-Soviet Review* 38, no. 2 (2011): 172–200, here: 185–88; Hill and Gaddy, *Mr Putin*, chapter 5; 'Putinu pokazali mogilu brata, pogibshego v blokadu', *MKRU*, (27 January 2014), http://

www.mk.ru/politics/article/2014/01/27/975982-putinu-pokazali-mogilu-brata-pogibshego-v-blokadu.html (accessed 10 February 2015).
33 'Stenograficheskii otchet o vstreche s delegatami Vserossiiskoi konferentsii prepodavatelei gumanitarnykh i obshchestvennykh nauk' (21 June 2007), Novo-Ogarevo, http://archive.kremlin.ru/text/appears/2007/06/135323.shtml (accessed 17 February 2014).
34 Medinskii, *Voina*, 643.
35 See Chapter 3. The term is Terry Martin's.
36 In addition to the works cited in notes above, see, for example, John Erickson, *The Road to Stalingrad: Stalin's War with Germany, Volume One* (New Haven, 1975), and *The Road to Berlin: Stalin's War with Germany, Volume Two* (New Haven, 1983); *pars pro toto* the immense oeuvre of Glantz: David M. Glantz and Jonathan House, *When Titans Clashed: How the Red Army Stopped Hitler* (Lawrence, 1995); Richard Overy, *Russia's War* (New York, 1997); Catherine Merridale, *Ivan's War: Life and Death in the Red Army, 1939–1945* (New York, 2006); David Stahel, *Operation Barbarossa and Germany's Defeat in the East* (Cambridge, 2010); Evan Mawdsley, *December 1941: Twelve Days That Began a World War* (New Haven, 2012); Jochen Hellbeck, *Stalingrad: The City That Defeated the Third Reich* (New York, 2015).
37 Phillips Payson O'Brien, *How the War Was Won: Air-Sea Power and Allied Victory in World War II* (Cambridge, 2015).
38 See chapters 3 and 5. On ambiguity, see Norman Davies, *No Simple Victory: World War II in Europe, 1939–1945* (London, 2006).
39 'Vstrecha s molodymi uchenymi i prepodavateliami istorii' (5 November 2014), Moscow, http://news.kremlin.ru/news/46951/print (accessed 22 January 2015).
40 Maria Lipman, 'How Putin Silences Dissent', *Foreign Affairs* 95, no. 3 (2016): 38–46.
41 Medinskii, *Voina*, 37–39, 50–52.
42 Yuen Foong Khong, *Analogies at War: Korea, Munich, Dien Bien Phu, and the Vietnam Decisions of 1965* (Princeton, 1992). For an early link by a Western historian of Munich and the Hitler–Stalin Pact, see Taylor, *The Origins of the Second World War*.
43 For two classic examples, see Bernard Wasserstein, *Barbarism & Civiliation: A History of Europe in Our Time* (Oxford, 2007), 271–79, quotation: 277; Eric Hobsbawm, *The Age of Extremes: A History of the World, 1914–1991* (New York, 1996), 153–54.
44 Medinskii, *Voina*, 37–39, 50–52.
45 On the Soviet position in the diplomatic jockeying of the interwar years, see Jackson, 'Europe', 223–27.
46 Robert Manne, 'Some British Light on the Nazi–Soviet Pact', *European Studies Review* 11, no. 1 (1981): 83–102.
47 Mark Edele, 'Russia Still Struggles with a Violent Past, 70 Years after the Defeat of Nazism', *The Conversation* (7 May 2015), http://theconversation.com/russia-still-struggles-with-a-violent-past-70-years-after-the-defeat-of-nazism-41031 (accessed 6 November 2019).
48 Carl Schreck, 'Transmission: Merkel's Remark on "Criminal" Annexation Omitted in Russian Translation', *Radio Free Europe/Radio Liberty* (12 May

2015), http://www.rferl.org/content/russia-merkel-putin-translation-criminal-word-omitted/27011285.html (accessed 15 May 2015).

49 'Zaiavleniia dlia pressy i otvety na voprosy zhurnalistov po itogam vstrechi s Federal'nym kantslerom Germanii Angeloi Merkel', 10 May 2015, 16:00, Moscow, Kremlin, http://kremlin.ru/events/president/transcripts/49455 (accessed 13 May 2015). For comparison of the wording, the German translation is available at: http://www.bundesregierung.de/Content/DE/Mitschrift/Pressekonferenzen/2015/05/2015-05-10-pk-merkel-putin.html (accessed 15 May 2015).

50 Sherlock, *Historical Narratives*, 161–65, quotation: 165.

51 See for example Elena Seniavskaia, *Protivniki Rossii v voinakh XX veka: Evoliutsiia 'obraza vraga' v soznanii armii i obshchestva* (Moscow, 2006); or Mel'tiukhov, *17 sentiabria 1939*. See also Inessa Jażborowska, 'Russian Historical Writing about the Crime of Katyn', *Polish Review* 53, no. 2 (2008): 139–57; David Brandenberger, Vladimir Solonari, Boris Mironov, Anton Fedyashin and Elena Zubkova, 'Toward a New Orthodoxy? The Politics of History in Russia Today', *Kritika: Explorations in Russian and Eurasian History* 10, no. 4 (2009): 825–68; and Karsten Brüggemann, 'Russia and the Baltic Countries: Recent Russian-Language Literature', *Kritika: Explorations in Russian and Eurasian History* 10, no. 4 (2009): 935–56.

52 Gregory Carlton, 'Victory in Death: Annihilation Narratives in Russia Today', *History & Memory* 22, no. 1 (2010): 135–68; Gregory Carlton, *Russia: The Story of War* (Cambridge, 2017).

53 Levada poll, 17 January 2019, https://www.levada.ru/2019/01/17/natsionalnaya-identichnost-i-gordost/ (accessed 30 January 2019).

54 Stephen M. Norris, 'Memory for Sale: Victory Day 2010 and Russian Remembrance', *Soviet & Post-Soviet Review* 38, no. 2 (2011): 201–29; Seth Bernstein, 'Remembering War, Remaining Soviet: Digital Commemoration of World War II in Putin's Russia', *Memory Studies* 9, no. 4 (2016): 422–36; Iva Glisic and Mark Edele, 'The Memory Revolution Meets the Digital Age: Red Army Soldiers Remember World War II', *Geschichte und Gesellschaft* 45, no. 1 (2019): 95–119.

55 In 2004, the Stalinist hardliner Vladimir Vasil'evich Sukhodeev denounced Putin's refusal to flatly deny the Soviet responsibility for the Katyn mass shootings as 'unobjective'. See his *Epokha Stalina: Sobytiia i liudi. Entsiklopediia* (Moscow, 2004), 129.

56 http://www.levada.ru/31-08-2014/vtoraya-mirovaya-i-velikaya-otechestvennaya-voiny (accessed 10 February 2015).

57 'Press-vypusk No. 1216: "Itogi Velikoi Otechestvennoi voiny: peresmotr nedopustim?"', http://wciom.ru/index.php?id=459&uid=11804 (accessed 13 February 2015).

58 Igor Torbakov, 'Divisive Historical Memories: Russia and Eastern Europe', in: *Confronting Memories of World War II: European and Asian Legacies*, ed. Daniel Chirot, Gi-Wook Shin and Daniel Sneider (Seattle, 2014), 253.

59 'USSR Didn't Need Allies to Win WWII – Survey', 23 October 2010, http://rt.com/usa/ussr-didnt-need-allies/ (accessed February 10, 2015). A good introduction to the question of the importance of Allied assistance is Alexander Hill, *The Great Patriotic War of the Soviet Union, 1941–45: A Documentary*

Reader (London, 2009), chapter 8. A broader view is provided by R. J. Overy, *Why the Allies Won* (New York, 1997). On the question of 'occupation', see Mark Edele, 'Soviet Liberations and Occupations, 1939–1949', *The Cambridge History of the Second World War*, 2:487–506.
60 See Mark Edele, *Stalinist Society, 1928–1953* (Oxford, 2011), 316–17, fn 97.
61 Torbakov, 'Divisive Historical Memories', 245. See also Chapter 9.
62 Torbakov, 'Divisive Historical Memories', 245.
63 See Zygar, *All the Kremlin's Men*; Ben Judah, *Fragile Empire: How Russia Fell in and out of Love with Vladimir Putin* (New Haven, 2013).
64 On the reconstruction of 'normal authoritarianism' under Putin, see also William Zimmerman, *Ruling Russia: Authoritarianism from the Revolution to Putin* (Princeton, 2014), esp. chapters 8–10.
65 Michael Shermer and Alex Grobman, *Denying History: Who Says the Holocaust Never Happened and Why Do They Say It?* Updated and expanded ed. (Berkeley, 2009).
66 See K. M. Aleksandrov's books, *Ofitserskii korpus armii general-leitenanta A. A. Vlasova 1944–1945*. 2nd ed. (Moscow, 2009); *Russkie soldaty Vermakhta: Geroi ili predateli* (Moscow, 2005); and *Armiia generala Vlasova 1944–1945* (Moscow, 2006).
67 The proceedings are available at http://www.spbiiran.nw.ru/защита-25/ (accessed 22 August 2016). The most important published account is Elena Kuznetsova, 'Zashchita s generalom Vlasovym', *Fontanka: Peterburgskaia internet-gazeta* (2 March 2016), http://www.fontanka.ru/2016/03/01/173/ (accessed 22 August 2016).
68 'O dvizhenii "Narodnyi Sobor"', http://www.narodsobor.ru/about (accessed 22 August 2016).
69 Kuznetsova, 'Zashchita s generalom Vlasovym'.
70 A. Iu. Plotnikov and V. V. Vasilik, '"Vlasovskoe dvizhenie" ili eshche raz ob istorii predatel'stva. (Na osnove analiza doktorskoi dissertatsii K. M. Aleksandrova)', *Klio* 1, no. 109 (2016): 197–202.
71 Kirill Chulkov, 'Spaset li VAK Rossiiu ot predatelei?', *Versiia na Neve* (27 March 2017), https://neva.versia.ru/istorik-vlasovec-kirill-aleksandrov-mozhet-ne-poluchit-stepen-doktora (accessed 12 April 2017).
72 http://vak.ed.gov.ru/documents/10179/0/834нк-Александров.pdf/9d2de054–0ce7–46fb-bdd2–58fb236f7d81 (accessed 14 February 2018).
73 'Nakazanie za pravdu', *Russkoe slovo* no. 6 (8 June 2017), http://ruslo.cz/index.php/component/k2/item/776-nakazanie-za-pravdu-6–2017 (accessed 8 June 2017).
74 https://www.facebook.com/andrei.b.zubov/posts/2014649635487044?pnref=story (accessed 14 February 2018). See also: 'Material istorika v "Novoi gazete" sud Peterburga priznal ekstremizmom', *Fontanka: peterpurgskaia internet-gazeta* (14 December 2017), https://www.fontanka.ru/2017/12/14/164/ (accessed 14 Feburary 2018).
75 'Kirill Aleksandrov: "Dlia nastoiashchego issledovatelia zapreta na professiiu byt' ne mozhet," Interv'iu', *Voice of America* (10 October 2017), https://www.golos-ameriki.ru/a/ai-historian-on-vlasov/4064158.html; '"Lozh' daet kratkovremennyi effect, a potom razrushaet." Interv'iu istorika Kirilla Aleksandrova, lishennogo doktorskoi stepeni za rabotu o vlasovskom dvizhenii', *Novaia gazeta*

(15 January 2018), https://www.novayagazeta.ru/articles/2018/01/12/75127-lozh-daet-kratkovremennyy-effekt-a-potom-razrushaet (accessed 14 February 2018).
76 For a succinct overview of the debate and the evidence, see Evan Mawdsley, 'Crossing the Rubicon: Soviet Plans for Offensive War in 1940–1941', *International History Review* 25, no. 4 (2003): 818–65.
77 See, for example, D. Khmel'nitskii, L. Liuks and L. Nemtsev, 'Professional'nyi spor ili istoricheskaia publitsistika? Stolknovenie po bolevym voprosam sovetskoi istorii: skreshchenny mechi', *Gefter. Zhurnal* (18 May 2016), http://gefter.ru/archive/18591 (accessed 14 February 2018).
78 'Rossianin sbezhal v Chekhiiu posle absurdnogo prigovora za repost v Vkontakte', *Russkii Monitor* (12 January 2017), https://rusmonitor.com/rossiyanin-sbezhal-v-chekhiyu-posle-absurdnogo-prigovora-za-repost-v-vkontakte.html (accessed 14 February 2018); 'Oppozitsioner Vladimir Luzgin: "Ia kak derevo, kotoromu obrubili korni"', *Radio Praha* (25 March 2017), https://inosmi.ru/politic/20170325/238958902.html (accessed 14 February 2018).

9

Holodomor: A transnational history

Catastrophe

The Second World War is not the only calamity from the Stalinist past which still matters today. The Great Famine of 1932–33 is another.[1] Three rural areas were particularly hard hit: Ukraine, the northern Caucasus and Kazakhstan. In absolute terms, Ukrainians suffered the largest losses. The Soviet census of 1937 showed 4.8 million fewer people than the census of 1927. Next came Kazakhs with a decline of 1.1 million, followed by Mordvinians (92,000), Germans (87,000), and Moldavians (55,000). In relative terms, however, the worst affected were Kazakhs, who lost 28 per cent between the censuses, ahead of Moldavians (20 per cent), and Ukrainians (15 per cent).[2]

The debate about the famine is among the most hard-fought controversies of contemporary scholarship on the Soviet Union. This polemic is transnational. It is both about the past and about the present. It is about historical evidence and its interpretation, but also about politics and ideology. It is often personal as much as political. It is about international politics and domestic struggles. Our story begins in the Soviet Union during the famine, moves to Britain, the United States, Canada and Australia during the Cold War, returns to the Soviet Union in the final years of its existence, to dissolve into a transnational debate in the new millennium.

It is wrong to claim that the famine had been 'forgotten' (see Figure 9.1). News of it filtered out nearly immediately and information accumulated over the decades. There were few scholars outside the Soviet Union who denied that a famine had occurred. Even in the Soviet Union, the veil of silence was lifted from time to time. The major controversy, thus, was and remains not over whether a famine happened, but what were its reasons. The extent of the famine, the number of victims, and the relative death toll of Ukrainians, Russians, Kazakhs, Poles and Jews also generated disagreement.

There are three broad interpretations of the origins of the catastrophe: the famine as an unintended calamity caused by utopian and callous grain collections; the famine as intentional genocide targeting the Ukrainian nation; the famine as a consciously employed weapon of class war. All three see the famine as man-made, but they diverge in their interpretation of the underlying logic. All three are plausible but unproven. Each makes sense of part of the evidence. Each requires assumptions about Stalin's state of mind.[3]

The first interpretation sees the famine as man-made, but not punitive. The brutal and total requisitioning methods of the Stalinist state stripped the peasants of food and even seed grain, leaving them to starve. The famine was a result of the clumsy methods of a rudimentary state attempting to extract the grain it needed for its overall development plans. This interpretation can agree that Stalin could have known about the famine, but interprets his utterances more literally than others: Stalin told a prominent writer who had reported the famine to him that the peasants were on strike against the Soviet regime;[4] he told a Ukrainian communist leader that reports of famine were 'fairy tales' only 'idiots' believed.[5] While he thus could have known about the famine, he refused to do so – like he wilfully ignored warnings about the German attack in 1941. This interpretation can accommodate Stalin's optimistic later statements about the size of the Soviet population. If Stalin really knew about the extent of the famine, why did he first announce figures which implied that no such calamity had occurred, and then commission a census in 1937 to prove them? The census returned such devastating numbers that the dictator had the statisticians shot and their work suppressed: the behaviour of a man who did not know that he had committed mass murder by starvation.[6]

This interpretation, however, is hard-pressed to account for the particularly vicious way the famine-causing requisitions were enforced in Ukraine. This fact is better accommodated by a second interpretation, originally promoted by the Ukrainian diaspora, later imported back to independent Ukraine to become a central part of the historical consciousness of this nation. This interpretation assumes that the famine was one prong of a broader Stalinist assault on the Ukrainian national movement. It targeted the peasantry – the foot soldiers of the nation. Purges of the intelligentsia and the state and party apparatus removed the brains and the political leadership. This interpretation notes that Stalin had always been hostile to the Ukrainian national movement; it reads his experience of the Civil War as forming this hostility; and it points out that Stalin could have known what happened in Ukraine at the time. The punitive removal of all foodstuffs is interpreted as intending to exterminate the Ukrainian peasantry, or at the very least break its will to ever resist Soviet (Russian) occupation. Scholars who embrace this interpretation need to explain the heavier death toll among Kazakhs, the continued existence of the Ukrainian Socialist Republic (as opposed to the dissolution of the administrative units of the deported populations in the Second World War), that Ukrainians remained the second largest group in the ruling Communist Party, that Khrushchev later promoted many Ukrainian cadres to top positions in Moscow, or that he 'gifted' Crimea to Ukraine in 1954: odd behaviours of a genocidal regime towards its victims.

A third interpretation also sees the famine as punitive, but diverges in the interpretation of the target. It assumes that Stalin and his leadership team were Marxists who thought, first of all, in class terms. The enemy was not the Ukrainian nation but the class enemy: peasants in the villages and the bourgeoisie in the cities. That in Ukraine the latter clothed itself in national garb was a minor consideration. The famine was imposed, in this reading, to break the will of the peasantry to resist the proletarian state from collecting the grain necessary to develop the country and make it ready for the inevitable war. Scholars who embrace this interpretation need to explain, on the one hand, why grain was diverted back to the villages and, on the other, why Ukraine and Kazakhstan were so much harder hit than much of Russia.[7]

Information seepage

At the beginning was denial. In 1932–33, Soviet newspapers reported famines, but in the evil capitalist part of the world.[8] In Stalin's lands, instead, the problem was that the local authorities failed to properly lead the village and fulfil the grain collection plans. Starving peasants were not mentioned.[9] Security troops manned checkpoints on train stations and roads preventing people from leaving the famine-stricken areas and spreading the word. This silence continued after Stalin's death. The Great Famine was not among Stalin's crimes Nikita Khrushchev would denounce in his Secret Speech in 1956. The general line towards the peasantry had been sound. Collectivization was a success. It helped win the war against the Nazis. By the end of Khrushchev's tenure the topic of the famine started to float to the surface, but only for a short while. *Pravda* mentioned the famine in passing,[10] and novelists began to broach the issue.[11] Such attempts to begin discussing this Stalinist crime were nipped in the bud once Khrushchev lost his position later in 1964. The major work on collectivization by Viktor Danilov and his team, which mentioned the unmentionable, could never be published.[12]

The Soviet authorities also tried to prevent a discussion of the famine abroad. Foreign correspondents were barred from travelling to the stricken areas.[13] They were briefed on what to write. Some bowed to the pressure, preferring their interesting life in Moscow over reporting the truth. The most scorned case was the *New York Times*'s Walter Duranty, a gushing admirer of Stalin. He would win a Pulitzer Prize for his reporting, but also the disgust of posterity.[14] Other journalists – Malcolm Muggeridge, Gareth Jones, Ralph Barnes and Henry William Chamberlin – did report, however, and eventually even ardent deniers like Duranty had to concede that something terrible had happened in the wake of collectivization.[15] By 1935, two major explanations had emerged: the famine as an unintended calamity caused by utopian and callous grain collections, peasant resistance, or both; and the famine as a consciously employed weapon of class war.[16]

Cold War

These two schools of thought would continue to develop over the decades to come In 1935 and 1936, the Baltic German activist Ewald Ammende published a major exposé.[17] Boris Souvarine's Stalin biography of 1939 included a section on the famine.[18] A widely read 1947 memoir by a Soviet defector included an entire chapter on the 'horror in the village' he had experienced as a collectivizer, and another one on the 'harvest in hell' – the famine, when he acted as a grain collector.[19] In 1949, the economic historian Naum Yasny mentioned 'the great famine in the winter of 1932–33 ... when millions died of starvation'. He called this calamity 'one of the worst famines' in the country's history and 'correctly characterized as man-made'.[20]

Later scholarship followed suit. In a seminal 1964 article, the agricultural specialist Dana Dalrymple systematized the then available evidence. Like almost everybody else up to this point, Dalrymple saw the famine as caused by 'the economic and social policies followed by the Soviet government during its first five-year plan'. It was thus clearly a 'man-made disaster', but not a planned one.[21] In 1969, Alec Nove spent six pages of his *Economic History of the USSR* on 'the 1932–3 crisis', which had a 'great tragedy' as its centre: 'the famine of 1933'. His account left no doubt that the death toll was the result of Stalin's agricultural policies.[22] 'The famine resulted from high government exactions and low grain production', wrote Lazar Volin in 1970, 'which was caused partly by the weather but mostly by the inefficiency of the new collective farms and the passive resistance of the bullied peasantry.' He placed the responsibility for this 'catastrophe' 'squarely on the Soviet government'.[23] Both Nikita Khrushchev's memoirs and Roy Medvedev's 1971 dissident history of Stalinism included descriptions of the famine.[24]

Soon, Moshe Lewin also discussed it. In a 1974 essay, widely read by scholars and students of Soviet history, he noted that crops at the time 'although poor, were not catastrophic'. Collectivization did disrupt production, and the 'slaughter of stock dealt a shattering blow to Soviet agriculture'. Nevertheless, the 'main factor' was overambitious grain procurements, which he described as 'a bloodletting'. Lewin stressed the responsibility of the regime. Grain procurement squads, he wrote, 'went berserk (with an unmistakable blessing from above: ... top leaders were on the spot) and stripped the recalcitrant villages of any grain they could lay their hands on'. This practice amounted to 'an obvious sentence to death by starvation'.[25] A 1977 essay based on the Smolensk Party archive built on this work, stating that the 'dark months' of starvation and terror in the winter and spring of 1932–33 'set the model for the exploitative police state of the years to come'.[26]

The famine was one area where socialist historians like Lewin, and totalitarian scholars like Adam Ulam, agreed. In 1973, Ulam also presented the famine as caused by bad weather, decline in the availability of draft animals (a result of collectivization), and overly greedy grain procurement goals. Clearly man-made, it was not orchestrated from above. Its results were mixed, from Stalin's point of view. It taught the peasants a lesson and broke resistance once and for all; but the death of so many potential industrial workers and soldiers must have pained the dictator.[27] Three years later, Ulam added details: at least five million peasants died, and the regime 'kept the news of starvation from spreading: in the most severely stricken regions, such as the Ukraine and North Caucasus, militia and GPU [police and state security] detachments barred people from leaving their villages'. Kazakhstan was 'hit by famine more severely than any other [region] in the USSR; between one third and one half of Kazakhs died in the terrible year 1932–33'.[28] Soon, participants like the communist true-believer-turned-dissident, Lev Kopelev, reported on what they had seen and done.[29] Standard textbooks also mentioned the calamity.[30]

Thus, between the famine itself and the start of the 1980s, specialists outside the Soviet Union wrote about the famine and saw it as man-made. The main disagreements among professionals were over the number of victims and the extent to which it had been consciously employed as a weapon of class war against the peasants. Most – on either side of academic politics – saw it as a man-made but unintentional calamity. Even the academic Left wrote about it, despite the fear that 'the cold warriors' might exploit it to slam the Soviet Union and advocate for more hawkish positions against it.[31] And the academic Right would soon do just that, edged on by Ukrainian diaspora organizations.

Diaspora

Ukrainians had left Eastern Europe in several waves. Already, before the First World War, they had settled in the United States and Canada. Smaller populations existed in Latin America. During and after the Russian Civil War, new refugees escaped Soviet terror and the economic hardships of life in the early Soviet Union. The Second World War brought a third wave of emigration. Australia was now added to the map of significant expatriate communities.[32]

Those who left during the Second World War would be particularly active in remembering the famine, among their most traumatic life experiences.[33] Their memories were of victimization by a regime that seemed intent on killing Ukrainians: men, women and children. This national interpretation of the famine was already evident in the displaced person camps, where some non-returnees were interviewed by the Harvard Interview Project.[34] As they left the DP camps and Europe behind, displaced Ukrainians brought this narrative with them.[35] 'Write down that the famine was artificial', one DP interviewed in New York in 1951 demanded. 'The crops in 1932 were very good in the Ukraine but the Communist Soviet government took by force all the crops from the Ukrainian peasants. There was no famine in Russia proper at that time.'[36]

Soon, some would organize to bring their national plight to the world's attention. In Australia in 1953, the twentieth anniversary of the famine was commemorated in a coordinated campaign by new Australians who had just emerged from the refugee camps which were their first destination after arrival, or returned from their two-year compulsory work contracts in remote Australia.[37] The demonstrations in Melbourne, Sydney and Adelaide on 28 June led to confusion among Canberra reporters writing about 'the 1932–33 Soviet invasion of Ukrainia', to clashes between Ukrainian Australians and communists in Sydney,[38] and the occasional competent article making the claim for the 'crime of genocide'.[39]

This argument was now made internationally in a growing number of document collections. The best-known was *The Black Deeds of the Kremlin*, published by the Canadian Ukrainian Association of Victims of Russian Communist Terror (vol. 1) and The Democratic Organization of Ukrainians Formerly Persecuted by the Soviet Regime in USA (vol. 2).[40] It was distributed worldwide through diaspora networks. In Australia, the first volume of 1953 was 'gifted to public and university libraries, only to gather dust on the shelves'. To the chagrin of Ukrainian activists, this book was 'not set down as prescribed reading in university courses'.[41] Neither was Mykola Haliy's pamphlet on the famine, which compiled reports by Western observers (Muggeridge, Chamberlin, Ammende) to conclude that 'the famine ... was deliberately planned and methodically carried out by the Communist Government of

Moscow' in order 'to destroy the separate individuality of the Ukrainian nation'.[42]

Critics would charge that the Ukrainian obsession with genocide was rooted in an attempt to relativize their own crimes during the war, when some of those who ended up in the West had made common cause with the Nazis or fought their own war against Poles and Jews.[43] In extremis, this line could flip into outright denial of the famine as dreamt up by Nazi collaborators – a position the Soviet Union took as late as 1983.[44] A slightly less radical version was to accept the famine as man-made, but denounce anybody as a Nazi who thought it was planned and targeted at Ukrainians.[45] Such critiques – as correct they might be in individual cases – ignored the real trauma the famine had caused to those who survived. Given that after 1945 'genocide' became the symbol for mass victimization by an inhumane regime, it was no surprise that the term would be mobilized by Ukrainians.

After the initial commemorations of 1953 and the source collections and book-length exposes of the 1950s and early 1960s, a lull ensued (see Figure 9.1). The Ukrainian community in Canada, the US and Australia focused its efforts on institution-building. At Harvard, an endowed chair in Ukrainian history was established in 1968, followed by a Ukrainian Research Institute (HURI) in 1973; the University of Alberta acquired a Canadian Institute for Ukrainian Studies in 1976; and Monash University in Melbourne received an endowed lectureship in 1983, followed by Macquarie University in Sydney a year later.[46] By the time of the fiftieth anniversary of the famine, the diaspora in North America successfully built 'the institutional base for raising the issue of the famine', and Australia was not far behind.[47]

Now, a major commemorative campaign was launched, involving publications of witness accounts, community meetings, and the promotion of scholars who worked on the famine. The genocide line was taken stridently. The famine was 'the least-known man-made holocaust of modern times' – 'politically motivated genocide'.[48] By now, the Jewish Holocaust had risen to prominence in public life (Figure 9.2), and the campaign tried to tag on to its status as the worst atrocity of the twentieth century.[49] Conceptual links were made with renewed vigour: the 'Great Famine in Ukraine' was 'the unknown holocaust'. It took place in 'Soviet-occupied Ukraine' (not in the Soviet Union as a whole), killed 'an estimated

7 million Ukrainians', and was 'the desired by-product of a deliberate political policy' to 'break the will of a nationally conscious Ukrainian peasantry' – 'mass murder by decree'.[50] This discourse was transnational: the diaspora in Canada, the United States and Australia used the same terms, the same numbers, the same narrative.[51]

Three projects stand out, two of them intimately connected with one central scholar: James Mace. Not of Ukrainian extraction, he had originally been drawn to Soviet history because of his political radicalism. He soon gravitated towards Ukrainian topics, completing a PhD on national communism in Ukraine, which later became a book.[52] Making the diaspora cause his own, he became a postdoctoral fellow at HURI in 1981. He would stay until 1986, playing pivotal roles in mainstreaming the Ukrainian national interpretation of the famine as genocide.[53]

Mace featured in the first major attempt to bring this view into the wider public sphere: the film *Harvest of Despair* (1984), which also interviewed Muggeridge and Kopelev, together with surviving victims of the famine. An impressive history from below, the documentary showed how the gestation of the famine looked from the perspective of the victims. In order to make the national point, it told Soviet history as Ukrainian history.[54] The documentary was shown throughout late 1984 across Canada, gaining 'considerable press coverage'. The following year, the Canadian public broadcaster aired the documentary, and after some controversy PBS followed suit for the US market in 1986. Surrounding news coverage further added to the reach of the programme.[55] Australia, too, saw a tour of the film in 1985, 'accompanied by the expert commentary of Dr James Mace', and a screening by the national broadcaster in 1987.[56] Thus, a broad audience in all major diaspora locations learned, for the first time, about this catastrophe in a distinctively Ukrainian interpretation.

Two other initiatives are worth mentioning. One was the US Commission on the Ukraine Famine, inaugurated in 1985; the other was an international commission on the same topic in 1988. The Commission was directed by Mace. Its actual work began in 1986, the year Mace's postdoc at Harvard ran out. Eschewing expert witnesses, whom he saw as tainted by 'the prevailing academic conventional wisdom', the Commission functioned 'like an oral history project in miniature', as Mace later remembered. 'We located or simply called for witnesses to come and tell their stories to the Commission', he described the process. This procedure increased the raw material describing the horrors of collectivization and the famine, while sidelining historians other than Mace himself. Unsurprisingly, the Commission found what Mace had already known: that the famine was 'caused by the maximum extraction of agricultural produce from the rural population'; that Stalin 'knew that people were starving to death in Ukraine by late 1932'; that he nevertheless intensified the procurements which 'maximized the loss of life'; and that 'Stalin and those around him committed genocide against Ukrainians in 1932–1933'. It was Mace and his two staff who drafted the final report in 1988. While, in his memoirs, he claims that it was only in his work for the Commission that he understood that 'the famine was a result of official policies', he had already called it a genocide much earlier. What the Commission allowed him to do was to document this claim with an impressive number of sources.[57]

The final initiative was the International Commission of Inquiry into the 1932–33 famine in Ukraine, convened by the World Congress of Free Ukrainians (today: Ukrainian World Congress), an organization, as critics noted, founded by exiled members of one faction of the Organization of Ukrainian Nationalists (OUN-M). The Commission was dominated by jurists and worked from 1988 to 1990. It found, to the slight disappointment of the initiators, what many historians also asserted: there was a famine caused by Soviet policies and it killed millions of people (4.5 million, according to the majority opinion). However, the Commission found insufficient evidence for a preconceived plan. On the question of genocide, three commissioners argued that the term, as defined by the UN, did apply, one found 'crimes against humanity' to be more appropriate, and another declared that the evidence did not support the claim.[58]

Mainstreaming

As the diaspora's campaign thus gained momentum, non-diaspora scholars took up the cause for their own political ends. Most prominent was Robert Conquest. Recommended by Ulam, he had accepted a commission by HURI.[59] His research assistant was the indefatigable Mace. On the famine's fiftieth anniversary, the duo joined the old pioneer, Dalrymple, at a conservative think tank in Washington DC. Their discussion of the 'man-made famine in Ukraine' marked one of those moments of amnesia we have observed in other chapters of this book: when specialists decide to forget what has come before, proclaim a clean slate, and thus their own originality. 'The famine has been forgotten', claimed Conquest in his initial statement.[60]

The debate marked the moment when the views of Ukrainian diaspora organizations began to be taken seriously by others. From now on, the original two interpretations – of the famine as an unintentional calamity, and the famine as a weapon of class warfare – were joined by a third: the famine as genocide. While Dalrymple was still unconvinced and non-committal, Conquest and Mace were edging towards the claim. Soon, Mace would make it explicitly. The famine was Stalin's way 'to impose a "final solution" on the most pressing nationality problem in the Soviet Union', he wrote in the respected *Problems of Communism* in the middle of 1984. 'According to internationally accepted definitions, this constitutes an act of genocide.'[61] In 1986, Conquest's massive study, *The Harvest of Sorrow*, used the term 'terror-famine', a concept which would soon become popular (Figure 9.1). Building on his earlier suggestion that the deportation of minority nations during the Second World War constituted genocide, he used direct analogies with the Holocaust: 'Fifty years ago as I write these words', he opened his book, 'the Ukraine and the Ukrainian, Cossack and other areas to its east ... was like one vast Belsen.'[62] This particular Nazi camp was skilfully chosen. There were no gas chambers in Bergen-Belsen, but some 50,000 inmates died of malnutrition, disease and exposure – typical famine deaths. And many readers would have heard of the camp, as the famous diarist Anne Frank ended her young life there.[63] But Conquest went beyond metaphors. He cited at length the UN Convention on the Prevention and Punishment of the Crime of Genocide, ratified by the USSR in 1954, and concluded that 'it certainly appears that a charge of genocide lies against the Soviet Union for its actions in the Ukraine'.[64] The book was reviewed widely and controversially, both in scholarly publications and, more importantly, in the general press.[65] Most important for the further discussion would be two claims: that Stalin 'planned the famine from the first', and that the Ukrainian nation (rather than the peasantry as a whole) was the intended victim. Both were based on conjecture – Conquest had no more direct access to Stalin's brain than anybody else.[66]

Thanks to Conquest's book and the consistent efforts of the Ukrainian diaspora,[67] by the late 1980s many in the English-reading world could have been at least dimly aware of the famine, the fact that it was man-made, and the claim that it was a genocide against the Ukrainian nation.[68] Textbooks routinely referred to it,[69] at times escalating their assessment over time.[70] By the early 2000s, some would include lengthy and nuanced passages which mentioned, but usually did not endorse, the genocide interpretation.[71]

As the famine rose and rose in prominence it acquired a new name. In 1983, one author was still struggling for words: 'How does one describe an event of such magnitude?'[72] Two terms were tried out in the 1980s: 'Ukrainian famine' and 'terror famine'. Finally, a new term won out: Holodomor (Figure 9.1), a compound of 'hunger' (Ukr: *holod*) and 'decimation' or 'pestilence' (Ukr: *mor*). Literally meaning 'decimation by starvation', its success in English-language literature is also due to its resonance with the term for the most iconic genocide of the twentieth century. The analogy with the Nazi genocide of the Jews – invoked repeatedly in the debate – was thus symbolically enshrined in both words and numbers: Holocaust (six million dead); Holodomor (seven million).

Ukraine vs Russia

Meanwhile, back in the USSR, politicians and historians began to react to the Western literature. A 1986 publication mentioned the famine 'in several regions of Ukraine', but blamed it on a drought.[73] In 1987, Soviet newspapers and magazines began to mention the famine, and at the end of the year the leader of the Ukrainian Communist Party, Volodymyr Shcherbytsky, attempted to pre-empt the findings of the US Commission. The famine, he claimed, was 'caused by a drought and a poor harvest'.[74] In August and September 1988, *Pravda* interviewed Danilov. The famine, he said, was 'Stalin's most terrible crime'. It victimized peasants in 'the grain-growing regions of the country', and was caused by unrealistic and forced grain procurements.[75] In parallel, he introduced a scholarly audience to Conquest's work.[76] In 1989, a first collection of primary sources was published,[77] and there was also

HOLODOMOR

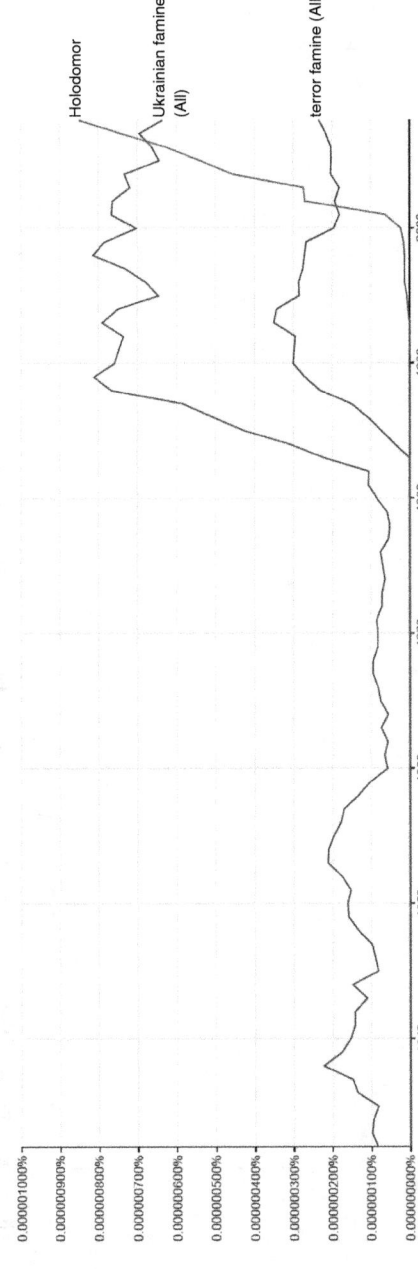

Figure 9.1 Google Ngram for 'Ukrainian famine' shows a first peak in English-language literature in the late 1930s, a second one in the 1950s, and a final upsurge from 1981, with a peak in 1988, followed by a plateau thereafter. During the 1980s peak, 'terror famine' became prominent before 'Holodomor' took over.

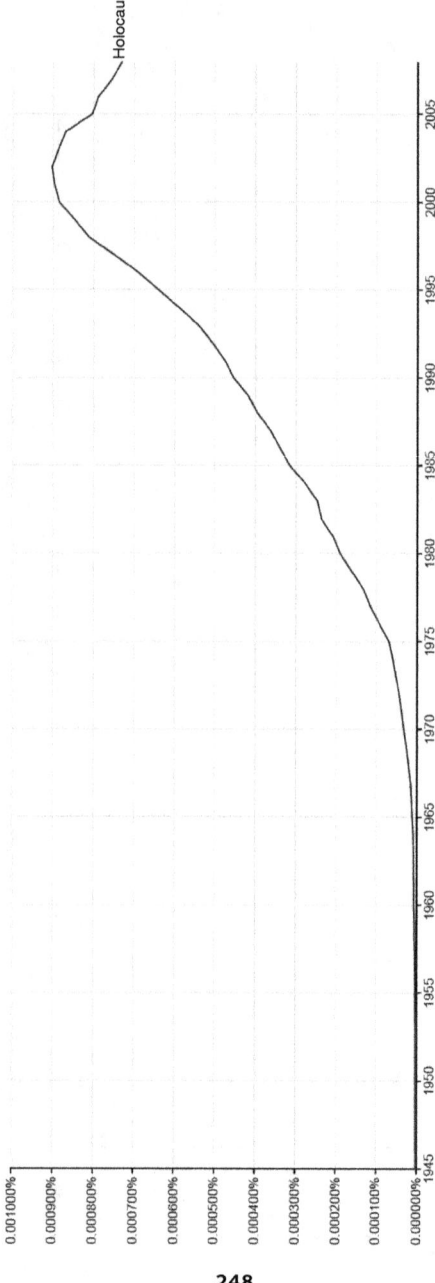

Figure 9.2 Google Ngram for 'Holocaust' shows the rise and rise of the concept.

HOLODOMOR

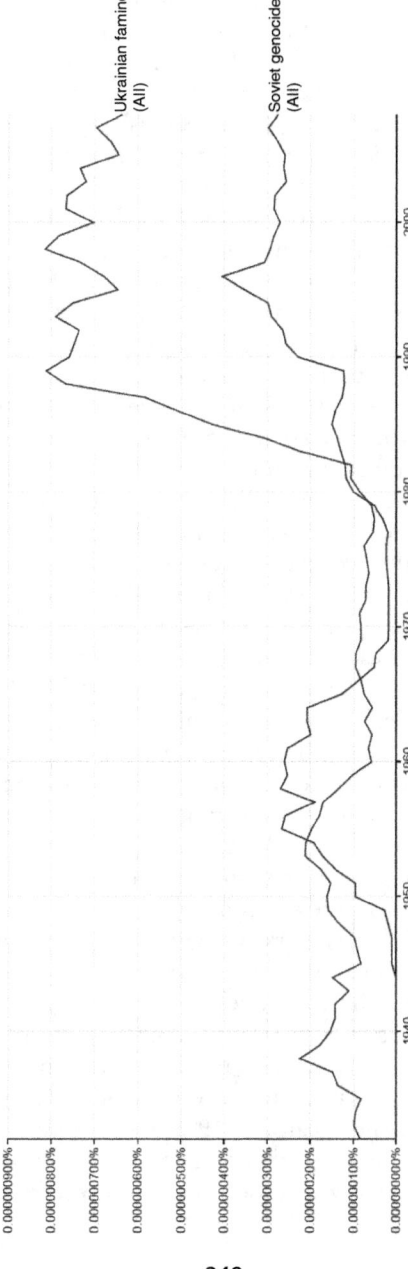

Figure 9.3 Google Ngram for 'Ukrainian famine' and 'Soviet genocide'.

an acknowledgement of the famine by the Soviet Union's leader, General Secretary Mikhail Gorbachev.[78] Soon, Conquest's work was published in Russian (in 1989–90) and in Ukrainian (in 1993).[79]

One of the leading Ukrainian historians in this unfolding debate was Danilov's Ukrainian student, Stanislav Kulchytsky. Writing both in an academic journal and a newspaper in 1988, his findings were 'noticeably cautious and conservative in tone'. The famine was caused by complex processes, he argued, explicitly condemning diaspora publications, including the film *Harvest of Sorrow*.[80] Soon, however, more critical voices made themselves heard, taking advantage of the new openness of discussion. By 1991, a variety of initiatives were underway in Soviet Ukraine to commemorate the victims and chart the location of mass graves. Even a film about the events was in the planning stages when the Soviet Union broke apart.[81] When the sixtieth anniversary of the famine rolled around, the largest commemoration was no longer held in Washington or Alberta, but in Kyiv. The narrative of the Ukrainian diaspora had taken root back in the homeland.[82]

So the breakdown of the Soviet Union, and the establishment of independent Russian and Ukrainian states, gave the historiography on the famine a massive boost. Now, the issue of genocide, long broached in the West, became a major bone of contention. In this transnational debate, both sides cited Western scholarship frequently. There was a tendency, however, to embrace those historians whose interpretation most furthered their own cause. Ukrainians were more likely to cite Mace, Conquest, or the findings of the US Commission on the Ukraine Famine, while Russians embraced experts like Sheila Fitzpatrick, R. W. Davies, Stephen Wheatcroft, or Lynne Viola, with whom they often collaborated as well.[83] Both sides of the debate could now, of course, explore the open archives; but while this work was going on, Ukrainian discourse developed independently in the broader public sphere. A growing number of survivor memoirs were published, driving home the entire horror of this past.[84] Newspaper editors, politicians and public intellectuals often took the lead in making sense of such material, boldly charging into interpretive terrain the historians were still trying to recover empirically. By 1993, the sixtieth anniversary of the famine, the conviction that the famine was genocide was well established. Demands were raised that Moscow 'take responsibility for its misdeeds'.[85]

It was at this juncture that Mace, who despite everything had never made much of a career, moved to Kyiv. His work fell on fertile soil there, and he became a celebrated public intellectual. When later in the decade his friend Kulchytsky emerged from the archives to report what he had found, public opinion on this atrocity was already well established. Experts still disagreed on the number of victims and the central question of whether the target of Moscow's assault was the Ukrainian nation or the peasantry. Slowly but surely, however, more and more Ukrainian scholars edged towards the interpretation that the famine was intended to destroy Ukrainians as a nation.[86] Collections of survivor testimony further solidified this tendency,[87] and by the end of the first decade of the new millennium the genocide interpretation was fully worked out.[88]

Their Russian colleagues saw things somewhat differently. They, too, had access to the archives, and pointed out that the famine affected non-Ukrainian regions as well. Within Ukraine it also killed people of other ethnicities.[89] Some dismissed the concept of the Holodomor as an 'ideological conception, a powerful tool to influence mass consciousness'.[90] Others were less confrontational, and debates at conferences usually remained civil. But there was a clear bifurcation: Russians tended to stress the all-Soviet nature of the famine and the lack of evidence for genocidal intent; Ukrainians focused on the specifically Ukrainian aspects and the fact that the famine coincided with a purge of the Ukrainian elite.[91]

Politicians also joined in. The Russian government first protested that Russia should not be confused with the Soviet Union,[92] then tried appeasement.[93] Soon, however, Russia's line hardened, as it did in other matters.[94] This tougher stance was a reaction to Ukraine's success in appropriating the famine as a Ukrainian event, and bringing a significant share of world opinion along. Countries with well-organized Ukrainian diasporas (Australia, Canada and the US), were at the forefront of this movement. Despite many national resolutions supporting a genocide interpretation, however, Ukraine did not completely win this fight. By 2017, it still lobbied to get the Holodomor recognized as genocide by the United Nations.[95]

It would be wrong, however, to see the political end of this debate merely as an international issue between Russia and Ukraine. In Ukraine, the debate on the Holodomor as genocide is divisive and entangled with larger tensions between pro- and anti-Russian forces. Attempts to outlaw 'Holodomor denial' stalled after Viktor Yanukovich became president in 2010. The new president tried to tread a careful middle path by avoiding the word 'genocide' (using 'tragedy', 'crime' or 'an Armageddon' instead), while using the term Holodomor.[96] After Yanukovich was removed from office by the Revolution of Dignity (or Euromaidan of 2013–14), the issue has not been revived. In the context of the undeclared war with Russia in the east of the country, and Russia's annexation of Crimea, the legal-historical front has shifted to commemoration of the Second World War (see Chapter 8).

Economic historians intervene

It was in this context of international efforts for and against legal recognition of the famine as a genocide against the Ukrainian people that two anglophone scholars from the old academic Left intervened in the debate. Stephen Wheatcroft, formerly part of the R. W. Davies team at Birmingham, and since 1985 at the University of Melbourne, had already reacted with some panache to Mace's original claims.[97] He developed this position over the coming two decades in a series of articles, and eventually in a co-authored book with Davies. Wheatcroft consistently argued against the genocide thesis, taking great delight in slugging both Conquest and Mace with more and more archival data. But he also began to distance himself from his one-time co-author, Mark Tauger, who had developed an extreme reaction to the genocide thesis: human action was relatively unimportant to the causation of the famine, while 'environmental disasters … have to be considered among the primary causes'.[98]

While Tauger was sidelined in a way reminiscent of the Thurston Affair discussed in Chapter 6, Conquest began edging himself away from his own extreme. In the discussion with Mace and Dalrymple in 1983 he said, unambiguously, that Stalin 'wanted a famine';[99] in *Harvest of Despair*, he also explicitly argued for a genocide interpretation. Then began a slow retreat. Already, in an exchange with Tauger, he acknowledged the reality of overall grain shortages. Eventually he abandoned his original position entirely, contacting Wheatcroft in 2003 to insist that he did not believe the famine was intentional. 'No', he wrote in a personal communication the Melbournian reproduced repeatedly. 'What I argue is that with the resulting famine imminent, he could have prevented it, and put "Soviet interests" other than feeding the starving first – thus consciously abetting it.'[100] This new position was remarkably close also to Fitzpatrick's.[101]

Genocide

By the end of the first decade of the new millennium, then, the contours of reasonable discourse in scholarly literature were fairly clear. Most historians agreed that the famine was man-made. The disagreement was if there were other factors – the weather in particular – which played a role in its genesis. The second was disagreement over the number of victims, which ranged from 3.5 to 7 million. Third was the debate of whether the famine was intentional, either in its entirety, or at least in 1933. If passions had not been so high, scholars could have agreed to disagree, given that no conclusive evidence was available. All positions relied on interpretation of often contradictory, and always fragmentary, data. Even the statistical discussion required making assumptions about accuracy of available numbers, underlying normal birth and death rates, and much else besides.[102]

A final discussion was more complex: whether the famine should be classified as genocide required judgements about evidence, definitions and politics. On the evidentiary front, the question came down to understanding Stalin's motivations – not an easy task. In sharp contrast to dekulakization, the Great Terror, or the mass execution of Polish officers in 1940, the archives did not provide a paper trail. No order to organize the famine, signed by Stalin or by anybody else, has come to light.[103] Thus, conclusions had to be drawn from behaviours.

The second axis of the genocide debate pointed out that the famine took place in the context of other anti-Ukrainian measures: a purge of the political elite in the Ukrainian party and state apparatus, and an onslaught on the cultural elite. The man-made famine could be seen in this context as the third prong, directed against the peasants as the foot soldiers of Ukrainian nationalism. The non-genocide camp, however, could point out that the causation between the grain requisitioning crisis (which led to famine) and anti-Ukrainian policies ran the other way: the grain requisitioning caused national resistance from peasants and elites alike, which led to an onslaught against Ukrainian nationalism.

'The famine was not an intentional act of genocide specifically targeting the Ukrainian nation', wrote the most prominent exponent of this line of research. 'It is equally false, however', Harvard's Terry Martin continued, 'to assert that nationality played no role whatsoever in the famine.' The famine was caused by anti-peasant policies with the goal of extracting as much grain as possible. Once resistance proved particularly strong in Ukraine, Moscow interpreted it as fuelled by Ukrainian nationalism: 'In brief, the grain requisitions terror triggered a nationalities terror that continued for over a year after the grain requisitions terror was halted (in May 1933).'[104]

This argument, however, could be adjusted to conform to the genocide interpretation. Usefully, Martin eventually did just that. In a 2004 essay, he built on his earlier interpretation, stressing that it was the 'national interpretation' Moscow developed of the resistance to grain requisitioning, which led 'to the Ukrainian terror in 1933, which in turn exacerbated the famine in ethnically Ukrainian territory'. New archival evidence could also show who the author of this 'personal idiosyncratic national interpretation' was: Stalin.[105] George Liber subsequently clarified this interpretation by reserving the term 'Holodomor' only for the 1933 famine in Ukraine. It was this famine, not the 1932 all-Soviet one, which was intentional, national, and hence genocidal.[106]

The third axis of the genocide debate was not evidentiary, but conceptual. It revolved around the question how 'genocide' was to be defined. Here, the anti-genocide group of scholars had originally the upper hand. The UN definition put enormous stress on the intentions of the perpetrators. It defined genocide as the *intent* to destroy, in whole or in part, a national group as a group. This definition had the advantage of allowing denunciation (and potential prosecution) of partial genocides: it was not necessary that the perpetrators succeeded in wiping out an entire ethnos; it was enough that they tried. But this definition had the disadvantage that intent is notoriously hard to demonstrate.

The reaction of the pro-genocide camp was to widen the definition.[107] If the man-made starvation of millions of helpless civilians did not qualify, then what would? Critics pointed out that such 'category creep' would upgrade very many atrocities to the status of genocide, in the process making the extraordinary crimes of the Nazis into fairly widespread affairs.[108] This consequence did not phase those arguing for a more flexible definition. Why was it, they asked, that only Jews and Armenians were victims of genocide, while other mass killings only qualified as crimes against humanity? Was Armenian and Jewish suffering worthier than the plight of Ukrainians or Native Americans? Did one really need to build Auschwitz to be labelled a genocidaire?[109] Those arguing for broadening the concept often appealed to the founding father, Raphael Lemkin, who in an unpublished paper from 1953 had referred to 'the destruction of the Ukrainian nation' as 'the classic example of Soviet genocide'. What is usually omitted is that Lemkin referred to a broader process beginning in the 1920s and targeting the national intelligentsia, the national church, and then, in 1932–33, the peasantry, followed by migration of non-Ukrainians to 'fragment' the Ukrainian people.[110] Still, he clearly intended a much broader interpretation than the one the UN eventually implemented.[111]

The 'Applebaum debate'

Thus, both the evidentiary and the conceptual aspects of the debate were deeply entangled with politics. Here, of course, things soon got muddled. Politics is highly dependent on context. To argue for subsuming both the Holocaust and the Holodomor under the label of genocide has radically different meanings in Moscow, Kyiv, Berlin, Warsaw, Washington or Tel Aviv.

How complex the politics of history in a transnational debate really are was demonstrated by the reactions to the latest Western intervention: journalist Anne Applebaum's carefully documented and well-written version of the two-level famine argument first developed by Martin, Liber and others: the calamity was originally unintended, but then Stalin 'twisted the knife further' in November and December 1932, launching a 'famine within the famine, a disaster specifically targeted at Ukraine and Ukrainians'.[112]

The ensuing controversy over the book was fuelled by personal animosities. Applebaum had prefaced her bestselling history of the Gulag with the claim that Western historians had ignored its existence, and that 'those who wrote "favourably" about the Soviet Union won more access to archives, more access to official information, longer visas in the country'.[113] As one of the pioneers of archival research, Fitzpatrick was an obvious target of this critique. Although in her memoirs she had conceded a similar point,[114] she now retaliated. *Gulag* was 'a good read', she quipped – 'if you held your nose through the introduction.' As far as the book under review was concerned, Fitzpatrick reiterated her own position that the famine was the unintended outcome of Stalin's bloody-minded pursuit of grain. She then sketched the Ukrainian nationalist position of famine-as-genocide, before declaring *Red Famine* 'a superior work of popular history'. She read the book as not endorsing the genocide interpretation. 'Though sympathetic to the sentiments behind it', Applebaum 'ultimately doesn't buy the Ukrainian argument that *Holodomor* was an act of genocide.' Finally, she chastised Applebaum for the 'odd quirk' of citing archival sources she had not inspected herself. 'This is not normal scholarly practice', she noted correctly, 'though graduate students sometimes do it for effect before they learn better.'[115]

Applebaum launched her counter-attack on social media. At the time, she had some 47,000 followers on Facebook and 206,000 on Twitter. Fitzpatrick did not even have an account on either platform. Applebaum skilfully exploited this power discrepancy, releasing a statement which quickly went viral. She had not, she claimed among other points, argued against the genocide interpretation.

> My argument is that the famine fits perfectly into the original definition of genocide, as conceived by the legal scholar Raphael Lemkin. ... I also explain that, during the United Nations debate about the genocide convention in the 1940s, the Soviet delegation altered the legal definition precisely in order to avoid the inclusion of the famine, which is why it is difficult to classify the famine as 'genocide' under existing international law.[116]

The usual niceties ensued. The public debate in North America in the 1980s had prepared audiences for claims that this was genocidal famine akin to the Holocaust, and that professional historians were liberal stooges of totalitarianism. Others defended Fitzpatrick, while a third category thought her too soft on the book. Eventually, Fitzpatrick also replied, tersely:

> I was pleasantly surprised ... to find that, rather than giving a black-and-white, politically-slanted interpretation of the famine as Stalin's

attempt to kill Ukrainians, Applebaum had offered a reasonable and nuanced account recognizing complexity. If I was mistaken in this reading ..., I apologize and unreservedly withdraw my praise.

Shared by a collaborator, this statement joined the Twitter storm.[117]

As usual, nobody won in this affair, reminiscent somewhat of the 1980s spat treated in the first chapter of this book. The scholarly arm of the discussion was more polite this time;[118] the social media commentary was all the more vicious. But it was not just new media which had made the context of scholarship more complex. In the 1980s, debates among Westerners only filtered through to Soviet audiences via illegal publications, sometimes by Western radio, or occasionally through the work of specialists charged with disputing the lies of the bourgeois falsifiers. In the post-Soviet world, Western books were read, translated and reviewed in the successor states.

Predictably, Russian audiences were dismissive. Academic journals ignored the volume, at least during the first year of its existence.[119] Online sources were scathing. 'There was no war of Stalin against Ukraine', opined one reviewer, accusing Applebaum of 'tendentious selection' of sources. Applebaum was nothing more than a cold warrior who activated the old lies in the new propaganda war against Russia.[120]

In Ukraine, the reception was initially better. In November 2017, President Petr Poroshenko met with the author.[121] A few days later, Kulchytsky published a positive review in a newspaper, using the occasion to lobby for a renewed effort to have the Holodomor recognized as 'genocide' by the United Nations.[122] In May of the following year, the book was launched to great fanfare in Ukrainian translation.[123] But Ukrainian nationalism had reached such a fever pitch in the context of Russia's annexation of Crimea and the hybrid war Putin waged in the east of the country, that Applebaum's embrace of the idea that the famine was a 'war on Ukraine' was no longer radical enough. In a twist both ironic and instructive, her book was declared a danger to the nation.

The charge was led in late 2017 by a wordy review in a nationalist weekly. The historian Vasil' Marochko disagreed in particular with Applebaum's use of statistics and her legal classification of the famine.[124] After the publication of the Ukrainian translation, the attacks got sharper. In the early summer of 2018, the veteran of the diaspora's memory wars, Roman Serbyn of the University of Quebec at Montreal, declared the book 'a step backwards' if compared to Conquest's original work. Writing on the website of the Memorial to the Victims of the Holodomor, a central institution in the official commemoration in Ukraine, he warned that the translation and distribution of the book among Ukrainians was 'harmful'.[125] Ten days later, Marochko upped the ante, comparing Applebaum to Duranty: both Pulitzer Prize winners, both 'Holodomor deniers!'[126] In early July, another prominent historian took exception to Applebaum's statistics and legal classification, exclaiming: 'Of course, we must thank all foreigners who raise their voice in defense of the rights of our people, especially during the current war of Russia against Ukraine. But that does not give them the right to tell our history to the world in an arbitrary manner, not according to the strictest truth.'[127] Finally, the Director-General of the Memorial complained in September that the 'Polish-American writer and journalist' Applebaum had not properly recognized the 'civilizational and ideological significance' of the 'Holodomor-genocide by the Bolshevik-Communist occupation regime' for 'the formation of the Ukrainian nation at the present [historical] stage'. As a 'weapon used in warfare' her book did not pass muster. Not only was it full of factual errors. Worse, it denied the 'genocidal character' of the Holodomor and contained statements which were 'anti-Ukrainian in their substance'. Reading this foreigner's book was 'harmful to the consciousness of Ukrainians'.[128]

What had Applebaum done to deserve such xenophobia? First, she had not given up on conceptual clarity. Under the strict UN definition, the famine did not qualify as genocide. Applebaum, of course, was among those who wanted to broaden the definition, but this point was lost on many readers. 'Why', wrote one online commentator, did the authorities 'not deport this writer Anne Applebaum for denying the genocide of the Ukrainian people?'[129] The foreigner had also not repeated the mystifications of Ukrainian nationalists, who wanted to follow the nation back to Kievan Rus, preferred to see Ukrainians united in their struggle against foreign oppression from Moscow, always victims, heroically resisting, never perpetrators. She had also shown remarkable restraint when it came to numbers. Rather than embracing the higher estimates of 7 million or more victims, she accepted the scholarly consensus of between 3.9 and 4.5 million.[130] Such scholarship was an affront to emotional attachments to the magical 7 million: one million more than in the Holocaust!

Third, while Applebaum was willing to push the evidence in one interpretive direction, she refused to give up on evidence altogether. The famine might have been man-made; it might have been directed against Ukrainians; it might have been Stalin's attempt to destroy resistance in Ukraine. But this was still *Stalin's* war on Ukraine, not Russia's. Still thinking in the context of the Cold War she had grown up in, her main point was not to indict Russia, but communism. The communists who inflicted the policies leading to the famine included Russians and Jews, but also Ukrainians. Indeed, 'the vast majority of members of the brigades that searched villages for food in 1932–3 were not outsiders. Nor were they motivated by hatred of Ukrainian peasants, because they were Ukrainian peasants themselves.'[131] Such historical accuracy made her book less useful for a nationalist politics of equating Stalin and Putin, the Soviet Union and contemporary Russia. This reluctance to adjust to the newly nationalized war zone of Eastern Europe could not be forgiven. And so Applebaum – a historian with strong political convictions – fell between all political chairs: to Russians she was a Russophobe, to Ukrainians an agent of Moscow, and to many in the West an unreconstructed cold warrior. Such is the fate of those who take positions in the history wars about Stalinism today.

Notes

1. For introductions, see David R. Marples, *Heroes and Villains: Creating National History in Contemporary Ukraine* (Budapest, 2007), chapter 2; David R. Marples, 'Ethnic Issues in the famine of 1932–1933 in Ukraine', *Europe–Asia Studies* 61, no. 3 (2009): 505–18; Rebakah Moore, '"A Crime against Humanity Arguably without Parallel in European History": Genocide and the "Politics" of Victimhood in Western Narratives of the Ukrainian Holodomor', *Australian Journal of Politics & History* 58, no. 3 (2012): 367–79.
2. V. B. Zhiromskaia, I. N. Kiselev and Iu. A. Poliakov, *Polveka pod grifom 'sekretno': Vsesoiuznaia perepis' naseleniia 1937 goda* (Moscow, 1996), 88.
3. 'Possible' but 'unproven' is what Michael Ellman called Anne Applebaum's interpretation. H-Diplo, H-Net Reviews (April 2018), http://www.h-net.org/reviews/showrev.php?id=51300 (accessed 5 November 2018).

4   Iurii Grigor'evich Murin, 'Sholokhov i Stalin. Prepiska nachala 30-kh godov', *Voprosy istorii*, no. 3 (1994): 3–25.
5   K. Kuznetsov and R. Terekhov, 'Vekha v zhisni leninskoi partii. K 40-letiiu XIII s"ezda RKP (b)', *Pravda* (26 May 1964): 2.
6   Catherine Merridale, 'The 1937 Census and the Limits of Stalinist Rule', *The Historical Journal* 39, no. 1 (1996): 225–40.
7   The debate on the origins of the Kazakh famine is just beginning. For two different views, see Matthew J. Payne, 'Seeing Like a Soviet State: Settlement of Nomadic Kazakhs, 1928–1934', in: *Writing the Stalin Era: Sheila Fitzpatrick and Soviet Historiography*, ed. Golfo Alexopoulos, Julie Hessler and Kiril Tomoff (New York, 2011), 59–86; and Sarah Cameron, *The Hungry Steppe: Famine, Violence, and the Making of Soviet Kazakhstan* (Ithaca, 2018).
8   For example, famine allegedly raged in non-Soviet Ukraine and Belarus: 'Golod v zapadnoi Ukraine i v zapadnoi Belorussii', *Izvestiia* (1 July 1932): 2; 'Golod in nishcheta v zakarpatskoi Ukraine', *Izvestiia* (12 November 1932): 2. In Japan, people sold their children because of the famine: 'Golod i nishcheta v iaponskoi derevne. Prodazha detei – rasprostranennoe iavlenie', *Izvestiia* (25 June 1932): 2; and in December, the paper asked 'will Americans die of famine?': 'Budut li Amerikantsy umirat' ot goloda?', *Izvestiia* (23 December 1932): 2.
9   For example: 'Itogi khlebozagotovok i zadachi KP(b)U v bor'be za podniatie sel'skogo khoziaistvaUkrainy', *Pravda* (15 February 1933): 3.
10 Kuznetsov and Terekhov, 'Vekha v zhisni leninskoi partii'.
11 Novels by Mikhail Alekseev and Vladimir Tendriakov published in 1964, quoted, with excerpts, in Roy Medvedev, *Let History Judge: The Origins and Consequences of Stalinism*, ed. David Joravsky and Georges Haupt (New York, 1971), 95–96.
12 See Chapter 5.
13 Zara Witkin, *An American Engineer in Stalin's Russia: The Memoirs of Zara Witkin, 1932–1934* (Berkeley, 1991), 207–08; Eugene Lyons, *Assignment in Utopia* (London, 1937), 576.
14 S. J. Taylor, *Stalin's Apologist: Walter Duranty. The New York Times's Man in Moscow* (Oxford, 1990).
15 Walter Duranty, *Stalin & Co.: The Politburo – the Men Who Run Russia* (New York, 1949), 78.
16 Malcolm Muggeridge, 'The Soviet and the Peasantry: An Observer's Notes. (I) Famine in North Caucasus', *Manchester Guardian* (25 March 1933): 13; Malcolm Muggeridge, 'The Soviet and the Peasantry. An Observer's Notes. (II) Hunger in the Ukraine', *Manchester Guardian* (27 March 1933): 9; Malcolm Muggeridge, 'The Soviet and the Peasantry. An Observer's Notes. (III) Poor Harvest in Prospect', *Manchester Guardian* (28 March 1933): 9. 'Famine Grips Russia, Millions Dying, Idle On Rise, Says Briton', *New York Evening Post* (29 March 1933): 1, 4; 'Famine in Russia: Englishman's Story. What he Saw on a Walking Tour', *Manchester Guardian* (30 March 1933): 12; Ralph Barnes, 'Millions Feared Dead of Hunger in South Russia', *New York Herald Tribune* (21 August 1935): 7; William Henry Chamberlin, *Russia's Iron Age* (London, 1935), 82–89.

17 Ewald Ammende, *Muß Rußland hungern? Menschen und Völkerschicksale in der Sowjetunion* (Vienna, 1935); Ewald Ammende, *Human Life in Russia* (London, 1936); Ewald Ammende, *Human Life in Russia*. 1st reprint ed. (Cleveland, 1984).
18 Boris Souvarine, *Stalin: A Critical Survey of Bolshevism* (New York, 1939), 551–54.
19 Victor Kravchenko, *I Chose Freedom: The Personal and Political Life of a Soviet Official* (London, 1947), 91–131.
20 Naum Jasny, *The Socialized Agriculture of the USSR: Plans and Performance* (Stanford, 1949), 52, 551–55, quotations: 52, 551.
21 Dana G. Dalrymple, 'The Soviet Famine of 1932–1934', *Soviet Studies* 15, no. 3 (1964): 250–84, quotations: 250, 257, 264; and Dana G. Dalrymple, 'The Soviet Famine of 1932–1934. Some Further References', *Soviet Studies* 16, no. 4 (1965): 471–74.
22 Alec Nove, *An Economic History of the USSR* (London, 1969; paperback edition 1972), 176–81, quotations 176, 179, 180.
23 Lazar Volin, *A Century of Russian Agriculture: From Alexander II to Khrushchev* (Cambridge, Mass., 1970), 232–33, quotations: 233.
24 Medvedev, *Let History Judge*, 94–96; Strobe Talbott (ed.), *Khrushchev Remembers* (London, 1971), 73–74.
25 Moshe Lewin, 'Taking Grain: Soviet Policies of Agricultural Procurements Before the War', in: *Essays in Honour of E. H. Carr*, ed. C. Abramsky and Beryl J. Williams (London, 1974), 281–323, on the famine: 291–96, quotations: 295–96. This essay was reprinted in one of the most widely read Lewin book (see Chapter 2): *The Making of the Soviet System: Essays in the Social History of the Interwar Years* (New York, 1985; 2nd ed.: 1994).
26 Daniel R. Brower, 'Collectivized Agriculture in Smolensk: The Party, the Peasantry, and the Crisis of 1932', *The Russian Review* 36, no. 2 (1977): 151–66, quotations: 165–66.
27 Adam Ulam, *Stalin: The Man and His Era* (New York, 1973), 344–49.
28 Adam Ulam, *A History of Soviet Russia* (New York, 1976), 97–98, quotations: 98. As late as 1985, Ulam was agnostic about the national interpretation, which saw the famine as an attack on Ukraine and Ukrainians. Adam Ulam, 'Introduction', in: Miron Dolot, *Execution by Hunger: The Hidden Holocaust* (New York, 1985), vii–xii, esp. xi.
29 Lev Kopelev, *I sotvoril sebe kumira* (Ann Arbor, 1978), 247–306; English translation: *The Education of a True Believer* (New York, 1980). The German edition added an extra chapter on 'the path into the catastrophic famine': Lew Kopelew, *Und schuf mir einen Götzen: Lehrjahre eines Kommunisten* (Hamburg, 1979), 289–369.
30 Donald W. Treadgold, *Twentieth Century Russia* (Chicago, 1959), 272. The statement was not altered in subsequent editions. See Donald W. Treadgold, *Twentieth Century Russia*. 7th ed. (Boulder, 1990), 252; Nicholas V. Riasanovsky, *A History of Russia* (Oxford, 1963), 551. It was unchanged in the 2nd ed. (1969), 551; 3rd ed. (1977), 551; 4th ed. (1984), 497; and 5th ed. (1993), 497. In the 6th edition (2000), the article was dropped to adjust the prose to current use: 'A frightful famine swept Ukraine' (not 'the Ukraine'

as in previous editions) (497). Basil Dmytryshyn, *USSR: A Concise History* (New York, 1965), 169. Sheila Fitzpatrick, *The Russian Revolution 1917–1932* (Oxford, 1984), 127, 137.

31 See Lewin's letter to Graziosi cited in Chapter 2. Also: Stephan Merl, 'Entfachte Stalin die Hungersnot von 1932–1933 zur Auslöschung des ukrainischen Nationalismus?', *Jahrbücher für Geschichte Osteuropas* 37, no. 4 (1989): 569–90, here: 570–71.

32 A. V. Zav'ialov, *Sotsial'naia adaptatsiia ukrainskikh immigrantov: Monografiia* (Irkutsk, 2017), 10–19. On Canada, see Lubomyr Y. Luciuk, *Searching for Place: Ukrainian Displaced Persons, Canada, and the Migration of Memory* (Toronto, 2000). On Australia: Michael Lawriwsky, 'Ukrainians', in: *The Australian People: An Encyclopedia of the Nation, its People and their Origins*, ed. James Jupp (Cambridge, 2001), 716–18.

33 The best account is Frank Sysyn, 'The Ukrainian Famine of 1932–3: The Role of the Ukrainian Diaspora in Research and Public Discussion', in: *Studies in Comparative Genocide*, ed. L. Chorbajian and G. Shirinian (London, 1999), 182–215.

34 Harvard Project on the Soviet Social System. Schedule A, Vol. 15, Case 285 (interviewer M.F., type A4). Male, 68, Ukrainian, Brigadier in kolkhoz. Widener Library, Harvard University, p. 22, http://nrs.harvard.edu/urn-3:FHCL:951544 (accessed 6 November 2019). Harvard Project on the Soviet Social System. Schedule A, Vol. 16, Case 314 (interviewer R.F., type A4). Male, 29, Ukrainian, Movie projectionist. Widener Library, Harvard University, p. 48. http://nrs.harvard.edu/urn-3:FHCL:954873 (accessed 6 November 2019). On the interview project see Chapter 7. On life in the DP camps, see Anna Holian, *Between National Socialism and Soviet Communism: Displaced Persons in Postwar Germany* (Ann Arbor, 2011).

35 Gerard Daniel Cohen, *In War's Wake: Europe's Displaced Persons in the Postwar Order* (Oxford, 2012).

36 Harvard Project on the Soviet Social System. Schedule A, Vol. 37, Case 622/(NY)1719 (interviewer W.T., type A4). Female, 53, Ukrainian, Kolkhoznik. Widener Library, Harvard University,p. 6, http://nrs.harvard.edu/urn-3:FHCL:982563 (accessed 6 November 2019).

37 Michael Lawriwsky, 'Australia and the *Holodomor*: 50 Years of Remembrance', paper presented at *The Great Famine of 1932–33. A Symposium*, National Europe Centre at the Australian National University and the Australian Federation of Ukrainian Organisations (22 October 2003), 2.

38 'Red Abuse at Ukrainians in Domain', *Canberra Times* (29 June 1953): 4.

39 G. Spolitakevych, 'Ukrainians Remember Fateful Days of 1933', *The West Australian* (26 June 1953): 3.

40 S. O. Pidhainy (ed.), *The Black Deeds of the Kremlin: A White Book*. Vol. 1: *Book of Testimonies* (Toronto, 1953), 222–305; Vol. 2: *The Great Famine in Ukraine in 1932–1933* (Detroit, 1955).

41 Lawriwsky, 'Australia and the *Holodomor*', 3.

42 Mykola Haliy, *Organized Famine in Ukraine 1932–1933* (Chicago, 1963), quotations: 5, 6.

43 See letter Moshe Lewin to Andrea Graziosi, cited in Chapter 2. More recently: John-Paul Himka, 'Encumbered Memory. The Ukrainian Famine of 1932–33',

Kritika: Explorations in Russian and Eurasian History 14, no. 2 (2013): 411–36, here: 435–36.

44 News release by Soviet Embassy in Ottawa, 28 April 1983, as quoted in Sysyn, 'The Ukrainian Famine of 1932–3: The Role of the Ukrainian Diaspora in Research and Public Discussion', 189.

45 Douglas Tottle, *Fraud, Famine and Fascism: The Ukrainian Genocide Myth from Hitler to Harvard* (Toronto, 1987). Despite its crass politics, the book is still well worth reading for its critical analysis of some of the source base, in particular photographs of often dubious origin.

46 Sysyn, 'The Ukrainian Famine of 1932–3', 187–88; Lawriwsky, 'Ukrainians', 718; Ihor Gordijew, 'The Ukrainian Studies Foundation in Australia. A Brief Survey', in: *Ukrainian Settlement in Australia: Second Conference. Melbourne, 5–7 April 1985*, ed. Marko Pavlyshyn (Melbourne, 1986), 141–48, here: 143–44.

47 Sysyn, 'The Ukrainian Famine of 1932–3', 188.

48 'Special Issue: The Great Famine in Ukraine', *Ukrainian Weekly* 51, no. 12 (20 March 1983), quotation: 3. On the Australian arm of the campaign, see Lawriwsky, 'Australia and the *Holodomor*', 4.

49 Peter Novick, *The Holocaust in American Life* (Boston, 1999).

50 *The Great Famine in Ukraine: The Unknown Holocaust: In Solemn Observance of the 50th Anniversary of the Ukrainian Famine of 1932–33* (Jersey City, 1983), editors' note (n.p.); and James Mace's essay 'The Man-Made Famine of 1932–33: What Happened and Why?', in: *The Great Famine in Ukraine*, 9–37. The term 'Ukrainian holocaust' appears repeatedly: 7, 9; direct comparison to the Holocaust: 38; claim that the famine 'occurred not throughout the Soviet Union, but largely in Ukraine and the North Caucasus': 49.

51 See, for example, the Holodomor monument in Canberra, Australia, erected in 1983, unveiled in 1985: http://monumentaustralia.org.au/themes/conflict/genocide/display/99823-execution-by-hunger-holodomor-1932-1933 (accessed 2 November 2018); the 1985 unveiling speech by then leader of the opposition and later Prime Minister John Howard is available at: https://parlinfo.aph.gov.au/parlInfo/download/media/pressrel/HPR03003432/upload_binary/HPR03003432.pdf;fileType=application%2Fpdf#search=%22media/pressrel/HPR03003432%22 (accessed 2 November 2018). On the unveiling: Lawriwsky, 'Australia and the *Holodomor*', 6.

52 James E. Mace, *Communism and the Dilemmas of National Liberation: National Communism in Soviet Ukraine, 1918–1933* (Cambridge, 1983).

53 James E. Mace, 'Facts and Values: A Personal Intellectual Exploration', in *Pioneers of Genocide Studies*, ed. Samuel Totten and Steven Jacobs (Piscataway, 2011), 59–74.

54 *Harvest of Despair: The 1932–33 Man-Made Famine in Ukraine*, dir. Slavko Nowytski, Toronto, 1984. Available online at: https://www.youtube.com/watch?v=n4T31lWq5ng (accessed 6 November 2019).

55 Sysyn, 'The Ukrainian Famine of 1932–3', 189–90.

56 Lawriwsky, 'Australia and the *Holodomor*', 6, 7.

57 Mace, 'Facts and Values', 67–70, quotations: 69, 70. The evidence is contained in the enormous tome of the final report: Commission on the Ukraine Famine, *Investigation of the Ukrainian Famine 1932–1933* (Washington, 1988), quotation:

vi–vii. The oral history component was documented in even more detail in James E. Mace and Leonid Heretz (eds), *Investigation of the Ukrainian Famine 1932–1933: Oral History Project*, 3 vols (Washington, 1990).
58. Sysyn, 'The Ukrainian Famine of 1932–33: The Role of the Ukrainian Diaspora in Research and Public Discussion', 194–95.
59. 'Conquest, Ulam discuss Harvard monograph on 1933 famine', *Ukrainian Weekly* no. 40 (3 October 1982): 4.
60. Robert Conquest, Dana Dalrymple, James Mace and Michael Novak, *The Man-Made Famine in Ukraine* (Washington and London, 1984), 7. This statement echoed what Dalrymple had already written in 1964: 'The Soviet Famine of 1932–1934', 250.
61. James E. Mace, 'Famine and Nationalism in Soviet Ukraine', *Problems of Communism* (May–June 1984): 37–50, quotation: 37.
62. Robert Conquest, *The Harvest of Sorrow: Soviet Collectivization and the Terror-Famine* (Oxford, 1986), 3.
63. 'Bergen-Belsen', in: *Holocaust Encyclopedia*. The United States Holocaust Memorial Museum, https://encyclopedia.ushmm.org/content/en/article/bergen-belsen (accessed 2 November 2018).
64. Conquest, *The Harvest of Sorrow*, 272.
65. For a list of reviews, see Frank Sysyn, 'Thirty Years of Research on the Holodomor: A Balance Sheet', in: *Contextualizing the Holodomor: The Impact of Thirty Years of Ukrainian Famine Studies*, ed. Andrij Makuch and Frank E. Sysyn (Toronto, 2015), 1–13, here: 10–13.
66. What he could show was that Stalin was informed of the famine, which is incontrovertible. See Conquest, *The Harvest of Sorrow*, 323–28, esp. 329 (summary), quotation: 326.
67. Roman Serbyn and Bohdan Krawchenko, *Famine in Ukraine 1932–1933* (Edmonton, 1986).
68. Another important contribution was Andrea Graziosi, '"Lettres de Kharkov". La famine en Ukraine et dans le Caucase du Nord à travers les rapports des diplomates italiens, 1932–1934', *Cahiers du Monde russe et soviétique* 30, no. 1/2 (1989): 5–106.
69. For example: Geoffrey Hosking, *A History of the Soviet Union* (London, 1985), 166–67.
70. M. K. Dziewanowski, *A History of Soviet Russia*. 2nd ed. (Eaglewood Cliffs, 1985), 194; 4th ed. (1993), 182; 54th ed., now titled *A History of Soviet Russia and its Aftermath* (1997), 177.
71. Catherine Evtuhov, David Goldfrank, Lindsey Hughes and Richard Stites, *A History of Russia: Peoples, Legends, Events, Forces* (Boston, 2004), 669; Manfred Hildermeier, *Geschichte der Sowjetunion 1917–1991: Entstehung und Niedergang des ersten sozialistischen Staates* (Munich, 1998), 399–401; Nicolas Werth, 'A State against its People: Violence, Repression, and Terror in the Soviet Union', in: *The Black Book of Communism: Crimes, Terror, Repression*, ed. Stephane Courtois and Nicolas Werth (Cambridge, Mass., 1999), 33–268, on the famine: 159–68.
72. Marco Carynnyk, 'Malcom Muggeridge on Stalin's famine: "deliberate" and "diabolical" starvation', in: *The Great Famine in Ukraine: the unknown holocaust*, 46–54, here: 49.

73 I. E. Zelenin, N. A. Ivnitskii, I. V. Rusinov and V. M. Selunskaia (eds), *Istoriia sovetskogo krest'ianstva*, vol. 2: *Sovetskoe krest'ianstvo v period sotsialisticheskoi rekonstruktsii narodnogo khoziaistva. Konets 1927–1937* (Moscow, 1986), 256.
74 Marples, *Heroes and Villains*, 36.
75 Kollektivizatsiia: kak eto bylo', *Pravda* (16 September 1988): 3. The first instalment was *Pravda* (26 August 1988): 3.
76 Viktor Danilov, 'Diskussiia v zapadnoi presse o golode 1932–1933 gg. i demograficheskoi katastrofe 30–40kh godov v SSSR', *Voprosy istorii* no. 3 (1988): 116–21.
77 V. P. Danilov and N. A Ivnitskii (eds), *Dokumenty svidetel'stvuiut: Iz istorii derevni nakanune i v khode kollektivizatsiia 1927–1932 gg.* (Moscow, 1989), on the famine: 491.
78 'Ob agrarnoi politike KPSS v sovremennykh usloviiakh. Doklad General'nogo sekretaria TsK KPSS M. S. Gorbacheva na Plenume TsK KPSS 15 marta 1989 goda', *Pravda* (16 March 1989): 1–4, here: 2.
79 The Russian publications are in *Novyi mir* no. 10 (1989); *Voprosy istorii* nos. 1 and 4 (1990). In Ukrainian: Robert Konkvest, *Zhnyva skorboty: Radian'ska kolektivizatsiia i Holodomor* (Kyiv, 1993).
80 Marples, *Heroes and Villains*, 36–37.
81 Marples, *Heroes and Villains*, 39–40.
82 Sysyn, 'The Ukrainian Famine of 1932–3', 199–200.
83 On the Ukrainian tendency, see Marples, *Heroes and Villains*, 40, on Mace and Conquest also 42. An excellent overview of the Ukrainian discussion is A. Kapustian, 'Ukrainskaia istoriografiia postsovetskogo perioda problemy goloda 1932–1933 gg', in: *Sovremennaia rossiisko-ukrainskaia istoriografiia goloda 1932–1933 gg. V SSSR*, ed. V. V. Kondrashin (Moscow, 2011), 72–106. On collaboration, see V. Danilov, R. Manning, L. Viola, R. Davies, Ha Yong-Chool, R. Johnson, V. Kozlov, Ia. Pogoniy, A. Sakharov, T. Shanin and S. Wheatcroft (eds), *Tragediia sovetskoi derevni: Kollektivizatsiia i raskulachivanie: Dokumenty i materialy v 5 tomakh 1927–1939*, vol. 3 (1930–1933) (Moscow, 2001).
84 On the memoirs, see Marples, *Heroes and Villains*, 45–48.
85 Marples, *Heroes and Villains*, 43–45.
86 Mace, 'Facts and Values', 72–73; Marples, *Heroes and Villains*, 48–50, 64–68. An important landmark was V. M. Lytvyn (ed.), *Holod 1932–1933 rokiv v Ukrainy: prychyny ta naslidky* (Kyiv, 2003). For a bibliography, see O. G. Liuta (ed.), *Holodomor 1932–1933 rr. v Ukrainy (do 70-rchchnia): Bibliohrafichnyi pokazhchyk*. 2nd rev. ed. (Uzhgorod, 2006).
87 Iurii Mitsik (ed.), *Ukrainskyi holokost 1932–1933: Svidchennia tykh, khto vyzhyv*, 4 vols (Kyiv, 2003–07).
88 Stanyslav Kul'chyts'kyi, *Holodomor 1932–1933 rr. iak henotsyd: trudnoshchi usvidomlennia* (Kyiv, 2008).
89 Viktor Kondrashin, *Golod 1932–1933 godov: tragediia Rossiiskoi derevni* (Moscow, 2008); V. V. Kondrashin (ed.), *Golod v SSSR 1929–1934*, 4 vols (Moscow, 2011–12).
90 Andrei Marchukov, 'Operatsiia "Golodomor"', *Rodina* 1 (2007). Some pointed to the culpability of the Ukrainian leadership: Ivan Chigirin, *Mif i pravda o*

DEBATES ON STALINISM

'*Stalinskom golodomore*'. *Ob ukrainskoi tragedii v 1932–1933 godakh* (Velikie Luki, 2009).

91 Good introductions are Stanislav Kulchytsky's review essay on Applebaum's famine book: *Ukrains'kyi istorichnyi zhurnal* no. 1 (2018): 184–204; and V. V. Kondrashin (ed.), *Sovremennaia rossiisko-ukrainskaia istoriografiia goloda 1932–1933 gg. v SSSR* (Moscow, 2011).

92 'Putin ne budet izviniat'sia pered ukraintsami za golodomor', *Pravda.ru* (28 January 2003), https://www.pravda.ru/politics/authority/kremlin/28-01-200 3/35218-putin-0/ (accessed 12 October 2018).

93 Vladimir Putin, 'Speech at the 58th session of the General Assembly of the United Nations' (25 September 2003), http://en.kremlin.ru/events/president/transcripts/22128 (accessed 12 October 2018).

94 See Chapter 8.

95 Statement by the president of Ukraine during the General Debate of the 72nd session of the united Nations General Assembly (20 September 2017), https://www.president.gov.ua/en/news/vistup-prezidenta-ukrayini-pid-chas-zagalnih-debativ-72-yi-s-43442 (accessed 5 November 2018).

96 Alexander J. Motyl, 'Yanukovych and Stalin's Genocide', *World Affairs* (29 November 2012), http://www.worldaffairsjournal.org/blog/alexander-j-motyl/yanukovych-and-stalin's-genocide (accessed 5 November 2018).

97 Stephen Wheatcroft, letter to the editors, *Problems of Communism* 34, no. 2 (1985): 132–34.

98 Mark Tauger, 'Natural Disasters and Human Actions in the Soviet Famine of 1931–1933', *The Carl Beck Papers in Russian & East European Studies* 1506 (2001), quotation: 6. Tauger had his own evolution. In 1991, while arguing that the famine was caused by food shortage due to a decreased harvest, he still assumed that this shortfall 'resulted from a series of economic, organizational, and political factors'. Mark B. Tauger, 'The 1932 Harvest and the Famine of 1933', *Slavic Review* 50, no. 1 (1991): 70–89, quotation: 84. The moment of co-authorship was R. W. Davies, Mark B. Tauger and S. G. Wheatcroft, 'Stalin, Grain Stocks and the Famine of 1932–1933', *Slavic Review* 54, no. 3 (1995): 642–57. R. W. Davies and S. G. Wheatcroft, 'The Soviet Famine of 1932–33 and the Crisis in Agriculture', in: *Challenging Traditional Views of Russian History*, ed. S. G. Wheatcroft (Basingstoke, 2002), 69–91, esp. 88. In the final version of the argument, bad weather plays a subsidiary role. See S. G. Wheatcroft, 'Towards Explaining Soviet Famine of 1931–3: Political and Natural Factors in Perspective', *Food and Foodways* 12, no. 2–3 (2004): 107–36; and R. W. Davies and Stephen G. Wheatcroft, *The Years of Hunger: Soviet Agriculture, 1931–1933* (Basingstoke, 2004), 431–41.

99 Conquest, Dalrymple, Mace and Novak, *The Man-Made Famine in Ukraine*, 7.

100 Wheatcroft, 'Towards explaining Soviet famine', 134 n. 26. Slightly different wording of the same direct quotation appears in Davies and Wheatcroft, *The Years of Hunger*, 4411 n. 145.

101 Sheila Fitzpatrick, *Stalin's Peasants: Resistance and Survival in the Russian Village after Collectivization* (Oxford, 1994), 69–79.

102 A good summary is Jeremy Smith, *Red Nations: The Nationalities Experience in and after the USSR* (Cambridge, 2013), 107–11.

103 Hiroaki Kuromiya, 'The Soviet Famine of 1932–1933 Reconsidered', *Europe–Asia Studies* 60, no. 4 (2008): 663–75; J. Arch Getty, 'New Sources and Old Narratives', *Contemporary European History* 27, no. 3 (2018): 450–55.
104 See Terry Martin, *The Affirmative Action Empire: Nations and Nationalism in the Soviet Union, 1923–1939* (Ithaca, 2001), chapter 7, quotations: 305, 306.
105 Terry Martin, 'The 1932–33 Ukrainian Terror: New Documentation on Surveillance and the Thought Process of Stalin', in: *Famine-Genocide in Ukraine, 1932–1933: Western Archives, Testimonies and New Research*, ed. Wsevolod W. Isajiw (Toronto, 2003), 97–114, quotations: 99, 114, Stalin as author: 107. Nicholas Werth (see fn. 71 above) also seems to have changed his mind along Martin's lines. See his discussion in 'Mass Deportations, Ethnic Cleansing, and Genocidal Politics in the Later Russian Empire and the USSR', in: *The Oxford Handbook of Genocide Studies*, ed. Donald Bloxham and A. Dirk Moses (Oxford, 2010), 395–98.
106 George O. Liber, *Total Wars and the Making of Modern Ukraine, 1914–1954* (Toronto, 2016), 141–59.
107 A prominent argument along these lines is Norman M. Naimark, *Stalin's Genocides* (Princeton, 2010), on the Holodomor: chapter 7.
108 Michael Ellman, 'Stalin and the Soviet Famine of 1932–33 Revisited', *Europe–Asia Studies* 59, no. 4 (2007): 663–93, esp. 681–88. 'Category creep' is Ben Shephard's term. See his *The Long Road Home: The Aftermath of the Second World War* (London, 2010), 5. Ellman's essay was a moment of a larger debate with Davies and Wheatcroft. See Michael Ellman, 'The Role of Leadership Perceptions and of Intent in the Soviet Famine of 1931–1934', *Europe–Asia Studies* 57, no. 6 (2005): 823–41; and R. W. Davies and Stephen G. Wheatcroft, 'Stalin and the Soviet Famine of 1932–33: A Reply to Ellman', *Europe–Asia Studies* 58, no. 4 (2006): 625–33.
109 This was the tenor of a debate at a panel I attended as part of the audience in 2007. It featured Don Filtzer, Michael Ellman, Mark Tauger and, as chair, Roberta Manning. Stephen Wheatcroft was meant to comment, but instead presented a long paper with ample statistics. Tempers flared, with one panel member waving the American Historical Association's code of conduct in the air, accusing another of misconduct. Ellman's cool delivery of a sharp analytical dissection of the consequences of widening the definition led to angry ripostes from the audience. Panel 9-09: 'Soviet Famines: 1924, 1933 and 1947'. American Association for the Advancement of Slavic Studies, National Convention 2007, 17 November 2007, New Orleans, Louisiana.
110 Rafael Lemkin, 'Soviet Genocide in Ukraine', *Holodomor Studies* 1, no. 1 (2009): 3–8.
111 See A. Dirk Moses, 'Raphael Lemkin, Culture, and the Concept of Genocide', in: *Oxford Handbook of Genocide Studies*, 19–41.
112 Anne Applebaum, *Red Famine: Stalin's War on Ukraine* (London, 2017), 193.
113 Anne Applebaum, *Gulag: A History* (London, 2003), 9.
114 Sheila Fitzpatrick, *A Spy in the Archives: A Memoir of Cold War Russia* (London, 2013), 210.

115 Sheila Fitzpatrick, 'Red Famine by Anne Applebaum Review – Did Stalin Deliberately let Ukraine Starve?' *Guardian* (25 August 2017), https://www.theguardian.com/books/2017/aug/25/red-famine-stalins-war-on-ukraine-anne-applebaum-review (accessed 29 August 2017).
116 Anne Applebaum, reply to Fitzpatrick review, 27 August 2017, https://www.facebook.com/anneapplebaumwp/posts/704110623118513?__xts__[0]=68.ARC6k1AovI2JLDfAAzGHPkGRvTedPmY_5aRzRHh6kMOUz5AMGR8UDK28iDt7QJ2jLXWrSTdKGJusJfPCYbLfcLLKxQvCktmSLRJfhifukgmzd_GqOArXsuYUGdh9wsHgWdj9ONECwdgRodD2FKt3ql2giNm_Yfv59_489FyzFXg_E7mc2tI8XJY0HeV1SmWZyvAeOqgnixptZKTL_WPWn3M2&__tn__=-R (accessed 29 August 2017).
117 https://twitter.com/jypersian/status/907936649354416128 (accessed 1 November 2018).
118 Norman Naimark, Niccolo Pianciola, Tanja Penter, J. Arch Getty, Alexander Etkind, Sarah Cameron, Stephen Wheatcroft, Andrea Graziosi and Ronald Suny, 'Roundtable on Soviet Famines', *Contemporary European History* 27, no. 3 (2018): 432–81.
119 Based on a search on 23 October 2018 of the following journals: *Otechestvennaia istoriia*; *Voprosy istorii*; *Sotsiologicheskie issledovaniia*; *Istoriia*; *Istoricheskie issledovaniia*; *Vestnik arkhivista*; *Istoricheskii arkhiv*; *Istorickeskii zhurnal*; *Nauchnye issledovaniia*; *Noveishaia istoriia Rossii*; *Novyi istoricheskii vestnik*; *Rodina*; *Russkii arkhiv*.
120 Vladislav Gulevich, 'Voiny Stalina protiv Ukrainy ne bylo', *Fond strategicheskoi kul'tury* (11 August 2018), https://www.fondsk.ru/news/2018/08/11/vojny-stalina-protiv-ukrainy-ne-bylo-46596.html (accessed 23 October 2018).
121 'Poroshenko vstretilsia s Enn Epplebaum – avtorom knigi 'Krasnyi golod. Voina Stalina protiv Ukrainy', *tsenzor.net* (21 November 2017), https://censor.net.ua/photo_news/463430/poroshenko_vstretilsya_s_enn_epplbaum_avtorom_knigi_krasnyyi_golod_voyina_stalina_protiv_ukrainy_fotoreportaj (accessed 22 October 2018).
122 Stanislav Kulchytsky, 'Holodomor 1933 roku. Ochyma Enn Epplbom', *den'* (24 November 2017), https://day.kyiv.ua/uk/article/istoriya-i-ya/golodomor-1933-roku (accessed 23 October 2018).
123 Enn Epplbom, *Chervonyj holod: Vijna Stalina proty Ukrainy* (Kyiv, 2018).
124 Vasil' Marochko, '"Chervonyj holod" Enn Epplbom: rozdumy pulittserivs'koho laureata', *Slovo Prosvity* (13 December 2017): 5.
125 Roman Serbyn, 'Nedoliky i shkidlyvist' monohrafiyi "Chervonyj holod" Enn Epplbom?', *Memorial Zhertv Holodomoru* (5 June 2018), http://memorialholodomor.org.ua/news/nedoliky-i-shkidlyvist-monografiyi-chervonyj-golod-enn-epplbom-roman-serbyn/ (accessed 23 October 2018).
126 V. I. Marochko, 'Zaprechennya Holodomoru-henotsydu pulittserivs'kymy laureatamy: Diuranti Uolter i Epplbom Enn', *Memorial Zhertv Holodomoru* (15 June 2018), http://memorialholodomor.org.ua/news/zaperechennya-golodomoru-genocidu-pulticerivskimi-laureatami-dyuranti-uolter-and-epplbom-enn/ (accessed 23 October 2018).
127 Volodymyr Serhijchuk, 'Iak nashi liudy "dopomohli" pulittserivs'komu laureatu', *Holos Ukrainy* (7 July 2018), http://www.golos.com.ua/article/304940 (accessed 23 October 2018).

128 Olesia Stasiuk, 'Holodomor buv henotsidom: retsenziia ukrains'kykh istorykiv na knyzhku Enn Epplbom', *Ukraina moloda* (19 September 2018), http://www.umoloda.kiev.ua/number/3362/196/126559/ (accessed 23 October 2018).
129 'Laureat Pulittserovskoi premii: Stalin ispol'zoval Golodomor, choby reshit' dlai sebia tak nazyvaemuiu ukrainskuiu problemu', *Gordon* (23 November 2017) and reader comment by Mikola Lukasevich, *Gordon* (23 November 2017), https://gordonua.com/news/society/laureat-pulitcerovskoy-premii-stalin-ispolzoval-golodomor-chtoby-reshit-dlya-sebya-tak-nazyvaemuyu-ukrainskuyu-problemu-218645.html (accessed 22 October 2018).
130 Applebaum, *Red Famine*, 284–85.
131 Applebaum, *Red Famine*, 233–54, quotation: 237.

NEW PERSPECTIVES ON STALINISM?
A CONCLUSION

The historiography of Stalinism was no journey from the darkness of ignorance to the light of understanding. Processes of learning went hand in hand with forgetting; concepts and approaches which had been 'overcome' in one era inspired scholars of a later period; increasing professionalization was challenged by repoliticization; global integration into a transnational scholarly debate was countered by renationalization. Today, scholars have more and better sources on all aspects of life under Stalin than ever before. But they also labour in a context where whatever they say about the Stalinist past will not only offend vocal and often powerful groups, but might well run foul of the law in one or other successor state of the Soviet Union. Thus, three and a half decades after the heated debate about 'new perspectives on Stalinism' which opened this book, researching and writing about Stalinism remains both challenging and stimulating.

It is more risky to forecast historiographical trends than it is predicting the weather. Nevertheless, five avenues of research are catching the attention of an increasing number of scholars: gender, the environment, the economy, the Second World War, and empire. Research in all of them is informed by political struggles in the present, which, as we have seen throughout this book, can serve as a positive incentive for intellectual work. All of them include a mix of the 'four levels of socio-cultural transformation' we can observe in Soviet society, and hence are conceptually interesting: pre-existing patterns following their own dynamic, structures formed through social engineering, including its non-intended consequences, forms which emerge through interactions not involving the state, and formations induced by interactions with the world outside the Soviet Union. All of them involve processes the Stalinists poorly understood and certainly did not control. And all of them will benefit if they embed Stalinism into the longer sweep of Soviet and post-Soviet history.[1]

NEW PERSPECTIVES ON STALINISM? A CONCLUSION

Gender

Like a submarine, gender has appeared and disappeared throughout this book. We encountered gendered dimensions in the interactions between historians (Chapter 1), in learned discussions about Stalin's penis (Chapter 5), but also in the debate about whether or not Sovietization was oppressive or liberating in non-Russian regions (Chapter 3). Gender resurfaced in Chapter 7 as a social phenomenon the scholars of 'Stalinist civilization' found hard to accommodate, and as one of the questions of state intervention which interested the 'modernity' school. Much more could have been said.[2]

Several reasons make the study of gender a likely future for research on Stalinism.[3] A renewed interest in gender and sexualities among students is fuelled by a new wave of the LGBT+ rights movement, the exploration of non-binary forms of gender identity, and a re-invigorated feminism. There is a lot of interesting work to be done for students of Stalinism whose sensibilities are sharpened by such political struggles. The history of gender relations and gender constructs is one sphere of life in Stalin's time where the relatively independent socio-cultural processes could be found, which Sheila Fitzpatrick had looked for in the 1980s (see Chapter 1).[4] As in other fields surveyed in this conclusion, such histories will benefit from breaking the chronological frame of Stalin's years in power and consider the longer arch of development from the nineteenth century to today.[5]

It is hard to refute that in the realm of gender and sexualities there was a retreat from revolutionary values during the Stalin years: divorce became harder, abortion was outlawed, and maternity celebrated.[6] The re-criminalization of male same-sex love entrenched homophobia for the long-term.[7] The massive increase in female employment did not raise the status of women, but rather imposed the double burden of work and family.[8] A 'glass ceiling' on female careers emerged fairly quickly in the Soviet Union,[9] and the war reinforced rather than weakened the established sexual and gender regime.[10]

And yet many women did experience social mobility, personal fulfilment and liberation from local patriarchy during the Stalin years.[11] Within the Communist Youth League, enough of the earlier revolutionary values were preserved that young women found nothing strange in volunteering for the army in the summer of

1941.[12] Women were prominent players in Soviet empire-building, as well as in the reform debates of the late Stalin years which anticipated later reforms.[13] And, in the long-term, the two largest successor states to the Soviet Union did rather well in the world index of economic equality between men and women. In 2017, Ukraine ranked thirty-fourth in the world with regards to economic equality between the sexes. The Russian Federation ranked forty-first. Both were ahead of societies priding themselves on their history of female emancipation: Australia (forty-second), Germany (forty-third), or the United Kingdom (fifty-third).[14] Russia is the world leader in employment of women in senior management positions.[15] And while politics in Russia remains a male domain, the same is not true for Ukraine, which had a female prime minister, Yulia Tymoshenko, between 2007 and 2010. Either the Stalinist retrenchment of the 1930s and 1940s had little long-term impact, or it was overcome much more successfully than usually imagined.

Ecology

The other contemporary problem which agitates intellectuals is the environmental crisis. For good reason, the environmental history of Stalinism (and of the USSR more generally) has been written as a tale of unmitigated disaster.[16] It should give intellectuals pause who think that our current predicament is simply an effect of capitalism. Indeed, Stalinism can work wonders for defenders of liberal economics. 'The Soviet government's imperatives for economic growth, combined with communal ownership of virtually all property and resources, caused tremendous environmental damage', reads one such polemic.[17] 'As socialist ideas capture the American imagination', warns another, 'it's important to remember socialism's dismal environmental legacy.'[18] Such use of Soviet environmental disaster to support capitalism has motivated the exploration of similarities between the two main forms of twentieth-century industrialism.[19] The history of Soviet environmental conservation and Stalinist environmental consciousness has also been excavated, with often surprising results.[20]

Economy

The environmental history of Stalinism is quite obviously entangled with a third field likely to see further growth in decades to come:

the history of the Stalinist economy. We have good studies now on the macro-economic history of pre-war Stalinism,[21] and important outlines of the Stalinist economy at war.[22] The economy of the Gulag, likewise, has found its historians.[23] We also understand the Soviet economy's place in the world much better.[24] But if we move beyond this general level, much remains to be done. Research into the micro-economics of daily life can build on recent studies of money and taxation,[25] corruption,[26] informal exchange,[27] food distribution and trade,[28] housing construction[29] and gardening.[30]

Understanding this history will be of profound importance to those who grope for alternatives to the current world economic system. Their number is rising among younger people in the richer economies of the world. As conservative pundits report with horror, many among the so-called 'millennials' – better educated, harder working, with larger savings than any generation before, but in many places locked out of the housing market and subjected to increasingly deregulated working conditions – find nothing frightening about the idea of socialism.[31] Some relatively high-profile middle-aged intellectuals are, likewise, celebrating the Russian Revolution as part of the positive history of their own struggle.[32] Like 'socialist historians' before them, they will have to come to terms with the relationships between socialism and Sovietism, as well as between Leninism and Stalinism. Their opponents already mobilize Stalinism as the dark future awaiting anybody daring to meddle in the economy: lines, scarcity and the Gulag. Thus, both the new socialists and their enemies will find Stalinism a fertile ground for both research and polemics. Both sides will gain an analytical edge if they keep the wider context of the economic transformation of the Soviet Union in view.[33]

The war

The greatest test for the Stalinist economy came during the Second World War. As we saw in Chapter 8, there is a large historiography to build on and many current political struggles to fuel debate. A large number of new sources – both from the archival and from the memory revolution – can release raw material for new histories of this war.[34] This emerging scholarship will have to grapple with the multiplicity of wartime experiences,[35] with the role of the home front,[36] the massive population displacements,[37] the question of loyalty and disloyalty,[38] the behaviour of Soviet citizens under German occupation,[39] the ways the regime tried to mobilize the population,[40] and the many reasons people worked and fought, often to the death.[41] Notwithstanding historians' increasing interest in violence,[42] any history of the Soviet Second World War will need to grapple with the more prosaic role of the economy and the extent to which Stalinist industrialization (and the women and children 'manning' the home front) ensured victory.[43]

In a world where Asia can no longer be ignored by Eurocentric historians, and where Eastern Europe has recovered its history independent of its Russian neighbour, historians will also have to come to terms with the fact that the Soviet Second World War was broader than the Great Patriotic War of 1941–45: The Soviet Union fought an undeclared border war with Japan in 1938–39, whose central role in the history of the Second World War is often forgotten, and it also joined the Allies in their fight against Japan at the end of the war. In the West, Stalin helped Germany dismantle Poland in 1939, and generally acted aggressively towards his neighbours, waging war on Finland in 1939–1940 and annexing the Baltic republics in 1940.[44] The later 'liberation' of the new western borderlands, then, was indeed a 're-occupation'.[45] Inevitably, such a history will be morally ambiguous, politically controversial, and empirically complex.

Empire

The two main results of the Soviet Second World War were the victory over Nazi Germany and the westward expansion of Stalin's empire. The debate about empire – if the USSR was one, and if so, what kind (Chapter 3) – was never about Stalinism alone. Most contributions put the Stalin years into a much wider chronological context. At stake was the entire Soviet experience, maybe even including earlier Russian imperial history as well. Stalinism was only one moment in this larger transformation.[46]

But the new studies of empire and nations have gone further. New research on Central Asia has brought the agency of indigenous groups, indigenous elites, and their longer-term cultural and social histories into view.[47] The literature on the western borderlands, likewise, has done much to liberate historians' imagination from the straitjacket of Russian history. Seen both from the vantage point of the post-Soviet world, and from the crucible of the Second World War, Stalinism became a transnational and trans-imperial moment. No longer located exclusively in the long-term history of the Russian Empire, it now resides at the intersection of the histories of the German, Habsburg and Russian empires, their successor states, and the various national, social and political movements entangled with them.[48]

Hence, we are witnessing a real postcolonial fracturing of the field of Soviet history.[49] In a growing number of studies, Soviet history is dissolved into histories of Ukraine,[50] Belarus,[51] the Baltic[52] and Central Asian republics,[53] the Caucasus[54] or Transcaucasus,[55] as well as, of course, Russia.[56] These new and multiple histories can build on precursors from the diasporas and their allies in the West, as we have seen in the case of Ukraine in Chapter 9. But the new reality of fifteen independent nation states has given this fragmentation a new logic, a new focus, and a new strength. Soviet history, then, is no longer only part of the history of Russia, but also of Armenia, Azerbaijan, Belarus, Estonia, Georgia, Kazakhstan, Kyrgyzstan, Latvia, Lithuania, Moldova, Tajikistan, Turkmenistan, Ukraine and Uzbekistan.

Bringing these histories back together is a challenge which historians are only just beginning to face. They have done so either by linking national histories to larger problematics of Soviet history,[57] or by combining them into multinational accounts of the Soviet Union written outside the framework of Russian history, which once held it together.[58] But these are no more than beginnings of a new history of the Soviet Union, and with it of Stalinism, which will be adequate for our times.

Notes

1 Mark Edele, 'Soviet Society, Social Structure, and Everyday Life. Major Frameworks Reconsidered', *Kritika: Explorations in Russian and Eurasian History* 8, no. 2 (2007): 349–73, here: 372–73. In contrast to the rest of this book, which has recovered the history behind contemporary debate, this chapter cites only recent literature published since 2000. The five fields, moreover, are not hermetically sealed silos. Many works could be listed under more than one subheading.

2 Sheila Fitzpatrick and Yuri Slezkine (eds), *In the Shadow of Revolution: Life Stories of Russian Women* (Princeton, 2000), and Melanie Ilic (ed.), *Women in the Stalin Era* (Basingstoke, 2001). On masculinity: Barbara Evans Clements, Rebecca Friedman and Dan Healey (eds), *Russian Masculinities in*

NEW PERSPECTIVES ON STALINISM? A CONCLUSION

History and Culture (Basingstoke, 2002); Mark Edele, 'Strange Young Men in Stalin's Moscow: The Birth and Life of the Stiliagi, 1945–1953', *Jahrbücher für Geschichte Osteuropas* 50, no. 1 (2002): 37–61. The pioneer in LGBT studies on Stalinism is Dan Healey, *Homosexual Desire in Revolutionary Russia: The Regulation of Sexual and Gender Dissent* (Chicago, 2001); Dan Healey, *Bolshevik Sexual Forensics: Diagnosing Disorder in the Clinic and Courtroom, 1917–1939* (DeKalb, 2009). A landmark collection charting the current state of research is Melanie Ilic, *The Palgrave Handbook of Women and Gender in Twentieth-Century Russia and the Soviet Union* (London, 2018).

3 For the state of the field, see Amy Randall, 'Gender and Sexuality', in: *Life in Stalin's Soviet Union*, ed. Kees Boterbloem (London, 2019), 139–66.
4 Mark Edele, *Stalinist Society 1928–1953* (Oxford, 2011), chapter 4.
5 For an overview: Barbara Alpern Engel, 'New Directions in Russian and Soviet Women's History', in: *Making Womens Histories Beyond National Narratives*, ed. Pamela S. Nadell and Kate Haulman (New York, 2013), 38–60.
6 Wendy Goldman, *Women, the State, and Revolution: Soviet Family Policy and Social Life, 1917–1936* (Cambridge, 2002).
7 Dan Healey, *Russian Homophobia from Stalin to Sochi* (London, 2018).
8 Thomas G. Schrand, 'Socialism in one Gender: Masculine Values in the Stalin Revolution', in: *Russian Masculinities*, 194–209.
9 Melanie Ilic, '"Equal Pay for Equal Work": Women's Wages in Soviet Russia', in: *The Palgrave Handbook of Women and Gender in Twentieth-Century Russia*, 101–15.
10 Greta Bucher, *Women, the Bureaucracy and Daily Life in Postwar Moscow, 1945–1953* (Boulder, 2006); Mark Edele, *Soviet Veterans of the Second World War: A Popular Movement in an Authoritarian Society, 1941–1991* (Oxford, 2008), 71–74; Steven G. Jug, 'Red Army Romance: Preserving Masculine Hegemony in Mixed Gender Combat Units, 1943–1944', *Journal of War & Culture Studies* 5, no. 3 (2012): 321–34; Erica L. Fraser, *Military Masculinity and Postwar Recovery in the Soviet Union* (Toronto, 2019).
11 Choi Chatterjee, *Celebrating Women: Gender, Festival Culture, and Bolshevik Ideology, 1910–1939* (Pittsburgh, 2002); Douglas Northrop, *Veiled Empire: Gender and Power in Stalinist Central Asia* (Ithaca, 2004); Marianne Kamp, *The New Woman in Uzbekistan: Islam, Modernity, and Unveiling under Communism* (Seattle, 2006); Mary Buckley, *Mobilizing Soviet Peasants: Heroines and Heroes of Stalin's Fields* (Lanham, 2006).
12 Anna Krylova, *Soviet Women in Combat: A History of Violence on the Eastern Front* (Cambridge, 2010).
13 Elena Shulman, *Stalinism on the Frontier of Empire: Women and State Formation in the Soviet Far East* (Cambridge, 2008); Beate Fieseler, 'Aufbruch der Frauen im Spätstalinismus? Hintergrund, Verlauf und Ergebnisse der ZK-Frauenkonferenz von 1950', in: *Stalinistische Subjekte: Individuum und System in der Sowjetunion und der Komintern 1929–1953*, ed. Brigitte Studer and Heiko Haumann (Zurich, 2006), 345–58.
14 World Economic Forum, 'Global Gender Gap Report 2017, Performance by Subindex: Economic Participation and Opportunity', http://reports.weforum.org/global-gender-gap-report-2017/performance-by-subindex/ (accessed 6 November

2019). Equality in the economy would receive an index of 1.0. No country has achieved such a rating.
15 'Russia is World's No. 1 Employer of Women Managers, Report Says', *Moscow Times* (18 June 2014), https://www.themoscowtimes.com/2014/06/18/russia-is-worlds-no-1-employer-of-women-managers-report-says-a36532 (accessed 19 December 2019); and Tim Smedley, 'Women in Leadership Roles – the West Finds itself Outshone', *Financial Times* (15 September 2015): 1.
16 Douglas R. Weiner, 'The Predatory Tribute-Taking State. A Framework for Understanding Russian Environmental History', in: *The Environment and World History*, ed. Edmund Burke and Kenneth Pomeranz (Berkeley, 2009), 276–315; Paul Josephson, Nicolai Dronin, Ruben Mnatsakanian, Aleh Cherp, Dmitry Dfremenko and Vladislav Larin (eds), *An Environmental History of Russia* (Cambridge, 2013); Klaus Gestwa, *Die stalinschen Grossbauten des Kommunismus: Sowjetische Technik- und Umweltgeschichte, 1948–1967* (Munich, 2010); Julia Obertreis, *Imperial Desert Dreams: Cotton Growing and Irrigation in Central Asia, 1860–1991* (Göttingen, 2017). For a critique of this negative approach, see David Moon, 'The Curious Case of the Marginalisation or Distortion of Russian and Soviet Environmental History in Global Environmental Histories', *International Review of Environmental History* 3, no. 2 (2017): 31–50.
17 Thomas J. DiLorenzo, 'Why Socialism Causes Pollution', *FEE: Foundation for Economic Education* (1 March 1992), https://fee.org/articles/why-socialism-causes-pollution/ (accessed 18 June 2019).
18 Shawn Regan, 'Socialism is Bad for the Environment', *National Review* (16 May 2019), https://www.nationalreview.com/magazine/2019/06/03/socialism-is-bad-for-the-environment/ (accessed 18 June 2019).
19 Kate Brown, *Plutopia: Nuclear Families, Atomic Cities, and the Great Soviet and American Plutonium Disasters* (Oxford, 2013); Andy Bruno, *The Nature of Soviet Power: An Arctic Environmental History* (New York, 2016); Serhii Plokhy, *Chernobyl: The History of a Nuclear Catastrophe* (New York, 2018).
20 For the cutting edge at the time of writing, see Stephen Brain, *Song of the Forest: Russian Forestry and Stalin's Environmentalism, 1905–1953* (Pittsburgh, 2011); Andy Bruno, 'Environmental Subjectivities from the Soviet North', and Johanna Conterio, 'Curative Nature: Medical Foundations of Soviet Nature Protection, 1917–1941', both in *Slavic Review* 78, no. 1 (2019): 23–49.
21 See Paul R. Gregory (ed.), *Behind the Facade of Stalin's Command Economy: Evidence from the Soviet State and Party Archives* (Stanford, 2001); Paul R. Gregory, *The Political Economy of Stalinism: Evidence from the Soviet Secret Archives* (Cambridge, 2004); and the concluding volume of R. W. Davies's seven-volume economic history of Stalinism: R. W. Davies, Mark Harrison, Oleg Khlevniuk and Stephen Wheatcroft, *The Soviet Economy and the Approach of War, 1937–1939* (London, 2018).
22 Mark Harrison, 'The USSR and Total War. Why Didn't the Soviet Economy Collapse in 1942?', in: *A World at Total War: Global Conflict and the Politics of Destruction, 1937–1945*, ed. Roger Chickering, Stig Förster, and Bernd Greiner (Cambridge, 2005), 137–56; Mark Harrison, 'Industry and the Economy', in: *The Soviet Union at War, 1941–1945*, ed. David R. Stone (Barnsley, 2010),

15–44; Lennart Samuelson, *Tankograd: The Formation of a Soviet Company Town: Cheliabinsk 1900s–1950s* (Basingstoke, 2011).
23 Galina Ivanova, *Labor Camp Socialism: The Gulag in the Soviet Totalitarian System* (Armonk, 2000); Simon Ertz, 'Trading Effort for Freedom: Workday Credits in the Stalinist Camp System', *Comparative Economic Studies* 47 (2005): 476–91; Leonid Borodkin and Simon Ertz, 'Forced Labour and the Need for Motivation: Wages and Bonuses in the Stalinist Camp System', *Comparative Economic Studies* 47 (2005): 418–36.
24 Oscar Sanchez-Sibony, *Red Globalization: The Political Economy of the Soviet Cold War from Stalin to Khrushchev* (New York, 2014); Special Issue: 'Economy and Power in the Soviet Union, 1917–39', ed. Andrew Sloin and Oscar Sanchez-Sibony, *Kritika: Explorations in Russian and Eurasian History* 15, no. 1 (2014).
25 Kristy Ironside, 'Rubles for Victory: The Social Dynamics of State Fundraising on the Soviet Home Front', *Kritika: Explorations in Russian and Eurasian History* 15, no. 4 (2014): 799–828; Kristy Ironside, 'Stalin's Doctrine of Price Reductions During the Second World War and Postwar Reconstruction', *Slavic Review* 75, no. 3 (2016): 655–77; Kristy Ironside, 'Between Fiscal, Ideological, and Social Dilemmas: The Soviet "Bachelor Tax" and Post-War Tax Reform, 1941–1962', *Europe–Asia Studies* 69, no. 6 (2017): 855–78. Marcie K. Cowley, 'The Right of Inheritance and the Stalin Revolution', *Kritika: Explorations in Russian and Eurasian History* 15, no. 1 (2014): 103–23.
26 James Heinzen, *The Art of the Bribe: Corruption under Stalin, 1943–1953* (Stanford, 2016).
27 Sheila Fitzpatrick, '*Blat* in Stalin's Time', in: *Bribery and Blat in Russia: Negotiating Reciprocity from the Middle Ages to the 1990s*, ed. Stephen Lovell, Alena Ledeneva and Andrei Rogachevskii (New York, 2000), 166–82; Alena Ledeneva, 'Blat and Guanxi: Informal Practices in Russia and China', *Comparative Studies in Society and History* 50, no. 1 (2008): 118–44.
28 Elena Osokina, *Our Daily Bread: Socialist Distribution and the Art of Survival in Stalin's Russia, 1927–1941* (Armonk, New York, London, 2001); Julie Hessler, *A Social History of Soviet Trade: Trade Policy, Retail Practices, and Consumption, 1917–1953* (Princeton, 2004); Amy Randall, *The Soviet Dream World of Retail Trade and Consumption in the 1930s* (New York, 2008).
29 Mark B. Smith, *Property of Communists: The Urban Housing Program from Stalin to Khrushchev* (DeKalb, 2010).
30 Stephen Lovell, *Summerfolk: A History of the Dacha, 1719–2000* (Ithaca and London, 2003).
31 According to a 2018 US poll, 46 per cent of 'millenials' would prefer to live under socialism and 6 per cent under communism: Victims of Communism Memorial Foundation, *Third Annual Report on US Attitudes Toward Socialism* (Washington, 2018), 4. Australian research found similar numbers: 58 per cent had a favourable view of socialism: Tom Switzer and Charles Jacobs, 'Millennials and Socialism: Australian Youth are Lurching to the Left', Policy Paper no. 7, The Centre for Independent Studies (Melbourne, 2018), 2.
32 China Mieville, *October: The Story of the Russian Revolution* (London, 2017). Mieville was born in 1972.

NEW PERSPECTIVES ON STALINISM? A CONCLUSION

33 Philip Hanson, *The Rise and Fall of the Soviet Economy: An Economic History of the USSR from 1945* (London, 2003).
34 Iva Glisic and Mark Edele, 'The Memory Revolution Meets the Digital Age: Red Army Soldiers Remember World War II', *Geschichte und Gesellschaft* 45, no. 1 (2019): 95–119.
35 Roger Reese, 'Ten Jewish Red Army Veterans of the Great Patriotic War: In Search of the Mythical Representative Soldier's Story', *The Journal of Slavic Military Studies* 27, no. 3 (2014): 420–29; Moritz Florin, 'Becoming Soviet through War: The Kyrgyz and the Great Fatherland War', *Kritika: Explorations in Russian and Eurasian History* 17, no. 3 (2016): 495–516; Sheila Fitzpatrick, *Mischka's War: A Story of Survival from War-Torn Europe to New York* (London, 2017); Brandon Schechter, *The Stuff of Soldiers: A History of the Red Army in World War II through Objects* (Ithaca, 2019).
36 Susanne Conze, *Sowjetische Industriearbeiterinnen in den Vierziger Jahren: Die Auswirkungen des Zweiten Weltkrieges auf die Erwerbstätigkeit von Frauen in der UdSSR, 1941–1950* (Stuttgart, 2001); Wendy Z. Goldman and Donald Filtzer (eds), *Hunger and War: Food Provisioning in the Soviet Union During World War II* (Bloomington, 2015); Wilson Bell, *Stalin's Gulag at War: Forced Labour, Mass Death, and Soviet Victory in the Second World War* (Toronto, 2018). On the war's impact on the legal regulation of sexual relations, see Mie Nakachi, 'N. S. Khrushchev and the 1944 Soviet Family Law: Politics, Reproduction, and Language', *East European Politics and Societies* 20, no. 1 (2006): 40–68; and Mie Nakachi, 'Population, Politics and Reproduction: Late Stalinism and its Legacy', in: *Late Stalinist Russia: Society between Reconstruction and Reinvention*, ed. Juliane Fürst (London, 2006), 167–91.
37 Mark Edele, 'The Second World War as a History of Displacement. The Soviet Case', *History Australia* 12, no. 2 (2015): 17–40.
38 For the state of play, see Mark Edele, '"What Are We Fighting For?" Loyalty in the Soviet War Effort, 1941–1945', *International Labor and Working-Class History* 84, Fall (2013): 248–68.
39 Johannes Due Enstad, *Soviet Russians under Nazi Occupation: Fragile Loyalties in World War II* (Cambridge, 2018).
40 Richard Bidlack, 'Propaganda and Public Opinion', in: *The Soviet Union at War*, 45–68; Karel C. Berkhoff, *Motherland in Danger: Soviet Propaganda During World War II* (Cambridge, Mass., 2012).
41 The best treatment is Roger Reese, *Why Stalin's Soldiers Fought: The Red Army's Military Effectiveness in World War II* (Lawrence, 2011). For a stress on ideology and self-mobilization, see Jochen Hellbeck, *Stalingrad: The City that Defeated the Third Reich* (New York, 2015); the role of coercion is stressed by Jörg Baberowski, *Scorched Earth: Stalin's Reign of Terror* (New Haven, 2016), 315–425.
42 Mark Edele, 'Take (No) Prisoners! The Red Army and German POWs, 1941–1943', *The Journal of Modern History* 88, no. 2 (2016): 342–79; Mark Edele and Filip Slaveski, 'Violence from Below: Explaining Crimes against Civilians across Soviet Space, 1943–1947', *Europe–Asia Studies* 68, no. 6 (2016): 1020–35; Kerstin Bischl, 'Presenting Oneself: Red Army Soldiers and Violence in the Great Patriotic War', *History* 101, no. 346 (2016): 464–79;

Vojin Majstorović, 'The Red Army in Yugoslavia, 1944–1945', *Slavic Review* 75, no. 2 (2016): 396–421.

43 The best overview of the economic, military and diplomatic history is Evan Mawdsley, *Thunder in the East: The Nazi–Soviet War 1941–1945*. 2nd rev. ed. (London, 2016). See also Alexander Hill, *The Red Army and the Second World War* (Cambridge, 2017).

44 Jan T. Gross, *Revolution from Abroad: The Soviet Conquest of Poland's Western Ukraine and Western Belorussia*. Expanded ed. (Princeton and Oxford, 2002); Evan Mawdsley, *World War II: A New History* (Cambridge, 2009); Tsuyoshi Hasegawa, 'Soviet Policy toward Japan During World War II', *Cahiers du monde russe* 52, no. 2–3 (2011): 245–71; Stuart D. Goldman, *Nomonhan, 1939: The Red Army's Victory That Shaped World War II* (Annapolis, 2012).

45 Mark Edele, 'Soviet Liberations and Occupations, 1939–1949', in: *The Cambridge History of the Second World War*, ed. Richard Bosworth and Joe Maiolo, vol 2 (Cambridge, 2015), 487–506.

46 Valerie A. Kivelson and Ronald G. Suny, *Russia's Empires* (Oxford, 2017). For an even broader view, see Jane Burbank and Frederick Cooper, *Empires in World History: Power and the Politics of Difference* (Princeton, 2011).

47 Shoshana Keller, *To Moscow, Not Mecca: The Soviet Campaign against Islam in Central Asia, 1917–1941* (Westport, 2001); Adrienne Lynn Edgar, *Tribal Nation: The Making of Soviet Turkmenistan* (Princeton, 2004); Adeeb Khalid, *Making Uzbekistan: Nation, Empire, and Revolution in the Early USSR* (Ithaca and London, 2015).

48 Shimon Redlich, *Together and Apart in Brzezany: Poles, Jews, and Ukrainians, 1919–1945* (Bloomington, 2002); Kate Brown, *A Biography of No Place: From Ethnic Borderland to Soviet Heartland* (Cambridge, Mass, 2003); Timothy Snyder, *The Reconstruction of Nations: Poland, Ukraine, Lithuania, Belarus, 1569–1999* (New Haven, 2003); Timothy Snyder, *The Red Prince: The Secret Lives of a Habsburg Archduke* (New York, 2008); Timothy Snyder, *Bloodlands: Europe between Hitler and Stalin* (London, 2010); Alexander V. Prusin, *The Lands Between: Conflict in the East European Borderlands, 1870–1992* (Oxford, 2010); Omer Bartov and Eric D. Weitz (eds), *Shatterzone of Empires: Coexistence and Violence in the German, Habsburg, Russian and Ottoman Borderlands* (Bloomington, 2013); Per Anders Rudling, *The Rise and Fall of Belarusian Nationalism, 1906–1931* (Pittsburgh, 2014); Tarik Cyril Amar, *The Paradox of Ukrainian Lviv: A Borderland City between Stalinists, Nazis, and Nationalists* (Ithaca, 2015).

49 For an attempt to come to terms theoretically with postcolonialism in the post-Soviet context, see Annus Epp, *Soviet Postcolonial Studies: A View from the Western Borderlands* (New York, 2018).

50 Serhy Yekelchyk, *Ukraine: Birth of a Modern Nation* (Oxford, 2007); Serhii Plokhy, *The Gates of Europe: A History of Ukraine* (New York, 2015); George O. Liber, *Total Wars and the Making of Modern Ukraine, 1914–1954* (Toronto, 2016).

51 David Marples, *Belarus: A Denationalized Nation* (London, 2012).

52 Mati Laur et al., *History of Estonia* (Tallin, 2000); Daina Bleierle et al., *History of Latvia: The 20th Century* (Riga, 2006); David J. Smith, David

NEW PERSPECTIVES ON STALINISM? A CONCLUSION

J. Galbreath and Geoffrey Swain (eds), *From Recognition to Restoration: Latvia's History as a Nation-State* (Amsterdam, 2010).
53 Peter L. Roudik, *The History of the Central Asian Republics* (Westport, 2007).
54 Alex Marshall, *The Caucasus under Soviet Rule* (New York, 2010).
55 Ronald G. Suny, *The Making of the Georgian Nation*. 2nd ed. (Bloomington, 1994); Ronald G. Suny, *Looking Toward Ararat: Armenia in Modern History* (Bloomington, 1993).
56 Geoffrey A. Hosking, *Rulers and Victims: The Russians in the Soviet Union* (Cambridge, Mass., 2006); David R. Marples, *Motherland: Russia in the 20th Century* (London, 2014); Serhii Plokhy, *Lost Kingdom: The Quest for Empire and the Making of the Russian Nation: From 1470 to the Present* (New York, 2017).
57 Olaf Mertelsmann, *Everyday Life in Stalinist Estonia* (Frankfurt, 2012); Sarah Cameron, *The Hungry Steppe: Famine, Violence, and the Making of Soviet Kazakhstan* (Ithaca, 2018).
58 Jeremy Smith, *Red Nations: The Nationalities Experience in and after the USSR* (Cambridge, 2013); Mark Edele, *The Soviet Union: A Short History* (Oxford, 2019).

FURTHER READING

The below list contains some suggestions for further reading by chapter. The list is deliberately short. Readers who desire to delve deeper into the literature should consult the endnotes for each chapter.

Debates on Stalinism: an introduction

Daly, Jonathan, 'The Pleiade: Five Scholars Who Founded Russian Historical Studies in the United States', *Kritika: Explorations in Russian and Eurasian History* 18, no. 4 (2017): 785–826.
Edele, Mark, *Stalinist Society 1928–1953* (Oxford, 2011).
—— *The Soviet Union: A Short History* (Oxford, 2019).
Engerman, David C., *Know Your Enemy: The Rise and Fall of America's Soviet Experts* (Oxford, 2009).
Gleason, Abbott, *Totalitarianism: The Inner History of the Cold War* (Oxford, 1995).
Jones, Polly, *Myth, Memory, Trauma: Rethinking the Stalinist Past in the Soviet Union, 1953–70* (New Haven, 2013).
Markwick, Roger, *Rewriting History in Soviet Russia: The Politics of Revisionist Historiography, 1956–1974* (Basingstoke, 2000).
Satter, David, *It was a Long Time Ago and it Never Happened Anyway: Russia and the Communist Past* (New Haven, 2012).
Sherlock, Thomas, *Historical Narratives in the Soviet Union and Post-Soviet Russia: Destroying the Settled Past, Creating an Uncertain Future* (New York, 2007).
Suny, Ronald G., *Red Flag Unfurled: History, Historians, and the Russian Revolution* (London, 2017).

Chapter 1: A 'withering crossfire': debating Stalinism in the Cold War

Cohen, Stephen F., 'Bolshevism and Stalinism', in: *Stalinism: Essays in Historical Interpretation*, ed. Robert C. Tucker (New York, 1977).
Fitzpatrick, Sheila, 'New Perspectives on Stalinism', *The Russian Review* 45, no. 4 (1986): 357–73; and the ensuing discussion in *The Russian Review* (1986, 1987).

FURTHER READING

Chapter 2: Marxism–Lewinism and the origins of Stalinism

Buskovitch, Paul, '[Interview with] Moshe Lewin', in: *Visions of History*, ed. Henry Abelove et al. (Manchester, 1983), 281–308.
Lewin, Moshe, *Lenin's Last Struggle: With a New Introduction* (Ann Arbor, 2005).
—— *Russian Peasants and Soviet Power: A Study of Collectivization* (New York, 1975).
—— *The Making of the Soviet System: Essays in the Soviet History of the Interwar Years* (New York, 1994).

Chapter 3: The Russian origins of totalitarianism: empire and nation

Brandenberger, David, *National Bolshevism: Stalinist Mass Culture and the Formation of Modern Russian National Identity, 1931–1956* (Cambridge, Mass., 2002).
—— *Propaganda State in Crisis: Soviet Ideology, Indoctrination, and Terror under Stalin, 1928–1941* (New Haven, 2011).
Conquest, Robert, *The Nation Killers: The Soviet Deportation of Nationalities* (London, 1970).
Daly, Jonathan, *Pillars of the Profession: The Correspondence of Richard Pipes and Marc Raeff* (Leiden, 2019).
Hirsch, Francine, *Empire of Nations: Ethnographic Knowledge and the Making of the Soviet Union* (Ithaca, 2005).
Igmen, Ali, *Speaking Soviet with an Accent: Culture and Power in Kyrgyzstan* (Pittsburgh, 2012).
Kamp, Marianne, *The New Woman in Uzbekistan: Islam, Modernity, and Unveiling under Communism* (Seattle, 2006).
Keller, Shoshana, *To Moscow, Not Mecca: The Soviet Campaign against Islam in Central Asia, 1917–1941* (Westport, 2001).
Khalid, Adeeb, *Making Uzbekistan: Nation, Empire, and Revolution in the Early USSR* (Ithaca, 2015).
Martin, Terry, *The Affirmative Action Empire: Nations and Nationalism in the Soviet Union, 1923–1939* (Ithaca, 2001).
—— 'The Origins of Soviet Ethnic Cleansing', *The Journal of Modern History* 70, no. 4 (1998): 813–61.
Massell, Gregory, *The Surrogate Proletariat: Moslem Women and Revolutionary Strategies in Soviet Central Asia* (Princeton, 1974).
Michaels, Paula, *Curative Powers: Medicine and Empire in Stalin's Central Asia* (Pittsburgh, 2003).

Michaels, Paula, Douglas Northrop, Francine Hirsch and Yuri Slezkine, 'Nationalities in the Soviet Empire', *The Russian Review* 59, no. 2 (2000): 159–234.

Nekrich, Aleksandr, *Foresake Fear: Memoirs of an Historian* (Boston, 1991).

—— *The Punished Peoples: The Deportation and Fate of Soviet Minorities at the End of the Second World War* (New York, 1978).

Northrop, Douglas, *Veiled Empire: Gender and Power in Stalinist Central Asia* (Ithaca, 2004).

O'Keeffe, Brigid, *New Soviet Gypsies: Nationality, Performance, and Selfhood in the Early Soviet Union* (Toronto, 2013).

Pipes, Richard, *The Formation of the Soviet Union: Communism and Nationalism, 1917–1923*. Rev. ed. (Cambridge, Mass., 1997).

—— *Vixi: Memoirs of a Non-Belonger* (New Haven, 2003).

Pohl, J. Otto, *Ethnic Cleansing in the USSR, 1937–1949* (Westport, 1999).

Polian, Pavel, *Against their Will: The History and Geography of Forced Migrations in the USSR* (Budapest, 2004).

Slezkine, Yuri, 'The Soviet Union as a Communal Apartment, or How a Socialist State Promoted Ethnic Particularism', *Slavic Review* 53, no. 2 (1994): 415–52.

Suny, Ronald G., *The Revenge of the Past: Nationalism, Revolution, and the Collapse of the Soviet Union* (Stanford, 1993).

Chapter 4: Unrevisionist revisionism

Alexopoulos, Golfo, Julie Hessler and Kiril Tomoff (eds), *Writing the Stalin Era: Sheila Fitzpatrick and Soviet Historiography* (Basingstoke, 2011).

Fitzpatrick, Sheila, *A Spy in the Archives: A Memoir of Cold War Russia* (London, 2014).

—— *Education and Social Mobility in the Soviet Union, 1921–1932* (Cambridge, 1979).

—— *Everyday Stalinism: Ordinary Life in Extraordinary Times: Soviet Russia in the 1930s* (Oxford, 1999).

—— *My Father's Daughter: Memories of an Australian Childhood* (Melbourne, 2010).

—— *On Stalin's Team: The Years of Living Dangerously in Soviet Politics* (Melbourne, 2015).

———— 'Revisionism in Retrospect: A Personal View', *Slavic Review* 67, no. 3 (2008): 682–704.
———— 'Revisionism in Soviet History', *History and Theory* 46, no. 4 (2007): 77–91.
———— 'Stalin and the Making of a New Elite, 1928–1939', *Slavic Review* 38, no. 3 (1979): 377–402.
———— *Stalin's Peasants: Resistance and Survival in the Russian Village after Collectivization* (Oxford, 1994).
———— *Tear Off the Masks!: Identity and Imposture in Twentieth-Century Russia* (Princeton, 2005).
———— *The Russian Revolution*. 3rd ed. (Oxford, 2008).

Chapter 5: Stalinism with Stalin left in

Deutscher, Isaac, *Stalin: A Political Biography*. 2nd ed. (London, 1967).
Gorlizki, Yoram and Oleg Khlevniuk, *Cold Peace: Stalin and the Soviet Ruling Circle, 1945–1953* (Oxford, 2004).
Khlevniuk, O. V., *Stalin: New Biography of a Dictator* (New Haven, 2015).
Kotkin, Stephen, *Stalin: Waiting for Hitler, 1929–1941* (New York, 2017).
Medvedev, Roy, *Let History Judge: The Origins and Consequences of Stalinism*, ed. David Joravsky and Georges Haupt (New York, 1971); 2nd rev. ed. (Oxford, 1989).
Radzinsky, Edvard, *Stalin: The First In-Depth Biography based on Explosive New Documents from Russia's Secret Archives* (New York, 1996).
Tucker, Robert C., *Stalin in Power: The Revolution from Above, 1928–1941* (New York, 1990).
Ulam, Adam B., *Stalin: The Man and His Era*. 2nd, expanded ed. (Boston, 1989).
Volkogonov, Dmitrii Antonovich, *Stalin: Triumph and Tragedy* (London, 1991).

Chapter 6: Totalitarianism and revisionism

Arendt, Hannah, *The Origins of Totalitarianism* (New York, 1951).
Bauer, A., Alex Inkeles and Clyde Kuckhohn, *How the Soviet System Works: Cultural, Psychological, and Social Themes* (Cambridge, Mass., 1956).

FURTHER READING

Borkenau, Franz, *The Totalitarian Enemy* (London, 1940).
Edele, Mark, 'Soviet Society, Social Structure, and Everyday Life. Major Frameworks Reconsidered', *Kritika: Explorations in Russian and Eurasian History* 8, no. 2 (2007): 349–73.
Fainsod, Merle, *Smolensk under Soviet Rule* (New York, 1958).
Friedrich, Carl J. and Zbigniew K. Brzezinski, *Totalitarian Dictatorship and Autocracy* (Cambridge, Mass., 1956).
Inkeles, Alex and Raymond Bauer, *The Soviet Citizen: Daily Life in a Totalitarian Society* (Cambridge, Mass., 1961).

Chapter 7: After revisionism

Amar, Tarik Cyril, *The Paradox of Ukrainian Lviv: A Borderland City between Stalinists, Nazis, and Nationalists* (Ithaca, 2015).
Brown, Kate, 'Gridded Lives: Why Kazakhstan and Montana are Nearly the Same Place', *The American Historical Review* 106, no. 1 (2001): 17–48.
Chatterjee, Choi and Karen Petrone, 'Models of Selfhood and Subjectivity: The Soviet Case in Historical Perspective', *Slavic Review* 67, no. 4 (2008): 967–86.
Courtois, S., N. Werth et al., *The Black Book of Communism: Crimes, Terror, Repression* (Cambridge, Mass., 1999).
Davies, Sarah, *Popular Opinion in Stalin's Russia: Terror, Propaganda, and Dissent, 1934–1941* (Cambridge, 1997).
Dunham, Vera S., *In Stalin's Time: Middleclass Values in Soviet Fiction*. Enlarged and updated ed. (Durham, 1990 [first edition: 1976]).
Edele, Mark, 'More Than Just Stalinists: The Political Sentiments of Victors 1945–1953', in *Late Stalinist Russia: Society between Reconstruction and Reinvention*, ed. Juliane Fürst (London, 2006).
Figes, Orlando, *The Whisperers: Private Life in Stalin's Russia* (New York, 2007).
Filtzer, Donald, *Soviet Workers and Late Stalinism: Labour and the Restoration of the Stalinist System after World War II* (Cambridge, 2002).
Garros, Veronique, Natalia Korenevskaya and Thomas Lahusen (eds), *Intimacy and Terror: Soviet Diaries of the 1930s* (New York, 1995).

FURTHER READING

Getty, J. Arch and Oleg V. Naumov, *The Road to Terror: Stalin and the Self-Destruction of the Bolsheviks, 1932–1939* (New Haven and London, 1999).

Geyer, Michael and Sheila Fitzpatrick (eds), *Beyond Totalitarianism: Stalinism and Nazism Compared* (Cambridge, 2009).

Halfin, Igal and Jochen Hellbeck, 'Rethinking the Stalinist Subject: Stephen Kotkin's "Magnetic Mountain" and the State of Soviet Historical Studies', *Jahrbücher für Geschichte Osteuropas* 44, no. 3 (1996): 456–63.

Heinzen, James, *The Art of the Bribe: Corruption under Stalin, 1943–1953* (Stanford, 2016).

Hellbeck, Jochen, *Revolution on My Mind: Writing a Diary under Stalin* (Cambridge, Mass., 2006).

Hessler, Julie, *A Social History of Soviet Trade: Trade Policy, Retail Practices, and Consumption, 1917–1953* (Princeton, 2004).

Hoffmann, David L., *Cultivating the Masses: Modern State Practices and Soviet Socialism, 1914–1939* (Ithaca, 2011).

Hoffmann, David L. and Yanni Kotsonis (eds), *Russian Modernity: Politics, Knowledge, Practices* (New York, 2000).

Johnston, Timothy, *Being Soviet: Identity, Rumour, and Everyday Life under Stalin 1939–1953* (Oxford, 2011).

Kotkin, Stephen, *Magnetic Mountain: Stalinism as a Civilization* (Berkeley, 1995).

Krylova, Anna, 'The Tenacious Liberal Subject in Soviet Studies', *Kritika: Explorations in Russian and Eurasian History* 1, no. 1 (2000): 119–46.

Lahusen, Thomas, *How Life Writes the Book: Real Socialism and Socialist Realism in Stalin's Russia* (Ithaca, 1997).

Lenoe, Matthew Edward, *Closer to the Masses: Stalinist Culture, Social Revolution, and Soviet Newspapers* (Cambridge and London, 2004).

Rossman, Jeffrey J., *Worker Resistance under Stalin: Class and Revolution on the Shop Floor* (Cambridge, Mass., 2005).

Siegelbaum, Lewis and Andrei Sokolov (eds), *Stalinism as a Way of Life: A Narrative in Documents* (New Haven, 2000).

Smith, Mark B., *Property of Communists: The Urban Housing Program from Stalin to Khrushchev* (DeKalb, 2010).

Viola, Lynne (ed.), *Contending with Stalinism: Soviet Power and Popular Resistance in the 1930s* (Ithaca and London, 2002).

FURTHER READING

Chapter 8: Fighting Russia's history wars

Bernstein, Seth, 'Remembering War, Remaining Soviet: Digital Commemoration of World War II in Putin's Russia', *Memory Studies* 9, no. 4 (2016): 422–36.

Carlton, Gregory, *Russia: The Story of War* (Cambridge, 2017).

Glisic, Iva and Mark Edele, 'The Memory Revolution Meets the Digital Age: Red Army Soldiers Remember World War II', *Geschichte und Gesellschaft* 45, no. 1 (2019): 95–119.

Horvath, Robert, *Putin's 'Preventive Counter-Revolution: Post-Soviet Authoritarianism and the Spectre of Velvet Revolution* (London, 2013).

Kirschenbaum, Lisa, *The Legacy of the Siege of Leningrad, 1941–1995: Myth, Memories, and Monuments* (Cambridge, 2006).

Lovell, Stephen, *The Shadow of War: Russia and the USSR 1941 to the Present* (Oxford, 2010).

Rudling, Per A., 'The OUN, the UPA and the Holocaust: A Study in the Manufacturing of Historical Myths', *The Carl Beck Papers in Russian & East European Studies* 2107 (2011).

Sherlock, Thomas, *Historical Narratives in the Soviet Union and Post-Soviet Russia: Destroying the Settled Past, Creating an Uncertain Future* (New York, 2007).

Tumarkin, Nina, *The Living and the Dead: The Rise and Fall of the Cult of World War II in Russia* (New York, 1994).

Youngblood, Denise J., *Russian War Films: On the Cinema Front, 1914–2005* (Lawrence, 2007).

Chapter 9 Holodomor: a transnational history

Applebaum, Anne, *Red Famine: Stalin's War on Ukraine* (London, 2017).

Conquest, Robert, *The Harvest of Sorrow: Soviet Collectivization and the Terror-Famine* (Oxford, 1986).

Davies, R. W. and S. G. Wheatcroft, *The Years of Hunger: Soviet Agriculture, 1931–1933* (Basingstoke, 2004).

Liber, George O., *Total Wars and the Making of Modern Ukraine, 1914–1954* (Toronto, 2016).

Luciuk, Lubomyr Y., *Searching for Place: Ukrainian Displaced Persons, Canada, and the Migration of Memory* (Toronto, 2000).

Mace, James E. and Leonid Heretz (eds), *Investigation of the Ukrainian Famine 1932–1933: Oral History Project*, 3 vols (Washington, 1990).

FURTHER READING

Marples, David R., *Heroes and Villains: Creating National History in Contemporary Ukraine* (Budapest, 2007).

Martin, Terry, 'The 1932–33 Ukrainian Terror: New Documentation on Surveillance and the Thought Process of Stalin', in: *Famine-Genocide in Ukraine, 1932–1933: Western Archives, Testimonies and New Research*, ed. Wsevolod W. Isajiw (Toronto, 2003).

Moore, Rebakah, '"A Crime against Humanity Arguably without Parallel in European History": Genocide and the "Politics" of Victimhood in Western Narratives of the Ukrainian Holodomor', *Australian Journal of Politics & History* 58, no. 3 (2012): 367–79.

New perspectives on Stalinism? A conclusion

Brain, Stephen, *Song of the Forest: Russian Forestry and Stalin's Environmentalism, 1905–1953* (Pittsburgh, 2011).

Bruno, Andy, *The Nature of Soviet Power: An Arctic Environmental History* (New York, 2016).

Clements, Barbara Evans, Rebecca Friedman and Dan Healey (eds), *Russian Masculinities in History and Culture* (Basingstoke, 2002).

Conterio, Johanna, 'Curative Nature: Medical Foundations of Soviet Nature Protection, 1917–1941', *Slavic Review* 78, no. 1 (2019): 23–49.

Cowley, Marcie, 'The Right of Inheritance and the Stalin Revolution', *Kritika: Explorations in Russian and Eurasian History* 15, no. 1 (2014): 103–23.

Davies, R. W., Mark Harrison, Oleg Khlevniuk and Stephen Wheatcroft, *The Soviet Economy and the Approach of War, 1937–1939* (London, 2018).

Edele, Mark, 'Strange Young Men in Stalin's Moscow: The Birth and Life of the Stiliagi, 1945–1953', *Jahrbücher für Geschichte Osteuropas* 50, no. 1 (2002): 37–61.

——— '"What Are We Fighting For?" Loyalty in the Soviet War Effort, 1941–1945', *International Labor and Working-Class History* 84, Fall (2013): 248–68.

Enstad, Johannes Due, *Soviet Russians under Nazi Occupation: Fragile Loyalties in World War II* (Cambridge, 2018).

Fraser, Erica L., *Military Masculinity and Postwar Recovery in the Soviet Union* (Toronto, 2019).

Healey, Dan, *Homosexual Desire in Revolutionary Russia: The Regulation of Sexual and Gender Dissent* (Chicago, 2001).

Hellbeck, Jochen, *Stalingrad: The City that Defeated the Third Reich* (New York, 2015).
Ironside, Kristy, 'Rubles for Victory: The Social Dynamics of State Fundraising on the Soviet Home Front', *Kritika: Explorations in Russian and Eurasian History* 15, no. 4 (2014): 799–828.
Jug, Steven G., 'Red Army Romance: Preserving Masculine Hegemony in Mixed Gender Combat Units, 1943–1944', *Journal of War & Culture Studies* 5, no. 3 (2012): 321–34.
Krylova, Anna, *Soviet Women in Combat: A History of Violence on the Eastern Front* (Cambridge, 2010).
Obertreis, Julia, *Imperial Desert Dreams: Cotton Growing and Irrigation in Central Asia, 1860–1991* (Göttingen, 2017).
Plokhy, Serhii, *Chernobyl: The History of a Nuclear Catastrophe* (New York, 2018).
Randall, Amy, 'Gender and Sexuality', in: *Life in Stalin's Soviet Union*, ed. Kees Boterbloem (London, 2019).
Reese, Roger, *Why Stalin's Soldiers Fought: The Red Army's Military Effectiveness in World War II* (Lawrence, 2011).
Sanchez-Sibony, Oscar, *Red Globalization: The Political Economy of the Soviet Cold War from Stalin to Khrushchev* (New York, 2014).

INDEX

Note: headings in italics are titles of publications. Page numbers in italics refer to figures and those followed by n. indicate a note on that page, followed by its number.

academic world
  conflict within 14, 82–3, 92, 98–102, 133, 168–9, 255–9
  leadership 51–5, 100
  teaching 69–70, 97
  see also *Russian Review* debate; scholarship
affirmative action 94, 97, 110–11, 179, 217
agrarian despotism 48–9, 50
Alberta, University of 242
Aleksandrov, Kirill Mikhailovich 226–7
Alexopoulos, Golfo 108
Alliluyeva, Nadya 138
Amendola, Giovanni 151
America *see* United States of America
American Association for the Advancement of Slavic Studies (AAASS) 98, 100, 106
Ammende, Ewald 238
Andrews, James 108
anti-Semitism 36, 64, 177, 183
appeasement 161–2, 220
Applebaum, Anne 255–9
Applebaum, Rachel 108
archives 109–10
  access to 26, 28, 108, 126, 181, 255–6, 273
  Communist Party 135, 176, 183–4
  Moscow 93, 94, 126, 136, 142
  NKVD (People's Commissariat for Internal Affairs) 176–7, 183
  Smolensk Party Archive 45, 158, 239
  Ukraine 81, 251
  see also diary sources; survivor testimony
Arendt, Hannah 152, 156, 158–9
Armenia 80, 255, 275
assimilation of ideas 6, 188, 190
atomization 48, 159, 181
Austin, University of Texas at 95, 98, 100, 107, 112
Australia 89, 91, 95
  Ukrainian diaspora 241, 242, 243

Baberowski, Jörg 139, 140, 141, 189
Ball, Alan 53
Baltic States 214, 223, 274
Bandera, Stepan 207–8, 209
Barber, John 19

Barenberg, Alan 108
Barnes, Ralph 238
Belsky, Natalie 108
Berkeley, University of California 67, 177–8, 183, 191
Birmingham, University of 43, 51, 95, 252
Bittner, Stephen 108
Boffa, Giuseppe 136
Bolshevism 40, 41, 71–2, 195
  and Fascism 153
  'speaking Bolshevik' 179, 180, 183, 190
  and Stalinism 49, 63, 97, 128, 130, 135–6, 195
  totalitarianism 63, 132, 133
Borkenau, Franz 153–6
Bourdieu, Pierre 178
Brandenberger, David 81
Braudel, Fernand 75
Brezhnev, Leonid 127, 215
Britain *see* United Kingdom
Brooks, Jeffrey 54
Brown, Kate 80
Brzezinski, Zbigniew 158–60, 163, 165
Bukharin, Nikolai 14, 27, 74, 128, 141
Burbank, Jane 53
Burton, Christopher 108

Canada 258
  Ukrainian diaspora 242, 243
capitalism 27, 74, 154, 186–7, 272
Carr, E. H. 17, 95
Chamberlin, Henry William 238
Chase, William 18, 21, 22, 23, 28
Chicago, University of 27, 96, 106, 112
  Chicago school 93, 107–9, 182, 192–3
China 191, 212, 213
Cohen, Stephen 27–8, 161
  and Fitzpatrick 98, 100
  Russian Review debate 14–16, 20, 23
Cohn, Edward 108
Cold War 23, 155–6, 161–2, 187
  effect on scholarship 5, 18–19, 25, 72, 94, 132, 133
collectivization 1, 96, 126
  development of policy 40, 48, 50, 135
  effects of 106, 131, 238, 239, 244
  grain requisitioning 46, 236, 253–4

291

INDEX

colonialism 78, 81, 183
Columbia University 42, 53, 96, 99, 184–5
   Columbia school 182–3, 192–3
communism 186, 191
   and fascism 152, 153–4
   see also Leninism; Marxism; Stalinism
Communist Party 191, 214–15
   archives 45, 158, 176, 183–4, 239
   attitudes within 98, 126, 164
   members of 94, 126
   Poland 123–4
Conquest, Robert 136, 162
   academic career 77–8, 244–6, 250, 252
   Russian Review debate 21, 22
   Thurston affair 168
Cossacks 245
Crimea 208, 221, 224, 237

Dalrymple, Dana 239, 245, 252
Danilov, Victor 126, 238, 246, 250
Danos, Michael 106
David-Fox, Michael 193
David, Michael 108
Davies, R. W. 17, 43, 95, 250, 252
Davies, Sarah 183–4
de Certeau, Michel 178
dekulakization 46, 125, 131, 253
deportations 77–80, 217, 218, 237, 245
   see also ethnic minorities
Deutscher, Isaac 110, 123–5, 131–3, 137, 190
diary sources 180–2, 194
   see also survivor testimony
dictatorships 41–2, 150–1, 153–4, 156, 186
Duranty, Walter 238, 258

Eastern Europe 124, 155, 189
economic policies 2, 40, 72, 143, 272–3
   First Five-Year Plan 239
   New Economic Policy (NEP) 27, 47, 98
Eley, Geoff 16–17
empiricism 93, 109, 156–8
Engelstein, Laura 54
Enlightenment 71, 73, 177, 184
environmental crisis 272
ethnic minorities 77–8, 165, 183, 274
   see also deportations
Euromaidan 28, 208, 252
everyday life 106–7, 157, 160, 166–7, 179, 273
   archive sources 45
   patronage networks 164
   for the political classes 109–10
   see also social history

Fainsod, Merle 18, 102, 157–8, 166, 168, 179–80, 190
   use of archive sources 158, 183
fascism 151, 153, 189
   opposition to 221
   and Stalinism 135–6, 152–3, 160–1
   victory over 142, 217
Field, Daniel 21, 22, 35, 69, 92, 101–2
Figes, Orlando 189
Filtzer, Donald 194
Finland 217, 218, 274
First World War 35 63, 76, 185, 217
Fischer, Louis 152, 155
Fitzpatrick, Brian 89, 90
Fitzpatrick, Sheila
   Applebaum debate 256–9
   and Cohen 98, 100
   early academic career 26–7, 92–3, 95–8
   and Lewin 55n.5, 95, 99–101, *104*
   personal background 89–95, 98, 106
   and Pipes 81, 82, *105*
   research methods 44, 69, 93–4, 111–12
   Russian Review debate 13–29, 34–5, 98, 101–3, 111, 160
   theoretical stance 90–2, 96–7, 134, 166, 187–8, 250
   at University of Chicago 106–12, 192
   at University of Texas, Austin 100, 103, 107
Five-Year Plan, First 96, 123, 124, 185, 239
forgetfulness 6, 110–11, 122, 179, 190, 245, 270
Foucault, Michel 25, 177–8, 196n.4
France 42, 45
   French scholarship 75, 122, 178, 189
Freud, Sigmund 127
Friedrich, Carl J. 158–60, 163
Furet, François 189

Galili, Ziva 53
gender 23, 81, 271–2
generational views of Stalinism 26, 162, 187–8
genocide 77–8, 79–80, 254–5
   Holodomor as 236, 241–6, *249*, 250–4, 255, 257
Gentile, Emilio 189
Gentile, Giovanni 151
Georgia 80, 224, 275
Germany 189
   attack on Soviet Union 38, 155
   German scholarship 79
   invasion of Poland 67–8, 124, 207
   Molotov-Ribbentrop pact 67–8, 124, 152–4, 209, 214, 218, 220–3
   Nazism 150, 158–9

INDEX

Getty, J. Arch 18, 19, 22, 25, 28, 29, 166, 168
glasnost 5
Goldman, Leah 108
Gorbachev, Mikhail 5, 27, 43, 46–7, 82, 134–5, 250
Great Famine (1932-33) 45, 127, 131, 247, 249
   death toll 235, 236, 259
   denial of 237–8
   interpretations of 236–40
   Russian perspective 246, 250–2, 257
   and Ukrainian diaspora 241–6
   see also Holodomor
Great Patriotic War 78, 168, 210–15, 222, 225–6
   see also Second World War
Great Terror (1937-38) 1, 15–16, 26, 97, 124
   Stalin's involvement 50, 123, 125, 133, 135, 140, 166–8
   see also purges
Green, Rachel 108
Gross, Jan 124
Gulag 255–6, 273

Hachten, Charles 108
Haimson, Leopold 66
Halfin, Igal 180–1, 184
Harris, James 108
Harris, Steven 108
Harvard Interview Project (HPSS) 46, 166, 168, 179, 180, 190
   data collection 156–7, 241
Harvard Ukrainian Research Institute (HURI) 242, 243, 244
Harvard University 66–7, 70, 72–3, 130, 132
Havel, Václav 189
Heinzen, James 195
Hellbeck, Jochen 180–2, 184, 189
Hessler, Julie 108
Highest Attestation Commission (VAK) 226
Hirsch, Francine 80
historiography 3–4, 5–7, 110, 150–1
   generational views of Stalinism 26, 162, 187–8
   Soviet/Russian 1–2, 126–7, 136–7
   Western 136–7, 141–2
history wars 208–11, 212–16, 222–3, 259
Hitler, Adolf 136, 152, 207, 209, 213, 220
Hitler-Stalin pact
   see Molotov-Ribbentrop pact (1939)
Hoffmann, David L. 184–6
Hoffmann, Joachim 136
Holocaust 68, 75, 242, 246, 248
   denial of 225–6

Holodomor 246, 247, 251–2, 257, 263n.51
   denial of 252, 258
   see also Great Famine (1932-33)
Holquist, Peter 185, 189
Hoover, J. Edgar 155
Horney, Karen 121–2, 128
Hosking, Geoffrey 162–6, 179, 188
Hough, Jerry 15, 98, 106, 110, 157–8, 161
HPSS *see* Harvard Interview Project (HPSS)
HURI *see* Harvard Ukrainian Research Institute (HURI)

'Icebreaker controversy' 227
iconoclastic revisionists 20, 111, 193
ideologies
   behind dictatorships 156, 186
   internalization of 179, 181
industrialization 1–2, 47, 50, 274
   industrialism 157
   at Magnitogorsk 176–9
   and modernity 192
   workers' attitudes 167, 178, 183
Institute of History, Russia 226
interest-group theory 191
internalization of ideology 179, 181
Ironside, Kristy 108
Islamic State 151
Israel 39
Italy 151, 153, 189, 220

Janco, Andrew 108
Japan, Second World War 212, 213, 274
Jews
   Holocaust 68, 75, 225–6, 242, 246, 248
   in Lithuania 35–9
   in Poland 35–6, 62–4, 75
   see also anti-Semitism
Joint Committee on Soviet Studies (JCSS) 100
Jones, Gareth 238
Jowitt, Ken 191
Jünger, Ernst 151

Karpovich, Michael 66–7, 71, 73, 75
Katz, Michael 100
Kazakhstan, Great Famine 235, 237, 240
Kenez, Peter 17–18, 19, 69, 188
Khlevniuk, Oleg 139, 142–4, 226
Khrushchev, Nikita 126, 214–15, 237, 239
   Secret Speech 79, 125, 128, 238
Kirov, Sergei 131
Kolarz, Walter 76
Kopelev, Lev 240, 243

INDEX

Kotkin, Stephen 54, 176, 182, 183–5
  biography of Stalin 139, 140–1
  perspectives on Stalinism 177–80, 183, 187–8
  and revisionists 25
Krylova, Anna 182
Kulchytsky, Stanislav 250, 251, 257
Kuromiya, Hiroaki 21

Labedz, Leo 132–3
Lapierre, Brian 108
Lemkin, Raphael 255, 256
Leninism 2, 14, 41
  continuity with Stalinism 73–4, 97, 124, 128–9, 140–1, 161
  isolation from Stalinism 42, 46, 50, 125
Lenin, Vladimir Il'ich 40, 41, 125
  relationship with Stalin 73, 128, 143
Lenoe, Matthew 108, 192–3
Levada Center polls 223–4
Lewin, Moshe
  academic career 23–4, 39–47, 51–5, 69
  and Fitzpatrick 55n.5, 95, 99–101, *104*
  personal background 35–9, 44
  political views 39, 41–2
  research methods 44–5
  and revisionism 75–6, 161, 188
  Russian Review debate 15, 17, 34–5
  theoretical stance 39–43, 45–50, 54, 239
Liber, George 254, 255
Lithuania 35–8
Lunacharsky, Anatoly 94
Luzgin, Vladimir 207–10, 225–6, 227

McCannon, John 108
McDonald, David 54
Mace, James 243–5, 250–1, 252
Macquarie University, Sydney 242
Magnitogorsk 176–7, 178, 180
Malia, Martin 177, 186–7, 189
  academic career 66–7, 71
  conservatism 73, 82, 184
Manning, Roberta 18, 102, 162, 168
Marochko, Vasil' 257, 258
Martin, Terry 81–2, 108, 191–2, 254, 255
Marxism 2, 41, 72, 74, 123, 130
Medinskii, Vladimir 211, 217
Medvedev, Roy 126–7, 136, 239
Melbourne, University of 89, 92, 110, 252
Memory Law (2014) 209, 210–13, 218, 223–7
memory politics 208, 273
Merkel, Angela 221
Meyer, Alfred G. 18
Michigan, University of 51, 52, 168

modernity 184–6, 192–3, 271
Molotov-Ribbentrop pact (1939) 214, 220, 221–2, 223
  breakdown of 38
  perspectives on 67–8, 124, 152–4, 218
Monash University, Melbourne 242
Monas, Sidney 103
Montefiore, Simon Sebag 138, 139
Moscow State University 126
Muggeridge, Malcolm 238, 243
Munich agreement (1938) 220, 222
Mussolini, Benito 64, 151, 153

Nakachi, Mie 108
Narodnyi Sobor 226
National Council for Soviet and East European Research 100
nationalism 76–7, 80–1, 183
  positive nationalism 228n.9
  Ukrainian nationalism 257, 258–9
National Security Council 67
National Seminar for the Study of Russia in the Twentieth Century 51–3, 55, 99, 100
Nazis 65, 124–5, 156, 215
  collaborators 208–9, 226, 242
  and Stalinism 125, 150, 152, 158–9, 160–1, 190
Nekrich, Alexander 77, 78–9
neo-conservatives 190
neo-Stalinism 140, 142
neo-totalitarianism 188–91
neo-traditionalism 191–4
New Economic Policy (NEP) 27, 47, 98
NKVD (People's Commissariat for Internal Affairs) 15, 176–7, 183
Nolte, Ernst 189
North Caucasus 235, 240
Nove, Alec 17, 239
Novyi mir 94

objectivity 20, 92, 218–19
oral history 67, 69, 79, 94, 182
Organization of Ukrainian Nationalists
  OUN-B 207, 209
  OUN-M 244
Oxford, University of 92–3

patrimonialism 63, 72, 73, 75
patronage networks 164
Payne, Matthew 108, 189
peasants 39–40, 49, 106–7, 185, 237
Pennsylvania, University of 34, 37, 43
People's Commissariat for Internal Affairs (NKVD) 15, 176–7, 183

294

INDEX

People's Council (Narodnyi Sobor) 226
perestroika 5, 215
Piłsudski, Józef 63–4, 151
Pipes, Mark 63–4
Pipes, Richard
  academic career 63, 65–7, 69–71, 76–7, 81
  conservatism 72–4, 82
  and Fitzpatrick 105
  personal background 63–7
  Polish line 72, 73, 74–5
  theoretical stance 18, 40, 49, 62–3
Pittsburgh, University of 28
Poland
  historians from 35–6, 62–4, 67–8, 75, 123–4, 130, 132
  Second World War 207, 209–10, 213, 214, 220, 274
Polian, Pavel 79
Politburo 109–10
population
  conformity 180–2
  control of 48–9, 150, 156, 160, 164–5, 219
  mood of 168, 182–4
  see also Great Terror (1937-38)
Poroshenko, Petr 257
post-revisionism 162, 177, 186–8, 190
power, nature of 178
property rights 74–5
Prusin, Alexander 189
psychoanalysis 121–2, 127–8
purges 163–4, 179, 237
  Ukraine 251, 253–4
  see also Great Terror (1937-38)
Putin, Vladimir 27–8, 151
  preventive counterrevolution 210–11, 225
  Second World War 142, 215–18, 219–24
  view of history 215–16, 217, 218–19
  see also Memory Law (2014)
Pyle, Emily 108

Radzinsky, Edvard 138, 142
Raeff, Marc 66
Raleigh, Don 54
Red Fascism 153, 155–6
Reece, B. Carroll 155
Reese, Roger 107
research methods 44–5, 69
  archival research 93, 109, 110
  oral history 67, 69, 79, 94
  see also archives; scholarship
revisionism 4–5, 96–7, 150, 168, 187–9
  post-revisionism 162, 177, 186–8, 190
  revisionist historians 14, 15, 18–22, 24–6, 28–9, 53–4, 80, 82

revisionist totalitarianism 166–9
Thurston affair 168–9
  see also Cohen, Stephen; Fitzpatrick, Sheila; Lewin, Moshe
Riasanovsky, Nicholas 66
Richmond, Steven 108
Rieber, Alfred 51
Rittersporn, Gabor 18, 19, 22, 29, 168
Roberts, Flora 108
Roh, Kyung Deok 108
Rosenberg, Bill (William) 51–2, 69, 168
Rossman, Jeffrey 183
Russian Federation 27
  gender equality 271–2
  nationalism narrative 216, 221
  see also Memory Law (2014); Putin, Vladimir
Russian Review debate 13–29, 34–5, 98, 101–3, 111, 160
Russian Revolution (1917) 1, 71–2, 96, 97

Sanborn, Joshua 108
Sats, Igor 94
Schapiro, Leonard 95, 136–7
Schmitt, Carl 151
scholarship
  assimilation of ideas 6, 188, 190
  forgetfulness 6, 110–11, 122, 179, 190, 245, 270
  Russian/Soviet 78–9, 126, 142, 246, 251
  Western 79, 133, 136–7, 142, 217–18, 241, 250, 255–6
  see also academic world; research methods
Second World War 133, 142, 155, 211–13, 273–4
  in Asia 213, 274
  Munich agreement (1938) 220, 222
  Russian perspective 210–11, 217–18, 221–4, 225–7, 274
  Ukraine 207–10
  views of Putin 142, 215–18, 219–24
  see also Great Patriotic War; Memory Law (2014)
Secret Speech (1956) 79, 125, 128, 159, 238
Serbyn, Roman 258
Service, Robert 139, 141, 189
Shcherbytsky, Volodymyr 246
Shearer, David 54, 194–5
Siegelbaum, Lewis 19
Slezkine, Yuri 80, 107
Smith, Jeremy 80
Smolensk Party Archive 45, 158, 239
Snyder, Timothy 189

INDEX

social history 16–17, 101–2, 163
  of Stalinism 13, 96, 99, 106–7, 156–7, 163–5, 167–8, 187–8
  see also everyday life
socialism 23, 36, 46–7, 70, 72
  future of 272, 273, 278n.31
social media 208, 256–7
social mobility 16, 55n.5, 110, 158, 271
social science perspective 14, 51, 109, 160, 162
socio-cultural transformation 270
Souvarine, Boris 122–3, 153, 190, 238–9
Soviet Union (USSR) 77, 178–9, 274–5
  attacked by Germany 38, 155
  breakdown of 5, 47, 82, 186, 194, 215, 250
  invasion of Poland 207, 210, 214, 274
  occupation of Lithuania 36–8
  scholarship in 78–9, 126, 246
'speaking Bolshevik' 179, 180, 183, 190
Stalingrad, Battle of (1942-1943) 182
Stalin, Iosif 49–50, 125
  biographies of 122–5, 129–33, 137–42
  and the Great Famine 236, 244, 245, 253
  and the Great Terror 168
  psychology of 121–3, 126–8, 129–31, 140
  relationship with Lenin 73, 128, 143
  Second World War 212, 214–15
  sex life 137–9
Stalinism 2–3, 46, 47–50
  and Bolshevism 49, 63, 97, 128, 130, 135–6, 195
  continuity with Leninism 73–4, 97, 124, 128–9, 140–1, 161
  deportations 77–8
  distinct from Leninism 2–3, 42, 46, 47, 50, 125
  economy 2, 154, 272–3
  and fascism 150, 158–9, 160–1, 190
  generational views of 26, 162, 187–8
  Second World War 142, 208–9, 219–21, 274–5
  Stalinist society 97, 179–82, 194–5
  'Stalinist subjectivity' 180–2, 183, 190
  successors to 195–6
Sukhodeev, Vladimir Vasil'evich 232n.55
Suny, Ronald G. 46, 70, 80, 159–60, 168
survivor testimony 79, 126, 194, 250, 251
  see also diary sources
Svanidze, Ekaterina 137

Tauger, Mark 252
teaching 69–70, 97
terror-famine 245, 247
Thaw (Khrushchev) 79, 125–7, 128, 135

Thomas, Norman 155
Thurston, Robert 168–9
Tomoff, Kiril 108
Toronto, University of 28
totalitarianism
  generational views of Stalinism 26, 162, 187–8
  historians 18, 75, 82, 91, 132, 150, 153–5
  and modernity 186
  neo-totalitarianism 188–91
  political system 65, 74, 151–6, 157–8, 165
  revisionist totalitarianism 166–9
  and social history 162–6
  of Stalinism 2–3, 6, 14, 19–20, 47–8, 101, 129, 150–4
  theory of 135, 158–62
  see also Conquest, Robert; Pipes, Richard
transnationalism 5, 7, 76, 95, 188–90, 194
transnational processes 185–6
Trotsky, Leon 15, 74, 141, 153
  biography of Stalin 123, 138–9
  view of Stalinism 14, 47, 152–3, 188
Tsarist empire 49, 76
  patrimonialism 63, 72, 73, 75
Tucker, Robert
  academic career 128–9, 135–7, 160–1
  personal background 121–3
  Russian Review debate 101
Tymoshenko, Yulia 272

Ukraine 77, 81, 272
  Crimea 221, 237
  fascism 215
  Great Famine (1932-33) 236–7, 240
  Holodomor 246, 247, 251–2, 257–8
  independence 250–1
  nationalism 257, 258–9
  purges 251, 253–4
  and Russian Federation 27–8
  Second World War 207–10
  Ukrainian diaspora 236, 240–2, 244–5, 250, 251
Ulam, Adam B. 129–33, 161, 190, 240, 244
United Kingdom 43, 75, 163, 189, 221
United Nations 77–8, 245, 256
United States of America
  academic world 163, 188–90
  American Association for the Advancement of Slavic Studies (AAASS) 98, 100, 106
  Ukrainian diaspora 242, 243
  United States Commission on the Ukraine Famine 243–4, 250

INDEX

USSR (Union of Soviet Socialist Republics)
  see Soviet Union (USSR)

VAK (Highest Attestation Commission) 226
vanden Heuvel, Katrina 27, 28
Vertinskii, Aleksandr 209
Vilnius (Vil'na/Wilno) 35–8, 39
Viola, Lynne 18, 22, 44, 164–5, 166, 188
  academic career 21, 28, 250
violence 185–6
VKontakte 208
Vlasov movement 226
Volin, Lazar 239
Volkogonov, Dmitri 134–5, 136, 137
von Hagen, Mark 53, 165
vulgarization 155–6

Walder, Andrew G. 191
Wcislo, Frank 53
Weiner, Amir 189
Weiner, Doug 53

Weissman, Neil 54
Werth, Nicolas 189
Westren, Michael 108
Wheatcroft, Stephen 250, 252
Wilno (Vilnius/Vil'na) 35–8, 39
workers 167, 178, 183
World Congress of Free Ukrainians 244
World War I
  see First World War
World War II
  see Second World War

Yanukovich, Viktor 252
Yasny, Naum 239
Yeltsin, Boris 27
Yezhov, Nikolai 29, 111

Zajicek, Benjamin 108
Zelnik, Reginald E. 177, 180, 183
Zemskov, V. N. 29
Zionism 36, 37, 39
Zubkova, Elena 194

EU authorised representative for GPSR:
Easy Access System Europe, Mustamäe tee 50,
10621 Tallinn, Estonia
gpsr.requests@easproject.com